PHYSICIAN LAW

EVOLVING TRENDS & HOT TOPICS
2021

Wes Cleveland, Editor

2021 Physicians Legal Issues Conference Planning Committee

ABA

AMERICAN**BAR**ASSOCIATION

Health Law Section

Cover design by Amanda Fry/ABA Design

The materials contained herein represent the opinions of the authors and/or the editors and should not be construed to be the views or opinions of the law firms or companies with whom such persons are in partnership with, associated with, or employed by, nor of the American Bar Association or the Health Law Section, unless adopted pursuant to the bylaws of the Association.

Nothing contained in this book is to be considered as the rendering of legal advice for specific cases, and readers are responsible for obtaining such advice from their own legal counsel. This book is intended for educational and informational purposes only.

Printed in the United States of America.

25 24 23 22 21   5 4 3 2 1

Library of Congress CIP

Discounts are available for books ordered in bulk. Special consideration is given to state bars, CLE programs, and other bar-related organizations. Inquire at Book Publishing, ABA Publishing, American Bar Association, 321 N. Clark Street, Chicago, Illinois 60654-7598.

www.shopABA.org

CONTENTS

Contents

CHAPTER 2

**Evolving Trends in Physician-Hospital Contracting: Integration,
Relationships, and Collaborations Toward Accountable
Care** **75**

BY: *VIOLET M. ANDERSON, J.D., HILARY H. BOWMAN, J.D., KELSEY U. JERNIGAN, J.D.,
GABRIEL SCOTT, J.D.*

Chapter 3
**Medical Professional Liability: Trends in Claims and Legislative
Responses 121**
By: *Michael C. Stinson, J.D.*

CHAPTER 9
The Alphabet Soup of Medicare and Medicaid Contractors 321
BY: *QUINN CARLSON, KARA SCHOONOVER, J.D., EMILY WEBER, J.D.*[1]

FOREWORD

This volume marks the eighth edition of the American Bar Association's *Physician Law: Evolving Trends and Hot Topics* series. This edition is based in part on the presentations given at the ABA's Health Law Section Physicians Legal Issues: Healthcare Delivery & Innovation Conference to be held in September 2021. The conference is a joint collaboration between the Health Law Section of the American Bar Association and the Chicago Medical Society.

We are very grateful to the 2021 planning committee of the ABA Physicians Legal Issues: Healthcare Delivery & Innovation Conference. Their input, guidance, and assistance in planning the conference will continue to serve as a springboard for future editions of this book and future conferences.

We also appreciate the hard work of Wes Cleveland with the American Medical Association for editing this publication. Furthermore, our annual conference and book production would also not be possible without hardworking staff of the ABA Health Law Section: Simeon Carson, Carol Simmons, Jason Billups, Sara Calvillo, Paige Rodenberg, and Daryl Taylor. Their energy and support have made each conference and book a success on many levels. We also express our gratitude to Theodore Kanellakes, Executive Director of the Chicago Medical Society, for his guidance, input, and support.

We would also like to thank all the speakers and presenters at this year's conference. We would not be able to put on such a successful conference without their hard work and devotion of time. This year's conference has been designed to be responsive to the unprecedented events of the COVID-19 pandemic and the business and legal issues that physicians continue to face in a rapidly evolving healthcare market—whether remaining independent, adapting to an employment arrangement with an integrated system, or changing practice patterns to include telehealth and other innovative models. This unique program and book offer attorneys, physicians, their administrative partners, and other industry stakeholders an opportunity to learn more about these issues. We hope you enjoy the conference and this book.

Co-Chairs

Elizabeth Greene, J.D.

Kathleen L. DeBruhl, J.D.

PHYSICIANS LEGAL ISSUES CONFERENCE 2021 PLANNING COMMITTEE

Co-Chairs

Kathleen L. DeBruhl	New Orleans, LA
Elizabeth Greene	Worcester, MA

Vice Chairs

Monique Anawis	Chicago, IL
Wes M. Cleveland	Chicago, IL
Adrienne Dresevic	Farmington Hills, MI
David Ellenbogen	Temple, TX
Jena M. Grady	New York, NY
Shannon Hartsfield	Tallahassee, FL

Health Law Section Staff:

Simeon Carson	Chicago, IL
Carol Simmons	Chicago, IL
Jason Billups	Chicago, IL
Sara Calvillo	Chicago, IL
Paige Rodenberg	Chicago, IL
Daryl Taylor	Chicago, IL

The Planning Committee Members from CMS:

Theodore D. Kanellakes, Executive Director, CMS	Chicago, IL
David Banayan, MD	Chicago, IL
Tripti C. Kataria, MD	Chicago, IL
Edward Linn, MD	Chicago, IL

Chapter 1

ENTREPRENEURIAL MEDICINE: FRAUD AND ABUSE RISK AREAS FOR PHYSICIAN BUSINESS RELATIONSHIPS

BY: *CLAY J. COUNTRYMAN, J.D. AND VIOLET ANDERSON, J.D.*

I.   Introduction

Physicians are potentially subject to significant liability under federal fraud laws and regulations that apply to common business relationships. There continues to be aggressive enforcement of federal fraud laws involving physician services that are paid by both government and private payors. The focus of this chapter is to provide an overview of federal fraud laws and regulations that apply to common physician business relationships and recent settlements under federal fraud laws and government guidance involving physicians.

In addition to federal fraud laws and regulations discussed in this chapter, physicians should consider potential application of a state's fraud laws and regulations application to their business arrangements.[1] Based on recent policy initiatives announced by the government, physicians and other providers should expect to continued scrutiny of their financial relationships with other providers and their business partners.

II.   Federal Fraud and Abuse Laws

Physician business relationships potentially raise several issues under different federal fraud and abuse laws. These issues may arise from business relationships such as physicians investing in other healthcare providers in which a physician investor is a source of patient referrals, or physician compensation arrangements with their own practice or with other healthcare providers. The Office of Inspector General (OIG) for the U.S. Department of Health and Services described the following statutory authorities as the five most important federal fraud laws that apply to physicians: the federal Anti-Kickback Statute,[2] the Physician Self-Referral Law (Stark Law),[3] the False Claims Act (FCA),[4] the Civil Monetary Penalties Law,[5] and the Federal statutory

---

1. Physicians should also consider whether a business arrangement would be affected by a particular state statute prohibiting the "corporate practice of medicine" in their particular state. Additionally, physicians should consider whether their state has laws that mirror the concepts expressed in the federal laws discussed in this chapter and whether those state laws would potentially impact or prohibit a business arrangement.

2. 42 U.S.C. § 1320a-7b(b).

3. 42 U.S.C. § 1395nn.

4. 31 U.S.C. § 3729.

5. 42 U.S.C. § 1320a-7a.

authorities under which an individual or entity may be subject to mandatory or permissive exclusion from participation in Federal healthcare programs.

A. The Federal Anti-Kickback Statute

The federal Anti-Kickback Statute (Anti-Kickback Statute) potentially applies to any physician business relationship or agreement to provide services that involve items or services provided to patients reimbursable under federal healthcare programs. The Anti-Kickback Statute is violated where individuals and entities knowingly and willfully offer, pay, solicit, or receive remuneration to induce or reward an individual for:

- referring an individual to a person or an entity for the furnishing, or arranging for the furnishing, of any item or service payable under a federal healthcare program; or

- purchasing, leasing or ordering, or arranging for, or recommending the purchasing, leasing, or ordering, of any item or service payable under the federal healthcare programs.

The Anti-Kickback Statute subjects both parties in an impermissible kickback arrangement to potential criminal liability and civil monetary penalties and fines for a violation of the Anti-Kickback Statute. A violation of the Anti-Kickback Statute constitutes a felony and is punishable by a maximum fine of up to $100,000, and imprisonment of up to ten years, or both. The OIG may initiate administrative proceedings to impose civil monetary penalties and may also seek to exclude a provider from the federal healthcare programs. A violation of the Anti-Kickback Statute may also result in liability under the False Claims Act.[6]

1. *Exceptions and Safe Harbors to the Anti-Kickback Statute*

a. Exceptions to the Anti-Kickback Statute

The Anti-Kickback Statute contains several statutory exceptions and regulatory "safe harbors" that describe payment and business practices that will not be subject to criminal prosecution under the Anti-Kickback Statute, the imposition of civil monetary penalties (CMPs), federal healthcare program exclusion, or liability under the FCA (31 U.S.C. §§ 3729-33). If an individual or entity satisfies all of the conditions of an applicable exception or safe harbor for a particular business arrangement, then that particular business arrangement will not be subject to an enforcement action under the Anti-Kickback Statute. Each type of

---

6. 31 U.S.C. §§ 3729-3733.

remuneration in a business arrangement will need to meet an applicable safe harbor.

Physicians should structure their business arrangements to fit within a safe harbor to the Anti-Kickback Statute. An arrangement must meet each condition of a safe harbor in order to be protected by that safe harbor. However, the OIG has emphasized in various guidance documents that an arrangement is not illegal or in violation of the Anti-Kickback Statute if it does not meet a safe harbor, but will be evaluated on the totality of its facts and circumstances to determine if the arrangement potentially violates the Anti-Kickback Statute or is considered to have a low risk of fraud or abuse.

The following are examples of statutory exceptions to the Anti-Kickback Statute that apply to common physician business relationships:

- payments to bona fide physician employees;
- properly disclosed discounts or other reductions in price;
- certain payments to group purchasing organizations;
- waivers of coinsurance for Medicare services for individuals who qualify for certain public health service programs; and
- certain risk-sharing and other arrangements with managed care organizations.[7]

b. Safe Harbors to the Anti-Kickback Statute

The OIG has also adopted several regulatory "safe harbor" regulations for particular business arrangements. The following "safe harbor" regulations apply to common physician business relationships:

- Investment interests safe harbor, 42 C.F.R. § 1001.952(a), this safe harbor protects remuneration in the form of returns on investments (i.e., profit distributions) paid to referral-source investors.
- Space rentals safe harbor, 42 C.F.R. § 1001.952(b)(c), this safe harbor applies to rental amounts paid between healthcare providers and other individuals or entities.
- Employee safe harbor, 42 C.F.R. § 1001.952(i), this safe harbor applies to compensation paid to individuals who are bona fide employees.

---

7. 42 U.S.C. § 1320a-7b(b)(3).

- Personal services and management contracts safe harbor, 42 C.F.R. § 1001.952(d), this safe harbor applies to compensation arrangements created by arrangements such as medical director agreements, independent contractor agreements, and management service agreements.

- Practitioner recruitment safe harbor, 42 C.F.R. § 1001.952(n), this safe harbor applies to physician recruitment agreements.

- Group purchasing safe harbor, 42 C.F.R. § 1001.952(j), this safe harbor applies to group purchasing arrangements.

- Ambulatory surgical centers (ASC) safe harbor, 42 C.F.R. § 1001.952(r), this safe harbor applies to profit distributions from an ownership or investment interest in an ASC.[8]

- Free or discounted transportation or shuttle services, 42 C.F.R. §1001.952(bb), this safe harbor protects free or discounted transportation services provided to federal healthcare program beneficiaries.

2. *OIG Special Fraud Alerts, Bulletins, and Other Guidance Involving Physicians*

   a. OIG Special Fraud Alert: Speaker Programs

   On November 16, 2020, the OIG issued a Special Fraud Alert regarding the fraud and abuse risks with receipt of remuneration relating to speaker programs by pharmaceutical and medical device companies. In this Special Fraud Alert, the OIG described its investigation of numerous fraud cases involving allegations that remuneration offered and paid in connection with speaker programs violated the Anti-Kickback Statute. According to the OIG, the cases alleged:

   - selected high-prescribing healthcare professionals to be speakers and rewarded them with lucrative speaker deals—with some receiving hundreds of thousands of dollars for speaking;

   - conditioned speaker remuneration on sales targets—requiring speakers to prescribe a minimum number of prescriptions as a condition to receive the honorarium;

---

8. Advisory opinions issued by the OIG involving the ASC safe harbors and recent enforcement actions related to physician ownership interests in ASCs should be considered in structuring physician business relationships with ASCs. *See* OIG Advisory Op. 03-02 (Jan 21, 2003) and OIG Advisory Op. 03-05 (Feb. 13, 2003); *see also* DeBartolo v. HealthSouth Corp., et al.,569 F.3d 736 (7th Cir., 2009).

- holding speaker programs at entertainment venues or during recreational events or otherwise in a manner not conducive to an education presentation—wineries, sports stadiums, fishing trips, golf clubs, and adult entertainment facilities;
- holding programs at high-end restaurants where expensive meals and alcohol were served—an example, average food and alcohol cost per attendee was over $500; and
- inviting an audience of healthcare professionals who had previously attended the same program or healthcare professionals' friends, significant others, or family members who did not have a legitimate business reason to attend the program.

The OIG expressed its skepticism of such programs and their education value and issued the following statement:

Our investigations have revealed that, often, healthcare professionals receive generous compensation to speak at programs offered under circumstances that are not conducive to learning or to speak to audience members who have no legitimate reason to attend. Such cases strongly suggest that one purpose of the remuneration to the healthcare professional speaker is to induce or reward referrals.[9]

The OIG and DOJ have investigated fraud cases involving allegations that remuneration offered and paid in connection with speaker programs violated the Anti-Kickback Statue. The federal government has also brought civil and criminal cases against companies and individual healthcare professionals involving speaker programs. The list of suspect characteristics is illustrative, not exhaustive, and the presence or absence of any one of these factors is not determinative of whether a particular arrangement would be suspect under the Anti-Kickback Statute.

The OIG included the following list of example suspect characteristics in speaker programs:

- A pharmaceutical or medical device company sponsors a speaker program where little or no substantive information is actually presented.
- Alcohol is available or a meal exceeding modest value is provided to the attendees of the program (the concern in heightened when the alcohol is free).

---

9. OIG Special Fraud Alert: Speaker Programs (November 16, 2020).

- The program is held at a location that is not conducive to the exchange of educational information (e.g., restaurants or entertainment or sports venues).

- The company sponsors a large number of programs on the same or substantially the same topic or product, especially in situations involving no recent substantive change in relevant information.

- There has been a significant period of time with no new medical or scientific information nor a new FDA-approved or cleared indication for the product.

- Healthcare providers attend programs on the same or substantially the same topics more than once (as either a repeat attendee or as an attendee after being a speaker on the same or substantially the same topic).

- Attendees include individuals who don't have a legitimate business reason to attend the program, including for example, friends, significant others, or family members of the speaker or healthcare provider attendee; employees or medical professionals who are members of the speaker's own medical practice; staff individuals with no use for the information.

- The company's sales or marketing business units influence the selection of speakers or the company selects healthcare provider speakers or attendees based on past or expected revenue that the speakers or attendees have or will generate by prescribing or ordering the company's product(s).

- The company pays healthcare provider speakers more than fair market value for speaking or pays compensation that takes into account the volume or value of past business generated or potential future business generated by a healthcare provider.

b. OIG General Policy Statement Regarding Gifts of Nominal Value to Medicare and Medicaid Beneficiaries

In December 2016, the OIG issued a general policy statement revising the monetary value of gifts considered "inexpensive" or of "nominal value" that are not considered remuneration likely to influence a beneficiary's selection of a particular provider.[10] Under Section 1128A(a)(5) of the Social Security Act, a person who offers or transfers to a Medicare or Medicaid beneficiary any

---

10. OIG General Policy Statement Regarding Gifts of Nominal Value to Medicare and Medicaid Beneficiaries, (Dec. 7, 2016).

remuneration that the person knows or should know is likely to influence the beneficiary selection of a particular provider, practitioner, or supplier of Medicare and Medicaid payable items or services may be liable for civil monetary penalties up to $20,000 for each wrongful act. For purposes of Section 1128A(a)(5), the statute defines "remuneration" to include waivers of co-payments and deductible amounts in transfers of items or services for free or for other that full amounts and transfers of items or services for free or for other than fair market value.

In this policy statement, the OIG adjusted the figures to interpret "nominal value" as having a retail value of no more than $15 per item or $75 in the aggregate per patient on an annual basis. If a gift has a value at or below these thresholds, then a gift need not fit into a statutory exception to the remuneration prohibition.

 c. 2015 OIG Fraud Alert: Physician Compensation Arrangements May Result in Significant Liability

In June 2015, the OIG released a Fraud Alert focused on compensation arrangements with physicians such as medical directorships. The OIG emphasized in the Fraud Alert that physicians will be held liable under the Anti-Kickback Statute for compensation payments that are not fair market value for bona fide services physicians actually provided.[11]

The OIG commented that compensation paid under "questionable medical directorships" in recent settlements constituted illegal remuneration under the Anti-Kickback Statute for several reasons, including that the payments took into account the physicians' volume or value of referrals and did not reflect the fair market value for the services to be performed, and in some cases the physicians did not actually provide the services described in the medical director agreements.

 d. 2014 OIG Special Fraud Alert Regarding Laboratory Payments to Referring Physicians

In June 2014, the OIG issued a Special Fraud Alert focused on compensation paid by clinical laboratories to referring physicians for: (1) blood specimen collection, processing, and packaging

---

11. OIG Fraud Alert: Physician Compensation Arrangements May Result in Significant Liability (June 9, 2015), *available at* https://oig.hhs.gov/compliance/alerts/guidance/Fraud_Alert_Physician_Compensation_06092015.pdf.

and (2) submitting patient data to a registry or database.[12] In this Fraud Alert, the OIG emphasized its belief that these arrangements are suspect under the Anti-Kickback Statute.[13]

The OIG noted that the Anti-Kickback Statute is implicated when a clinical laboratory pays a physician for services. Whether an actual violation has occurred depends on the intent of the parties (if one purpose of the payment is to induce or reward for referrals, OIG believes that the Anti-Kickback Statute has been violated). The probability that the payment is for an illegitimate purpose is increased if the payment exceeds the fair market value of the services provided by the physician or physician group.

The OIG listed the following as some of the characteristics in a specimen processing arrangement that may indicate an unlawful purpose under the Anti-Kickback Statute:

- Payment exceeds fair market value for services actually rendered by the party receiving the payment.
- Payment is made directly to the ordering physician, rather than the practice bearing the overhead.
- Payment is made on a per-specimen basis for more than one specimen collected during a single patient encounter or any other basis that would indicate that the payment takes into account the volume or value of referrals.
- Payment is offered on the condition of a specified volume or type of test ordered.
- Payment is made to the physician or the group practice despite the fact that the work is being performed by a phlebotomist placed in the office by the laboratory or a third party.
- Payment is for services for which payment is also made by a third party, such as Medicare.

The OIG also described arrangements where laboratories are establishing, coordinating, and maintaining databases purport-edly to collect data on patients who have undergone tests performed by the laboratory (Registry Arrangements). The OIG described the following characteristics of Registry Arrangements that may be evidence of an unlawful purpose:

---

12. OIG Special Fraud Alert: Laboratory Payments to Physicians (June 25, 2014), *available at* http://oig.hhs.gov/compliance/alerts/index.asp.

13. 42 U.S.C. § 1320a-7b(b).

- the laboratory requires or recommends that physicians who enter into Registry Arrangements perform the test with a stated frequency to be eligible to receive, or not to receive, a reduction in compensation;
- compensation is paid on a per-patient basis or other basis that takes into account the volume or value of referrals;
- compensation paid to physicians is not fair market value for the physician's efforts in collecting and reporting data;
- no documentation is maintained or submitted of the physician's efforts in performing the services; and
- when a test is performed by multiple laboratories, the laboratory collects data only from the test it performs.

3. *Proposed Changes to the Anti-Kickback Statute for Value-Based Arrangements and Other Areas (October 17, 2019)*

On December 2, 2020, the OIG published a Final Rule, amending the safe harbors to the Anti-Kickback Statute, by adding safe harbors for certain coordinated care and value-based arrangements among physicians, providers and modifying certain existing safe harbors.[14] In this Final Rule, the Secretary of Health and Human Services (HHS) identified the purpose for the changes to the Anti-Kickback Statute as "transforming the U.S. healthcare system to one that pays for value as a top priority" and facilitating enhanced collaboration among providers.[15]

The OIG finalized the following new Anti-Kickback Statute safe harbors:

- Safe harbors for value-based arrangements including (1) care coordination arrangements to improve quality, health outcomes, and efficiency; (2) value-based arrangements with substantial downside financial risk; and (3) value-based arrangements with full financial risk.
- A new safe harbor for patient engagement and support furnished by a value-based arrangement to patients in a target population to improve quality, health outcomes, and efficiency.
- A new safe harbor to protect certain remuneration provided in connection with certain models sponsored by CMS that would

---

14. Medicare and State Healthcare Programs: Fraud and Abuse; Revisions to Safe Harbors Under the Anti-Kickback Statute, and Civil Monetary Penalty Rules Regarding Beneficiary Inducement, 854 Fed. Reg. 77684 (December 2, 2020).

15. *Id.*

reduce the need for HHS to issue individualized fraud and abuse waivers for each model.

- A new safe harbor for donations of cybersecurity technology and services that are "necessary and used predominantly to implement and maintain effective cybersecurity".

The OIG modified the following existing safe harbors:

- *Personal Services and Management Contracts Safe Harbor.* The OIG added greater flexibility for part-time and outcomes-based arrangements by removing the part-time schedule requirement and the aggregate compensation set-in-advance requirement.
- *Local Transportation.* The OIG expanded mileage limits for local transportation to within 25 miles of the healthcare provider or supplier to or from which the patient would be transported, or within 75 miles if the patient resides in a rural area.
- *Electronic Health Records Items and Services Safe Harbor.* The OIG extended protection for certain related cybersecurity technology, update the interoperability provisions and made the safe harbor permanent by removing the "sunset" date, December 31, 2021.
- *Warranties.* The OIG protected bundled warranties for one or more items and related services, exclude beneficiaries from the reporting requirements applicable to buyers, and added a definition of "warranty" to the Anti-Kickback Statute safe harbor regulations.

B. The False Claims Act

There are several federal statutes that impose criminal or civil penalties for the submission of false claims to the government or other payers. The False Claims Act or FCA[16] is the primary federal civil statutory authority used by the government to bring a case against a healthcare provider for submitting false claims to federal healthcare programs. Most FCA cases are resolved through settlement agreements in which the government alleges fraudulent conduct and the settling parties do not admit liability.

Under the FCA, any person who knowingly submitted false claims to the government is liable for double the government's damages (the amount of the false claims) plus a minimum penalty of $11,665 up to $23,331 for each false or fraudulent claim. The FCA also prohibits knowingly making or us-

---

16. 31 U.S.C. §§ 3729-3733.

ing (or causing to be made) a false record or statement to get a false or fraudulent claim paid by a federal healthcare program.

The FCA defines "knowingly" to include when a person has actual knowledge that the claim is false or instances in which the person acted in *deliberate ignorance* or *reckless disregard* of the truth or falsity of the information. Under the FCA, no specific intent to defraud is required.

1.   *Whistleblower Actions under the FCA*

The FCA also allows private citizens to file suits on behalf of the government called "qui tam" or "whistleblower suits" against individuals or entities that allegedly defrauded the government. Private citizens (i.e., whistleblowers) who successfully bring qui tam suits under the FCA may receive a portion of the government's recovery. For example, 672 qui tam suits were filed in 2020, an average of nearly 13 new cases each week.[17]

The Department of Justice obtained over $2.2 billion in settlements and judgments from civil cases involving fraud and false claims against the government in the fiscal year ending September 30, 2020. Over $1.8 billion relates to matters involving the healthcare industry, including drug and medical device manufacturers, managed care providers, hospitals, pharmacies, hospice organizations, laboratories and physicians. "Even in the face of a nationwide pandemic, the dedicated employees continued to investigate and litigate cases involving fraud against the governments and to ensure that citizen's tax dollars are protected from abuse and are used for their intended purposes," according to Acting Assistant Attorney General Bossert Clark. In 2020, one of the largest recoveries came from a pharmaceutical company, over $591 million, to resolve claims that it paid kickbacks to doctors to induce them to prescribe its drugs by selecting high-volume prescribers to serve as paid "speakers" to induce the physicians to prescribe the pharmaceutical company's drugs.[18]

Of the $2.2 billion in settlements and judgments reported by the government in fiscal year 2020, over $1.6 billion arose from lawsuits filed under the qui tam provision of the False Claims Act. During the same period, the government paid out $309 million to individuals who exposed fraud and false claims by filing these actions and recognized that whistleblowers with insider information are critical to

---

17.   www.justice.gov/opa/pr/justice-department-recovers-over-22-billion-false-claims-act-cases-fiscal-year-2020.

18.   *Id.*

identifying and pursuing new and evolving fraud schemes that might otherwise go undetected.

2. *Examples of Potential False Claims for Items and Services*

The OIG and other government agencies have generally described the following as examples of false claims for services or supplies that were not provided as specifically as described in a claim:

- a claim for a service or supply that was never provided;
- a claim indicating the service was provided for some diagnosis code other than the true diagnosis code in order to obtain reimbursement;
- a claim indicating a higher level of service than was actually provided; and
- a claim for services provided by an unlicensed individual.

3. *Penalties for Violation of the FCA*

There are significant damages and penalties for violations of the FCA. In addition to the treble damages and penalties mention above, the Patient Protection and Affordable Care Act of 2010 (ACA) expanded the potential liability under the FCA by specifically providing that:

- a claim submitted for items or services that were provided as a result of a violation of the Anti-Kickback Statute are false claims under the FCA and
- a person or entity that does not report and return an overpayment within 60 days of discovery or by the date a cost report is due, if that date is later, may be liable under the FCA.

4. *The 60-Day Overpayment Report and Refund Obligation*

The ACA expanded potential liability under the FCA by making it a reverse false claims violation of the FCA if a person or entity fails to report and return an overpayment to the Medicare or Medicaid program by the later of 60 days after the overpayment is identified or the date a corresponding cost report is due (generally referred to as the 60-Day Overpayment Rule).[19]

On February 12, 2016, CMS issued a Final Rule interpreting the 60-Day Overpayment Rule for Medicare Parts A and B.[20] The Final Rule provides that identification of an overpayment occurs when the provider has, or should have, through the exercise of reasonable

---

19. ACA, § 6402.
20. 81 Fed. Reg. 7654 (Feb. 12, 2016).

diligence, determined that it has received an overpayment and quantified the amount of the overpayment. CMS provided in this Final Rule that acknowledged that the investigation and quantification of a potential overpayment may take up to six months. After a provider has credible evidence of receipt of a potential overpayment, providers will have up to six months to investigate possible overpayments before the 60-day reporting period begins. CMS also finalized a six-year look back period for investigating potential overpayments.

In a recent notable settlement, a Jacksonville cardiovascular practice agreed to pay more than $440,000 to resolve FCA allegations for failing to reimburse government healthcare programs of more than $175,000 in overpayments owned to Medicare, Medicaid, TRICARE, and the Department of Veterans Affairs. The cardiovascular group had accrued credit balances or overpayments owed to federal healthcare programs, and despite several warnings from the government, had failed to pay the money back.[21]

C. The Stark Law

The Stark Law[22] affects a wide range of physician business arrangements, including ownership interests in other providers and compensation arrangements for a physician's professional services. The Stark Law is similar to a strict liability statute because an arrangement subject to the Stark Law must meet an exception or it will be in violation of the Stark Law self-referral prohibition. Accordingly, the Stark Law should be considered by physicians in structuring almost any business relationships with other healthcare providers, including their own group practice.

1. Scope of the Stark Law Physician Self-Referral Prohibition

The Stark Law prohibits physicians from making referrals for the furnishing of certain designated health services payable by Medicare or Medicaid to an entity with which a physician (or an immediate family member) has a financial relationship, unless an exception applies. The Stark Law also prohibits the entity (i.e., provider receiving the referral) from presenting or causing to be presented a claim for payment to Medicare or Medicaid (or billing another individual, entity, or third-party payer) for any designated health services furnished pursuant to a prohibited referral.

---

21. Press Release, U.S. Dep't of Justice, Jacksonville Cardiovascular Practice Agrees to Pay More Than $440,000 to Resolve False Claims Act Allegations For Failing to Reimburse Government Health Care Programs, (Oct. 13, 2017) *available at* https://www.justice.gov/usao-mdfl/pr/jacksonville-cardiovascular-practice-agrees-pay-more-440000-resolve-false-claims-act.
22. 42 U.S.C. § 1395nn.

The Stark Law applies indirectly to referrals for Medicaid covered services. Specifically, the Stark Law authorizes the federal government to deny state programs the federal matching funds for any Medicaid services provided pursuant to a prohibited referral if the patient had been a Medicaid beneficiary.[23] Although CMS has not finalized proposed regulations with respect to the application of the referral prohibition to the Medicaid program, courts have recently recognized the application of the Stark Law to Medicaid services in FCA litigation.[24]

The Stark Law defines a "financial relationship" as an ownership or investment interest or a compensation arrangement. The Stark Law broadly defines a "referral" as any request for, order of, or certification or recertification of the need for, or establishment of a plan of care that includes a designated health service. The definition of "referral" does not include any services personally performed by the referring physician, such as the professional interpretation of an imaging service.

The Stark Law applies specifically to physician referrals for the furnishing of an item or service that falls within one of the following categories of designated health services or DHS:

(1) clinical laboratory services;

(2) physical therapy, occupational therapy, and outpatient speech-language pathology services;

(3) radiology and certain other imaging services;

(4) radiation therapy services and supplies;

(5) durable medical equipment and supplies;

(6) parenteral and enteral nutrients, equipment, and supplies;

(7) prosthetics, orthotics, and prosthetic devices and supplies;

(8) home health services;

(9) outpatient prescription drugs; and

(10) inpatient and outpatient hospital services.

Clinical laboratory services, physical therapy, occupational therapy and speech-language pathology services, radiology and certain other imag-

---

23. Most states have false claims acts that would also apply to the state portion of funds from a state's Medicaid program.

24. *See, e.g.,* United States ex rel. Schubert v. All Children's Health System, Inc. No. 8:11-cv-01687-T-27EAJ2013 WL 6054803 (M.D. Fla. Nov. 15, 2013), in which a Florida Federal District Court denied a motion to dismiss and rejected the defendant hospital's argument that the Stark Law did not apply to Medicaid.

ing services, and radiation therapy services and supplies are defined entirely by reference to a list of specific CPT and HCPCS codes. These codes are listed on the CMS website and are published and updated annually in the Medicare physician fee schedule final rule.

2. *Examples of Physician Relationships Subject to the Stark Law*

The following are examples of common physician relationships that are construed to be a financial relationship under the Stark Law:

- a physician's referral of his or her patients to the physician's group practice for a service or item subject to the Stark Law (i.e., x-ray, lab work, or MRI);
- compensation methods in physician group practices for distributing profits from ancillary services such as MRI and CT diagnostic imaging, nuclear stress tests, x-rays, and clinical laboratory services;
- a physician providing medical director services for a hospital;
- a physician having an investment or ownership interest in another healthcare provider that provides any of the designated health services (i.e., hospital, diagnostic imaging center) subject to the Stark Law;
- a physician's lease of space or equipment from a hospital or other healthcare provider that provides designated health services;
- a physician's receipt of compensation through an employment relationship;
- a physician's receipt of an electronic medical records subsidy or e-prescribing system from a hospital;
- a physician's receipt of a holiday gift from a hospital or other healthcare provider that provides designated health services; and
- a physician's receipt of cybersecurity technology.

3. *Penalties for Stark Law Violations*

Penalties for violations of the Stark Law include denial of payment for any *designated health services* and an obligation to refund any amounts collected for any *designated health services* furnished pursuant to a prohibited referral. Referring physicians may be sanctioned with the imposition of civil monetary penalties of up to $25,820 per claim for knowing violations of the Stark Law A provider is also obligated to refund to a Medicare beneficiary any coinsurance or deductible amounts paid by the beneficiary.

Any person who submits or causes to be submitted a claim for a service that the person knows or should know is for a service that results from a prohibited self-referral, or does not make a refund, may be subject to a civil monetary penalty of up to $25,820 for each service plus three times the amount of the claims,[25] and may be excluded from Medicare or Medicaid participation. A civil monetary penalty of up to $172,137 and exclusion may be imposed on persons who enter into circumvention schemes (such as a cross-referral arrangement). A Stark Law violation may also be a basis for liability under the False Claims Act.

4. *Exceptions to the Stark Law Physician Self-Referral Prohibition*

The Stark Law contains statutory exceptions to the general physician self-referral prohibition, and CMS has adopted several regulatory exceptions. In general, there are three categories of exceptions to financial relationships that are subject to the Stark Law, which include:

- exceptions for certain ownership arrangements and certain types of compensation arrangements (i.e., referrals for ancillary services provided through a referring physician's own practice);
- exceptions for certain types of ownership interests, such as in rural providers and hospitals (i.e., physician-owned hospitals); and
- exceptions for certain compensation-related arrangements, such as office and equipment leases, employment relationships, and personal service arrangements.

Some commonly used Stark Law exceptions that apply to physician business relationships include:

(a) in-office ancillary services exception;

(b) bona fide employment relationships exception;

(c) personal services arrangements exception;

(d) ownership or investment interests in a rural provider (rural provider exception);

(e) ownership in a hospital (whole hospital exception);

(f) office space and equipment rental exceptions;

(g) temporary period of noncompliance;

(h) risk-sharing arrangements exception; and

(i) physician recruitment exception.

---

25. 42 C.F.R. § 1003.310.

5. *Differences between Stark Law and the Federal Anti-Kickback Statute*

There are several significant differences between the Stark Law and the federal Anti-Kickback Statute, including:

- The Stark Law only applies to physician referrals for certain items or services payable by Medicare and Medicaid patients, and the Anti-Kickback Statute applies to all referrals for items or services payable by a federal healthcare program.

- The Stark Law only applies to physician referrals and the Anti-Kickback Statute applies to referrals from anyone.

- The Stark Law physician self-referral prohibition is like a strict liability statute in that a financial relationship must meet one of the exceptions to the Stark Law, and the Anti-Kickback statute has voluntary safe harbors where failure to meet a particular safe harbor does not make an arrangement necessarily illegal.

6. *Stark Law and Hospital Ownership*

The Stark Law contains an exception for physician ownership of a hospital, commonly known as the whole hospital exception.[26] This exception applies to a physician's ownership interest in an entire hospital as long as: (1) the referring physician is authorized to perform services at the hospital and (2) the ownership interest is in the hospital as a whole and not a department. One of the most important changes to the Stark Law in the ACA is the changes to the whole hospital exception relating to physician ownership in hospitals. Specifically, Section 6001 of the ACA limited the *whole hospital and rural provider exceptions*, restricting new and expanded physician ownership and investment in hospitals. Some of the important changes to the *whole hospital and rural provider exceptions* include:

(a) physician owners or investors and a provider agreement must be in effect no later than December 31, 2013;

(b) the facility cannot increase capacity beyond the number of operating rooms, procedure rooms, and beds for which the hospital was licensed as of March 23, 2010, unless an exception is granted by the HHS Secretary;

(c) the facility must comply with certain reporting and disclosure requirements and not condition any physician ownership or investment interests directly or indirectly on a physician making or influencing referrals to or generating other business for the hospital;

---

26. 42 U.S.C. § 1395nn(d)(3)(C).

(d) the facility must comply with certain requirements designated to ensure that all ownership and investment interests in the hospital are bona fide;

(e) patients must be informed before admission if the hospital does not have a physician available on the premises during all hours and receive a signed acknowledgment that the patient understands this fact; and

(f) the facility cannot have been converted from an ASC on or after March 23, 2010.[27]

In November 2015, CMS adopted several changes to the whole hospital exception to the Stark Law, including requiring that a physician-owned hospital to disclose that the hospital has physician ownership on any public hospital website and in any public advertising for the hospital.[28] CMS requires ownership or investment interests held by both referring and non-referring (i.e., retired) physicians should be included for determining a physician-owned hospital's baseline bona fide investment level held by physicians for compliance with the whole hospital exception. This effectively means that a physician who is retired but still holds his or her license to practice medicine must be included in the calculation of physician ownership in the hospital.

7. *Recent Stark Law Changes and Clarifications*

On December 2, 2020, CMS modernized the Stark law by finalizing significant changes. The changes became effective January 19, 2021.[29] The following are some of the key new exceptions and changes to the Stark Law regulations:

a. New Stark Law Compensation Exceptions:

(1) Value-Based Care Exceptions. CMS adopted several new defined terms that work together to describe the universe of value-based arrangements that are potentially eligible for new proposed value-based arrangement exceptions.

(2) New Exception for Limited Remuneration to a Physician. CMS adopted a new exception to protect compensation not exceeding an aggregate of $5,000 per calendar year.

(3) New Exception for Cyber Security Technology and Related Services. CMS adopted a new exception to protect arrange-

---

27. Health Care and Education Reconciliation Act of 2010, Pub. L. No. 111-152, §1106(1), 124 Stat. 1029 (2010).
28. 42 C.F.R. § 411.362(b)(3)(ii)(C).
29. 85 Fed. Reg. 77492 (December 2, 2020).

ments involving the donation of certain cyber security technology and related services.

b. New Defined Terms and Regulatory Modifications

(1) New or Modified Definitions. CMS adopted several new definitions of key concepts, including commercial reasonableness, the volume/value standard and fair market value, in an effort to establish clear bright-line rules. CMS also modified the definition of designated health service (DHS) to make clear that an inpatient hospital service is only DHS if the furnishing of the service affects the amount of Medicare's payment to the hospital under the Inpatient Prospective Payment System.

(2) Clarifications to "Group Practice" Requirements. CMS adopted clarifications to the regulations defining a "group practice" for purposes of the Stark Law, including revisions that make clear that group practices may not use DHS-specific pods for purposes of distributing DHS profits.

(3) Modifications to Various Compensation Exceptions. CMS proposed several modifications to various compensation exceptions, including the space lease exception, recruitment exception, fair market value exception and others.

(4) Temporary Non-Compliance. CMS adopted an expanded grace period for certain writing and signature requirements.

(5) Period of Disallowance. CMS deleted the period of disallowance rules to address the confusion these rules have created as to when a financial relationship has ended.

(6) Modification of Electronic Health Records Items and Services. CMS extended protection for certain related cyber security technology, updated the interoperability provisions, and made this exception permanent by removing the "sunset" date of December 31, 2021.

8. *Stark Law Self-Referral Disclosure Protocol*

The ACA established the Voluntary Self-Referral Disclosure Protocol (SRDP) that provides a process for providers and suppliers to self-disclose actual or potential violations of the Stark Law. An incentive for physicians and other providers to use the SRDP is that the ACA gives CMS the authority to reduce amounts owed by providers for actual or potential violations of the Stark Law disclosed under the SRDP.[30]

CMS has also provided special instructions for self-disclosures by a physician-owned hospital and rural provider solely involving non-compliance with the requirements to disclose on any public website and in any public advertising that the hospital or rural provider is owned or invested in by physicians. [31]

D. The Civil Monetary Penalties Law

Under the Civil Monetary Penalties Law (CMPL) of the Social Security Act, 1128A, the OIG has the authority to impose civil monetary penalties, assessments, and exclusion against any individual or entity based on several different types of prohibited conduct. For example, the OIG may seek to impose civil monetary penalties on any person who submits, or causes to be submitted, claims to a federal healthcare program that the persons knows or should know were false or fraudulent.

1. Civil Monetary Penalties Law—False or Fraudulent Claims

For example, under the CMPL, a person who submits, or causes to be submitted, to a federal healthcare program a claim for items and services that the person knows, or should know, is false or fraudulent is subject to a penalty of up to $ 20,866[32] for each item or service falsely or fraudulently claimed, an assessment of up to three times the amount falsely or fraudulently claimed, and exclusion from participation in federal healthcare programs.[33]

For the purposes of the CMPL, "should know" is defined to mean that the person acted in reckless disregard or deliberate ignorance of the truth or falsity of the claim. The CMPL also authorizes actions for a variety of other violations, including submission of claims for items or services furnished by an excluded person; requests for payment in violation of an assignment agreement; violations of rules regarding the possession, use, and transfer of biological agents and toxins; and payment or receipt of remuneration in violation of the Anti-Kickback Statute (42 U.S.C. §1320a7b(b)).

---

30. Additional information on Stark Law Self-Referral Disclosure Protocol is available on the CMS website at http://www.cms.gov/Medicare/Fraud-and-Abuse/PhysicianSelfReferral/Self-Referral-Disclosure-Protocol-Settlements.html.

31. See https://www.cms.gov/Medicare/Fraud-and-Abuse/PhysicianSelfReferral/Self_Referral_Disclosure_Protocol.html.

32. See https://www.ecfr.gov/cgi-bin/text-idx?SID=78a3e90ced07ef07cb7593828bfa1cb8&mc=true&node=pt45.1.102&rgn=div5%23se45.1.102_13.

33. 42 U.S.C. § 1320a-7a(a); 42 C.F.R. § 1003.210(a)(1).

Examples of activities that may be a basis for the imposition of a fine or penalty under the CMPL include:

- presenting a claim for services of a physician or services provided "incident to" a physician's service if the physician: (a) was not licensed as a physician; (b) obtained his or her license through misrepresentation; or (c) falsely represented to the patient at the time the service was furnished that he or she was certified by a medical specialty board;

- submission of a claim for items or services furnished by an excluded person;

- offering remuneration to a Medicare or Medicaid beneficiary that the person knows or should know is likely to influence the beneficiary to obtain items or services billed to Medicare or Medicaid from a particular provider; or

- employing or contracting with an individual or entity that that person knows or should know is excluded from participation in a federal healthcare program.

The OIG may also seek to impose civil monetary penalties under the CMPL against any person who violates provisions of the CMPL, the federal Anti-Kickback Statute, or the Stark Law. For example, the OIG may seek to impose CMPs against any person who violates the Anti-Kickback Statute by knowingly and willfully offering or paying any type of remuneration for referrals of federal healthcare program business, or for soliciting or receiving remuneration for referrals of federal healthcare program business.

2. *Examples of Recent CMPL Settlements Involving Physicians*

The following are examples of recent settlements by healthcare providers involving physician services:

- Fee Reductions and Payments for Services: On February 7, 2019, Amputee Associates, LLC (AA), in Nashville, Tennessee, entered into a $681,774 settlement agreement with OIG. The settlement agreement resolved allegations that AA offered and paid illegal remuneration to two surgical practices and a prosthetist in the form of fee reductions and payments. Specifically, OIG alleged that AA reduced its monthly fee to a Texas surgical practice by an amount equal to the monthly salary the practice paid its prosthetist, in order to induce the practice to refer prosthetics business to AA. OIG also alleged that AA made payments to a prosthetist employed by a Georgia surgical practice in order to induce the prosthetist to refer prosthetics business to AA.

- <u>Free Point-of-Care Test Cups:</u> On December 21, 2018, Tulsa Pain Consultants, Inc., Martin Martucci, M.D., and Andreas Revelis, M.D. (collectively, TPC), Tulsa, Oklahoma, entered into a $98,942.50 settlement agreement with OIG. The settlement agreement resolves allegations that TPC received remuneration from Millennium Health, LLC f/k/a Millennium Laboratories, Inc., in the form of point-of-care test cups, which resulted in prohibited referrals. OIG further alleged that the referrals were prohibited because the remuneration created a financial relationship and TPC caused Millennium to present claims for designated health services that resulted from the prohibited referrals.

- <u>Payments for Processing Lab Specimens</u> In December 2017, the Heart Center of Philadelphia, P.C. (Heart Center) agreed to pay $50,000 for allegedly violating the CMPL, including provisions applicable to physician self-referrals and kickbacks. The OIG alleged that Heart Center received remuneration from a laboratory company in the form of "process, handling, and collection" payments related to the collection of blood and "consulting" fees in exchange for Heart Center referring patients for laboratory testing services.

- <u>Payment for Processing Lab Specimens:</u> In November, 2017, the Arkansas Family Care Network, P.A., Michael Beard, M.D., and Michael Kittell, M.D. (collectively, AFCN), agreed to pay $50,000 for allegedly violating the CMPL, including provisions applicable to physician self-referrals and kickbacks. The OIG alleged that AFCN solicited and received remuneration from a laboratory company in the form of "process and handling" payments related to the collection of blood in exchange for AFCN referring Medicare patients for laboratory testing services.

- <u>Patient Travel Assistance:</u> In April 2015, Laser Spine Institute, LLC (Laser Spine) in Florida, agreed to pay $145,127.45 for allegedly violating the CMPL provisions applicable to physician self-referrals and kickbacks. The OIG alleged Laser Spine paid remuneration to Medicare and TRICARE beneficiaries in the form of hotel and travel assistance to induce referrals to Laser Spine.

E. Exclusion Authorities

The OIG has authority to exclude physicians and other healthcare providers from participation in federal healthcare programs, including the Medicare and Medicaid programs. An important distinction is that exclusion is mandatory in some circumstances, and permissive in other cases, according to the OIG's discretion.

1. *Mandatory Exclusion*

Individuals or entities convicted of any of the following crimes must be excluded from participation in federal healthcare programs for a minimum of five years:

- a criminal offense related to the delivery of an item or service under Medicare or Medicaid;[34]
- a criminal offense related to the neglect or abuse of a patient in connection with the delivery of a healthcare item or service;[35]
- any felony related to fraud, theft, embezzlement, breach of fiduciary responsibility, or other financial misconduct under federal or state law related to healthcare fraud for an offense that occurred after August 21, 1996;[36] and
- any felony conviction under federal or state law occurring after August 21, 1996, relating to the unlawful manufacture, distribution, prescription, or dispensing of a controlled substance.[37]

2. *Permissive Exclusion*[38]

There are several bases for which the OIG has the authority (known as *permissive exclusion*) to exclude an individual or entity from the federal healthcare programs for a minimum of three years. The following is a list of some of the most frequently used grounds for the permissive exclusion of a physician or other healthcare provider:

- fraud, kickbacks, and other similar prohibited activities;
- license revocations or suspensions;
- submitting claims for unnecessary or substandard services;
- submitting false or improper claims;
- convictions relating to fraud in non-healthcare programs;
- defaulting on a health education loan or scholarship obligation;
- entities controlled by an individual who is subject to mandatory exclusion; and
- failure to take corrective action.

In January 2017, the OIG finalized a rule to implement the ACA's expansion of the OIG's permissive exclusion authority to include: exclusions

---

34. 42 U.S. Code § 1320a–7(a)(1).
35. 42 U.S. Code § 1320a–7(a)(2).
36. 42 U.S. Code §1320a–7(a)(3).
37. 42 U.S. Code §1320a–7(a)(4).
38. See 42 U.S. Code § 1320a–7(b).

for obstruction of a government audit; failure to provide certain payment information when requested by the federal healthcare programs; and making false statements, omissions, or misrepresentations in federal healthcare program enrollment applications.[39]

3. Exclusion Liability

A provider that participates in a federal healthcare program may only contract with or employ an excluded person under a limited set of circumstances without being liable for civil money penalties. The payment prohibition is not violated when the excluded person furnishes items or services solely to non-federal healthcare program beneficiaries, and the federal healthcare programs do not pay for any items or services, directly or indirectly. However, a provider may be liable for civil monetary penalties, even if it does not pay the excluded person for his or her services.

4. OIG Guidance on Permissive Exclusion

On May 8, 2013, the OIG issued an Updated Special Advisory Bulletin (2013 Exclusion Bulletin). The 2013 Exclusion Bulletin describes the scope and effect of the prohibition on payment by federal healthcare programs for items or services furnished (1) by an excluded person or (2) at the medical direction or on the prescription of an excluded person.[40] The OIG commented that the effect of an exclusion is that no payment may be made, directly or indirectly, by a federal healthcare program (e.g., Medicare) for any items or services furnished: (i) by an excluded person or (ii) at the medical direction or on the prescription of an excluded person.

The OIG specifically commented in the 2013 Exclusion Bulletin that:

- The prohibition on payment by federal healthcare programs for items or services furnished by an excluded individual includes items and services constituting direct patient care, regardless of whether the items and services are separately billable or are included in a bundled payment. Examples in the Updated Exclusion Bulletin include an excluded individual who provides services such as strategic planning, billing, accounting, and staff training; transportation services provided by excluded individuals; and an excluded individual who inputs prescription information for pharmacy billing.

---

39. 82 Fed. Reg. 4, 100 (Jan. 12, 2017).

40. This Updated Bulletin replaced a Special Advisory Bulletin originally published by the OIG in 1999 regarding the effect of exclusion from participation in federal healthcare programs. 64 Fed. Reg. 52791 (Sept. 30, 1999). The Updated Bulletin is available at https://oig.hhs.gov/exclusions/files/sab-05092013.pdf.

- Excluded persons are prohibited from furnishing administrative and management services, regardless of whether such services are separately payable by a federal healthcare program (e.g., billing and accounting services, staff training, health information technology services, and support).

- Healthcare providers (e.g., laboratories, imaging centers, durable medical equipment suppliers) that furnish items or services to a federal healthcare program beneficiary on the basis of an order or a prescription written by an excluded provider may be responsible for overpayments and civil monetary penalty liability for such items or services even though they relied on a third party (e.g., Medicare Part D plan, state agency) to determine whether the ordering provider was excluded.

- Exclusion does not directly prohibit an excluded person from owning a provider that participates in federal healthcare programs. However, the provider entity would be subject to permissive exclusion and the excluded provider would be subject to civil monetary penalties if an excluded individual retained greater than 5 percent control of the entity.

F. Eliminating Kickbacks in Recovery Act of 2018 (EKRA)

The Eliminating Kickbacks in Recovery Act (EKRA) was enacted by Congress on October 24, 2018, and was part of the Substance Use Disorder Prevention that Promotes Opioid Recovery and Treatment for Patients and Communities Act (the SUPPORT Act) into law. Section 8122 of the SUPPORT Act contains the Eliminating Kickbacks in Recovery Act (EKRA). EKRA added an all payor anti-kickback rule to the healthcare fraud laws concerning improper remuneration for patient referrals to, or in exchange for an individual using the services of, a recovery home, clinical treatment facility or clinical laboratory.

EKRA is important to physicians for several reasons, including the enactment of federal legislation that applies to healthcare services covered by all payors, including Medicare, Medicaid, and commercial insurance health plans.

The Department of Justice (DOJ) had several investigations and prosecutions in 2020 of EKRA violations. In January 2020, an office manager of a substance abuse treatment clinic pled guilty to soliciting kickbacks from a toxicology lab in exchange for referrals.[41] On September 15, 2020, two men

---

41. See Press Release, U.S. Attorney's Office for the Eastern District of Kentucky, Jackson Woman Pleads Guilty to Soliciting Kickbacks, Making False Statements to Law Enforcement Agents, and Tampering With Records (January 10, 2020).

admitted to having a role in a multi-state recovery home patient brokering scheme involving kickbacks.[42]

III. Fraud Risk Areas with Physician Business Relationships

Physician business relationships to provide professional services, administrative services, joint ventures and other arrangements, potentially raise several compliance issues under federal fraud laws and regulations. Physicians and the entities that employ physicians are both subject to liability for compensation arrangements that violate a particular law or regulation. A challenge for physicians and other providers is to structure compensation arrangements to avoid or minimize potential liability. Examples of different physician compensation arrangements involving professional and administrative services by physicians include employment agreements, service line co-management arrangements, medical directorships, and call-coverage agreements. Physicians should also keep in mind that there are other types of common business arrangements that may implicate fraud and abuse laws, such as joint ventures, space or equipment rental agreements, and management agreements.

A. Physician Employment and Professional Service Agreements

1. Employment Relationship

Physicians have been increasingly entering into employment arrangements with hospitals and health systems since the enactment of the ACA. Many factors have contributed to the hospitals' employment of physicians, including healthcare reform initiatives, rising costs to operate an independent physician practice and the consolidation of different types of healthcare providers.

There are several different types of compensation formulas in physician employment agreements, which may impact different compliance requirements. Generally, compensation formulas include a base salary amount and an incentive or productivity-based component to incentivize an employed physician. Examples of commonly used incentive compensation approaches include production bonuses, quality bonuses, and retention bonuses. A commonly used productivity-based compensation approach is to pay an employed physician a fixed dollar amount per work relative value unit (wRVU) for the services personally performed by a physician.[43]

---

42. See Press Release, U.S. Attorney's Office District of New Jersey, Two California Men Admit Roles in Multi-State Recovery Home Patient Brokering Scheme (September 15, 2020).

43. Medicare uses a physician fee schedule to determine payments for physician services. The fee for each service depends on its relative value units or RVUs. RVUs are based on the resources used to provide a service. These resources include the physician's work, the expenses of the physician's practice, and professional liability insurance. For each service, Medicare determines RVUs for three types of resources, including wRVUs.

2. *Fraud and Abuse Concerns*

Depending on the structure and background, an employment arrangement for a physician is considered to be one of the simplest approaches
to avoid or minimize compliance risk. For example, the Anti-Kickback
Statute has an exception for bona fide employees.[44] The Stark Law
also has an exception for bona fide employment relationships provided that compensation is based on fair market value and satisfies
other conditions.[45] However, a physician's employment or other compensation arrangement may be subject to scrutiny under the Anti-Kickback Statute, Stark Law, and CMPL, as well as other fraud and abuse
laws and regulations. As discussed below, there has been a significant
increase in enforcement activity (i.e., cases and settlements) based on
compensation paid to physicians under employment and professional
service arrangements.

A potential concern under the Anti-Kickback Statute is whether
compensation paid to a physician is consistent with the fair market
value for the physician's services and whether it does not take into
account, directly or indirectly, the value or volume of any past or
future referrals or other business between the parties.[46] The OIG has
also commented that a legitimate business arrangement, such as a
physician-compensation arrangement, may violate the Anti-Kickback
Statute if *one purpose* of the arrangement is to compensate the
physician for past or future referrals.

Because an employment or professional services arrangement creates a
financial relationship for purposes of the Stark Law, a physician's
employment or professional services arrangement must fit within an
exception to the Stark Law, or the physician will be prohibited from
referring Medicare patients to that provider for the furnishing of any
of the "designated health services."

The OIG has further raised concerns regarding incentive or productivity-based compensation arrangements (i.e., through employment or
other arrangement such as a service line co-management agreement)
that are structured in part to improve efficiency and quality of care
may result in conduct prohibited under the CMPL.[47]

Hospitals and other physician employers should consider the
implications of the federal Third Circuit Court of Appeal's decision on

---

44. 42 C.F.R. § 1001.952(i)(2016).
45. 42 C.F.R. § 411.357(c)(2016).
46. 70 Fed. Reg. 4858, 4866 (Jan. 31, 2005).
47. OIG Adv. Op. No. 08-16 (Oct. 7, 2008).

September 17, 2019, in *Bookwalter v. UPMC, et al.* in which the court concluded that the mere allegation that a surgeon is paid productivity-based compensation is enough to survive a motion to dismiss a False Claims Act complaint based on alleged Stark Law violations. The Third Circuit reasoned that the amount of productivity-based compensation paid to a surgeon employed by an affiliated medical center arguably correlates with the volume of the surgeon's referrals for inpatient hospital services.[48]

A common condition in the exceptions and safe harbors applicable to physician compensation arrangements for professional services is that the compensation must be based on the fair market value for the physician's services. However, the Anti-Kickback Statute has a statutory exception and a safe harbor for bona fide employment relationships that allows for the payment of any amount of compensation paid by an employer to an employee (who has a bona fide employment relationship with such employer) for the provision of covered services or items, and there is not an express requirement that compensation be "fair market value."[49] The OIG safe harbor regulations provide that the term "remuneration," as well as used in the Anti-Kickback Statute, does not include any amount paid by an employer to a bona fide employee for employment to furnish services paid for in whole or in part by a federal healthcare program. In contrast, the Stark Law employment exception requires that the amount of remuneration under the employment arrangement is consistent with fair market value, is not determined in a manner that takes into account (directly or indirectly) the volume or value of any referrals by a referring physician, and is provided under an agreement that would be commercially reasonable even if no referrals were made to the physician's employer.[50]

Besides the payment of cash compensation to physicians, the OIG and other federal agencies have raised concerns with the following items that may also be considered compensation to a physician:

- payment for non-compete agreements;
- bonus payments and/or retention payments; and
- the payment to physicians for other services provided contemporaneously to an employment arrangement (generally referred to as

---

48. U.S. ex rel. J. William Bookwalter, III, M.D. et al. v. UPMC et al. (3rd Cir. Sept. 17, 2019) (No. 18-1693).
49. 42 U.S.C. § 1320a-7b(b)(3)(B).
50. *See* OIG Adv. Op. No. 08-22 (Dec. 8, 2008).

"Stacking"), such as compensation for medical director services, call coverage, and service line management agreements.[51]

3. *Compliance Recommendations*

To address potential concerns under the federal fraud and abuse laws, a physician's compensation arrangement should be structured to the extent possible to:

- satisfy a statutory exception or safe harbor to the Anti-Kickback Statute;

- include any safeguards or other aspects that the OIG considers to mitigate against the risk of fraud or abuse; and

- be based on a valuation opinion of the fair market value of the compensation in the arrangement.

If a compensation arrangement implicates the Stark Law that arrangement must fit within an applicable Stark Law exception.

a. Exceptions and Safe Harbors to the Anti-Kickback Statute for Employing Physicians and Contracting for Professional Services

The Anti-Kickback Statute contains the following exceptions and safe harbors that are commonly used to structure physician employment or professional service arrangements:

- employee safe harbor (42 U.S.C. § 1320a-7b(b)(3)(B), 42 C.F.R. § 1001.952(i)) and

- personal services and management contracts safe harbor (42 C.F.R. § 1001.952(d)).

b. Stark Law Exceptions Related to Compensation Arrangements[52]

The following are statutory and regulatory exceptions to the Stark Law that have generally been used for physician employment or professional service arrangements:

(i) bona fide employment relationships exception (42 U.S.C. § 1395nn(e)(2), 42 C.F.R. § 411.357(c));

(ii) personal services arrangements exception (42 U.S.C. § 1395nn(e)(3), 42 C.F.R. § 411.357(d)); and

(iii) fair market value compensation (42 C.F.R. § 411.357(l)).

---

51. The OIG and other agencies may consider amounts received by physicians from all sources, such as a lease, medical directorship, co-management agreement, etc., as a physician's total compensation in scrutinizing the fair market value and commercial reasonableness of a compensation arrangement.

52. 42 C.F.R. § 411.357.

The *bona fide employment exception* and *personal services arrangements* exceptions to the Stark Law require the following:

(1) a written agreement signed by the parties;

(2) the agreement covers all of the services to be furnished by the physician (or an immediate family member of the physician) to the entity;

(3) the aggregate services contracted for do not exceed those that are reasonable and necessary for the legitimate business purposes of the arrangement;

(4) the term of the arrangement is at least one year;

(5) the compensation to be paid over the term of each arrangement is set in advance, does not exceed fair market value, and is not determined in a manner that takes into account the value or volume of any referrals or other business generated between the parties; and

(6) the services to be furnished under the arrangement do not involve the counseling or promotion of a business arrangement or other activity that violates any federal or state law.

4. *Recent Settlements Based on Compensation by Physician Practices to Owner and Employed Physicians*

- *On August 15, 2019,* Baldwin Bone & Joint, P.C. in Daphne, Alabama, agreed to pay $1.2 million to settle allegations of violating the Stark Law based on the practice's direct compensation arrangements with shareholder physicians. The alleged Stark Law violations involved compensation paid to physicians that was directly or indirectly related to the volume of each shareholder physician's referrals for physical therapy, x-rays, and MRIs.[53]

- *Cardiovascular Specialists, P.C., d/b/a New York Heart Center* agreed in 2014 to pay $1.3 million to resolve allegations that the practice violated the FCA and the Stark Law by knowingly compensating its physicians in a manner that violated the Stark Law. This settlement resolved allegations that compensation paid to each partner-physician was determined using a formula that

---

53. See Press Release, U.S. Dep't of Justice, Qui Tam Lawsuit and Federal Investigation Results in Settlement and $1.2 Million Payment by Baldwin Bone & Joint, P.C. (August 15, 2019), *available at* https://www.justice.gov/usao-sdal/pr/qui-tam-lawsuit-and-federal-investigation-results-settlement-and-12-million-payment

took into account the volume or value of that physician's referrals for nuclear scans and CT scans, in violation of the Stark Law and the FCA.[54]

5. *Recent Cases and Settlements Based on Compensation to Employed or Contracted Physicians*

There have been several recent settlements involving violations of the Stark Law from physician compensation arrangements that exceeded the fair market value of the physician's services. The following are some recent settlements:

- *On September 9, 2020,* the DOJ announced that Wheeling Hospital, Inc., an acute care hospital, agreed to pay $50 million to resolve claims that it violated the FCA by knowingly submitting claims to the Medicare program that resulted from violations of the Stark Law and the Anti-Kickback Statute. In this case, the government alleged that under the direction and control of its prior management, Wheeling Hospital systematically violated the Stark Law and Anti-Kickback Statute by knowingly and willfully paying improper compensation to referring physicians that was based on the volume or value of the physicians' referrals or was above fair market value.[55]

- *On November 15, 2019*, as part of a larger settlement, Sutter Health agreed to pay $15,177,516 to resolve Stark Law violations that Sutter self-disclosed to the government, which included: (1) compensation paid to referring physicians under personal service arrangements that exceeded the fair market value of the services provided; (2) leased office space to physicians at below market rates; and (3) reimbursed physician-recruitment expenses that exceeded the actual recruitment expenses at issue.[56]

---

54. See Press Release, U.S. Dep't of Justice, Northern District of New York, New York Heart Center to Pay More Than $1.3 Million to Settle Allegations of False Claims Act and Stark Law Violations (Aug. 14, 2014), *available at* https://www.justice.gov/usao-ndny/pr/new-york-heart-center-pay-more-133-million-settle-allegations-false-claims-act-and.

55. See Press Release, U.S. Department of Justice, (September 9, 2020), West Virginal Hospital Agrees to Pay $50 Million to Settle Allegations Concerning Improper Compensation to Referring Physicians

56. See Press Release, U.S. Dep't of Justice, California Health System and Surgical Group Agree to Settle Claims Arising from Improper Compensation Arrangements (November 15, 2019), *available at* https://www.justice.gov/opa/pr/california-health-system-and-surgical-group-agree-settle-claims-arising-improper-compensation#:~:text=As%20part%20of%20the%20settlementsto%20whom%20it%20paid%20amounts.

- *On December 11, 2018, an integrated healthcare system* located in Wisconsin, Illinois, and Michigan agreed to pay $12 million to settle allegations that it entered into improper compensation arrangements with two physicians in violation of the Stark Law when acquiring their practice and employing the physicians.[57]

- *On September 28, 2018, a Montana-based regional healthcare system* and six subsidiaries agreed to pay $24 million to settle allegations that they submitted claims to Medicare for services referred in violation of the Stark Law and federal Anti-Kickback Statute. The healthcare system allegedly paid excessive compensation to more than 60 physicians, paid excessive compensation to induce referrals, and provided administrative services to physicians at below fair market value.[58]

- *On August 2, 2018, a Detroit-based regional hospital system* agreed to pay $84.5 million to resolve allegations that it maintained improper relationships with eight referring physicians, submitted claims for services provided to illegally referred patients in violation of the federal Anti-Kickback Statute and Stark Law, and misrepresented the qualifications of a radiology center to federal programs.[59]

- *In July 2016, Lexington Medical Center* agreed to pay $17 million to settle allegations that it violated the Stark Law and FCA when it entered into asset purchase agreements for the acquisition of physician practices and related physician employment agreements because these agreements allegedly took into account the volume or value of physician referrals, were not commercially reasonable or provided compensation in excess of fair market value. A whistleblower had alleged that the physicians were paid inflated salaries for seeing patients at

---

57. See Press Release, U.S. Atty's Office for the Eastern Dist. of Wis., Aurora Health Care, Inc. Agrees to Pay $12 Million to Settle Allegations Under the False Claims Act and the Stark Law (Dec. 11, 2018), *available at* https://www.justice.gov/usao-edwi/pr/aurora-health-care-inc-agrees-pay-12-million-settle-allegations-under-false-claims-act.

58. See Press Release, Office of Pub. Affairs, U.S. Dep't of Justice, Kalispell Regional Healthcare System to Pay $24 Million to Settle False Claims Act Allegations (Sept. 28, 2018), *available at* https://www.justice.gov/opa/pr/kalispell-regional-healthcare-system-pay-24-million-settle-false-claims-act-allegations.

59. See Press Release, Office of Pub. Affairs, U.S. Dep't of Justice, Detroit Area Hospital System to Pay $84.5 Million to Settle False Claims Act Allegations Arising From Improper Payments to Referring Physicians (Aug. 2, 2018), *available at* https://www.justice.gov/opa/pr/detroit-area-hospital-system-pay-845-million-settle-false-claims-act-allegations-arising.

satellite campuses and were expected to refer the patients back to the hospital.[60]

- *In 2016, Memorial Medical Center* agreed to pay $9.89 million, with $2.29 million going to a whistleblower who was the hospital's former CEO, to resolve allegations that the Medical Center violated the FCA by submitting claims in violation of the Stark Law based on the acquisition of a physician practice for compensation in excess of fair market value, and that the acquisition resulted in a projected financial loss of $670,000 for Memorial Medical Center.[61]

- *In 2015, Columbus Regional Healthcare System* and Dr. Andrew Pippas agreed to pay $35 million to resolve allegations that they violated the FCA by submitting claims in violation of the Stark Law by providing compensation to a physician that was in excess of fair market value and was based in part on the number of the physician's referrals.

- *In September 2015, North Broward Hospital District* agreed to pay $69.5 million to resolve allegations that multiple employed physicians were paid excessive compensation that exceeded fair market value for their services, was not commercially reasonable, and was based on the volume or value of referrals to Broward Health. The evidence cited in support of these allegations included: records that indicated that the employment compensation resulted in substantial losses to Broward Health; logs tracking hospital contribution margins from the physicians' referrals; compensation to collections ratios that were in some instances more than double 90th percentile benchmarks; and allegations that Broward Health permitted free or below fair market value leasing of physician office space.[62]

- *Adventist Health System* agreed in 2015 to pay $115 million to resolve allegations that it violated the FCA by maintaining improper financial relationships with referring physicians and by

60. See Press Release, U.S. Dep't of Justice, South Carolina Hospital to Pay $17 Million to Resolve False Claims Act and Stark Law Allegations (July 28, 2016), *available at* https://www.justice.gov/opa/pr/south-carolina-hospital-pay-17-million-resolve-false-claims-act-and-stark-law-allegations.

61. See Press Release, U.S. Dep't of Justice, Government Settles Alleged False Claims Act Violations with Memorial Health, Inc., (Dec. 23, 2015), *available at* https://www.justice.gov/usao-sdga/pr/government-settles-alleged-false-claims-act-violations-memorial-health-inc.

62. United States ex rel. v. North Broward Hospital District, et al., Case No. 10-60590 (S. O. Fla).

miscoding claims. The allegations included: physician employment compensation arrangements with above-fair market value, non-commercially reasonable compensation through high compensation amounts for part-time physicians with low productivity work; excessive productivity bonuses reflecting inflated and improperly calculated wRVU values, based in some cases on upcoded services; excessive benefits and remuneration that were not properly accounted for, including payment of physician car payments; provision of office staff; equipment and supplies without fair market value charge; payments to physicians for drugs and ancillary items that were provided by Adventist and not the physicians; and pro formas and records that indicated that the employment compensation was expected to result and actually resulted in substantial losses to Adventist.[63]

- *Citizen's Medical Center* agreed in 2015 to pay $21.75 million to resolve allegations that its physician compensation practices violated the FCA. The hospital allegedly paid a group of cardiologists much more in salary than they earned in private practice, and provided abnormally generous benefits. The settlement also resolved allegations that the hospital paid cash bonuses to emergency department physicians to induce referrals and bonuses paid to gastroenterologists on referrals.[64]

- *Halifax Hospital Medical Center and Halifax Staffing, Inc.* agreed to pay in 2014 $85 million to settle allegations that compensation arrangements with six employed medical oncologists and three neurologists violated the Stark Law. The government alleged that the physicians' compensation improperly took into account the volume or value of referrals of designated health services because the revenue pool for incentive bonuses included facility fees paid to Halifax Hospital for referrals of Medicare patients for designated health services in violation of the Stark Law. The bonus pool was generated from an incentive compensation pool equaling 15 percent of the operating margin of the hospital's oncology program, including fees for designated health services not personally performed by the physicians, such as fees for services related to the administration

---

63. See Press Release, U.S. Dep't of Justice, Adventist Health System Agrees to Pay $115 Million to Settle False Claims Act Allegations (Sept. 21, 2015), *available at* https://www.justice.gov/opa/pr/adventist-health-system-agrees-pay-115-million-settle-false-claims-act-allegations.

64. See Press Release April 21, 2015, of the U.S. Department of Justice regarding Texas-Based Citizen's Medical Center, *available at* https://www.justice.gov/opa/pr/texas-based-citizens-medical-center-agrees-pay-united-states-2175-million-settle-alleged.

of chemotherapy. The hospital argued that the compensation agreements met the bona fide employment exception, or alternatively the indirect compensation exception, and were not prohibited by the Stark Law. The court disagreed with the hospital and concluded that the bonus pool was based on factors in addition to personally performed services and included revenue from referrals made by the medical oncologists for designated health services.[65]

- *Tuomey Healthcare System* agreed in 2015 to pay $72.4 million to resolve a $237 million judgment against the hospital based on FCA violations for violating the Stark Law arising from part-time employment relationships with physicians that the government alleged were above fair market value and varied with the volume or value of referrals.[66]

B. Payments to Physicians for Other Than Professional Services

1. General Description and Compliance Recommendations

Physicians and physician practices enter into many arrangements that may include a physician directly or indirectly receiving something of value, other than direct cash payments, that the OIG and other enforcement agencies may consider to constitute remuneration under the fraud and abuse laws. Similar to the general compliance recommendations for physician employment and professional service agreements, any type of arrangement that arguably provides remuneration to a physician practice should be structured to meet an applicable safe harbor to the Anti-Kickback Statute, and include as many safeguards recognized by the OIG in similar arrangements to minimize the risk of violating a fraud and abuse law.

2. Recent Enforcement Actions and Settlements

The following cases involve alleged violations of the Anti-Kickback Statute based on payments to physicians to induce referrals of Medicare patients:

---

65. Press Release, U.S. Dep't of Justice, Florida Hospital System Agrees to Pay the Government $85 Million to Settle Allegations of Improper Financial Relationships with Referring Physicians (Mar. 11, 2014) *available at* http://www.justice.gov/opa/pr/2014/March/14-civ-252.html.

66. Press Release, U.S. Dep't of Justice, United States Resolves $237 Million False Claims Act Judgment against South Carolina Hospital that Made Illegal Payments to Referring Physicians (Oct. 2015), *available at* https://www.justice.gov/opa/pr/united-states-resolves-237-million-false-claims-act-judgment-against-south-carolina-hospital.

- On October 29, 2020, the DOJ announced that Minnesota-based medical device maker Medtronic USA, Inc. agreed to pay $8.1 million to resolve allegations that it violated the FCA by paying kickbacks to induce a South Dakota neurosurgeon to use certain Medtronic products. Medtronic also agreed to pay an additional $1.11 million to resolve allegations that it violated the Open Payments Program by failing to accurately report payments it made to the neurosurgeon to CMS. The settlement also resolved allegations that Medtronic agreed to the requests of the South Dakota neurosurgeon to pay for social events at a restaurant Medtronic knew the neurosurgeon owned. [67]

- On October 14, 2020, the DOJ announced that medical device maker Merit Medical Systems, Inc. (MMSI), agreed to pay $189 million to resolve FCA allegations that the company caused the submission of false claims to the Medicare, Medicaid, and TRICARE programs by allegedly paying kickbacks to physicians and hospitals to induce the use of MMSI products. MMSI allegedly provided remuneration to healthcare providers in the form of millions of dollars in free advertising assistance, practice development, practice support, and purported unrestricted "educational" grants to induce the healthcare providers to purchase and use a wide variety of MMSI products. Despite publicly claiming that its financial assistance was designed to "increase the awareness" of medical treatments, MMSI allegedly provided financial assistance only to select healthcare providers to reward past sales, induce future sales, and steer business to MMSI and away from MMSI's competitors.[68]

- On July 1, 2020, the DOJ settled a civil fraud lawsuit against Novartis Pharmaceuticals Corporation, alleging that Novartis violated the FCA and Anti-Kickback Statute by providing doctors with cash payments, recreational outings, lavish meals, and expensive alcohol to induce them to prescribe Novartis cardiovascular and diabetes drugs reimbursed by federal healthcare programs. The government alleged that

---

67. See Press Release, U.S. Department of Justice (October 29, 2020), Medtronic to Pay Over $9.2 Million to Settle Allegations of Improper Payments to South Dakota Neurosurgeon.
68. See Press Release, U.S. Department of Justice (October 14, 2020), Medical Device Maker Merit Medical to Pay $18 Million to Settle Allegations of Improper Payments to Physicians.

Novartis organized tens of thousands of sham educational events at high-end restaurants and other venues, paid exorbitant speaker fees to doctors who gave no meaningful presentations, and provided expensive meals and alcohol to doctor attendees and their guests.[69]

- On August 8, 2018, a pharmaceutical company agreed to pay at least $150 million to resolve allegations that it improperly paid medical practitioners to prescribe its opioid medication, in violation of the Anti-Kickback Statute.[70]

- In August 2018, Beaumont Hospital in Detroit agreed to pay $84.5 million to settle allegations that Beaumont Hospital provided compensation substantially in excess of fair market value and free or below-fair market value office space and employees to certain physicians to secure their referrals of patients in violation of the Anti-Kickback Statute and the Stark Law.[71]

- On February 19, 2019, a Tulsa doctor agreed to pay the government $84,666.42 for allegedly accepting illegal kickback payments from OK Compounding, LLC. OK Compounding paid a physician what was characterized by the parties as "medical director fees" based upon an hourly rate. However, the payments the physician received from the company were alleged by the government to be, in actuality "kickbacks."

- In December 2017, Pine Creek Medical Center, a physician-owned hospital in the Dallas/Fort Worth area, agreed to pay $7.5 million to resolve claims that it violated the FCA by paying physicians kickbacks in the form of *marketing services* in exchange for surgical referrals. The government alleged that this physician-owned hospital paid on behalf of

69. See Press Release, U.S. Attorney's Office So. Dist. of New York (July 1, 2020), Acting Manhattan U.S. Attorney Announces $678 Million Settlement of Fraud Lawsuit Against Novartis Pharmaceuticals for Operating Sham Speaker Programs Through Which it Paid Over $100 Million to Doctors to Unlawfully Induce Them to Prescribe Novartis Drugs.

70. See Press Release, U.S. Department of Justice, Insys Agrees to pay $150 million to Settle U.S. Opioid Kickback Probe, (Aug. 8, 2018), *available at* https://www.reuters.com/article/us-insys-opioids/insys-to-pay-150-million-to-settle-u-s-opioid-kickback-probe-idUSKBN1KT1G5.

71. See Press Release, Office of Pub. Affairs, U.S. Dep't of Justice, Detroit Area Hospital System to Pay $84.5 Million to Settle False Claims Act Allegations Arising From Improper Payments to Referring Physicians (Aug. 2, 2018), *available at* https://www.justice.gov/opa/pr/detroit-area-hospital-system-pay-845-million-settle-false-claims-act-allegations-arising.

physicians for radio and television advertising, pay-per-click advertising campaigns, billboards, website upgrades, brochures and business cards to induce physicians to refer patients to the hospital for medical services.[72]

- In March 2015, Robinson Health System, an Ohio-based health system agreed to pay $10 million to settle FCA, Stark Law, and Anti-Kickback Statute violations based on financial relationships with certain referring physicians who allegedly failed to provide sufficient bona fide management services to justify payments the physicians received under management agreements.[73]

- In January 2015, Daiichi Sankyo Inc., a pharmaceutical company, agreed to pay $39 million to resolve allegations that it violated the FCA by paying kickbacks to induce physicians to prescribe Daiichi drugs.[74] The government had alleged that Daiichi paid physicians improper kickbacks in the form of speaker fees, and such payments were allegedly made to physicians even when physicians took turns speaking on duplicative topics at Daiichi-paid dinners, a physician spoke only to members of his or her own office staff in his or her own office, or the associated dinner was extremely lavish and exceeded Daiichi's own internal cost limitations per physician.

3. Joint Ventures

The following are recent settlements based on violations of the Anti-Kickback Statute that involved alleged improper financial incentives provided to physicians in joint ventures with hospitals and other healthcare companies:

- On July 8, 2020, the DOJ announced that the Oklahoma Center for Orthopaedic and Multi-Specialty Surgery (OCOM), a specialty

---

72. Press Release, U.S. Dep't of Justice, Dallas-Based Physician-Owned Hospital to Pay $7.5 Million to Settlement Allegations of Paying Kickbacks to Physicians in Exchange for Surgical Referrals, (Dec. 1, 2017) *available at* https://www.justice.gov/opa/pr/dallas-based-physician-owned-hospital-pay-75-million-settle-allegations-paying-kickbacks.

73. Press Release, U.S. Dep't of Justice, Ohio-Based Health System Pays United States $10 Million to Settlement False Claims Act Allegations (Mar. 31, 2015), *available at* https://www.justice.gov/opa/pr/ohio-based-health-system-pays-united-states-10-million-settle-false-claims-act-allegations.

74. Press Release, U.S. Dep't of Justice, Daiichi Sankyo Inc. Agrees to Pay $39 Million to Settle Kickback Allegations Under the False Claims Act (Jan. 9, 2015), *available at* https://www.justice.gov/opa/pr/daiichi-sankyo-inc-agrees-pay-39-million-settle-kickback-allegations-under-false-claims-act.

hospital, its part-owner and management company, USP OKC, Inc., and USP OKC Manager, Inc., and , Southwest Orthopaedic Specialists, PLLC (SOS), an Oklahoma City-based physician group, and two SOS physicians, agreed to pay $72.3 million to resolve allegations under the FCA and the Oklahoma Medicaid False Claims Act of improper relationships between OCOM and SOS resulting in the submission of false claims to the Medicare, Medicaid, and TRICARE programs. This settlement resolved allegations that OCOM and USP provided improper remuneration to SOS and certain of its physicians in exchange for patient referrals to OCOM in the form of (i) free or below-fair market value office space, employees, and supplies, (ii) compensation in excess of fair market value for the services provided by SOS and certain of its physicians, (iii) equity buyback provisions and payments for certain SOS physicians that exceeded fair market value, and (iv) preferential investment opportunities in connection with the provision of anesthesia services at OCOM. The settlement also resolved issues arising out of USP's preferential offering of investment opportunities to physicians at four surgery facilities in Texas.[75]

- On December 18, 2020, the Department of Justice announced that Texas Heart Hospital of the Southwest LLP, a partially physician-owned hospital, and its wholly owned subsidiary, THHBP Management Company, LLC (collectively, the Heart Hospital) agreed to pay $48 million to resolve claims that the Heart Hospital violated the FCA by knowingly submitting claims to the Medicare program that resulted from violations of the Stark Law Physician Self-Referral Law and the Anti-Kickback Statute. The settlement resolved allegations that the Heart Hospital violated the Stark Law and the Anti-Kickback Statute by requiring physician owners to satisfy the Heart Hospital's yearly 48 patient-contract requirement in order to maintain ownership in the hospital.[76]

- On September 28, 2020, the Department of Justice announced that Lakeway Regional Medical Center LLC (LRMC) agreed to pay $13,580,822.79, and Surgical Development Partners LLC,

---

75. See Press Release, U.S. Department of Jusitce (July 8, 2020), Oklahoma City Hospital, Management Company, and Physician Group to Pay $72.3 Million to Settle Federal and State False Claims Act Allegations Arising From Improper Payments to Referring Physicians.

76. See Press Release, U.S. Department of Justice (December 18, 2020), Texas Heart Hospital and Wholly-Owned Subsidiary THHBP Management Company LLC to Pay $48 Million to Settle False Claims Act Allegations Related to Alleged Kickbacks.

Surgical Development Partners of Austin Enterprises LLC, G. Edward Alexander, Frank Sossi, and John Prater collectively agreed to pay $1.8 million, to resolve allegations they violated the FCA and other statutes in connection with the development of Lakeway Regional Medical Center, a hospital in Lakeway, Texas. LRMC had been formed to develop and operate the hospital. The settlement resolved allegations that, when applying for a mortgage loan insured by the Federal Housing Administration to fund construction of the hospital, the defendants made numerous false statements and material omissions in order to overstate physician support for the hospital and understate other key credit risks, in order to obtain the loan under false pretenses.[77]

- In November 2019, Boston Heart Diagnostics agreed to pay $26.67 million to resolve allegations that Boston Heart conspired with others to pay doctors kickbacks disguised as investment returns. Boston Heart set up management service organizations with hospitals that were allegedly used to make payments to referring physicians disguised as investment returns.[78]

- In October 2014, DaVita Healthcare Partners, Inc., agreed to pay $350 million to resolve allegations that it violated the Anti-Kickback Statute and the FCA by entering into joint ventures with physicians in dialysis clinics in which the physicians may not have been charged fair market value.[79]

- In December 2013, a Montana hospital paid $3.85 million to settle allegations that it violated the Anti-Kickback Statute, Stark Law, and the FCA by providing improper financial incentives to physicians who were involved in a medical office building joint venture with the hospital on its campus. The alleged improper incentives included a payment to the joint venture by the hospital that increased the share values for the physicians and resulted in below market value lease rates for the physicians who rented space in the medical office building.

---

77. See Press Release, U.S. Department of Justice (September 28, 2020), Lakeway Regional Medical Center LLC and Co-Defendants Agree to Pay Over $15.3 Million to Resolve Allegations They Fraudulently Obtained Government-Insured Loan and Misused Loan Funds.

78. See Press Release, U.S. Dep't of Justice, Laboratory to Pay $26.67 Million to Settle False Claims Act Allegations of Illegal Inducements to Referring Physicians, (November 26, 2019), *available at* Laboratory to Pay $26.67 Million to Settle False Claims Act Allegations of Illegal Inducements to Referring Physicians | OPA | Department of Justice.

79. See Press Release, U.S. Dep't of Justice, DaVita to Pay $350 million to Resolve Allegations of Illegal Kickbacks (Oct. 22, 2014), *available at* http://www.justice.gov/opa/pr/davita-pay-350-million-resolve-allegations-illegal-kickbacks.

C. Service Line Co-Management Arrangements

1. General Description

An increasingly common approach used by hospitals and physicians to align their efforts to improve the quality and efficiency of hospital service lines are service line co-management agreements. Similar to gainsharing arrangements, service line co-management agreements generally consist of a management contract or joint venture through which physicians are paid compensation for managing and improving the quality of care and outcomes in a specific hospital service line. Some examples of hospital service lines in which hospitals and physicians have entered into co-management service line arrangements include orthopedic surgery, cardiology, and oncology.

The actual structure and services provided through a service line co-management agreement will depend on many factors, including the specific circumstances and current opportunities of a hospital's service line. However, these types of agreements are generally structured to reward the achievement of certain clinical outcomes and the attainment of specific quality metrics and operational efficiencies.

a. Structures of Service Line Co-Management Agreements

Service line co-management agreements have typically been structured under one of the following three approaches:

(1) a new joint venture, e.g., through a corporate entity, such as a limited liability company, is formed by a hospital and participating physicians through which certain management and other services are provided for a hospital's service line;

(2) a new joint venture, e.g., a limited liability company, is formed only by the participating physicians through which certain management and other services are provided for the overall improvement of a particular hospital service line; and

(3) a hospital may contract directly with a physician group practice (e.g., generally a single specialty group) to provide certain management and other services related to a particular hospital service line.

b. Services and Compensation

Service line co-management agreements generally consist of incentive-based management services that are based on very specific objectives and agreed upon metrics between a hospital and physicians. Examples of services provided by physicians under a service line co-management agreement include: development of clinical

pathways, credentialing activities, medical staff committee participation and leadership, and overall management of a hospital's service line.

There are typically two types of compensation paid under a service
line co-management agreement, which include a base fee and incentive compensation. A base fee is generally a fixed amount, paid
monthly, that provides compensation to participating physicians
consistent with fair market value for their time and efforts in over-
seeing, managing, and improving a hospital's service line. The incentive compensation is generally only payable to the extent that
certain pre-determined service line objectives and metrics are satisfied and are not directly based on hourly based services by physicians. Incentive or performance-based metrics should be set in
advance and reset at the end of each contract year for the following
year of a service line co-management agreement.

2. *Fraud and Abuse Concerns*

In OIG Advisory Opinion No. 12-22 (issued December 31, 2012), the
OIG addressed whether a co-management agreement for a hospital's cardiac catheterization labs between the hospital and a cardiology group
would violate the Anti-Kickback Statute or result in the imposition of
civil monetary penalties on the parties involved. Although the OIG commented that properly structured arrangements that compensate physicians for achieving hospital cost savings may increase efficiency, such
arrangements may also have a detrimental effect on patient care. The
OIG listed the following concerns:

(a) stinting on patient care;

(b) "cherry picking" healthy patients and steering sicker (and more
costly) patients to hospitals that do not offer such arrangements;

(c) payments to induce patient referrals; and,

(d) unfair competition among hospitals offering incentive compensation programs to foster physician loyalty and to attract more
referrals.

In the OIG's legal analysis in Advisory Opinion No. 12-22, the OIG
commented that hospital cost-savings programs with physicians and the
cardiac catheterization co-management agreement at issue may implicate concerns under the following federal fraud and abuse statutes:

• the civil monetary penalty for reductions or limitations of services
provided to Medicare and Medicaid beneficiaries, sections
1128A(b)(1)-(2) of the Social Security Act;

- the federal Anti-Kickback Statute;

- the Stark Law; and

- in the case of nonprofit hospital arrangements, there may be issues of private inurement and private benefit under the Internal Revenue Service's income tax regulations under section 501(c)(3) of the Internal Revenue Code.

3. *Compliance Issues and Recent Guidance*

The OIG issued a favorable advisory opinion on December 31, 2012, regarding a co-management agreement between a hospital and a cardiology group described above that may be used as a basis to structure a service line co-management arrangement.[80] In this advisory opinion, the OIG discussed certain safeguards in the co-management agreement upon which the OIG considered the arrangement to have a low risk of fraud or abuse under the Anti-Kickback Statute, and other fraud and abuse statutory authorities.

a. <u>Co-Management Services and Compensation</u>

Under the co-management agreement described in Advisory Opinion No. 12-22, a cardiology group would provide management and medical direction services for the hospital's cardiac cath labs for: (1) a guaranteed, fixed payment per year (the fixed fee) and (2) an annual performance-based payment (the performance fee). The hospital would pay an installment of the fixed fee and an estimated installment of the performance fee to the group quarterly. Every year, the hospital would reconcile the quarterly installment payments of the performance fee under the arrangement.

Under the co-management agreement, the cardiology group would perform the following duties: oversee lab operations; provide strategic planning and medical direction services; develop the hospital's cardiology program; serve on medical staff committees; provide staff development and training; provide credentialing for lab personnel; recommend lab equipment, medical devices, and supplies; consult with the hospital regarding information systems; provide assistance with financial payer issues; and provide public relations services.

The Performance Fee consisted of the following components: hospital's employee satisfaction (Employee Satisfaction Component); patient satisfaction with the hospital's labs (Patient Satisfac-

---

80. OIG Adv. Op. 12-22 (Dec. 31, 2012).

tion Component); and implementation of certain measures to reduce costs attributable to lab procedures (Cost Savings Component). The hospital selected performance measures within these components based on its financial, purchasing, employee satisfaction, patient satisfaction, and quality measurement data systems, as well as certain national cardiology quality measures.

b. Concerns under the Civil Monetary Penalties Law

The OIG determined that the Cost-Savings Component implicated the CMPL because the payments under the program for standardization and limitation of devices and supplies might induce the physicians to reduce or limit services furnished to Medicare and Medicaid patients. The OIG concluded that the Fixed Fee, Employee Satisfaction, Patient Satisfaction, and Quality Components did not implicate the CMPL. The OIG also concluded that the arrangement included the following safeguards, which were sufficient to avoid sanctions under the CMPL:

- Patient care had not been adversely affected due to the hospital monitoring the performance of the cardiology group and the implementation of the Cost Savings Component to protect against inappropriate reductions or limitations in patient care or services.

- A low risk of inappropriate application of a specific cost-savings measure existed because physicians had access to clinically appropriate devices or supplies.

- The Performance Fee payment was based on aggregate performance, not treatment of individual patients.

- The Performance Fee had an annual cap and the term was limited to three years.

- The Performance Fee payment was conditioned on the cardiology group not: (1) stinting on care; (2) increasing referrals to the hospital; (3) cherry-picking healthy patients or patients with desirable insurance; or (4) accelerating patient discharges.

c. The Federal Anti-Kickback Statute

The OIG also concluded that, although the arrangement could result in illegal remuneration if the requisite intent to induce referrals were present, the OIG would not impose sanctions under the Anti-Kickback Statute for the following reasons:

(1) The hospital certified that the compensation paid under the arrangement to the cardiology group was fair market value and the group provided substantial services.

(2) The compensation paid to the group did not vary with the number of patients treated in or referred to the cath labs.

(3) Because the hospital operated the only cardiac catheterization labs within a 50-mile radius, and the cardiology group did not provide cardiac catheterization services at other hospital facilities it was unlikely that the co-management agreement was an inducement of the group's referrals.

(4) The specificity of the measures in the arrangement ensured that the purpose was to improve quality, rather than reward referrals.

(5) The management agreement was in writing with a limited duration of a three-year term.

4. *General Recommendations to Address Fraud and Abuse Concerns*

    a. *Medical Director Services:* Hospitals and physicians entering into service line co-management agreements should review the number and services provided by medical directors to ensure that they meet the *commercially reasonable* conditions in any applicable Stark Law exceptions or Anti-Kickback Statute safe harbors.

    b. *Fair Market Valuation Concerns:* An independent valuation should be obtained to establish the fair market value basis of any compensation paid to physicians under a service line co-management arrangement. A determination of fair market value for compensation paid under a co-management arrangement should generally consider: (i) other arrangements between the hospital and the physicians; (ii) the method used to track and compensate physicians for the achievement of day-to-day management tasks; (iii) the scope of the hospital's service line being managed; and (iv) the integration of designated medical directors.

    c. *Documentation:* Another important compliance-related task in a service line co-management arrangement is to ensure that any base management tasks and incentive-based performance metrics are tracked to document their achievement, and support the payment of any compensation to physicians.

    d. *Service Overlap Concerns:* Hospitals and physicians entering into co-management arrangements should ensure that any physicians are not receiving compensation for tasks that are also being performed in part by others.

    e. *Annual Review:* The base management and medical director tasks under any co-management arrangement generally should be reviewed on an annual basis to ensure that such tasks are still relevant and appropriate for succeeding years under a co-management arrangement.

D. Gainsharing Arrangements

Physicians considering entering into arrangements commonly referred to as "gainsharing arrangements" with healthcare facilities will need to consider the Gainsharing Civil Monetary Penalty prohibition in the Social Security Act and the Anti-Kickback Statute. "Gainsharing" typically refers to an arrangement in which a hospital agrees to share with a group of physicians a percentage of cost savings resulting from certain cost-reduction measures implemented by the physicians. The Gainsharing CMP prohibits a hospital from knowingly making payments, directly or indirectly, to a physician to induce the physician to reduce or limit medically necessary services provided to Medicare or Medicaid beneficiaries who are under the physician's direct care.[81]

On December 29, 2017, the OIG issued a favorable advisory opinion, Advisory Opinion 17-09, relating to an arrangement for a medical center than would pay certain neurosurgeons a share of three years of cost savings attributable to changes the neurosurgeons would make when selecting and using products during spinal fusion surgeries.[82]

In reviewing concerns under the Gainsharing CMP, the OIG concluded that the overall features of the arrangement appeared reasonable and reduced the risk that payments by the medical center to the neurosurgeons would induce the neurosurgeons to limit or reduce *medically necessary services*. These features included the methodology used to develop the cost-savings recommendations, the monitoring and documentation safeguards in the arrangement, and the methodology to calculate each year's savings.

The OIG also concluded that the arrangement had a sufficiently low risk of fraud or abuse under the Anti-Kickback Statute based on several safeguards included in the overall arrangement. These safeguards included: the incentive payments would be distributed to the neurosurgeons on a per capita basis; the potential savings were capped based on the number of spinal fusion surgeries performed by the neurosurgeons on federal healthcare program beneficiaries in the relevant base year; the aggregate payment to the neurosurgeon group would not exceed 50 percent of the projected cost savings estimated by the program administrator at the beginning of the agreement; and the program's committee would collect and review data to confirm a historically consistent selection of patients.

---

81. 42 U.S.C. §1320a-7a(b)(1).
82. OIG Advisory Op. No. 17-09 (Dec. 29, 2017).

E. Medical Directorships

1. General Description

Many physicians have medical director agreements with hospitals and other healthcare providers to provide administrative services relating to patient care service. Some providers, such as hospitals, are required by Medicare to have medical directors for certain departments, such as psychiatric units and rehabilitation units. Medical director agreements have also been used by providers to engage physicians to provide administrative and management services in order to improve the quality and efficiency of the delivery of certain healthcare services. (See the discussion on service line co-management agreements.)

A medical director agreement between a physician and a provider, in which the physician is a referral source, potentially raises issues under several federal fraud and abuse statutes. For example, a medical director agreement creates a financial relationship between a physician and a hospital or other entity that may be furnishing a designated health service under the Stark Law. A medical directorship and resulting compensation under a medical director agreement must be structured to fall within an exception to the Stark Law or the physician will be prohibited from referring any Medicare patients to the hospital for the furnishing of any inpatient or outpatient hospital services, which are *designated health services* under the Stark Law.

2. Fraud and Abuse Concerns

A common concern expressed by the OIG and other governmental agencies is that a medical director agreement may be used as a vehicle to provide remuneration to physicians as an inducement to refer patients to a provider for services that are covered under a federal healthcare program. In the past few years, there have been numerous investigations and prosecutions targeting improper medical directorship arrangements between physicians and healthcare providers (i.e., hospitals, hospice, home health, and nursing facilities), which have resulted in significant financial liability against physicians and healthcare providers.

For example, a federal district judge ordered a home health agency and its owners to pay $5 million in damages and serve 15 months in federal prison for filing false claims to the Medicare program, which were premised on payments that the home health agency made to physicians for providing medical director services while serving on an advisory board to the home health agency.[83] The court concluded that the physicians did not perform any compensable services for the home health agency, but were instead paid for taking care of their own patients, which was separately reimbursable by Medicare.

The OIG has also commented on several occasions that compensation arrangements between hospitals and physicians, such as medical director agreements, may violate the Anti-Kickback Statute if one purpose of the arrangement is to compensate physicians for past or future referrals, regardless of whether the agreement is a legitimate business arrangement.[84] In June 2015, the OIG described settlements with 12 physicians who had entered into medical director agreements as examples of physician compensation arrangements that may result in significant liability when they are structured in a way that does not comply with federal fraud and abuse laws.[85]

An often overlooked criterion of the compensation exceptions to the Stark Law is that any arrangement must be also be *commercially reasonable*. In the context of medical directorships, a primary concern with medical directorships is whether a hospital or another provider already has several medical directors and it may not be *commercially reasonable* to engage the services of another physician to provide medical director services. As an example, the OIG recommends that a hospital review whether the hospital has multiple arrangements with different physicians so that in the aggregate the services provided by all physicians may exceed the hospital's actual needs.[86]

3. Compliance Guidance

In regard to medical directorships, and for any physician compensation arrangements, steps should be taken to ensure that any compensation is within a range of fair market value for actual and necessary services provided by a physician and that any compensation does not take into account the value or volume of referrals between the parties. In addition, physicians should structure their medical director agreements to fit within an applicable safe harbor to the Anti-Kickback Statute, an exception to the Stark Law, as well as including any safeguards recognized by the OIG to minimize the risk of violating the

---

83. Press release Jan. 8, 2008, of the U.S. Attorney's Office for the Western District of Louisiana regarding Aging Care Home Health, *available at* https://www.justice.gov/sites/default/files/usao-wdla/legacy/2013/02/27/wdl20080108.pdf.
84. 70 Fed. Reg. 4858, 4866 (Jan. 31, 2005).
85. OIG Special Fraud Alert, June 2015.
86. 70 Fed. Reg. at 4866.

Anti-Kickback Statute, Stark Law or any other fraud and abuse law applicable to medical director arrangements.

a.   Anti-Kickback Safe Harbors

The potentially applicable safe harbor to the Anti-Kickback Statute for medical director agreements is the *personal services and management contracts* safe harbor.[87] Medical director services are typically provided on a sporadic basis according to the availability of the physician. As a result, medical director agreements generally are unable to satisfy all of the requirements of this safe harbor, which require the exact schedule, precise length, and exact charge for the services and the aggregate compensation paid over the term of the agreement be set in advance.

However, the OIG has concluded in several advisory opinions that the risk of fraud or abuse with a physician's medical director agreement is greatly reduced where the compensation is:[88]

- certified to be consistent with fair market value according to an independent valuation;
- based upon a specified hourly rate;
- subject to a monthly payment cap; and
- paid only if there is written documentation of the hours and services provided by the physician under a written agreement.

b.   Stark Law Exceptions

Generally, hospitals and physicians primarily focus on a medical director agreement meeting an exception to the Stark Law. The following two exceptions to the Stark Law are potentially applicable for medical director agreements:

- personal services arrangements exception and
- bona fide employment relationships exception, which allows a hospital to employ a medical director, full or part time, as long as the amount paid is fair market value, does not relate to the volume or value of referrals made by the physician, and the physician is paid pursuant to a commercially reasonable agreement that specifically identifies the services rendered.[89]

---

87. 42 U.S.C. § 1001.952(d).
88. *See* OIG Adv. Op. No. 01-07 (Oct. 10, 2001).
89. 42 U.S.C. § 1395nn(e)(2).

<u>c.</u> General Recommendations

The following are common recommendations for medical director agreements to minimize the risk of noncompliance under federal fraud and abuse statutes:

(1) *Written Agreement:* Ensure there is a written agreement signed by all of the parties with a current effective date. The agreement should specify that the medical director services are administrative services related to patient care, and that the physician is not being compensated for any services that are separately reimbursable under a federal healthcare program or other third-party payer.

(2) *Time Sheets and Documentation:* Time sheets and/or other documentation should be kept by the physician contemporaneously and used as a basis to make monthly payments for the medical director services.

(3) *Commercial Reasonableness:* It should be commercially reasonable to enter into a medical director agreement, which requires in part establishing the necessity for a hospital or other provider to justify that services under the medical director agreement do not exceed the actual needs of a hospital or other provider. For example, does a hospital have medical director agreements with other physicians for the same or similar services?

(4) *Compensation:* Another common compliance concern is the actual compensation and the compensation formula used to pay physicians for medical director services. It is generally recommended that physician medical directors are paid on an hourly basis, and such hourly rate be based on the fair market value for the administrative services provided by a physician according to that physician's particular medical specialty.

4. *Recent Cases and Settlements Involving Medical Director Agreements*

The following are examples of some recent cases and settlements based in part on physician medical director agreements:

• On November 20, 2020, the DOJ announced that Doctor's Choice Home Care, Inc. and its former executives have agreed to pay $5.15 million to resolve allegations that the home health agency provided improper financial inducements to referring physicians through sham medical director agreements and bonuses to physicians' spouses who were Doctor's Choice employees. The settlement also resolved allegations that Doctor's Choice provided unnecessary services to Medicare patients in order to increase the number of skilled service visits provided during a home health episode to avoid the Medicare Low Utilization Payment Adjustment which otherwise would have decreased Doctor's Choice Medicare reimbursement.[90]

- August 2016, DaVita Health Partners agreed to pay $5,008,732 for allegedly violating the CMPL based on payments to physicians for medical director services that were in excess of fair market value.

- October 2016, WakeMed Health and Hospitals agreed to pay $146,235 for allegedly violating the CMPL provisions applicable to physician self-referrals and kickbacks based on remuneration paid to one medical director.

- December 2015, Memorial Health Services and Saddleback Memorial Medical Center agreed to pay $1,143,750 for allegedly violating the CMPL provisions applicable to physician self-referrals and kickbacks by paying remuneration to a surgical practice for services that were not adequately documented or were beyond the scope of their medical director agreements, including services provided at third-party facilities.

F. Free or Discounted Items and Services

1. General Description

Another common area subject to scrutiny under federal fraud and abuse laws for physicians is the provision of free or discounted items or services to physician practices from providers to which physicians are referral sources. This type of fraud and abuse concern applies to several different types of arrangements including:

- a laboratory company providing a computer to a physician practice;

- hospitals providing free or discounted electronic health record systems to physicians (see discussions below);

- the provision of free insurance pre-authorization services to physician practices; and

- hospitals providing personnel, at the hospital's cost, to perform certain administrative services in a physician's office.

---

90. See Press Release, U.S. Department of Justice (November 20, 2020), Home Health Agency and Former Owner to Pay $5.8 Million to Settle False Claims Act Allegations.

2. Fraud and Abuse Concerns

The OIG has expressed concerns on the provision of free or below-market goods and services to actual or potential referral sources (e.g., physicians) in several advisory opinions and compliance guidance documents. An arrangement where hospitals or other providers provide physicians with items or services for free or less than fair market value, which relieve physicians of financial obligations they would otherwise incur, are viewed as posing a significant risk of fraud or abuse under the Anti-Kickback Statute.

The general basis articulated by the OIG for determining whether an arrangement for free or discounted items or services violates the Anti-Kickback Statute is whether the goods or services would eliminate an expense that the physician would have otherwise incurred (i.e., if there is an independent value to the physician), or if the items or services are sold to a physician at less than fair market value.

3. Recent Guidance

The OIG has issued two favorable advisory opinions regarding the provision of free insurance pre-authorization services to patients and physicians.[91] These advisory opinions offer guidance to physicians in evaluating an arrangement for the receipt of free or subsidized goods or services from hospitals and other providers to which they refer patients.

The OIG cited the following factors in reaching its conclusion in these advisory opinions:

- *Availability.* The free insurance pre-authorization services would be offered to all physicians and not targeted to any particular referring physicians.
- *Safeguards.* No payments would be made to physicians and there would be no other ancillary agreements that could be used to reward physicians for referrals.
- *Transparency.* The pre-authorization services would operate transparently, in that individuals providing the services would identify themselves as working for an imaging center or radiology group.
- *Legitimate Business Interest.* The OIG considered there to be a legitimate business interest in providing the free insurance

---

91. OIG Adv. Op. No. 12-12 (Aug. 23, 2012); OIG Adv. Op. No. 10-04 (April 30, 2010); OIG Adv. Op. No. 10-20 (Sept. 21, 2010).

pre-authorization services because the providers of the pre-authorization services are attempting to ensure payment for their services.

4. *Recent Settlements and Voluntary Self-Disclosures*

- On January 30, 2019, pathology laboratory company Inform Diagnostics agreed to pay $63.5 million to settle allegations that the company violated the Anti-Kickback Statute and the Stark Law by providing to referring physicians subsidies for electronic health records (EHR) systems and free or discounted technology consulting services.

- On March 11, 2019, Covidien LP agreed to pay $17,477,947 to resolve allegations that it violated the FCA by providing free or discounted practice development and market development support to physicians to induce purchases of Covidien's vein ablation products. The practice and market development support Covidien provided included customized marketing plans for specific vein practices; scheduling and conducting "lunch and learn" meetings and dinners with other physicians to drive referrals to specific vein practices; and providing substantial assistance to specific vein practices in connection with planning, promoting, and conducting vein screening events to cultivate new patients for those practices.[92]

G. Call Coverage Agreements

1. *General Relationship*

Many hospitals have entered into call coverage agreements with physicians to secure coverage for their emergency departments. Common call coverage compensation arrangements with physicians include hourly or "per diem" payments to be available for call payment for time or services actually provided in response to call, in exchange for assignment of the physician's professional fees.

Because on-call coverage agreements are generally entered into between physicians and hospitals with which the physician is a referral source, several concerns under fraud and abuse statutes generally will arise. For example, similar to a medical director agreement, an on-call coverage

---

92. See Press Release, U.S. Dep't. of Justice, Covidien to Pay Over $17 Million to the United States for Allegedly Providing Illegal Remuneration in the Form of Practice and Market Development Support to Physicians (Mar. 11, 2019), *available at* https://www.justice.gov/opa/pr/covidien-pay-over-17-million-united-states-allegedly-providing-illegal-remuneration-form.

agreement will create a financial relationship for purposes of the Stark Law between a physician and a hospital. From a federal Anti-Kickback Statute prospective, an on-call-coverage agreement with a physician may be viewed as a mechanism to provide additional remuneration to a physician to induce or reward a physician for referrals of federal healthcare program patients to a particular hospital or other provider.

2. *Fraud and Abuse Concerns*

    a. Anti-Kickback Concerns

    The OIG has commented that the key inquiry regarding whether compensation to physicians for on-call coverage may violate the Anti-Kickback Statute is whether such compensation is: (i) fair market value in an arm's length transaction for actual and necessary items or services and (ii) not determined in any manner that takes into account the volume or value of referrals or other business generated between the parties.

    According to the OIG, suspect call coverage agreements include:

    - "lost opportunity" or similarly designed payments that do not reflect bona fide lost income;
    - payment structures that compensate physicians when no identifiable services are provided;
    - aggregate on-call payments that are disproportionately high compared to the physician's regular medical practice income;
    - payment structures that compensate the on-call physician for professional services for which the physician receives separate reimbursement from insurers or patients, resulting in the physician essentially being paid twice for the same service; or
    - payments made in response to threats that the physician will refuse to continue to use the hospital or refer nonemergency patients to the hospital unless call payments are provided.

    b. Stark Law Concerns

    There are similar concerns under the Stark Law with call coverage agreements between hospitals and physicians. The compensation paid to physicians under a call coverage agreement creates a financial relationship for purposes of the Stark Law. Accordingly, a coverage agreement will need to be structured to fit within an exception to the Stark Law, or the physician providing the call coverage services will be prohibited from referring any Medicare patients to that particular hospital for the furnishing of any designated health services (i.e., which includes services billed to Medicare as inpatient and outpatient services).

3. *Guidance Involving Call Coverage Agreements*

The following are compensation structures for call coverage agreements that were included in advisory opinions that the OIG concluded would result in a low risk of fraud or abuse:

- per diem payment structure based on physician specialty (No. 07-10);
- per service payment structure for services to uninsured patients (No. 09-05); and
- per diem fee, calculated annually in advance, to specialist physicians to provide unrestricted call coverage for a hospital's emergency department (No. 12-15).

In addition, the OIG noted the following reasons as to why a proposed arrangement for call coverage would result in a low risk of fraud and abuse under the Anti-Kickback Statute:

(1) *Valuation of Pier Diem Payments.* The hospital certified that the per diem payments were commercially reasonable, consistent with fair market value, did not take into account the volume or value of referrals, and that the payments were tailored to reflect the call coverage burden applicable to each specialty.

(2) *Implementation.* The hospital would calculate and allocate the payments in advance each year, and administer the coverage agreements without regard to physician referral patterns.

(3) *Payment for Actual Services Rendered.* The participating physicians would provide actual and necessary services for which they are not otherwise compensated (e.g., follow-up care if the patient is admitted).

(4) *Offered to all Staff Physicians.* The hospital would offer the opportunity to participate in the on-call arrangements to all specialists on the hospital's medical staff required to provide unrestricted call coverage under the hospital's bylaws.

(5) *Hospital Absorbs Costs.* No costs of the coverage arrangements would accrue to federal healthcare programs.

H. FCA Cases Based on Physicians Providing Medically Unnecessary Services

The government has recently brought or intervened in lawsuits against hospitals, physicians, and other healthcare providers under the FCA for billing Medicare for medically unnecessary procedures and other services. These lawsuits have generally been filed under the qui tam, or whistleblower provisions of the FCA, under which a private party may file suit on behalf of the government when the private party has evidence that the defendants have submitted false claims to the government.

- In January 2015, the DOJ intervened in two lawsuits against a Florida cardiologist and his physician group alleging that the physician and group billed Medicare for medically unnecessary peripheral artery interventions and paid kickbacks to patients by waiving Medicare copayments irrespective of financial hardship.[93]

- In May 2014, the King's Daughter's Medical Center in Ashland, Kentucky, agreed to pay $40.9 million to resolve allegations that it had billed federal healthcare programs for medically unnecessary heart procedures. The government had alleged that the medical center had billed the Medicare and Kentucky Medicaid program for numerous unnecessary coronary stents and diagnostic catheterizations performed by the medical center's physicians.[94]

I. Recent Settlements Related to Physician Billing

- On September 9, 2020, the DOJ announced that William M. Kelly, Inc., and Omega Imaging, Inc., agreed to pay the United States $5 million to resolve allegations that they violated the FCA by knowingly submitting claims to Medicare and TRICARE for unsupervised radiology services and services provided at unaccredited facilities. This settlement resolved allegations that the defendants submitted claims for CT scans and MRIs involving contrast injections that were not properly supervised by a physician.[95]

---

93. Press Release, U.S. Dep't of Justice, Government Intervenes in Lawsuit Against Florida Cardiologist Alleging Unnecessary Peripheral Artery Interventions and Payment of Kickbacks (Jan. 5, 2015), *available at* https://www.justice.gov/opa/pr/government-intervenes-lawsuit-against-florida-cardiologist-alleging-unnecessary-peripheral .

94. Press Release, U.S. Dep't of Justice, Ashland Hospital to Pay Nearly $41 Million to U.S. Government As Part of Landmark Settlement (May 28, 2014), *available at* https://www.justice.gov/usao-edky/pr/ashland-hospital-pay-nearly-41-million-us-government-part-landmark-settlement.

95. See Press Release, U.S. Department of Justice (September 9, 2020), William M. Kelly, M.D., Inc. and Omega Imaging, Inc. Agree to Pay $5 Million to Resolve Alleged False Claims for Unsupervised and Unaccredited Radiology Services.

- On February 2, 2021, the DOJ announced that Collier Anesthesia Pain, LLC, a pain management clinic located in Fort Myers, Florida, and Tampa Pain Relief Center, Inc., agreed to pay $1,665,000 to resolve allegations that they violated the FCA and Anti-Kickback Statute. As part of the settlement, the government alleged that Collier Anesthesia and Tampa Pain engaged in an illegal kickback scheme by causing affiliated surgery centers to waive copayments for surgical facility fees in order to induce patients to receive injection procedures and they submitted false claims by improperly billing for evaluation and management services and physiological testing services.[96]

- On February 4, 2020, Southeastern Retina Associates paid $1.5 million to resolve FCA allegations that the practice improperly used the modifier 25 billing code to charge Medicare and Medicaid for exams that were not separately billable from other procedures performed on the same day.[97] The settlement also resolved allegations that the practice charged for exams at higher levels than appropriate.

- On December 11, 2018, a Pennsylvania-based health system and its chief executive officer agreed to pay $12.5 million to settle allegations that the health system submitted inflated claims for orthopedic surgeries by unbundling and separately billing for services that were part of the same surgery.[98]

- On September 25, 2018, a Florida-based hospital chain, agreed to pay over $260 million to resolve criminal and civil charges for allegedly billing for inpatient services that should have been billed as outpatient services, remunerating physicians for referrals, and inflating claims for emergency department fees, as well as allegations hospital administrators and executives set mandatory admission-rate benchmarks and pressured physicians to meet them by admitting patients in non-medically necessary cases.

96. See Press Release, U.S. Attorney's Office Middle District of Florida (February 1, 2021), Pain Clinic Pays More Than $1,6 Million to Settle False Claims Act and Kickback Allegations.

97. See Press Release, U.S. Department of Justice, U.S. Settles False Claims Act Allegations against Southeastern Retina Associates (February 4, 2020), available at htts://www.justice.gov/usdao-edtn/pr/u-s-settles-false-claims-act-allegations-against-southeastern-retina-associates.

98. See Press Release, U.S. Atty's Office for the Eastern Dist. of Pa., Coordinated Health and CEO Pay $12.5 Million to Resolve False Claims Act Liability for Fraudulent Billing (Dec. 11, 2018), https://www.justice.gov/usao-edpa/pr/coordinated-health-and-ceo-pay-125-million-resolve-false-claims-act-liability.

IV. Concierge Medicine

A. General Description

"Concierge medicine" generally describes a model for a physician practice that has a contractual arrangement between a physician and a patient during which the patient pays the physician a fixed fee in exchange for enhanced services, access, and benefits beyond those services covered under a patient's insurance policy. Concierge medicine is generally limited to between 50 and 600 patients[99] and provides increased access, as well as additional benefits such as wellness assessments, annual physicals, or other preventative care. The federal government has demonstrated a concern for potential liabilities under the model, and several physicians have entered into settlements with the OIG based on an alleged breach of the CMPL as a result of their concierge medicine practice structure.[100]

While there are many different models, there are three primary structures for creating a concierge medicine practice. One model is the Fee for Extra Services Model, in which a patient pays a smaller fixed fee (monthly or annual) to be part of a physician's patient "panel." The patient receives increased access and wellness services, but continues to pay for office visits other than the wellness services and other extra care, either through Medicare or private insurance. Another model is the Fee for Health Care Services Model, in which the patient pays a larger fixed fee, and the physician covers all (or potentially just primary) care for the patient. Generally these physicians do not accept private insurance or Medicare. Finally, hybrid models allow physicians to offer a choice of the two options or additional features.

B. Concierge Medicine vs. Direct Primary Care

Another physician practice model that has grown recently in use that is similar to "concierge medicine" is called direct primary care. The growth of the direct primary care model has been motivated by the requirement in the ACA that most people have insurance, and that the ACA identifies direct primary care as an acceptable option. In the direct primary care model, patients generally pay a fixed monthly fee to a physician for comprehensive primary care, including basic medication, lab tests, and follow-up visits, in comparison to the "concierge medicine" model in which physician practices bill insurers for routine care while also charging a retainer.

---

99. *See* U.S. Government Accountability Office, Concierge (GAO), Care Characteristics and Considerations for Medicare, GAO-05-929 (August 2005).

100. 42 U.S.C. § 1320a-7a(a).

C. Compliance Concerns

1. General Description

A significant compliance concern for a physician considering a concierge-type physician practice is whether a type of concierge practice used by the physician may violate the Medicare assignment rules if the physician is a Medicare enrolled provider and accepts assignment of Medicare benefits. Physicians who bill in violation of the assignment rules or the limiting charge rules for nonparticipating Medicare providers may be subject to prosecution under the FCA. The OIG issued a Fraud Alert March 31, 2004,[101] warning physicians that charging Medicare beneficiaries more that the Medicare-authorized coinsurance and deductible amounts can potentially lead to violations of the assignment regulations describing the potential liability posed by billing Medicare patients for services already covered by Medicare in a concierge type practice.

This Fraud Alert also described some of the OIG's recent enforcement activity. Citing a recent settlement for the violation of a Medicare assignment agreement by a concierge physician, the OIG stated that "if participating physicians decide they want to charge patients additional fees they should be mindful that they are subject to civil money penalties if they request payment of already covered services from Medicare patients other than the applicable deductible and coinsurance." In particular, each contract presented to the physician's patients was a separate violation of the Medicare assignment agreement, because it acted as a request for payment for already covered services.

D. Compliance Issues and Recent Government Guidance

Physicians accepting Medicare reimbursement have the option of accepting assignment and billing Medicare directly for their services. If a physician does not accept assignment, the physician must seek payment from the patient, who then seeks reimbursement from Medicare.[102] If a physician agrees to accept assignment, the physician "agrees to accept the Medicare payment as payment in full for the services furnished to the beneficiary and is precluded from charging the beneficiary more than the deductible and coinsurance based on the approved Medicare fee amount."[103] As a result, the physician is not allowed to separately bill a patient for any services that are covered by

---

101. OIG Alert, OIG Alerts Physicians about Added Charges for Covered Services (Mar. 31, 2004) *available at* https://oig.hhs.gov/fraud/docs/alertsandbulletins/2004/fa033104assignviolationi.pdf.

102. 42 U.S.C. § 1395u(i).

103. 42 C.F.R. § 402.

Medicare. A breach of the terms of this assignment by charging for Medicare covered services may subject the physician to civil monetary penalties, including a penalty of up to three times the amount charged, and potential exclusion from federal healthcare programs.

Physicians with a concierge practice who do not wish to accept Medicare patients at all must formally opt out of their participation in Medicare. This process includes signing an opt-out affidavit and having any patient who previously participated in Medicare sign an opt-out as well. As part of the affidavit, the physician must agree not to submit any claims to or receive payment from Medicare for two years.

1. Private Payor Compliance Issues

Certain concierge medicine models may also violate contractual provisions included in network provider agreements. For example, provider agreements between a physician and private insurance companies or third-party payers generally contain a provision requiring the physician to accept payment from the insurer as "payment in full," thereby prohibiting the physician from seeking payment from the insured beyond co-pays, deductibles, or co-insurance.

Similar to the Medicare payment requirements, the key consideration is whether the services provided in exchange for the fixed fee charged by the physician are covered by the insurer. When the concierge model used by the physician includes services that are covered by the patient's private insurance, the physician is acting in violation of his provider agreement by billing the patient for any amounts beyond the patient's cost-sharing obligations. In addition, many states ban in-network providers from billing insured patients beyond co-payments or co-insurance required by the plan, viewing this as a deceptive business practice.

2. Recent Civil Monetary Penalty Settlements

The following settlements were based on physician practices using a concierge medicine model to provide services to their Medicare patients.

In 2007, a physician paid $107,000 to resolve potential liability under the CMPL for charging patients, including Medicare beneficiaries, an annual fee. In exchange for the annual fee, the physician provided: (1) an annual comprehensive physical examination; (2) same-day or next-day appointments; (3) support personnel dedicated exclusively to members; (4) 24 hours a day and seven days a week physician availability; (5) prescription facilitation; (6) coordination of referrals and expedited referrals, if medically necessary; and (7) other service amenities.

In 2013, a physician practice paid $170,260 for allegedly violating the CMPL for sending letters to 5,474 of its Medicare patients asking for a $50 annual fee because "the federal government (Medicare) continues to increase the amount of paperwork we are required to fill out to assure you receive the benefits to which you're entitled."

V.   Physician-Owned Medical Device Distributorships

A.   Fraud and Abuse Concerns

The OIG issued a Special Fraud Alert on March 26, 2013, regarding physician-owned entities that sell and distribute implantable medical devices.[104] In this Special Fraud Alert, the OIG specifically addressed "physician-owned entities that derive revenue from selling, or arranging for the sale of, implantable medical devices ordered by their physician owners for use in procedures the physician-owners perform on their own patients at hospitals or ASCs." This Special Fraud Alert underscores the significant increase in attention that the OIG and other government agencies are giving to this type of business relationship by physicians.

B.   OIG Special Fraud Alert Physician-Owned Entities

The OIG emphasized that its comments in the Special Fraud Alert Physician-Owned Entities would be applicable in evaluating similar arrangements involving other types of physician-owned entities that sell or distribute healthcare items or services paid for in part by federal healthcare programs.

The OIG listed the following "suspect" characteristics of a physician-owned entity that distributes medical devices that may be indicative of violating the Anti-Kickback Statute in its operations:

- The size of the investment offered to each physician varies with the expected or actual volume or value of devices used by the physician.

- Distributions are not made in proportion to ownership interest, or physician-owners pay different prices for their ownership interests, because of the expected or actual volume or value of devices used by the physicians.

- Physician-owners condition their referrals to hospitals or ASCs on their purchase of the physician-owned distributorship's (PODs) devices through coercion or promises, for example, by stating or implying they will perform surgeries or refer patients elsewhere if

---

104.   OIG Special Fraud Alert: Physician-Owned Entities (March 26, 2013).

a hospital or an ASC does not purchase devices from the POD, by promising or implying they will move surgeries to the hospital or ASC if it purchases devices from the POD, or by requiring a hospital or an ASC to enter into an exclusive purchase arrangement with the POD.

- Physician-owners are required, pressured, or actively encouraged to refer, recommend, or arrange for the purchase of the devices sold by the POD or, conversely, are threatened with, or experience, negative repercussions (e.g., decreased distributions, required divestiture) for failing to use the POD's devices for their patients.

- The POD retains the right to repurchase a physician-owner's interest for the physician's failure or inability (through relocation, retirement, or otherwise) to refer, recommend, or arrange for the purchase of the POD's devices.

- The POD is a shell entity that does not conduct appropriate product evaluations, maintain or manage sufficient inventory in its own facility, or employ or otherwise contract with personnel necessary for operations.

- The POD does not maintain continuous oversight of all distribution functions.

- When a hospital or an ASC requires physicians to disclose conflicts of interest, the POD's physician-owners either fail to inform the hospital or ASC of, or actively conceal through misrepresentations, their ownership interest in the POD.

C. Cases and Settlements Involving PODs

- On May 3, 2021, a South Dakota neurosurgeon and two medical device distributorships owned by this neurosurgeon agreed to pay $4.4 million to resolve False Claims Act allegations related to illegal payments made to the neurosurgeon to induce him to use certain medical devices in violation of the Anti-Kickback Statute and the Stark Law. This settlement resolved allegations that the neurosurgeon used kickback schemes with medical device distributorships to pay him profit distributions in exchange for using certain medical devices in spine surgeries.[105]

- In September 2014, the DOJ announced that it had intervened in a whistleblower suit under the FCA against a physician, a spinal implant company, and two distributorships owned by the spinal implant com-

---

105. Press Release, U.S. Dep't of Justice, Neurosurgeon and Two Affiliated Companies Agree to Pay $4.4 Million to Settle Healthcare Fraud Allegations, (May 3, 2021).

pany and physician investors.[106] The complaints filed by the government allege that the spinal implant company paid physician investors to use their spinal implants in surgeries they performed. The government also alleged that a physician using the spinal implants performed medically unnecessary or excessive surgeries.

- In October, 2019, the DOJ announced that Sanford Health and related hospital entities agreed to pay $20.25 million to resolve False Claims Act allegations that they knowingly submitted false claims to federal programs resulting from violations of the Anti-Kickback Statute and medically unnecessary spinal surgeries. The settlement resolved allegations that Sanford knew that one of its top neurosurgeons was improperly receiving kickbacks from his use of implantable devices distributed by his physician-owned distributorships.[107]

VI. Fraud and Abuse Risks with Electronic Health Records Arrangements and Electronic Health Record Billing Arrangements

A. Fraud and Abuse Concerns with Electronic Health Record Arrangements

Several concerns have been raised by the healthcare industry that assistance or donations of electronic health record (EHR) hardware and software provided by hospitals or other healthcare entities to physicians may constitute remuneration under the Anti-Kickback Statute or create a compensation relationship under the Stark Law. CMS, in 2006, established an exception to the Stark Law, the Electronic Health Records Items and Services exception, allowed for the donation of interoperable electronic health records software or information technology and training services to providers, such as physicians.[108] The Electronic Health Records Items and Services exception was set to expire on December 31, 2021. As part of the modernization of the Stark Law, CMS removed the sunset, or December 31, 2021, expiration of the Electronic Health Records Items and Services exception.[109] Additionally, CMS modified elements of the exception, by incorporating into the exception cybersecurity software and services and items and services that protect electronic health records, allowing for the donation of replacement items and services are reasonable intervals, and modifying the interoperability

---

106. United States v. Reliance Medical Systems, LLC, et al., CV14-6979 (USDC–Southern District of California).

107. Press Release, U.S. Dep't of Justice, Sandford Health Entities to Pay $20.25 Million to Settle False Claims Act Allegations Regarding Kickbacks and Unnecessary Spinal Surgeries, (October 28, 2019).

108. 71 FR 45140.

109. 85 FR 77608.

element of the exception to deem software interoperable if, on the date of the donation, the software is certified by a certifying body authorized by the National Coordinator for Health Information Technology.[110]

B. Stark Law and Applicable Exceptions

There are four exceptions to the Stark Law related to the provision of electronic information systems, prescribing systems, health records, cybersecurity items, and services to physicians by healthcare providers. These exceptions enable hospitals, group practices, prescription drug plan sponsors, and Medicare Advantage organizations to provide certain technology and other non-monetary remuneration to their medical staffs, physician members, and physicians if certain conditions are met.

The CMS and OIG EHR regulations do not preclude donations of health information technology (HIT) that comply with other safe harbor exceptions. For example, the prepaid plan exception provides that Stark Law designated health services furnished to enrollees of a Medicare Advantage (MA) and other specified risk plans are exempt from the Stark Law prohibitions. Accordingly, financial relationships arising from HIT donations by MA organizations to referring physicians should not trigger the Stark Law prohibitions and there should not be a need to use the new donation exception.

1. EHR Exception

The EHR exception to the Stark Law permits certain individuals and entities to donate EHR software, information technology and training services to physicians provided certain conditions are satisfied.[111]

The donated EHR technology must be *necessary and used predominantly* to create, maintain, transmit, receive, or protect a patient's EHR. It is important for physicians to ensure that an EHR arrangement meets all of the conditions of the EHR exception to address potential liability under the Stark Law.[112]

The following are some of the conditions for donations of EHR items and services that must be satisfied:

- the arrangement is set forth in a written agreement and signed by the parties;

---

110. *Id.*

111. 42 C.F.R. § 411.357(w).

112. On June 6, 2013, CMS agreed to a settlement under the Stark Self-Disclosure Protocol for violations of various provisions of the Stark Law, including an arrangement with a physician to provide EHR subject matter expert services, *available at* https://www.cms.gov/Medicare/Fraud-and-Abuse/PhysicianSelfReferral/Self-Referral-Disclosure-Protocol-Settlements.

- The agreement must specify the items and services provided, the donor's cost of the items and services, and the amount of the physician's contribution;

- the donation must be part of or be used to access an electronic prescription drug program that meets Medicare Part D standards at the time of donation;

- the donor cannot restrict the use or compatibility of the donation with other e-prescribing or EHR systems;

- the donor cannot take into account the volume or value of referrals or other business between the parties when determining eligibility for, or amount or nature of, donations;

- the recipient cannot make the donation a condition of doing business with the donor;

- donated software must be interoperable at the time provided to the physician;

- the recipient must share 15 percent of the donor's cost before the receipt of the initial donation of the items and services or the donation of the replacement items and services;

- the donor must not finance the physician's payment or loan funds to be used bythe physician to pay for the items and services;

- donations cannot include staffing the physician's office or items and services primarily used to conduct personal business or business unrelated to the physician's medical practice; and

2. *Electronic Prescribing Exception*[113]

The Stark Law also contains an e-prescribing exception for items and services that are necessary and used solely to receive and transmit electronic prescription information. This exception protects donations of hardware, software, internet connectivity, and training and support services, provided that the technology meets the applicable standards under Medicare Part D at the time the items and services are donated. A donor entity may provide computers, software, equipment, and technical training to its physicians as long as the items and services are provided as part of or are used to access an electronic prescription drug program that meets the standards of Part D at the time the items and services are provided. The definition of e-prescribing items and services includes software programs that link the two entities' prescribing systems, but excludes billing, scheduling, or administrative software. Non-monetary remuneration that is necessary and used solely to receive and

---

113.   42 C.F.R. § 411.357(v).

transmit electronic prescriptions will not be considered a compensation arrangement that constitutes a financial relationship if eight conditions are met.

The goal of the EHR and e-prescribing exceptions is to encourage physicians to integrate EHR and e-prescribing into their general practices. As a result, the e-prescribing and EHR exceptions mandate that the donor entity may not take any action to limit or restrict the use or compatibility of the donated items or services with external e-prescribing systems. The donor entity must be sure that neither the eligibility of a physician nor the amount or nature of the items or services can be determined in a manner that takes into account the volume or value of referrals or other business generated between the parties.

3. *Community-Wide Health Information Exception*[114]

The community-wide health information exception allows hospitals, group practices, or health plans to give physicians access to their computer network for use of technology that is dedicated specifically to the services of the donor entity and provision of healthcare to its patients. The donor entity may even provide the physician or physician practice with a computer, modem, software, or other information technology items necessary to allow the physician to connect and participate meaningfully in the network. Provision of such goods unnecessarily (i.e. giving a computer to a physician practice that already has a computer system) would constitute improper remuneration, but providing necessary software and technical expertise to assist the provider in joining the network would be appropriate. To the extent that the physician can use the equipment for purposes unrelated to the donor entity, the exception will not protect the entity from exposure to the Stark Law. A donor entity must ensure that the computer or software provided is only capable of interfacing with the specific network for which it is designed. If the computer system is capable of being used for purposes unrelated to the community network, the donor entity must charge the physician fair market value for the equipment or services. An entity may provide access to and sharing of EHR and related information to any community physician as long as:

- the items and services are available as necessary to enable the physician to participate in the system and are not provided in any manner that takes into account the volume or value of referrals and

- the system is available to all providers, practitioners, and residents of the community who desire to participate, and the arrangement does not violate any other laws.

114. 42 C.F.R. § 411.357(u).

4. The Cybersecurity Technology and Related Services Exception[115]

The Cybersecurity Technology and Related Services Exception allows hospitals and group practices to give to physicians and physician practices software or other types of information technology necessary and used predominantly to implement, maintain, or reestablish cybersecurity, provided neither eligibility nor the amount or nature of the technology or services is determined in any manner that directly takes into account the volume or value of referrals or other business generated between the parties. Additionally, the donor is prohibited from making the donation of the technology or services a condition of doing business with the donor.

C. Anti-Kickback Statute

The Anti-Kickback Statute has two safe harbors that are similar in scope to the Stark Law exceptions for e-prescribing and EHR.[116] The exceptions and safe harbors both allow hospitals, group practices, prescription drug plan sponsors, and MA organizations to act as donors of the EHR. The differentiating factor is who may receive donations. The Stark Law exceptions limit recipients to physicians—physician members of the hospital medical staff, physician members of group practices, and prescribing physicians for drug plans and MA plans. The OIG, in its final rule, "Revisions to the Safe Harbors Under the Anti-Kickback Statute and Civil Monetary Penalty Rules Regarding Beneficiary Inducements" modified, in similar manner to CMS's revision of the Stark Law's EHR exception the Anti-Kickback Statute's EHR safe harbor to add protections for related cybersecurity technology, remove he sunset date of the exception, and to update provisions regarding interoperability.[117] The Anti-Kickback Statute safe harbors address donations to other recipients in addition to physicians.

The Anti-Kickback Statute e-prescribing safe harbor allows group practices to donate to prescribing healthcare professional members and health plans to donate to network pharmacists and pharmacies, as well as prescribing healthcare professionals. The EHR safe harbor allows any individual or entity engaged in the delivery of healthcare to receive the donation. In practice, physicians are usually the target of the donations, not only because of the limitations of the Stark Law exceptions but also because they are the primary consumers of the services.

While there is no corresponding exception for the community-wide health information exception, the OIG has described its position on community-

---

115. 42 C.F.R. § 411.357(bb)
116. 42 C.F.R. § 1001.952(x) and (y).
117. 42 C.F.R. § 1001.952(y).

wide interfaces in a 2012 advisory opinion.[118] Where the company that donates the hospital-specific electronic interface provides free access to all providers who request it, the Anti-Kickback Statute will not be implicated.

The OIG added a new safe harbor, Cybersecurity Technology and Services. This new safe harbor allows for certain donations of cyber security technology and services.

D. Recent Government Settlements, Advisory Opinions, and Guidance

1. Recent Settlements Involving EHR Systems

- On January 28, 2021, the DOJ announced that Athenahealth, Inc., a developer of EHR services, agreed to pay $18.25 million to resolve allegations that it violated the FCA by paying illegal kickbacks to generate sales of its EHR product, AthenaClinicals through three marketing programs. The marketing programs included: all-expense paid sporting, entertainment and recreational events; payment of illegal fees to its customers through its "Lead Generation" program designed to identify new prospective customers; and deals with competing companies that had decided to discontinue their HIT products and refer their clients to Athena.[119]

- In June, 2016, Dr. Jonathon Oppenheimer, former owner and CEO of Nashville drug testing laboratory ProstData, Inc., (OURLab) and other related parties agreed to pay $9.35 million to resolve FCA allegations based on alleged violations of the Anti-Kickback Statute and the Stark Law related to donations that OURLab made toward electronic EHR purchased by their client physician practices from EHR vendors. OURLab had made these contributions pursuant to the Anti-Kickback Statute safe harbor and Stark Law exception that allowed labs to contribute to a practice's purchase of an EHR system before drug testing labs were removed from the scope of these EHR safe harbors in 2013. The government had alleged that OURLab had violated the EHR safe harbors by specifically taking actions to improperly consider the amount of Medicare business when making the donation payments throughout their arrangement.[120]

---

118. OIG Adv. Op. No. 12-20 (2012).

119. See Press Release, U.S. Attorney's Office District of Massachusetts (January 28, 2021), Athenahealth Agrees to Pay $18.25 Million to Resolve Allegations that it Paid Illegal Kickbacks.

120. Press Release, U.S. Dep't of Justice, Former CEO-Physician and Drug Testing Laboratory Pay $9.35 Million to Settle False Claims Act Allegations, (June 1, 21016), *available at* https://www.justice.gov/usao-mdtn/pr/former-ceo-physician-and-drug-testing-laboratory-pay-935-million-settle-false-claims.

- On July 7, 2016, the DOJ announced that MD2U, a regional provider of home-based care and its principal owners admitted to violating the False Claims Act and knowingly submitting false claims to Medicare and other federal programs. The government's complaint alleged that MD2U cloned medical records (a cut, copy, paste electronic program) in order to justify patient visits. Specifically, the government's complaint alleged that MD2Uutilized an electronic medical records (EMR) system that permitted the Nurse Practitioners to easily electronically cut, copy, and paste medical notes from prior visits. The ability to migrate notes from visits that occurred weeks, months, or even years prior to the current patient encounter created the illusion that MD2U's Nurse Practitioners were performing a significant amount of work during their patient encounters when, in fact, they were not. If the documentation was deficient to bill the highest level code, MD2U would direct Nurse Practitioners to go back and change the medical record after the encounter had occurred and to falsely show that more work was performed during the visit in order to support the highest level billing.[121]

2. *OIG Advisory Opinion 12-20*[122] *Free Access to an Electronic Interface to Physicians*

In Advisory Opinion 12-20, the OIG addressed a proposed arrangement for a hospital to provide free access to an electronic interface to community physicians and physician practices that would allow those physicians and practices to transmit orders for certain services to, and receive the results of those services from, the hospital. The hospital would provide free access to the interface to all physicians who requested it. The interface would be used by the physicians only to transmit orders and receive results for laboratory and diagnostic services. The free access therefore had no independent value outside of the arrangement. As a result, the OIG concluded that the proposed arrangement would not generate prohibited remuneration under the Anti-Kickback Statute.

3. *CMS Stark Law Advisory Opinion 2008-01*

A hospital system proposed to pay a third-party vendor to develop a physician practice interface customized to each affiliated physician practice's existing EHR software. The proposed software would be used only to order or communicate the results of tests and procedures furnished by the

---

121.   Press Release, U.S. Dep't of Justice, Louisville Based MD2U, a Regional Provider of Home-Based Care, and its Principal Owners Admit to Violating the Federal False Claims Act and Being Liable for Millions, (July 7, 2016).

122.   OIG Adv. Op. No. 12-20 (2012).

123.   *Id.*

hospital system and could not perform any other function or are altered in any way. The advisory opinion cited an exception from the Social Security Act[124] related to the creation of a compensation arrangement. The exception states that "the provision of items, devices, or supplies that are used solely to order or communicate the results of tests or procedures for the entity" does not create a compensation arrangement under the Stark Law. As a result, this type of provision of electronic record services acts as another exception to the Stark Law. While the advisory opinion did not consider the Anti-Kickback Statute, which does not have such an exception, it is probable that under this rationale the service would not generate prohibited remuneration under the Anti-Kickback Statute even if the provided services did not fall under a safe harbor.

4. *OIG Alert—Information Blocking and the Federal Anti-Kickback Statute*

On October 6, 2015, the OIG issued an alert reminder that EHR systems furnished to referral services may not meet the federal Anti-Kickback Statute EHR system safe harbor if the system has limited or restricted interoperability. The OIG specifically noted that donations of items or services that have limited or restricted interoperability due to action taken by the donor or by any person on the donor's behalf would fail to meet one of the conditions of the EHR safe harbor.[125] This alert cites several examples of information blocking that would threaten protection under the EHR safe harbor, e.g., precluding a competitor from interfacing with the donated system, or charging high EHR interface fees to non-recipient providers or suppliers.

5. *Information Blocking Final Rule*

On May 1, 2020, the U.S. Department of Health and Human Services' (HHS) Office of the National Coordinator for Health IT (ONC) published the Information Blocking Final Rule, which is a part of the 21st Century Cures Act focused on ensuring access, exchange and use of electronic health information. The Information Blocking Final Rule became effective on April 5, 2021.[126] Physicians and other providers should ensure that their practices are in compliance with these new federal regulations.

The Information Blocking Final Rule did not provide an exhaustive list or comprehensive description of practices that may implicate the

---

124. Social Security Act § 1877(h)(1)(C).

125. 42 C.F.R § 1001.952(y)(3).

126. 85 Fed. Reg. 25642 (May 5, 2020); https://www.federalregister.gov/documents/2020/11/04/2020-24376/information-blocking-and-the-onc-health-it-certification-program-extension-of-compliance-dates-and.

information blocking prohibition, but does provide some examples, such as imposing unreasonable fees that would prevent patients from accessing their health information. Physicians may experience information blocking when trying to access patient records from other providers, connecting their Electronic Health Record systems to local health information exchanges, migrating from one system to another, and linking with a clinical record data registry.

F. EHR Billing Concerns

1. *General Description*

With technology as sophisticated as the EHR systems, there is a concern that billing errors may be made both intentionally and unintentionally. Increased guidance and discussion emerging from different avenues indicate that the federal government may be focusing some of its resources toward fraud and abuse related to the provision of EHR and other resources used for medical services.

2. *Compliance Concerns*

There are two primary areas of concern with regard to EHR billing: using the EHR to up-code charges and cloning information. Up-coding generally consists of listing more services than were done or listing a service with a higher reimbursement rate than the services done. Cloning occurs when physicians document patient visits by cutting and pasting notes from previous visits in their EHR systems for current visits.

CMS administrators have noted an increase in up-coding from physician offices and hospital emergency departments, and expressed concern that the increased use of EHR systems may be the cause.[127] CMS has announced that there will be ongoing audits conducted of providers' billing practices using EHR systems. These "small, targeted audits" are taking place in parallel with the meaningful use audit program that started in July 2012, and are designed to determine whether providers are properly receiving meaningful use incentive payments and complying with program rules.

3. *Compliance Issues and Recent Government Guidance*

a. Up-Coding and Cloning

The Secretary of HHS and the U.S. Attorney General released a joint letter on September 24, 2012, to address concerns with po-

---

127. Remarks by acting CMS Administrator Marilyn Tavenner at a March 5, 2013, meeting of the Federation of American Hospitals.

tential up-coding and cloning through the use of EHR. In the letter, they commented, "a patient's care information must be verified individually to ensure accuracy; it cannot be cut and pasted from a different record of the patient, which risks medical errors as well as overpayments."[128] This concern was reiterated by the OIG[129] in a December 2013 report on recommended fraud safeguards in hospital EHR technology. The OIG's report emphasized that while most hospitals had recommended audit functions in place, many were not maximizing their potential. As an example, the report partially targeted hospital cloning technology, stating that "the copy-paste feature in EHR technology, if used improperly, is vulnerability to fraud, and only one quarter of hospitals have policies to prevent this technology from being improperly used."[130]

b.   OIG Concerns

The focus on cloning is part of an effort by the OIG to prevent Medicare overpayments by policing how physicians document and bill, particularly for evaluation and management (E/M) services. In its past work plans, the OIG has commented that it would review "multiple E/M services for the same providers and beneficiaries" to identify EHR practices linked to potentially improper payments.[131] The OIG also released a video in July 2017 on its website highlighting concerns with EHR companies falsely representing that its software has functions that the software actually does not include.

In 2014, the OIG issued a report highlighting two examples of EHR documentation practices that could be used to commit fraud: (1) copy-pasting and (2) over-documentation.[132] Copy-pasting enables providers to select information from one source and duplicate it in another location. Fraud occurs when providers inappropriately copy and paste one patient's information into another patient's records to support claims. Over-documentation occurs when providers include irrelevant documentation to

128.   Letter from Obama Administration on hospital billing, NY Times, (Sept. 24, 2012), *available at* https://archive.nytimes.com/www.nytimes.com/interactive/2012/09/25/business/25medicare-doc.html

129.   U.S. Office of Inspector General Report, "Not All Recommended Fraud Safeguards Have Been Implemented in Hospital EHR Technology" (December 2013), *available at* http://oig.hhs.gov/oei/reports/oei-01-11-00570.pdf.

130.   *Id.* at 3.

131.   OIG 2013 Work Plan, p. 25; OIG 2012 Work Plan, p. 20.

132.   OIG Report, "CMS and Its Contractors Have Adopted Few Program Integrity Practices to Address Vulnerabilities in EHRs" (OEI-01-11-00571, Jan. 7, 2014).

support billing for higher-level services. Because some EHR systems auto-populate fields when using templates or create extensive documentation after a single click of a checkbox, a medical record can become inaccurate.

c. OIG 2017 Audit Report on Payment of Meaningful Use Incentive Payments

As an incentive for using certified EHR technology, the federal government made incentive payments to eligible healthcare professionals and hospitals that attest to the "meaningful use" of EHRs. The OIG released an audit report in June 2017 that covered an audit period from May 2011 to June 2014. The OIG concluded that incentive payments to providers totaling $291,222 did not meet with the "meaningful use" requirements of the law. Based upon an extrapolation, the OIG estimated that CMS had inappropriately paid approximately $700 million in incentive payments to physicians and hospitals.

The following are some recommendations by the OIG as a result of this audit:

- recover the $291,000 in payments made to the sampled eligible providers who did not meet the meaningful use requirements,
- review the incentive payments to eligible providers to attempt recovery of the estimated approximately $700 million in inappropriate incentive payments, and
- recover the estimated $2,300,000 in overpayments made to eligible providers due to switching the incentive programs between Medicare and Medicaid.

d. Medicare Contractor Warnings

National Government Services, a Medicare contractor in Indianapolis, warned providers in September 2012 that individualized patient notes for each patient are required, and that cloned notes may cause a provider to overlook new information that may result in safety or quality issues. It stated that "cloned documentation will be considered misrepresentation of the medical necessity requirement for coverage of services due to the lack of specific individual information for each unique patient. Identification of this type of documentation will lead to denial of services for lack of medical necessity and the recoupment of all overpayments made." Other Medicare contractors have released similar statements regarding cloned patient records, focusing on the fact that identical medical documentation from patient to patient will be viewed with suspicion.[133]

---

133. Robert Lowes, *Cloned EHR Notes Jeopardize Medicare Payment,* MEDSCAPE MED. NEWS (Sept. 25, 2012).

Evolving Trends in Physician-Hospital Contracting: Integration, Relationships, and Collaborations Toward Accountable Care

UPDATE BY: *VIOLET M. ANDERSON, J.D.,*
HILARY H. BOWMAN, J.D.,
KELSEY U. JERNIGAN, J.D.,
GABRIEL SCOTT, J.D.[1]

I.   INTRODUCTION

Physicians and hospitals, as well as other physician employers, have a long and often complex history of negotiating how their relationships will be governed. The tone and outcome of negotiations can be affected by a variety of factors, including the sophistication of the parties, geography, competition, management style, hospital governance, the professional liability market, and the current economic climate.

Beginning in the early 2000s, the number of physicians in private practice rapidly decreased. In 2012, 60 percent of all physicians were independent.[2] In 2016, only 32.7 percent of the physicians surveyed were owners, partners, and/or associates of private practices.[3] In a recent survey from 2018, only 31.4 percent were partners or

---

1.   The original edition of this chapter was written by Almeeta E. Cooper and Christopher Mayfield; the 2016 version was updated by Timothy M. Moore and R. Christopher Raphaely; the 2018 version was updated by Robert W. McAdams, Jr., Violet M. Anderson, and Christina Hultsch. In 2019, Hilary H. Bowman, Kelsey U. Jernigan, and Gabriel Scott of K&L Gates LLP provided additional editorial support.

2.   Carol K. Kane, AMA, *Policy Research Perspectives—Updated Data on Physician Practice Arrangements: Inching Towards Hospital Ownership* (2015).

3.   Merritt Hawkins, The Physicians Foundation, 2016 Survey of America's Physicians Practice Patterns & Perspectives (Sept. 2016), *available at* https://physiciansfoundation.org/wp-content/uploads/2017/12/Biennial_Physician_Survey_2016.pdf. . Note that this number may not include physician employed by physician-owned medical groups.

4 Merritt Hawkins, The Physicians Foundation, 2018 Survey of America's Physicians: Practice Patterns and Perspectives (Sept. 2018), *available at* https://www.merritthawkins.com/news-and-insights/thought-leadership/survey/2018-survey-of-americas-physicians-practice-patterns-and-perspectives/.

owners in their practice and Merritt Hawkins remarked that this was "the lowest percent recorded in this survey since it was first conducted in 2012."[4]

Traditionally, physicians leaving private practice sought employment with hospitals either as an individual or through acquisition of their medical practice. In 2013, Deloitte reported that hospital ownership of medical group practices increased by 65.3 percent between 2003 and 2010.[5] In 2014, the American Medical Association (AMA) found through its Physician Practice Benchmark Survey that 25 percent of physicians worked in practices that were at least partly hospital-owned, while an additional 7 percent were directly employed by hospitals.[6] By 2016, however, the AMA discovered that hospital ownership of group practices and hospital employment of physicians had reached its height in 2014 and the survey results showed no significant change in hospital-employed physicians since then.[7]

Even though the physician employment trend has slowed in recent years, a more detailed analysis of workforce data reveals that physicians who are younger and practicing in the area of primary care are more likely to be employed compared to their counterparts.[8] In particular, the AMA found that "[y]ounger physicians were more than three times as likely as older physicians to be employed by hospitals."[9] When physicians are asked why they move to hospital-based employment, they typically say that hospital employment offers guaranteed salaries, accommodation of life style and schedule preferences, and less administrative burden with business operations.

For many years, one key factor that drove hospitals to employ physicians was pressure to develop innovative ways to provide more cost-efficient delivery

---

5. *Physician-Hospital Employment: This Time It's Different* (Deloitte Consulting, 2013) (citing data from D. Gans, *Changes in Ownership for MGMA Practices 2003-2010*, which is an unpublished paper from Medical Group Management Association in 2011)), *available at* https://www2.deloitte.com/content/dam/Deloitte/us/Documents/life-sciences-health-care/us-chs-physician-hospital.pdf.

6. Kane, *supra* note 2; *Policy Research Perspectives—Updated Data on Physician Practice Arrangements: Physician Ownership Drops Below 50 Percent* (2017), *available at* https://www.ama-assn.org/sites/ama-assn.org/files/corp/media-browser/public/health-policy/PRP-2016-physician-benchmark-survey.pdf.

7. In both 2014 and 2016, AMA found that the percentage of practices with some hospital ownership and the percentage of physicians employed by hospitals was 32.8%. Carol K. Kane, AMA, *Policy Research Perspectives: Updated Data on Physician Practice Arrangements: Physician Ownership Drops Below 50 Percent* (2017), *available at* https://www.ama-assn.org/sites/ama-assn.org/files/corp/media-browser/public/health-policy/PRP-2016-physician-benchmark-survey.pdf.

8. Merritt Hawkins, *The Physicians Foundation, 2018 Survey of America's Physicians: Practice Patterns and Perspectives* (Sept. 2018), *available at* https://www.merritthawkins.com/news-and-insights/thought-leadership/survey/2018-survey-of-americas-physicians-practice-patterns-and-perspectives/.

9. Kane, *supra* note 7, at 3.

models. As participation in value-based care has grown, hospitals have believed that they can exert greater influence on the delivery of care and thereby reduce costs, if physicians are employed.[10] For physicians who are compensated on a value-based model, Merritt Hawkins reported that on average only 14.2% of their total compensation is value-based.[11] Even more surprising, one health system (*i.e.*, Geisinger Health System) has already reverted back to salary-based compensation after pursing a value-based model for some time.[12] This data suggests that hospitals are coming to realizations of their own about the limitations of their ability to change practice behaviors of physicians through value-based compensation.

At the height of the recent physician employment trend, hospitals appeared to have the upper hand in contract negotiations. A significant portion of the physician population was, and still is, facing burnout.[13] Physicians were eager to seek employment with hospitals, which gave hospitals the ability to control various aspects of negotiations, such as the timeline for due diligence in acquiring a physician practice or the imposition of more restrictive covenants (*e.g.*, non-compete or non-solicitation provisions) in an employment agreement.

Now that the physician employment trend may be waning, the negotiating advantage hospitals once held may shift to physicians. The key reason for such shift is the growing shortage of physicians. By 2030, the Association of American Medical Colleges (AAMC) estimates there will be a shortage of 49,300 primary care physicians and 72,700 specialty physicians.[14] These shortages are driven by several factors, including a decreasing supply of physicians caused by an aging workforce and an increasing demand for services caused by an aging population and desire to improve population health.[15]

Hospitals are not the only employers that may find themselves in a changing landscape when it comes to contract negotiations. Physicians are increasingly more likely to be affiliated with or employed by new types of entities, including accountable care organizations (ACOs), clinically-integrated networks (CINs), retail clinics, telemedicine companies, and insurance companies.[16] These new types of

---

10. Even though there has been a lot of discussion in the health care industry about compensating physicians in part by certain quality and outcome-based factors, Merritt Hawkins reported that less than half of physicians are compensated on a value-based model. Merritt Hawkins, *supra* note 8, at 44.

11. *Id.* at 45.

12. *Id.*

13. *Id.* at 14.

14. AAMC, *The Complexities of Physician Supply and Demand: Projections from 2016 to 2030* (Mar. 2018), *available at* https://aamc-black.global.ssl.fastly.net/production/media/filer_public/85/d7/85d7b689-f417-4ef0-97fb-ecc129836829/aamc_2018_workforce_projections_update_april_11_2018.pdf.

15. Merritt Hawkins, *supra* note 8, at 35.

16. *Id.* at 26.

employers will face the same contracting and negotiating challenges as traditional hospital employers as a result of the shortage.

This chapter is not intended to be a comprehensive review of every aspect of physician arrangements.[17] Instead, it will address the current regulatory framework for physician arrangements and potential future changes to such framework. This chapter will also address common contractual provisions in physician arrangements and discuss how changing market factors may affect related negotiations.

II. REGULATORY FRAMEWORK OF PHYSICIAN ARRANGEMENTS

The relationships between physicians and hospitals often present a regulatory minefield.[18] The primary federal laws regulating physician recruitment, employment, and staffing are the physician self-referral law, also known as the Stark Law,[19] which is a civil statute, and the Anti-Kickback Statute (AKS), which is a criminal statute.[20] Violations of these laws, in addition to triggering their own penalties, may lead to investigations and litigation by the federal government or a *qui tam* relator claiming a violation of the False Claims Act.[21]

The Stark Law prohibits a physician from referring Medicare patients for certain designated health services (DHS) to an entity with which that physician (or the physician's immediate family member) has a financial relationship, unless an exception applies.[22] The Stark Law contains a long list of exceptions which protect

---

17. Some excellent sources have been written that address the general subject matter. *See generally, e.g.,* EUGENE NELSON & KAY B. STANLEY, PHYSICIAN RECRUITMENT AND EMPLOYMENT: A COMPLETE REFERENCE GUIDE, 2d ed. (Coker Group, 2007); MARIA K. TODD, PHYSICIAN EMPLOYMENT CONTRACT HANDBOOK, 2d ed. (CRC Press, 2011); BERNARD D. HIRSH & DONALD P. WILCOX, HOW TO NEGOTIATE A PHYSICIAN'S EMPLOYMENT CONTRACT (American Medical Association, 1995). This subject was discussed in detail more than 30 years ago. HARRY E. OLSON, JR., PHYSICIAN RECRUITMENT AND THE HOSPITAL (American Hospital Association, 1980).

18. In addition to the federal fraud and abuse laws discussed herein, tax-exempt health systems should also be aware of the regulatory requirements, as well as the significant guidance from the Internal Revenue Service (IRS), as to recruitment and employment arrangements. For example, while outside the scope of this book, it is prudent to ensure that a tax-exempt hospital's recruitment and employment arrangements comply with IRS guidance regarding private inurement issues, which address *e.g.*, loan forgiveness for physicians, and fair market value compensation.

19. 42 U.S.C. § 1395nn; 42 C.F.R. § 411.350–.389.

20. 42 U.S.C. § 1320a-7b.

21. 31 U.S.C. §§ 3729–3733.

22. Recently, some courts have concluded that the Stark Law also applies to Medicaid claims. *See, e.g.*, United States ex rel. Osheroff v. Tenet Healthcare Corp., No. 09–22253–CIV, 2012 WL 2871264, at *1 n.2 (S.D. Fla. July 12, 2012); United States ex rel. Baklid–Kunz v. Halifax Hosp. Med. Ctr., No. 6:09–CV–1002–Orl–31DAB, 2012 WL 921147, at *4 (M.D. Fla. Mar. 19, 2012); Fresenius Med. Care Holdings, Inc. v. Francois, 832 F. Supp. 2d 1364, 1367 (N.D. Fla. 2011), *aff'd as* Fresenius Med. Care Holdings, Inc. v. Tucker, 704 F.3d 935 (11th Cir. 2013); United States ex rel. Schubert v. All Children's Health Sys., No. 8:11-CV-01687-T-27EAJ, 2013 WL 6054803, at *5 (M.D. Fla. Nov. 15, 2013).

remuneration between a referring physician and DHS entity, such as a hospital, to the extent that all requirements of the applicable exception are met. Violations of the Stark Law are punishable through repayment of reimbursements from Medicare for the referring physician's DHS referrals, as well as substantial fines. The Stark Law is a strict liability statute; intent is not a factor.

Similarly, the AKS prohibits, among other things, certain direct and indirect consideration intended to induce the referral of patients to, the arranging for services by, or the recommending of a particular provider of healthcare items or services payable in whole or in part by a federal healthcare program. The AKS also has a list of exceptions and safe harbors that, if satisfied, protect the parties involved from AKS liability.[23]

But the AKS differs from the Stark Law in several respects. Unlike the Stark Law, the AKS is an intent-based statute. Federal courts have held that if the facts and circumstances demonstrate that one purpose of the remuneration was to illegally induce referrals, there will be a violation of the AKS.[24] Furthermore, the AKS is not limited to physicians and their immediate family members. In addition, violations of the AKS may be punished by civil fines *and* criminal penalties.

Below is an overview of common exceptions that apply to recruiting agreements, employment agreements, and professional services agreements.

A. Recruiting Agreements

1. Stark Law

Under the Stark Law, hospitals, federally qualified health centers (FQHC), and rural health clinics are permitted to pay a physician in order to induce the physician to relocate to the entity's geographic service area and become a member of the medical staff.[25]

To comply with the Stark Law recruitment exception, the recruitment arrangement must meet the following criteria: (1) the arrangement is set out in writing and signed by both parties; (2) the arrangement is not conditioned on the physician's referrals; (3) the amount of remuneration under the agreement may not be determined in a manner that takes into account (directly or indirectly) the volume or value of any actual or anticipated referrals by the physician or other business generated between the parties; and (4) the physician must be allowed

---

23. 42 C.F.R § 1001.952.
24. United States v. Davis, 132 F.3d 1092, 1094 (5th Cir. 1998); United States v. Kats, 871 F.2d 105, 108 (9th Cir. 1989); United States v. Greber, 760 F.2d 68, 71-72 (3d Cir. 1985).
25. 42 U.S.C. § 1395nn(e)(5); 42 C.F.R. § 411.357(e).

to establish medical staff privileges at any other hospital and to refer business to other entities.[26]

To meet the recruitment exception's relocation requirement, the physician must relocate the physician's medical practice from outside the hospital, FQHC, or rural health clinic's geographic area, and (a) move the practice a minimum of 25 miles and into the hospital's geographic area or (b) relocate into the hospital's geographic area and the physician's new medical practice derives at least 75 percent of revenue from care provided to new patients, not seen or treated in the last three years. [27] Residents, new physicians and physicians most recently employed by certain federal or state agencies are exempted from the requirement that they have "relocated" their practice but must meet the other requirements.[28]

When recruiting a physician to join an existing physician practice, the following additional criteria must be met in order to fit within the Stark Law recruitment exception: (1) the written agreement must also be signed by the physician practice; (2) except for the actual costs incurred by the physician practice during recruitment, the remuneration must be passed directly through to, or remain with, the recruited

---

26. *See id.* CMS has also provided guidance in several Advisory Opinions as to the Stark Law's recruitment exception, specifically addressing whether a recruited physician who practices outside of the geographic area served by the hospital on a part-time basis has "relocated" their medical practice, see CMS, Advisory Opinion No. CMS-AO-2006-01 (November 2006); whether an excess receipts provision is required to be included in a recruitment agreement with an income guarantee, see CMS, Advisory Opinion No. CMS-AO-2007-01 (September 2007); and whether certain non-competition provisions included in a physician's recruitment agreement are permissible, see CMS, Advisory Opinion No. CMS-AO-2011-01 (May 2011).

27. The geographic area served by the hospital is the area containing the fewest contiguous zip codes from which the hospital draws at least 75 percent of its inpatients. When the hospital draws fewer than 75 percent of its inpatients from contiguous zip codes, the geographic area served by the hospital is the area comprised of all of the contiguous zip codes from which the hospital's inpatients are drawn. For rural health clinics and FQHCs, the area served is the lowest number of contiguous or noncontiguous zip codes from which the FQHC or rural health clinic draws at least 90 percent of its patients, as determined on an encounter basis. The area served may include one or more zip codes from which the FQHC or rural health clinic draws no patients, provided that such zip codes are entirely surrounded by the area from which it draws at least 90 percent of its patients. A similar definition applies to determine a rural hospital's geographic area. 42 C.F.R. § 411.357(e)(2); 42 C.F.R. §411.357(e)(6)(ii).

28. 42 C.F.R. § 411.357(e)(3). Qualifying recent government employment includes, for example, recently working for a federal or state agency in which the physician would not have established a community medical practice, such as a bureau of prisons, the Department of Veterans Affairs, and the Indian Health Service.

physician; (3) in the case of an income guarantee[29] made by the hospital, costs allocated by the physician practice to the recruit may not exceed the actual additional incremental costs to the practice attributable to the recruit; (4) records of the actual costs and the passed through amounts must be maintained for a period of at least six years; (5) the remuneration from the hospital may not be determined in a manner that takes into account (directly or indirectly) the volume or value of any referrals (actual or anticipated) by the recruit or by the practice receiving the direct payments from the hospital (or any physician affiliated with the practice); (6) the practice receiving the hospital payments may not unreasonably restrict the recruit's ability to practice in the geographic area served by the hospital; and (7) the arrangement does not violate the AKS or any federal or state law governing billing or claims submission.[30]

2. *Anti-Kickback Statute*

The "remuneration" generally prohibited by the AKS does not include any payment or exchange of anything of value by an entity in order to induce a practitioner who has been practicing within his or her current specialty for less than one year to locate, or to induce any other practitioner to relocate, his or her primary place of practice into a health professional shortage area (HPSA) for his or her specialty area and that is served by the entity if:

(1) The arrangement is set forth in a written agreement signed by the parties that specifies the benefits provided by the entity, the terms under which the benefits are to be provided, and the obligations of each party.

(2) If a practitioner is leaving an established practice, at least 75 percent of the revenues of the new practice must be generated from new patients not previously seen by the practitioner at his or her former practice.

---

29. The requirements in § 411.357(e)(4)(iii) are triggered by an income guarantee, whether gross income, net income, revenues, or some other variation.

30. 42 C.F.R. § 411.357(e)(4)(vi). However in commentary to the Stark Law recruitment exception, CMS has indicated that certain restrictions imposed by a physician practice on a recruited physician may be permissible, including restrictions related to moonlighting, prohibitions on soliciting patients or employees, requiring the recruit to repay losses on his/her practice absorbed by the practice, and requiring liquidated damages if the physician leaves the practice and remains in the community. CMS noted, however, that a liquidated damages clause that provides for a significant or unreasonable payment may have a substantial effect on the recruit's ability to remain in the service area, thus, may not be permitted. 72 Fed. Reg. 51,012, 51,053–54 (Sept. 5, 2007).

(3) The benefits are provided by the entity for a period not in excess of three years, and the terms of the agreement are not renegotiated during this three-year period in any substantial aspect; provided, however, that if the HPSA to which the practitioner was recruited ceases to be a HPSA during the term of the written agreement, the payments made under the written agreement will continue to satisfy this paragraph for the duration of the written agreement (not to exceed three years).

(4) There is no requirement that the practitioner make referrals to, be in a position to make or influence referrals to, or otherwise generate business for the entity as a condition for receiving the benefits; provided, however, that, for purposes of this paragraph, the entity may require as a condition for receiving benefits that the practitioner maintain staff privileges at the entity.

(5) The practitioner is not restricted from establishing staff privileges at, referring any service to, or otherwise generating any business for any other entity of his or her choosing.

(6) The amount or value of the benefits provided by the entity may not vary (or be adjusted or renegotiated) in any manner based on the volume or value of any expected referrals to or business otherwise generated for the entity by the practitioner for which payment may be made in whole or in part under Medicare, Medicaid, or any other federal healthcare programs.

(7) The practitioner agrees to treat patients receiving medical benefits or assistance under any federal healthcare program in a nondiscriminatory manner.

(8) At least 75 percent of the revenues of the new practice must be generated from patients residing in a HPSA or a Medically Underserved Area or who are part of a Medically Underserved Population.

(9) The payment or exchange of anything of value may not directly or indirectly benefit any person (other than the practitioner being recruited) or entity in a position to make or influence referrals to the entity providing the recruitment payments or benefits of items or services payable by a federal healthcare program.[31]

B. Employment Agreements

1. Stark Law

Under the Stark Law, amounts paid by an employer to an employee pursuant to a bona fide employment relationship are excepted from the

---

31. 42 C.F.R § 1001.952(n).

general prohibition on compensation relationships between a physician and DHS entity (such as a hospital) if: (1) the employment is for identifiable services; (2) the remuneration is consistent with the fair market value of the services and not determined in a manner that takes into account (directly or indirectly) the volume or value of referrals by the employed physician; and (3) the remuneration is provided under an agreement that would be commercially reasonable even if no referrals were made to the employer.[32] The Stark Law employment exception does not prohibit a productivity bonus based on services personally performed by the physician or the physician's immediate family member.[33] Notably, unless the employment contains a directed referral provision,[34] the Stark Law employment exception does not require that the compensation to the employee be set in advance, or set forth in a signed, written agreement. However, it is necessary to ensure that all remuneration to the physician is consistent with fair market value, in order to fit within the Stark Law exception.

As the Stark Law exception requires that employees be paid "fair market value" for the services rendered,[35] it is important to carefully

---

32. 42 U.S.C. § 1395nn(e)(2); 42 C.F.R. § 411.357(c).

33. 42 C.F.R. § 411.357(c)(4). A highly publicized case involving the employment exception to the Stark Law is *United States of America ex rel. Elin Baklid-Junz v. Halifax Hosp. Medical Center*, No. 09-CV-1002, 2013 WL 6017329 (M.D. Fla. Nov. 13, 2013), in which the court concluded that a bonus methodology did not fit within the Stark employment exception, when such methodology was based on pooling a certain percentage of the profit margin of a hospital service line, and distributing such pool based on each physician's personally performed services. The court concluded that the bonus was based on factors in addition to personally performed services, including revenue from referrals for designated health services. *Id.*

34. *See* 42 C.F.R. § 411.354(d)(4) for additional requirements in the event the employment includes a directed referral provision in which the employer conditions an employed physician's compensation on the employee's referrals to a certain supplier or provider.

35. While the AKS safe harbor for employment arrangements does not require that remuneration paid to the bona fide employee is consistent with fair market value, employee compensation in excess of fair market value may raise regulatory scrutiny under the AKS as to the intent of the compensation, in part based on guidance from federal agencies. For example, CMS has previously commented that in certain instances, compensation exceeding fair market value may be considered to take into account the volume or value of the physician's referrals. *See* 69 Fed. Reg. 16,054, 16,059 (January 4, 2001) (discussing when fixed aggregate compensation takes into account the volume or value of referrals, "for example, the fixed compensation exceeds fair market value for the items or services provided or is inflated to reflect the volume or value of a physician's referrals or other business generated."). Further, to deduct employee compensation, the IRS generally requires total compensation to an employee to be reasonable, for services performed, and based on the amount that a similar business would pay for the same or similar services, and "excessive pay" is disallowed as a deduction. *See* IRS Publication 535, Business Expense, Ch. 2 (2018). For this reason and to minimize the potential for regulatory scrutiny generally, hospitals should always review employed physician compensation against fair market value benchmarks.

consider how that fair market value amount is calculated. The Stark Law specifies a definition of fair market value that differs from the traditional definition of that term in other business contexts:

> *Fair market value* means the value in arm's-length transactions, consistent with the general market value. "General market value" means the price that an asset would bring as a result of bona fide bargaining between well-informed buyers and sellers who are not otherwise in a position to generate business for the other party, or the compensation that would be included in a service agreement as the result of bona fide bargaining between well-informed parties to the agreement who are not otherwise in a position to generate business for the other party, on the date of acquisition of the asset or at the time of the service agreement. Usually, the fair market price is the price at which bona fide sales have been consummated for assets of like type, quality, and quantity in a particular market at the time of acquisition, or the compensation that has been included in bona fide service agreements with comparable terms at the time of the agreement, where the price or compensation has not been determined in a manner that takes into account the volume or value of anticipated or actual referrals.[36]

The determination of fair market value under healthcare laws and rules is not necessarily consistent with generally accepted appraisal standards and definitions and may, in fact, prohibit the use of certain data normally relied upon in the classical valuation arena.[37] For instance, the methodology must exclude valuations where the parties to the transactions are at arm's length but are in a position to refer to one another.[38] Additionally, the government intends:

> [t]o accept any method that is commercially reasonable and provides . . . evidence that the compensation is comparable to what is ordinarily paid for an item or service in the location at issue, by parties in arm's-length transactions who are not in a position to refer to one another. (As discussed in section V of [the final rule at 66 Federal Register 856], in most instances the fair market value standard is further modified by language that precludes taking into account the "volume or value" of

---

36. 42 C.F.R. § 411.351.

37. 69 Fed. Reg. 16,054, 16,107 (Mar. 26, 2004) ("Moreover, the definition of 'fair market value' in the statute and regulation is qualified in ways that do not necessarily comport with the usage of the term in standard valuation techniques and methodologies.").

38. *Id.*

referrals, and, in some cases, other business generated by the referring physician. Depending on the circumstances, the "volume or value" restriction will preclude reliance on comparables that involve entities and physicians in a position to refer or generate business.)[39]

The Centers for Medicare and Medicaid services (CMS) has provided additional facts to consider in the determination of whether compensation under an employment arrangement is fair market value. For example, objective compensation surveys compiled by independent, third party valuation companies are a prudent resource to consult when evaluating fair market value. But while that evidence of compensation being within the bounds of objective, benchmarked compensation data may be relevant to a party's intent, it does not establish the ultimate issue: the fair market value for the service provided by the employed physician.[40] When considering fair market value in healthcare transactions and physician relationships, several approaches should be considered, including the income, market, and cost approaches. The analysis also should address all payments and inducements between the parties. Namely, the hospital or health system must consider all clinical, administrative, and other compensation paid to the physician in order to accurately and fairly determine whether the totality of such compensation is fair market value. CMS has clearly acknowledged there are potential differences between the fair market value of clinical and administrative services.[41]

The Stark Law further requires remuneration to be "commercially reasonable" in order to satisfy the requirements of the employment exception, which has been interpreted as:

> An arrangement will be considered "commercially reasonable" in the absence of referrals if the arrangement would make commercial sense if entered into by a reasonable entity of similar type and size and a reasonable physician (or immediate family member or group practice) of similar scope and specialty, even if there were no potential DHS referrals.[42]

---

39. 66 Fed. Reg. 856, 944 (Jan. 4, 2001).

40. 72 Fed. Reg. 51,015 (citing 69 Fed. Reg. 16,107).

41. 72 Fed. Reg. 51,016 ("A fair market value hourly rate may be used to compensate physicians for both administrative and clinical work, provided that the rate paid for clinical work is fair market value for the clinical work performed and the rate paid for administrative work is fair market value for the administrative work performed. We note that the fair market value for the administrative services may differ from the fair market value of clinical services.")

42. 69 Fed. Reg. 16,054, 16,093 (Mar. 26, 2004).

Physicians and hospitals should avoid the appearance of impropriety when establishing the fair market value of physician compensation. For example, if a health system "stacks" the physician's duties and compensation so that the total compensation corresponds to more than a 100 percent full-time employee, this may weaken the validity of the fair market value valuation. Physicians and hospitals are cautioned to avoid potential abuses such as stacking compensation in the fair market value process.

Care should also be taken to avoid the appearance of shopping for a valuation among multiple third party valuators. The ultimate valuator selected and relied upon should be independent and reputable. Careful documentation should be maintained to support the fair market value analysis, in the event it is ever challenged.

2. *AKS*

The AKS is simpler: "Remuneration" does not include any amount paid by an employer to an employee with a bona fide employment relationship with the employer and for employment in the furnishing of any item or service for which payment may be made in whole or in part under Medicare, Medicaid, or other federal healthcare programs.[43]

C. Professional/Personal Services Agreements—Physician Staffing Models

Rather than direct employment, hospitals and health systems may also choose to contract with a physician or physician group to staff a physician practice, a hospital clinic, or a hospital service. Under these arrangements, the group commits to staff the practice, clinic, or service in return for an agreed-upon compensation arrangement. This relationship is typically documented through a professional/personal services agreement (PSA).

A PSA can take many forms, but in the hospital/physician context, a PSA is generally an independent contractor agreement between a hospital and a physician or group of physicians that sets forth the responsibilities of both parties and the corresponding compensation and billing arrangements. PSAs often include provisions addressing physician criteria, hours of service, and use of mid-levels and support staff. Other important contractual provisions could include how performance will be measured, assignment of collections, and insurance.

Over the last decade, federal health care programs and commercial insurers have instituted a number of payment mechanisms that calculate payment

---

43. 42 C.F.R § 1001.952(i). Note that "employee" in the context of the AKS has the same meaning as it does in 26 U.S.C. § 3121(d)(2). *Id.*

to providers based on value of services, not volume alone.[44] These changes have called into question the utility of physician compensation methodologies that pay physicians and physician groups on volume of hours or wRVUs instead of value. For this reason, hospitals are increasingly moving to the second compensation model, which incorporates methodologies that condition payments on the physician or physician group meeting performance-based measures agreed to by the parties. These measures typically are related to the quality of services, patient care considerations, or cost savings metrics. For example, a PSA that is based in part on value measures might require the physician group to be at-risk for a portion of its payment that would be based on the group's physicians achieving certain benchmark scores on 30-day mortality measures.[45] Where the group's physicians do not collectively achieve a qualifying score, the portion of payment tied to that measure would not be paid.

1. Stark Law

A PSA between a hospital and physician or physician group raises a number of potential Stark Law issues, because the arrangement is between a referring physician and a DHS entity. Thus, agreements should be carefully drafted to comply with an applicable Stark Law exception, such as the personal services exception or fair market value (FMV) exception. As discussed in previous sections, meeting all elements of a Stark Law exception is mandatory in order to protect referrals between the parties from the significant legal and financial exposure raised by noncompliance with the Stark Law and False Claims Act.[46]

The Stark Law personal services exception[47] requires:

(1) The arrangement is set out in writing, signed by the parties, and specifies the services covered by the arrangement;

---

44. *See, e.g.,* CMS, Hospital-Acquired Conditions, https://www.cms.gov/medicare/medicare-fee-for-service-payment/hospitalacqcond/hospital-acquired_conditions.html.

45. *See, e.g.,* CMS, Outcome Measures, https://www.cms.gov/medicare/quality-initiatives-patient-assessment-instruments/hospitalqualityinits/outcomemeasures.html

46. The U.S. Department of Justice continues to vigorously prosecute False Claims Acts cases based on violations of the Stark Law. *See, e.g.*, Department of Justice, "Aurora Health Care, Inc. Agrees to Pay $12 Million" (Dec. 11, 2018), *available at* https://www.justice.gov/usao-edwi/pr/aurora-health-care-inc-agrees-pay-12-million-settle-allegations-under-false-claims-act; and Department of Justice, "Detroit Area Hospital System to Pay $84.5 Million" (Aug. 2, 2018), *available at* https://www.justice.gov/opa/pr/detroit-area-hospital-system-pay-845-million-settle-false-claims-act-allegations-arising

47. 42 C.F.R. § 411.357.

(2) The arrangement covers all of the services to be furnished by the physician (or immediate family member);[48]

(3) The aggregate services covered by the arrangement do not exceed those that are reasonable and necessary for the legitimate business purposes of the arrangement(s);

(4) The term of each arrangement is for at least one (1) year;[49]

(5) The compensation to be paid over the term of each arrangement is set in advance, does not exceed fair market value, and, except in the case of a physician incentive plan,[50] is not determined in a manner that takes into account the volume or value of any referrals or other business generated between the parties;

(6) The services to be furnished under each arrangement do not involve the counseling or promotion of a business arrangement or other activity that violates any federal or state law;

(7) If the arrangement terminates after at least one year, a holdover arrangement immediately following the arrangement's termination is permissible if the holdover arrangement is on the same terms and conditions as the immediately preceding arrangement, the previous arrangement complied with (1)-(6) above, and the holdover arrangement remains compliant.[51]

Similarly, the Stark Law FMV exception may be used to protect compensation under a PSA to a referring physician. It shares a number of similarities with requirements under the personal services exception but need not be at least one year in duration. Specifically, the FMV exception requires:

(1) The *arrangement* is in writing, signed by the parties, and covers only identifiable items or services;

(2) The writing specifies the timeframe for the *arrangement*, which can be for any period of time and contain a termination clause,

---

48. This requirement is met if all separate arrangements incorporate each other or if they cross-reference a master list of contracts that is maintained and updated centrally and is available for review upon request. 42 C.F.R. § 411.357(d)(1)(ii).

49. For arrangements terminated before their one-year anniversary, this element is still considered fulfilled if the parties do not enter into another agreement within the original one-year period. 42 C.F.R. § 411.357(d)(1)(iv) ("To meet this requirement, if an arrangement is terminated with or without cause, the parties may not enter into the same or substantially the same arrangement during the first year of the original arrangement.").

50. For a description of the physician incentive plan exception, see 42 C.F.R. § 411.357(d)(2).

51. 42 C.F.R. § 411.357(d)(vii).

provided that the parties enter into only one *arrangement* for the same items or services during the course of a year;[52]

(3) The writing must specify the compensation that will be provided under the *arrangement*; compensation must be set in advance, consistent with fair market value, and not determined in a manner that takes into account the volume or value of *referrals* or other business generated by the *referring physician*;

(4) The *arrangement* must be commercially reasonable (taking into account the nature and *scope* of the transaction) and furthers the legitimate business purposes of the parties;

(5) The *arrangement does not violate the anti-kickback statute*, or any federal or state law or regulation governing billing or claims submission; and

(6) The services to be performed under the *arrangement* do not involve the counseling or promotion of a business *arrangement* or other activity that violates a federal or state law.

Finally, while the personal services and FMV exceptions require that the compensation to the physician be fair market value, the exceptions themselves do not explicitly define what constitutes fair market value compensation. Parties to a PSA should utilize the same definition of fair market value discussed above in the employment context. Obtaining a valuation from an independent third-party valuator is a best practice and highly recommended, particularly for PSAs with a physician group that could involve dozens of referring physicians.

2. *AKS*

As addressed above, because the AKS prohibits the payment of remuneration to induce or reward patient referrals involving services payable by the federal health care programs, a PSA involving hospital and physician parties should be reviewed for compliance with an applicable AKS safe harbor. The safe harbor most often used in the PSA context is the personal services and management contracts safe harbor.

The AKS personal services and management contracts safe harbor[53] requires:

(1) The agency agreement is set out in writing and signed by the parties;

---

52. An arrangement may be renewed any number of times if the terms of the arrangement and the compensation for the same items or services do not change. 42 C.F.R. § 411.357(l)(2).
53. 42 C.F.R. §1001.952(d).

(2) The agency agreement covers all of the services the agent provides to the principal for the term of the agreement and specifies the services to be provided by the agent;

(3) If the agency agreement is intended to provide for the services of the agent on a periodic, sporadic, or part-time basis, rather than on a full-time basis for the term of the agreement, the agreement specifies exactly the schedule of such intervals, their precise length, and the exact charge for such intervals;

(4) The term of the agreement is for not less than one (1) year;

(5) The aggregate compensation paid to the agent over the term of the agreement is set in advance, is consistent with fair market value in arms-length transactions, and is not determined in a manner that takes into account the volume or value of any referrals or business otherwise generated between the parties for which payment may be made in whole or in part under Medicare, Medicaid, or other federal healthcare programs;

(6) The services performed under the agreement do not involve the counseling or promotion of a business arrangement or other activity that violates any state or federal law;

(7) The aggregate services contracted for do not exceed those that are reasonably necessary to accomplish the commercially reasonable business purpose of the services.

D. Potential Changes to the Regulatory Framework

The existing regulatory landscape, especially the Stark Law, contemplates fee-for-service financial incentives for physicians. As healthcare reform continues its focus on reducing health care delivery costs while improving patient outcomes, efforts to expand value-based reimbursement will continue. While today's physician-hospital contracting largely takes the form of employing physicians or group practices, physician-hospital contracting also occurs with CINs or ACOs. All forms of contracting will continue to play significant roles as healthcare reform continues, but hospitals will continue to change compensation and recruitment strategies to contract with team-oriented physicians prepared to work in ACOs and other value-based payment models, perhaps at a more rapid pace than they have to date.

1. Risk-Sharing and Value-Based Reimbursements

Physicians contracting with hospitals should take into account the realities of healthcare reform: Resource-sharing and patient population health management will play prominent roles. In fact, the U.S. Department of Health and Human Services (HHS) for the first time set explicit goals for alternative payment models and value-based payments. In January 2015, HHS announced that it intended to tie 30 percent of traditional, or fee-for-service, Medicare payments to quality or value through alternative payment models, such as ACOs or bundled payment arrangements by the end of 2016 and to tie 50 percent of payments to these models by the end of 2018.[54] HHS also set a goal of tying 85 percent of all traditional Medicare payments to quality or value by 2016 and 90 percent by 2018 through programs such as the Hospital Value Based Purchasing and the Hospital Readmissions Reduction Programs.[55]

<u>*a. Value-Based Contracting Arrangements*</u>

Hospitals under value-based contracting arrangements pay providers for results based on quality, access, and efficiency metrics. Hospitals and physicians will need to meet threshold performance levels in order to qualify for benefits from shared savings plans and other types of value-based contracting arrangements. Failure to meet those levels puts the hospitals and physicians at risk for reduced payment, no payment, or even exclusion from payer networks.[56]

A hospital or health system pursuing designation as an ACO may need to further integrate its employed and private practice physicians. Integration of information technology, management of payer relationships, coordination of care delivery, streamlining of data collection and analytics, and alignment of providers with a hospital's strategic objectives are necessary steps in developing the infrastructure for value-based contracting arrangements.[57] Additionally, organizations should demonstrate their value-driving capacity to attract competent physicians.

<u>*b. Changes in Recruitment Strategies*</u>

Despite national physician shortages, hospitals designing ACOs continue seeking only the best hires who have a high tolerance for changing environments. A survey from the Mediscus Firm

---

54. Press release, U.S. Dep't of Health and Human Servs. (Jan. 26, 2015), *available at* https://www.hhs.gov/about/news/2015/01/26/better-smarter-healthier-in-historic-announcement-hhs-sets-clear-goals-and-timeline-for-shifting-medicare-reimbursements-from-volume-to-value.html.

55. *Id.*

56. Scott J. Cullen et al., A Guide to Physician Integration Models for Sustainable Success (Kaufman Hall, Sept. 2012), *available at* http://www.hpoe.org/Reports-HPOE/guide_to_physician_integration_models_for_sustainable_success.pdf.

57. *Id.*

reveals that 73 percent of healthcare executives involved in ACOs believe their physician recruitment processes and goals will change with new delivery models. A majority of these executives further state that they have increased their recruitment efforts for nurse practitioners and physician assistants.[58]

With new patients under expanded health insurance coverage, hospitals are seeking physicians who can accommodate larger patient volumes. To that effect, recruiters want to know whether prospective physician candidates can adapt to the hospital's business model. They also want highly collaborative physicians with team-oriented outlooks who have the ability to seamlessly interact with advance practitioners and hospital staff. Hospital executives indicate that a physician's use of evidence-based practices, familiarity and competence with technology, and understanding of quality-based incentives all influence hospitals' recruitment strategies.[59]

> c. *Possible Changes in Law to Facilitate New Compensation Models in Hospital-Physician Contracts*

In December 10, 2015, the Senate Committee on Finance and the House Committee on Ways and Means a Senate convened a roundtable concerning whether changes to Stark are necessary to implement the Medicare Access and CHIP Reauthorization Act of 2015 (MACRA), Pub. L. No. 114-10 (2015) and other health care reform.[60] The roundtable's discussion was summarized in the Finance Committee Majority Staff Report, "Why Stark, Why Now? Suggestions to Improve the Stark Law to Encourage Innovative Payment Models" (the "Report").

Recognizing the reluctance of many providers to move toward value-based payment of MACRA and other health care reform because of the "tension between the Stark Law and alternative payment models and the possibility of devastating penalties if they guess wrong," the Report acknowledged Stark's complexity and scope and referenced James A. Wynn of the United States Court of Appeals for the Fourth Circuit, who stated, "'even for well-intentioned health care providers, the Stark Law has become

---

58. Molly Gamble, *How Has the Rise of Physician Employment Changed Hospitals' Recruitment Strategies?*, BECKER'S HOSPITAL R. (Nov. 29, 2012), *available at* http://www.beckershospitalreview.com/hospital-physician-relationships/how-has-the-rise-of-physician-employment-changed-hospitals-recruitment-strategies.html.

59. *Id.*

60. *Id.* at 1.

a booby trap rigged with strict liability and potentially ruinous exposure—especially when coupled with the False Claims Act.'"[61] With respect to implementing value-based payment models that Congress and CMS have promoted, Stark has been a significant impediment.

Before Congress passed health care reform, the health care industry recognized that the Stark Law would be an obstacle to hospitals' and other providers' efforts to align incentives with physicians for certain alternative payment models, including pay-for-performance, gainsharing, bundled payment or outcomes measures. During the American Health Lawyers Association's (AHLA) 2009 Stark discussion, many participants noted that alternative payment programs inevitably link physician payments to the volume or value of referrals – a payment formula that will generally not pass muster under the compensation arrangement exceptions to the Stark Law.[62]

While the Affordable Care Act authorizes the HHS Secretary to issue regulatory payment waivers from Stark for innovative payment and service delivery models and while MACRA modifies the Civil Monetary Penalties law (CMP), 42 U.S.C. § 1320a-7a, to specify that gainsharing applies only to inducement made to reduce or limit medically necessary services to beneficiaries and removes some barriers to gainsharing and pay-for-performance programs, the waivers and the modification of the CMP do not protect all alternative payment models under MACRA or with commercial payers.[63]

In 2018, CMS issued a Request for Information focused on identifying the regulatory burdens of the Stark Law, aiming to determine whether revising Stark was necessary to eliminate regulatory impediments to implementing value-based reimbursement.[64] CMS sought information on alternative payment models, proposals for additional Stark Exceptions to facilitate innovation, proposals to modify existing Stark Law provisions, proposals to change compensation approaches, and changes to protect ACOs

---

61. *Id.* at 2. (citing United States ex rel. Drakeford v. Tuomey Healthcare Sys. Inc., No. 13-2219 U.S. App. LEXIS 11460 at *56, *69 (4th Cir. July 2, 2015)).

62. *Id.* at 2-3.

63. *Id.* at 3.

64. *Medicare Program; Request for Information Regarding the Physician Self-Referral Law*, 83 Fed. Reg. 29,524 (June 25, 2018).

and bundled payment models.[65] After hearing concerns raised by stakeholders in the healthcare industry, Seema Verma, Administrator of CMS, in March 2019, at the Federation of American Hospitals 2019 Public Policy Conference, recognized:

> This Administration is focused on driving competition and unleashing the forces of innovation to help us drive down costs and improve health outcomes. This starts with payment innovation to better align financial incentives for providers to deliver efficient, high quality care. When providers have responsibility for managing a budget and their reimbursement is tied to the results they produce, they will be incentivized to find innovative ways to keep people healthy and lower costs.[66]

Verma highlighted that only 14 percent of providers in Medicare were in value-based arrangements and further recognized the movement toward value-based reimbursement was slow and needed to speed up.[67] Verma identified the enactment of the Stark Law in a largely fee-for-service context and distinguished paying for value, "where the provider, ideally, is taking on some risk for outcomes and cost overruns" mitigates the need to interfere with compensation models to prevent physicians from ordering services based on their financial interests.[68] Accordingly, Verma announced an update to the Stark Law that would be issued later in 2019 to "spur better care coordination and help support our work to remove barriers to innovation."[69]

The Stark Law has largely shaped the parameters for physician-hospital contracting. It appears CMS is moving toward allowing more flexibility in creating compensation models, provided those models center on value-based reimbursement. The upcoming Stark Law modifications are likely to be the catalyst for the next generation of hospital-physician contracts.

---

65. *Id.*

66. Press Release. "Speech: Remarks by Administrator Seema Verma at the Federation of American Hospitals 2019 Public Policy Conference" (March 4, 2019). https://www.cms.gov/newsroom/press-releases/speech-remarks-administrator-seema-verma-federation-american-hospitals-2019-public-policy-conference.

67. *Id.*

68. *Id.*

69. *Id.*

III. AMA PHYSICIAN EMPLOYMENT PRINCIPLES

In addition to the regulatory landscape, the parties involved in physician arrangements should also be aware of AMA's guiding principles concerning physician employment. In 2017,[70] the American Medical Association (AMA) House of Delegates (House) reaffirmed[71] the "Principles for Physician Employment," first adopted in 2012.[72] The House wrote the principles as a way to "address select, potentially problematic aspects of the employer-employee relationship" rather than to comprehensively explain all physician-hospital contractual matters. While the principles aid physicians in negotiating employment arrangements, the AMA designed the principles to benefit physicians and those who employ physicians alike.[73] Specifically, the House approved positions on conflicts of interests, patient and profession advocacy, contracting, hospital medical staff relations, peer review and performance evaluations, and payment agreements. (A copy of the principles is attached as Appendix 1.)

A. Potentially Problematic Aspects of Employer-Employee Relationships[74]

1. *Conflicts of Interests*

The AMA cautions physicians that contractual standards must signify a clear delineation between the physician's professional judgment and financial needs of his or her employer. This means that the patient-physician relationship should not be altered by the health care system or setting in which a physician practices, or the methods by which he or she is compensated. While certain checks and balances between the cost and quality are necessary for provision of heath care services, the AMA principles underscore the need for the medical staff to play an important role in striking the balance between operating a business and providing high-quality care. To avoid the type of economic credentialing that some managed care organizations conducted in the 1990s, the AMA advises against provisions where non-clinicians cast the deciding votes in credentialing decisions.

---

70. AMA, "Reports of the Council on Medical Service," 2017 Annual Meeting, *available at* https://www.ama-assn.org/sites/ama-assn.org/files/corp/media-browser/public/hod/a17-cms-reports.pdf

71. AMA, Principles for Physician Employment H-225.950, *available at* https://policysearch.ama-assn.org/policyfinder/detail/AMA%20Principles%20for%20Physician%20Employment%20?uri=%2FAMADoc%2FHOD.xml-0-1535.xml.

72. AMA, Principles for Physician Employment, *available at* https://www.ncmedsoc.org/wp-content/uploads/2013/09/ama-principles-for-physician-employment.pdf.

73. *Id.*

74. *Id.*

2. *Advocacy for Patients and the Profession*

The AMA principles note that patient advocacy is a fundamental element of the patient-physician relationship. Accordingly, physician employment contracts should delineate whether malpractice insurance covers volunteer clinic work, and contracts should address a physician's ability to teach and provide expert witness testimony.

3. *Contracting*

It is commonplace for physicians to tell their lawyers, "I've already negotiated most of my contract; I just want to know if my compensation looks okay." The AMA principles advise that physicians retain attorneys to examine the entire contract. An employment contract should be reviewed holistically, with consideration given to whether it restricts or infringes on the physician's ability to practice medicine. Specifically, the contract should provide formulas and examples for compensation, including hourly fees and other arrangements related to professional services, education, expertise, and skills.

Effective financial incentives for work productivity include satisfactory patient surveys, billing, meeting certain quality indicators, and personal performance of services in excess of a certain threshold. Suspect incentives may include payment for keeping patient referrals internal; meeting financial benchmarks that reduce care, such as reduced lab testing or less imaging; and other strategies for reducing costs, particularly those that correspond to reductions in the provision of medically necessary services.

Contracts regularly state that "medical records are the property of the hospital." Most states' laws provide that hospitals are legal custodians of medical records.[75] However, where physician possession of all medical records of his or her patients is not already required by state law, the AMA principles recommend that an employment agreement specify that the physician is entitled to copies of patient charts and records upon a specific request in writing from any patient, or when

---

75. *See, e.g.*, 10A NCAC 13B .3903, Preservation of Medical Records (2018) (stating that medical records in North Carolina remain the property of the hospital). However, a state medical board may establish obligations upon physicians relative to disposition of medical records independent of the hospital's custodial obligations. *See* NORTH CAROLINA MEDICAL BOARD, POSITION STATEMENT ON MEDICAL RECORDS, *available at* https://www.ncmedboard.org/resources-information/professional-resources/laws-rules-position-statements/position-statements/medical-records-documentation-electronic-health-records-access-and-retentio (imposing a duty on physicians to be able to be able to provide a copy of a patient's medical record, upon request, in a timely manner, including medical records maintained by other health care facilities).

such records are necessary for the physician's defense in malpractice actions, administrative investigations, or other proceedings against the physician. If a physician is either terminated or leaves a hospital, the AMA advises that contract language clarify who notifies patients, the content and timing of the notification, and the hospital response when patients call for an appointment with the departed physician.

4. *Hospital Medical Staff Relations*

The AMA principles suggest that contracts' duty of loyalty provisions should not be written broadly. The concern is that overreaching with respect to the duty of the physician to the hospital or hospital system may come at the expense of the patient and violate the physician's ethical responsibilities. The AMA states that employment contracts should include provisions to protect a physician's right to due process before termination for cause, and hospitals should not be allowed to terminate physician employees without medical staff approval. The AMA policies underscore the importance of the medical staff as the collegial self-governance mechanism for monitoring and improving patient care in the hospital.

5. *Peer Review and Performance Evaluations*

Contractual language should distinguish, to the extent possible, between medical staff-based peer review conducted solely for the purpose of enhancing quality and reducing mortality and morbidity, medical staff-based peer review associated with potential corrective action, and employed physician performance evaluations. This means that peer review of employed physicians should be conducted independently of and without interference from any human resources activities of the employer, and employers should provide employed physicians with regular performance evaluations, which should be presented in writing and accompanied by an oral discussion with the employed physician.

6. *Payment Agreements*

The AMA counsels that a hospital's perspective on matters relating to patient care may differ from those of the medical staff and the physician members of the medical staff, particularly in the areas of cost containment, allocation of resources, managed care contracting, scope of services provided, and contract exclusivity. Although physicians typically assign their billing privileges to their employers, employed physicians have a responsibility to assure that bills issued for services they provide are accurate. Physicians should be prospectively involved if the employer negotiates agreements for them for professional fees, capitation or global billing, or shared savings. Additionally, employed physicians should be informed about the actual payment amount allocated to the professional fee component of the total payment received by the contractual arrangement.

B. Related Codes of Medical Ethics

Additional opinions within the AMA Code of Medical Ethics elaborate on elements of the AMA physician employment principles. Opinion 11.2.1 states that compensation incentives should, among other things, be "based on appropriate comparison groups and cost data and adjusted to reflect complexity, case mix, and other factors that affect physician practice profiles."[76] Opinion 11.2.3.1 discourages restrictive covenants that are excessive in geographic scope or duration.[77] Additionally, Opinions 10.2[78] and 11.2.3[79] speak to hospital-physician employment arrangements.

IV. CONTRACTUAL ISSUES WITH PHYSICIAN ARRANGEMENTS

A. Standard Contract Provisions and Process

1. Standard Provisions

Despite the variety of physician-hospital arrangements, certain terms appear in nearly every contract. Physicians and hospitals can expect to see terms covering compensation, professional expenses, paid time off, employment benefit programs, professional liability insurance, billing practices, confidentiality, termination, and arbitration, and, when contracting with religious-affiliated hospitals, physicians can also expect to see terms covering ethical and religious directives. Despite common use, the terms may be negotiable. Attorneys and physicians should carefully consider even standard terms when drafting a physician-hospital contract.

---

76. AMA, Opinion 11.2.1: Professionalism in Health Care Systems (2016), *available at* https://www.ama-assn.org/sites/default/files/media-browser/code-of-medical-ethics-chapter-11.pdf.

77. AMA, Opinion 11.2.3.1: Restrictive Covenants and the Practice of Medicine (2016), *available at* https://www.ama-assn.org/sites/default/files/media-browser/code-of-medical-ethics-chapter-11.pdf.

78. AMA, Opinion 10.2: Physician Employment by a Non-physician Supervisee (2016), *available at* https://www.ama-assn.org/sites/default/files/media-browser/code-of-medical-ethics-chapter-10.pdf.

79. AMA, Opinion 11.2.3: Contracts to Deliver Health Care Services (2016), *available at* https://www.ama-assn.org/sites/default/files/media-browser/code-of-medical-ethics-chapter-11.pdf.

Chapter 2

2. *Contracting Process*

Hospitals and physicians must consider general contract principles when negotiating and executing agreements. In addition to considering general contract principles, hospitals and physicians must abide by federal healthcare regulatory laws and certain state laws, such as state corporate practice of medicine laws and state fee-splitting laws. Even though large, multi-specialty medical groups, hospitals, health systems, and clinics may not permit significant departure from standard contractual provisions, physicians should ask for clarification of any unclear contractual provision and work with the hospitals or other contracting parties to revise ambiguous provisions to clearly express the contractual arrangement. All changes should contemplate the physician's provision of services under the agreement as well as the physician's specialty.[80] Regardless of an employer's oral explanation of ambiguous language or oral promise to change contractual provisions, the written contract is, in most cases, the final word. While verbal promises may be comforting at the time, the written contract almost always controls. It is imperative to appropriately modify agreements to eliminate or modify ambiguous provisions before the parties sign the contract.

3. *Physician and Hospital Interests*

Physicians and hospitals have individual interests to protect when signing contracts. By understanding the other side's concerns, each can reach more productive agreements.

a. *Physician's Perspective*

Compensation. From the physician's perspective, compensation is often the dominant factor in assessing the value of an offer. As the hospital and the physician negotiate compensation, physicians may consider asking the hospital to identify which regulatory considerations govern the arrangement. Knowledge of the legal parameters used to define compensation may assist the physician in negotiating compensation terms with the hospital. For example, if the physician intends to enter into an employment relationship with a hospital, awareness of Stark's employment exception remuneration elements (fair market value for the services, no consideration of the volume or value of referrals made by the physician, and commercial reasonableness) may aid the physician in inquiring about and negotiating compensation.

---

80. BERNARD D. HIRSH & DONALD P. WILCOX, HOW TO NEGOTIATE A PHYSICIAN'S EMPLOYMENT CONTRACT (American Medical Association, 1995).

The physician may also consider asking the hospital to identify the appraisal reports or other guidance used to establish the fair market compensation rate and question whether the appraisal reports or other guidance sufficiently contemplate the services the physician is to perform, the physician's anticipated productivity, and market demands. Concerning compensation under any value-based arrangement/alternative payment model, the physician should ask the hospital to specifically identify: the activities to be undertaken under the arrangement; the target population for the arrangement; the nature of the payment; metrics or perfor- . mance standards that trigger payments; the frequency quality or efficiency will be measured and the methodology used for such measurements; the physician's data reporting duties; and the extent to which the physician is to participate in or facilitate audits by the hospital. And, perhaps most important from the physician's perspective, the physician should understand whether the physician is exposed to downside risk.

A well-drafted compensation provision will quantify the physician's base compensation (whether hourly, per diem, per annum, etc.), and, when useful, delineate the elements contemplated in the compensation, for example, minimum work relative value units (wRVUs) and wRVU conversion factor. As well as clearly establishing the compensation rate, the contract must identify when the physician is to receive payment. Beyond base compensation, the contract should address any incentive payment opportunities, for example, productivity incentives tied to exceeding threshold relative value units. When assessing compensation for services, physicians should carefully consider which elements of compensation are outside of the physician's control as well as consider which elements the hospital will rebase and under which conditions the hospital will adjust compensation. Ideally, the contract will define the conditions under which the hospital will adjust compensation, the frequency the hospital will examine whether an adjustment is necessary, and the timeframe within which the adjustment will become effective. Finally, as health systems implement more alternative payment/ value-based compensation arrangements, the physician must always consider whether compensation is at risk and whether performance standards and metrics are measured in a defensible manner and whether goals are reasonable.

Compliance with Hospital's Medical Staff Bylaws, Policies and Procedures. Contracts commonly contain provisions that establish the physician's duty to abide by all applicable policies and procedures. Physicians should seek clarification about all policies and procedures that will apply and should consider having those policies identified in an exhibit to the contract and included in the contract language.[81]

Hospitals' policies and procedures often cover: deadlines to document the provision of clinical services; coding responsibilities; the manner in which the physician is to submit demands for payment and reimbursement of expenses; obligations to perform administrative services; and duties to attend quality and compliance meetings. Physicians should always request a copy of the hospital's medical staff bylaws and explore additional duties mandated under the bylaws. Some medical staff bylaws may require physicians to provide specified hours of uncompensated emergency room call coverage and identify duties to attend administrative meetings. In most cases, policies govern the physician's benefits, including, without limitation: health, dental, and vision insurance; malpractice insurance; disability insurance; sick leave; paid time off; retirement plans; professional membership dues; relocation expenses; and student loan repayment. Related to medical staff bylaws and hospital policies, when working with religious-affiliated hospitals, expect the hospital to provide services in accordance with the direction provided by its religious sponsor. Religious-affiliated hospitals may, by specific contractual terms, policies and procedures, or medical staff bylaws provisions obligate physicians to abide by ethical and religious directives that may impact the physician's ability to perform certain medical services. Often compliance with such directives is non-negotiable. When examining the religious mandates, a physician should assess the extent to which restrictions impact the physician's provision of services, assessing specifically whether the religious restrictions prohibit the physician from providing elective abortions, elective sterilization, research on aborted fetuses, or whether the religious restrictions affect any other research activities or clinical activities. Particularly when a physician contracts with a religious-affiliated hospital and the physician remains an independent contractor, the physician should determine whether the hospital requires the physician to comply with religious mandates only when providing services on the hospital's campus only or whether the

---

81. MARIA K. TODD, PHYSICIAN EMPLOYMENT CONTRACT HANDBOOK, 2d ed. (CRC Press, 2011), at page 9.

mandates extend to the physician's performance of services off-campus at other hospitals or in the physician's private office. A physician contracting with a religious-affiliated health system should determine whether "scandalous" activity, often defined by the health system, allows for immediate termination of the agreement. If so, the physician should strive to have the health system clearly define in the agreement the activities that may fall within the health system's definition of "scandal."

When determining the value of an offer, obligations under medical staff bylaws, policies, and ethical and religious directives are significant considerations that may impact paid time off, establish uncompensated call coverage duties, require uncompensated administrative duties and meeting attendance, limit the physician's ability to perform certain services, limit the physician's ability to conduct certain forms of research, and define behavioral expectations through religious affiliations. Awareness of duties established in medical staff bylaws and hospital policies and procedures helps the physician understand additional duties beyond treatment that, if not satisfied, afford the hospital an opportunity to assert breach of contract.

Outside Activities. Outside activities provisions define the parameters under which the physician may provide clinical services or other professional services outside the physician's arrangement with the hospital. Many outside activities provisions are designed to restrict the physician from providing any service that may limit the physician's ability to be available to perform services under the contract with the hospital. An outside activities provision may impact a physician's ability to conduct research activities, consult, and provide medical director services outside of the hospital contract. In addition to limiting a physician's ability to work outside the practice, an outside activities policy, within the context of an employment agreement with a hospital, may also establish whether income related to the outside activities is considered compensation that may be paid directly to the physician or must be paid to the physician's employer. The physician should determine whether an outside activities provision permits the physician to undertake outside activities upon the hospital's consent and the physician should also determine whether the hospital has a duty to act "reasonably" in deciding to deny the physician's request to perform outside activities.

Assignment. Physicians should also examine assignment clauses. Physicians may want to ensure that a hospital cannot assign the contract to a third party without prior written authorization, to prevent the hospital from assigning the physician's contract to an organization with fewer management and financial resources or a different patient base.[82] If a hospital refuses to omit an assignment provision that allows the hospital to assign the contract without receiving the physician's prior consent, the physician may pursue a compromise. The physician may consider asking the hospital to modify the assignment provision so that the hospital may only assign the agreement, without the physician's prior written consent, to an entity affiliated with the hospital by ownership or control, or allow the physician to terminate the arrangement, without cause, upon brief (for example, 10 days) written notice.

Additional issues the physician may want to address:[83]

(1) What is the employer's status with the Bureau of Workers' Compensation?

(2) Are all physicians in good standing with the medical board?

(3) What is the malpractice experience of physicians in the practice? What was the outcome in those cases?

(4) Will the new employer assist the physician in the licensure process?

(5) Does the physician need to apply for medical staff privileges before the physician begins employment?

(6) Are all physicians required to be board-certified?

(7) Does the contract state how leave is accruable in hours per pay period?

(8) To what extent will the physician be required to contract with certain managed care payors?

(9) To what extent will the physician be required to provide charity care services?

(10) What is the frequency of administrative meetings that the physician is required to attend?

(11) Does the arrangement require the physician to participate in any CIN or ACO activities?

---

82. *Id.*

83. *See also* Steven M. Hacker, *Physician Employment Agreements: Read the Fine Print,* THE STUDENT DOCTOR NETWORK (Apr. 3, 2011).

(12) What data must the physician provide to the hospital and why?

(13) If the physician is an independent contractor, what, if any, access to the physician's personal records must the physician provide the hospital?

b. *Hospital's Perspective*

Background Information. Hospitals will want background information about the physician. A key fact for the hospital to determine is whether the physician is excluded from federal healthcare programs or has been subject to discipline.[84] In addition to determining whether the physician is excluded from federal healthcare program participation, hospitals frequently contractually obligate the physician to disclose adverse actions taken against the physician by any state licensing board, medical society, specialty board, any claim of negligence or malpractice asserted against the physician, as well as any denial of privileges.

Insurance. Hospitals will also require documentation of malpractice insurance if the physician is contractually obligated to obtain insurance. A minority of states have medical malpractice patient compensations funds, state-administered funds used to compensate patients. For example, the Louisiana patient compensation fund basically plays the role of an "excess insurer" of private healthcare providers. Louisiana's patient compensation fund laws allow a provider to have financial responsibility for the first $100,000 of exposure per medical malpractice claim whether through insurance or security deposit and enroll in the fund for the excess coverage.[85] Once enrolled in the fund, Louisiana law limits recovery for malpractice claims to $500,000 plus interests and costs, excluding future medical care and related benefits.[86] Hospitals in patient compensation fund states may conclude that if the physician's liability is capped through the state's fund a coordinated defense to a medical malpractice lawsuit is more likely, believing the physician and hospital may be more inclined to either negotiate a settlement or mount a common defense. Physicians who perform services in states that have patient compensation funds should expect hospitals to strongly encourage participation in the fund and should also expect a representa-

---

84. The federal exclusion database is *available at* https://exclusions.oig.hhs.gov/.

85. *See* DOA Louisiana Patient's Compensation Fund, *available at* https://www.doa.la.gov/Pages/pcf/index.aspx.

86. *See* La. R.S. 40:1231.2 and La. R.S. 40:1231.3.

tion in the contract centered on participation in the patient compensation fund.

Immediate Termination. Contracts often establish the hospital's ability to immediately terminate the agreement upon the occurrence of any of the following: the physician's exclusion from a state or federal healthcare program; the physician's failure to satisfy malpractice insurance requirements set forth in the agreement; the physician's loss or restriction of medical state licensure; if a material representation becomes false; or the physician's conviction of a felony or a misdemeanor involving moral turpitude.

Selection of Equipment and Supplies. Additionally, hospitals may have a preferred equipment supplier. Hospitals should disclose to physicians this information about their purchasing programs to avoid misunderstanding later if the new physician has preferences for particular brands of supplies and equipment.[87]

B. Current Contractual Hot Spots

Some contract provisions are straightforward. Others generate debate as physicians and hospitals negotiate for favorable contractual arrangements. While state-specific contract law and statutes drive many of these issues, an understanding of physician-hospital contracting helps physicians and hospitals better navigate these complicated issues.

Contractual elements that prove especially contentious are due diligence terms (including confidentiality clauses), non-competition terms, and non-solicitation provisions. Clauses concerning terms and the standard of care, disability insurance, and extended reporting "tail" policy upon termination of the contractual arrangement also cause some negotiation, though are more manageable.

1. Due Diligence and Related Terms When Acquiring the Physician Practice in Conjunction with Employment/Contracting

General due diligence terms. These terms will allow the recruiting health system access to otherwise confidential information—such as data, records, information, and vendor agreements—to determine whether to move forward with recruiting the physician.

Information technology and systems remediation. Typically, during the due diligence phase and prior to completing a transaction, the health system will review the physician group's information technol-

---

87. HARRY E. OLSON, JR. PHYSICIAN RECRUITMENT AND THE HOSPITAL 71 (1980).

ogy and systems. The health system may also choose to begin running T-1 lines and placing the necessary infrastructure into the existing practice so the practice is on the new systems and can hit the ground running. Often, deals become delayed or do not happen. What happens with the deployed infrastructure and the costs to restore the practice to its pre-deal condition? Parties should address this during negotiations in a letter of intent, specifically, in a binding provision that survives the letter of intent's termination.

Confidentiality. Before the parties dive into a deal, they must determine what each considers confidential and whether the other party can legitimately gain access to that confidential information. The parties may contractually agree to keep the discussions and negotiations confidential, including information sharing during meetings and the due diligence process. However, a physician may be prohibited from revealing any of the business aspects of his or her current employment agreement, the financial or other proprietary data and information of his or her existing employer and/or group, or other information that may be pertinent to the recruiting health system in making a decision about whether to recruit/employ the physician. All of the effort expended on developing a deal can become meaningless if the disclosing party did not have the right to grant access to the confidential information and the deal is therefore ultimately thwarted. Moreover, it can lead to needless legal costs and headaches.

No shop clauses. Typically, the recruiting health system will require the physician to agree not to talk or negotiate with any other recruiting health system or potential party with which the physician may contract, including, without limitation, a physician group for a time long enough to allow the health system to complete due diligence, including valuations on assets and consideration of compensation, review of vendor agreements, review of employee credentials and background checks, and other items.

Representations and warranties. Representation and warranty provisions are intended to provide assurance that the physician is eligible for employment or contacting and under no arrangements restricting discussions and offers by the recruiting health system.

These terms also attempt to mitigate risk regarding tortious interference claims. Tortious interference occurs when a person or business damages another person's or business's contractual relationships or other business relationships intentionally. These claims are often pursued in actions between competing businesses. Typical actions giving rise to liability include inducing customers to breach contracts, enticing employees to leave, and making false statements about the competing business.[88]

Courts have required that the plaintiff in a tortious interference case provide proof that the defendant acted improperly, purposefully, and maliciously with intent to cause harm to the plaintiff by inducing a third party or parties to discontinue or refrain from a business relationship with the plaintiff. Furthermore, the defendant must have caused economic injury to the plaintiff.[89]

Several defenses against tortious interference lawsuits exist, including the right of fair competition. Fair competition is always permitted. Former employees may seek employment from a competing business or start new businesses themselves. They can make use of expertise from a former employer and compete for the same customer base so long as they do not use proprietary information or make misleading statements. To guard against competition from a former employee, many employers put restrictive covenants in their employment contracts.[90]

Avoidance of bad press during the recruiting process. Recruitment efforts and disputes often end up in local and regional media outlets, resulting in potentially embarrassing and often hostile reactions from interested parties. The health system and the recruit must be aware of this issue as they proceed in the recruitment process. Confidentiality provisions can go a long way towards mitigating this risk.

Health Insurance Portability and Accountability Act compliance. Having an agreement in place provides adequate documentation for protection under the Health Insurance Portability and Accountability Act that the parties are intending on an arrangement for the physician(s) to join the health system.

2. *Non-Competition and Non-Solicitation*

Non-competition and non-solicitation provisions limit the ability: (1) to leave an existing employer or group and join another employer or group within the same geographical market and (2) to hire existing staff in a new practice setting. State law varies considerably about the enforcement and effectiveness of non-compete and non-solicitation laws.

---

88. RESTATEMENT (SECOND) OF TORTS § 766; Penna v. Toyota Motor Sales, 902 P.2d 740 (Cal. 1995) (outlining the development of the tort).
89. RESTATEMENT (SECOND) OF TORTS § 766.
90. *Id.*

Many physicians have "heard" that non-competition and non-solicitation clauses are unenforceable and therefore can be ignored. Some physicians claim their lawyers have told them to sign without worry because a court will *never* enforce them. Physicians believing this urban legend are ill advised. In many states, non-competition language is enforceable. While courts will make case specific determinations about enforceability, and every case is unique, *courts are enforcing them.* The general rule of thumb continues to be that a non-competition or non-solicitation clause is more likely to be upheld if the limitation is reasonable in geographic scope and duration and the limitation specifically identifies the activities the physician is not to perform. Thus, physicians should know the standards in the physician's state. Generally, the more ambiguous the description of limited services, the greater the duration and geographic limitation, and the more adverse impact upon the departing physician, the more likely a court may be to "reform" or overturn the limitation.

From a purely practical perspective, counsel advising his or her client should emphasize that the client cannot expect verbal promises made by unauthorized parties to be binding or persuasive in court. Further, counsel should communicate that a hospital's leniency with another physician three, two, or even one year ago does not mean the hospital will extend the same to the client. In addition, non-competes tend to be specialty specific. One specialty at the same hospital may have a five-mile radius limitation while another specialty may have a ten-mile radius limitation.

Careful advice must be given to both the party enforcing the non-compete as well as the party subject to the non-compete. When one is before a judge in a temporary restraining order hearing, the hospital representative must be able to articulate a rational, reasonable basis for the limitation. There should be some evidence-based analysis to support the hospital's alleged harm. That analysis should focus on how allowing the departing physician to reestablish a practice immediately in the same locale will unduly compromise the hospital's human and financial investment. Supporting documentation should be reasonably current and updated at least every three years.

A few practice pointers: Careless e-mails and memos that contradict either side's position can carry the day. Administrative oversight should include periodic review of whether the non-competition and/or non-solicitation limitations are being fairly and consistently applied. Anecdotal recollection will be trumped by the cold, hard facts unearthed in the discovery process. Beliefs that only one exception has been made in many years when in fact there have been multiple exceptions for "insiders" and friends hurt a party's consistency and fair application argument.

Further, if there is an option to buy out a non-competition or non-solicitation limitation, careful thought should be given in advance as to how that amount should be calculated, and if breach of the non-competition or non-solicitation provision triggers a liquidated damages payment, the potential amount due should be carefully examined. The amount should be significant enough to enforce the limitations of the non-competition or non-solicitation provision. Practice managers and fiscal staff should keep their eyes on this issue.

3. Terms and Standards of Care

The contract should include a detailed list of the duties required, including hospital visits, surgeries, surgical assists, and weekend and night calls. The terms should also specify whether duties are exclusive. Some contracts require physicians to provide care "of the highest quality." As this standard of care is higher than that required by many states' laws,[91] physicians should be aware of this wording when contracting.

4. Disability Insurance

Many physicians overlook disability insurance. This provision is often misunderstood. It is important for physicians to ask whether disability insurance is portable and to what types of injuries and accidents it extends.

5. Extended Reporting "Tail" Policy

Contracts should specify if malpractice insurance coverage continues after the physician-hospital relationship is terminated. Tail insurance provides the physician continued coverage on the employer's malpractice policy for future claims that may occur related to the particular period of employment. A physician's ability to know best practices regarding the purchase of tail and reasonableness of post-employment restrictions is well worth attorneys' fees for reviewing the physician-hospital contract.[92]

---

91. TODD, *supra* note 82, at 85.

92. *See also* Steven M. Hacker, *Physician Employment Agreements: Read the Fine Print,* THE STUDENT DOCTOR NETWORK, Apr. 3, 2011, *available at* http://www.studentdoctor.net/2011/04/physician-employment-agreements-read-the-fine-print/.

Appendix 1

AMA Principles for Physician Employment

The following "AMA Principles for Physician Employment" are intended to help physicians, those who employ physicians, and their respective advisors identify and address some of the unique challenges to professionalism and the practice of medicine arising in the face of physician employment. These principles are not intended to serve as a comprehensive listing of the professional and ethical obligations of employed physicians; such obligations—which are the same for all physicians, regardless of employment status—are more fully delineated in the *AMA Code of Medical Ethics*. Nor are these principles a comprehensive treatment of contractual matters such as work hours, compensation models, employee benefits, and other issues typically the subject of negotiation between physicians and employers; such issues are addressed elsewhere in the body of AMA policy and in the American Medical Association's model employment agreements. Rather, it is hoped that the "AMA Principles for Physician Employment," in addressing select, potentially problematic aspects of the employer-employee relationship, will provide broad guidance for employed physicians and their employers as they collaborate to provide safe, high-quality, and cost-effective patient care.

I.   AMA Principles for Physician Employment

1.   Addressing Conflicts of Interest

(a)   A physician's paramount responsibility is to his or her patients. Additionally, given that an employed physician occupies a position of significant trust, he or she owes a duty of loyalty to his or her employer. This divided loyalty can create conflicts of interest, such as financial incentives to over- or under-treat patients, which employed physicians should strive to recognize and address.

(b)   Employed physicians should be free to exercise their personal and professional judgment in voting, speaking, and advocating on any matter regarding patient care interests, the profession, healthcare in the community, and the independent exercise of medical judgment. Employed physicians should not be deemed in breach of their employment agreements, nor be retaliated against by their employers, for asserting these interests.

(c)   In any situation where the economic or other interests of the employer are in conflict with patient welfare, patient welfare must take priority.

(d)   Physicians should always make treatment and referral decisions based on the best interests of their patients. Employers and the physicians they employ must assure that agreements or understandings (explicit or implicit) restricting, discouraging, or encouraging particular treatment or referral options are disclosed to patients.

(e) Assuming a title or position that may remove a physician from direct patient-physician relationships—such as medical director, vice president for medical affairs, etc.—does not override professional ethical obligations. Physicians whose actions serve to override the individual patient care decisions of other physicians are themselves engaged in the practice of medicine and are subject to professional ethical obligations and may be legally responsible for such decisions. Physicians who hold administrative leadership positions should use whatever administrative and governance mechanisms exist within the organization to foster policies that enhance the quality of patient care and the patient care experience.

Refer to the AMA Code of Medical Ethics (ama-assn.org/go/code)[94] for further guidance on conflicts of interest.

2. Advocacy for Patients and the Profession

(a) Patient advocacy is a fundamental element of the patient-physician relationship that should not be altered by the healthcare system or setting in which physicians practice, or the methods by which they are compensated.

(b) Employed physicians should be free to engage in volunteer work outside of, and which does not interfere with, their duties as employees.

3. Contracting

(a) Physicians should be free to enter into mutually satisfactory contractual arrangements, including employment, with hospitals, healthcare systems, medical groups, insurance plans, and other entities as permitted by law and in accordance with the ethical principles of the medical profession.

(b) Physicians should never be coerced into employment with hospitals, healthcare systems, medical groups, insurance plans, or any other entities. Employment agreements between physicians and their employers should be negotiated in good faith. Both parties are urged to obtain the advice of legal counsel experienced in physician employment matters when negotiating employment contracts.

(c) When a physician's compensation is related to the revenue he or she generates, or to similar factors, the employer should make clear to the physician the factors upon which compensation is based.

(d)   Termination of an employment or contractual relationship between a physician and an entity employing the physician does not necessarily end the patient-physician relationship between the employed physician and persons under his or her care. When a physician's employment status is unilaterally terminated by an employer, the physician and his or her employer should notify the physician's patients that the physician will no longer be working with the employer and should provide them with the physician's new contact information. Patients should be given the choice to continue to be seen by the physician in his or her new practice setting or to be treated by another physician still working with the employer. Records for the physician's patients should be retained for as long as they are necessary for the care of the patients or for addressing legal issues faced by the physician; records should not be destroyed without notice to the former employee. Where physician possession of all medical records of his or her patients is not already required by state law, the employment agreement should specify that the physician is entitled to copies of patient charts and records upon a specific request in writing from any patient, or when such records are necessary for the physician's defense in malpractice actions, administrative investigations, or other proceedings against the physician.

(e)   Physician employment agreements should contain provisions to protect a physician's right to due process before termination for cause. Physician employment agreements should specify whether or not termination of employment is grounds for automatic termination of hospital medical staff membership or clinical privileges.

(f)   Physicians are discouraged from entering into agreements that restrict the physician's right to practice medicine for a specified period of time or in a specified area upon termination of employment.

(g)   Physician employment agreements should contain dispute resolution provisions. If the parties desire an alternative to going to court, such as arbitration, the contract should specify the manner in which disputes will be resolved.

Refer to the "AMA Annotated Model Physician-Hospital Employment Agreement" and the "AMA Annotated Model Physician-Group Practice Employment Agreement" for further guidance on physician employment contract.[95]

4.   Hospital Medical Staff Relations

(a)   Employed physicians should be members of the organized medical staffs of the hospitals or health systems with which they have contractual or financial arrangements, should be subject to the bylaws of those medical staffs, and should conduct their professional activities according to the bylaws, standards, rules, and regulations and policies adopted by those medical staffs.

(b)   Regardless of the employment status of its individual members, the organized medical staff remains responsible for the provision of quality care and must work collectively to improve patient care and outcomes.

(c)   Employed physicians who are members of the organized medical staff should be free to exercise their personal and professional judgment in voting, speaking, and advocating on any matter regarding medical staff matters and should not be deemed in breach of their employment agreements, nor be retaliated against by their employers, for asserting these interests.

(d)   Employers should seek the input of the medical staff prior to the initiation, renewal, or termination of exclusive employment contracts.

5.   Peer Review and Performance Evaluations

(a)   All physicians should promote and be subject to an effective program of peer review to monitor and evaluate the quality, appropriateness, medical necessity, and efficiency of the patient care services provided within their practice settings.

(b)   Peer review should follow established procedures that are identical for all physicians practicing within a given healthcare organization, regardless of their employment status.

(c)   Peer review of employed physicians should be conducted independently of and without interference from any human resources activities of the employer. Physicians – not lay administrators – should be ultimately responsible for all peer review of medical services provided by employed physicians.

(d)   Employed physicians should be accorded due process protections, including a fair and objective hearing, in all peer review proceedings. The fundamental aspects of a fair hearing are a listing of specific charges, adequate notice of the right to a hearing, the opportunity to be present and to rebut evidence, and the opportunity to present a defense. Due process protections should extend to any disciplinary action sought by the employer that relates to the employed physician's independent exercise of medical judgment.

(e)   Employers should provide employed physicians with regular performance evaluations, which should be presented in writing and accompanied by an oral discussion with the employed physician. Physicians should be informed before the beginning of the evaluation period of the general criteria to be considered in their performance evaluations, for example: quality of medical services provided, nature and frequency of patient complaints, employee productivity, employee contribution to the administrative/operational activities of the employer, etc.

(f) Unless specified otherwise in the employment agreement, upon termination of employment with or without cause, an employed physician should not be required to resign his or her hospital medical staff membership or any of the clinical privileges held during the term of employment, unless an independent action of the medical staff calls for such action, and the physician has been afforded full due process under the medical staff bylaws.

6. Payment Agreements

(a) Although they typically assign their billing privileges to their employers, employed physicians or their chosen representatives should be prospectively involved if the employer negotiates agreements for them for professional fees, capitation or global billing, or shared savings. Additionally, employed physicians should be informed about the actual payment amount allocated to the professional fee component of the total payment received by the contractual arrangement.

(b) Employed physicians have a responsibility to assure that bills issued for services they provide are accurate and should therefore retain the right to review billing claims as may be necessary to verify that such bills are correct. Employers should indemnify and defend, and save harmless, employed physicians with respect to any violation of law or regulation or breach of contract in connection with the employer's billing for physician services, which violation is not the fault of the employee.

Adopted at the 2012 Interim Meeting of the AMA House of Delegates (Board of Trustees Report 6).

Visit the AMA website to learn more about AMA resources for employed physicians, https://www.ama-assn.org/life-career/understanding-employment-contracts.

This work was created and produced by James DeNuccio and Keith Voogd of the Organized Medical Staff Section, Barney Cohen of the Office of General Counsel, of the AMA, and/or Sidney Welch, of Arnall Golden Gregory LLP.

Appendix 2

Standard Provisions in a Physician-hospital Contract Govern the Following Areas

(i) Terms of Employment—A contract must specify the terms of employment, including relevant dates, a description of clinical and administrative responsibilities, and any employment restrictions.

    (1) Dates—The contract must list the effective start date, length of commitment, and whether the physician works full- or part-time.

    (2) Job Description—A statement of employment should include what duties the physician will perform and where.

    (3) Restrictive Covenants or Noncompetition Clauses

(ii) Compensation—Hospitals and health systems can compensate physicians vis-à-vis a number of financial structures. Compensation can be predicated on straight productivity, an equal-share of receipts, a salary, a salary plus discretionary bonus, or a salary plus productivity or quality-based bonus.

(iii) Professional expenses—Contracts should spell out how a hospital pays a physician's professional licensing fees, fees associated with prescriptive authority and obtaining a DEA number, certification costs, continuing medical education (CME) tuition, professional membership dues, medical subscriptions and professional books, and travel for medical conferences and other professional meetings.

(iv) Billing—Physician-hospital agreements should contain a provision explaining a physician's right to review and make corrections to claims. Physicians should ask to see a hospital's compliance plan and what it says about the right to review the outcomes of claims.

(v) Paid time off (PTO)—Paid time off provisions for vacation, illness, parental leave, educational leave, and other Family Medical Leave Act (FMLA) scenarios should be included in standard contracts.

(vi) Employment benefit programs—Standard employee benefits—in addition to leave policies, professional expenses, and professional liability insurance—include health, dental, and vision care for self/family; disability insurance; hospital dues; long-term care; and moving expenses.

(vii) Facilities support—Any promised specific items or personnel need to be in writing in the contract.

(viii) Professional liability insurance

    (1) Coverage—Minimum coverage should provide limits up to $1,000,000 per occurrence and up to $3,000,000 annual aggregate.

(2)   Tail Policy—Contracts should specify if coverage continues after the physician-hospital relationship is terminated. This includes who pays for a "tail policy," or the assured continued coverage on the employer's malpractice policy for future claims that may occur related to the particular period of

(ix)   Confidentiality

(x)   Termination clause—Contracts should provide for termination with and without cause. Moreover, contracts contain provisions that outline situations triggering immediate termination and others giving an option for termination. Several incidents can result in an immediate termination of a physician-hospital relationship. These include[96]:

(1)   The loss or suspension of a physician's license to practice medicine;

(2)   The resignation, expulsion, or suspension of the physician from the medical staff;

(3)   The loss of malpractice insurance with respect to the physician, other than that as a result of the employer's termination of such coverage as a result of some other act by the employer;

(4)   The physician's death or permanent disability;

(5)   The dissolution of the employer; or

(6)   The physician's conviction of a felony or another crime involving immoral conduct.

Appendix 3

Physician Recruitment and Generic Checklist

DEPARTMENT or Lead person
the physicians will contact for
questions as noted in
second paragraph
Phone and Address

**Wexner
Medical
Center**

We are excited to have this opportunity to talk with you about The Ohio State University Wexner Medical Center. OSU Wexner Medical Center has had unprecedented success in physician recruitment in support of our mission of improving people's lives though innovation in research, education and patient care.

To help simplify the process we have provided you with two checklists to help you prepare for the recruitment process. Please review these documents before you provide us any information or documents and do not hesitate to contact us if you have any questions.

We look forward to working with you to support our vision of shaping the future of medicine by creating, disseminating and applying knowledge and by personalizing health care to meet the needs of each individual.

Please sign below indicating your interest and confirmation that there are no restrictions or confidentiality provisions preventing our discussions. Please return a copy of this document to me at the above address.

_____

Physician Signature

_____

Print Name

_____

Date

List of Arrangements to Review

1. Employment Agreement
2. Medical Director Agreements/Appointments
3. Recruitment Agreement/Student Loan Agreement
4. Right of First Refusal to Purchase Practice
5. Lease Arrangements
6. Real Estate Ownership
   o Operating Agreements
7. Practice Management Agreements
8. Professional or Administrative Service Agreements
9. Co-Management Agreements
   o Operating Agreements
10. Ambulatory Surgery Center Ownership
    o Operating Agreements
11. Ancillary Services Ownership
    o Operating Agreements
12. Affiliation Agreements
13. Teaching Contracts

List of Potential Restrictions to Review

1. Confidentiality Clauses
2. Restrictive Covenant (i.e. non-compete clauses)
3. Right of First Refusal
4. Lease Restriction
5. Notification of Negotiation
6. Recruitment Agreement Restrictions to Maintain Staff Privileges
7. Ambulatory Surgery Center or Ancillary Ownership Restrictions
8. Medical Director – Provision of Same or Similar Services
9. Exclusive Provider Agreements
10. Co-Management Agreement Restrictions
11. Exclusive Negotiation Discussions
12. Trade Secret Document of Competitor
13. Term of Agreement

Appendix 4

OSU Wexner Medical Center Office of Legal Services Guidelines for Interactions with Physicians for Recruitment Purposes

OSU Wexner Medical Center has had unprecedented success in physician recruitment in support of our mission of improving people's lives though innovation in research, education and patient care. In addition to these benefits, there are some risks. These materials are intended to assist you in bringing professionals to the OSU Wexner Medical Center while minimizing the legal risks.

The following graphic illustrates a few ways in which risk may vary in the recruitment process.

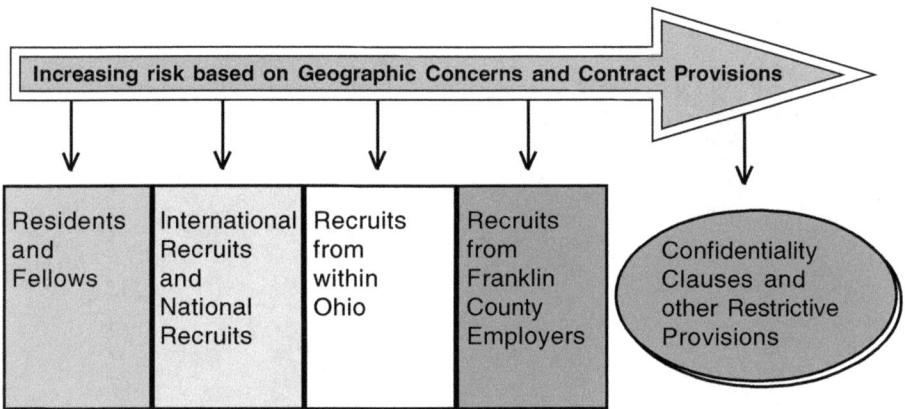

Increasing risk based on Geographic Concerns and Contract Provisions

| Residents and Fellows | International Recruits and National Recruits | Recruits from within Ohio | Recruits from Franklin County Employers | Confidentiality Clauses and other Restrictive Provisions |

Restrictive provisions in the recruit's employment related documents with their current employer determine one aspect of recruitment risk level. This risk is addressed in these guidelines and accompanying checklists which cover restrictive arrangements and various types of restrictive clauses encountered.

Chapter 3

MEDICAL PROFESSIONAL LIABILITY: TRENDS IN CLAIMS AND LEGISLATIVE RESPONSES

BY: MICHAEL C. STINSON,[1] J.D.

Introduction

The U.S. healthcare system continues to transform, and as it does the medical liability environment changes with it. While many have experienced these changes first-hand—from the dominance of sole practitioners to the growth of employed physicians, and from the advent of managed care to the creation of Accountable Care Organizations—change has also come to what happens after care is delivered. Over the years we have seen substantial increases in the frequency of medical professional liability (MPL) claims, and dramatic surges in awards to those who have suffered a suboptimal medical outcome (whether the result of negligence or not). We have seen several MPL crises (when premiums rise significantly while fewer insurers remain in the market to provide coverage), and, more recently, a sustained period of relative calm in the litigation environment. Below, I will review what has happened in the MPL environment over time, and how government has, or has not, responded.

This chapter will examine the trends in MPL claims since 1985, with a particular emphasis on the changing nature of claims and payments in that time frame. In addition, it will examine claims reported to a national MPL repository and the

1. Michael C. Stinson is the Vice President of Government Relations and Public Policy for the Medical Professional Liability (MPL) Association, where he oversees all aspects of the Association's interactions with the federal and state governments. He also serves as Chair of the Health Coalition on Liability and Access, which brings together insurers, medical organizations, and other stakeholders to form the largest coalition in Washington, D.C., dedicated to addressing federal medical professional liability issues. Prior to joining the MPL Association, Mr. Stinson had extensive federal public policy experience having worked on the legislative staffs of four U.S. senators, including six years as the health and judiciary policy advisor to Sen. Dirk Kempthorne (R-ID). He later served as the associate director for health and welfare in Governor Mark Schweiker's (R-PA) federal affairs office.
Mr. Stinson received a bachelor of science degree from the University of New Hampshire and a juris master degree from the George Mason University School of Law. He wishes to acknowledge the tremendous assistance of Divya Parikh, MPL Association Vice President of Research and Education, and Kwon Miller, MPL Association Research Database Manager, for their assistance in preparing this document.

severity of indemnity paid, as well as the cost of defending those claims, and look at how changes in all of these areas have affected both MPL insurers and self-insured entities and the healthcare providers/facilities that they cover. This chapter will also review the legislative trends at both the state and federal levels that have resulted from changes in the MPL environment and will address how these trends may foretell future legislative trends in the MPL arena.

Part A—Medical Professional Liability Claims Trends[2]

Introduction to the Data Sharing Project

While the MPL environment over the last 30+ years has sometimes resembled a roller coaster, the Medical Professional Liability (MPL) Association[3] recognized that trends existed, and that collecting claims data would be a critical tool in understanding those trends.

The data by which this article will analyze claims in MPL trends is taken from the MPL Association Data Sharing Project (DSP). The DSP collects and accumulates claims data from participating domestic member companies of the MPL Association, and its focus is to provide the intelligence needed to enhance risk management and patient safety in medicine and to track MPL claim costs. The DSP was initiated in 1985 and is now the largest independent database of MPL claims worldwide. This data has been reported by more than 40 MPL Association members located all across the nation. By the end of 1987, over 10,000 paid claims had been reported representing over $1 billion in indemnity payments. By the end of 2019, more than 331,000 closed claims and lawsuits were reported to the DSP, totaling in excess of $46 billion in indemnity and expense payments on more than 97,000 paid claims.

---

2. Taken in whole or in part from the annual MPL Association Closed Claim Comparative and Specialty Specific Series reports, as well as MPL Association special data queries. Additional data from MPL Association archived data, including PIAA Risk Management Review, PIAA Semiannual Report, and PIAA Claims Trend Analysis. Most materials are *available at* www.MPLassociation.org. All data and data analysis come from these sources. Policy analysis based on this data is solely the opinion of the author.

3. The Medical Professional Liability Association (formerly the Physician Insurers Association of America or PIAA) is the leading trade association representing insurance companies, risk retention groups, captives, trusts, and other entities owned and/or operated by their policyholders, as well as other insurance carriers with a substantial commitment to the MPL line who support the quality delivery of healthcare. MPL Association members insure more than 2 million healthcare professionals worldwide—doctors, nurses and nurse practitioners, and other healthcare providers—including more than two-thirds of America's private practice physicians. MPL Association members also insure more than 200,000 dentists and oral surgeons, 2,500 hospitals, and 8,000 medical facilities.

Data Sharing Project Data: Claims Analysis

The following sections provide an overview of major areas of interest in the DSP database.[4]

Claim Details

The primary focus of MPL insurers when reviewing the finances associated with such claims are indemnity and expenses. Indemnity represents the amount paid to a claimant as the result of the claim.

The data submitted to the DSP is captured on a *per claim* basis—not a per physician basis. Therefore, the compiled data in this report comprises MPL claims in which a specific healthcare provider was involved; there may be multiple claims for any given provider. This compilation of data is then compared with that of all medical specialties, combined, to observe deviations of a particular specialty group from the calculations derived from the population of all medical specialties in the DSP.

Trend Analysis of Claims by Close of Year

When DSP data is aggregated into five-year bands, we find that the average indemnity payment from 1990-1994 was nearly $314,000. Average indemnity continued to grow for many years, reaching a high of more than $434,000 in the 2000-2004 time period. The subsequent decline in such payments has been attributed to many factors, including an increased focus on patient safety and the enactment of effective medical liability reforms in numerous states. Whatever the reason, there was a distinct reduction in indemnity payments resulting in a stabilizing of such costs for a number of years. Most recently, however, average indemnity payments have again begun to climb, rising to nearly $380,000 in the 2015-2019 time period.

Unlike indemnity payments, expenses involved in closed claims climbed substantially since the early 1990s, only leveling off most recently. The average amount spent to defend claims closed between 2015 and 2019 was $53,808. Even after adjusting for inflation, this average is a notable increase compared with the figures reported 15 years prior (2000-2004), when expenses averaged "just" $39,954. In addition, expense costs can increase substantially when one focuses solely on claims in which an indemnity payment was made, as will be noted later.

---

4. This information is to be considered an aid to those who study MPL claims; it is not intended to be a formal position statement of the MPL Association on the interpretation of the data found here. The MPL Association does not intend the data from the DSP to be interpreted as defining standards of care attributable to the MPL Association and makes no recommendations for the use of the data for this purpose.

Figure 1. Average Payments and % Paid-to-Closed by Close Year for All Specialties (1990-2019) 2019 Dollars

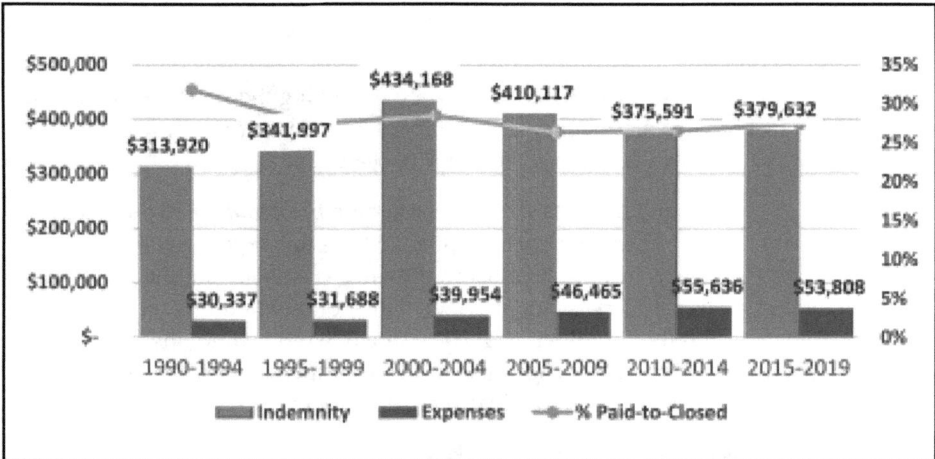

Figure 1 illustrates the average indemnity and average expenses in 2019 dollar values, and the paid-to-closed ratio, for the last 30 years in five-year intervals. As noted, one sees a steady increase in both the average indemnity and average expense for closed claims for many years. More recently, we see a dip in average indemnity before it rises once again, while the average defense expense only stabilized in the most recent years. It is very important to note that these numbers are already adjusted for inflation, so even with the previous reduction in indemnity payments, one still sees a nearly 21 percent increase in medical liability indemnity payments over the last 30 years. At the same time, the expenses associated with defending medical liability claims have jumped more than 75 percent.

Comparative Payment Analysis by Close Year

Figure 2 provides an overview of claims closed by year at four indemnity-payment thresholds: $100,000, $250,000, $500,000, and $1,000,000 (in 2019 dollars). The percentage of claims with $1 million or more in indemnity payment has increased from just over 4 percent of all paid claims in 1985 to more than 13 percent in 2019. Claims resulting in a payment of $500,000 or more have increased from 9 percent of total claims in 1985 to 27 percent in 2019. As one might expect, along with the upward shift in large dollar payments comes a consistent decline in the lower end of the spectrum where, from 1985 to 2019, indemnity payments of less than $100,000 have fallen from 57 percent of all paid claims to 37 percent of paid claims.

Figure 2. Percentage of Paid Claims by Indemnity Payment Threshold by Close Year (1985-2019)
2019 Dollars

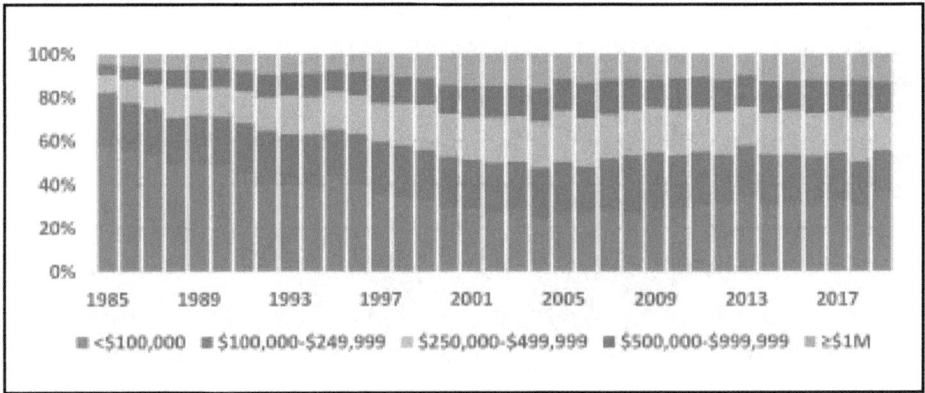

■ <$100,000   ■ $100,000-$249,999   ■ $250,000-$499,999   ■ $500,000-$999,999   ■ ≥$1M

Comparative Payment Threshold Analysis by Specialty

While tracking general trends in MPL insurance is certainly beneficial, these trends merely paint an overall picture of the liability environment. To gain a complete understanding of what healthcare providers face, it is appropriate, even necessary, to look at the claims faced by individual specialties. This gives a clearer picture of the threats faced by certain types of healthcare providers and how those threats have changed, if at all, over the years.

Figure 3. Total and Average Indemnity Paid by Medical Specialty (1985-2019) 2019 Dollars

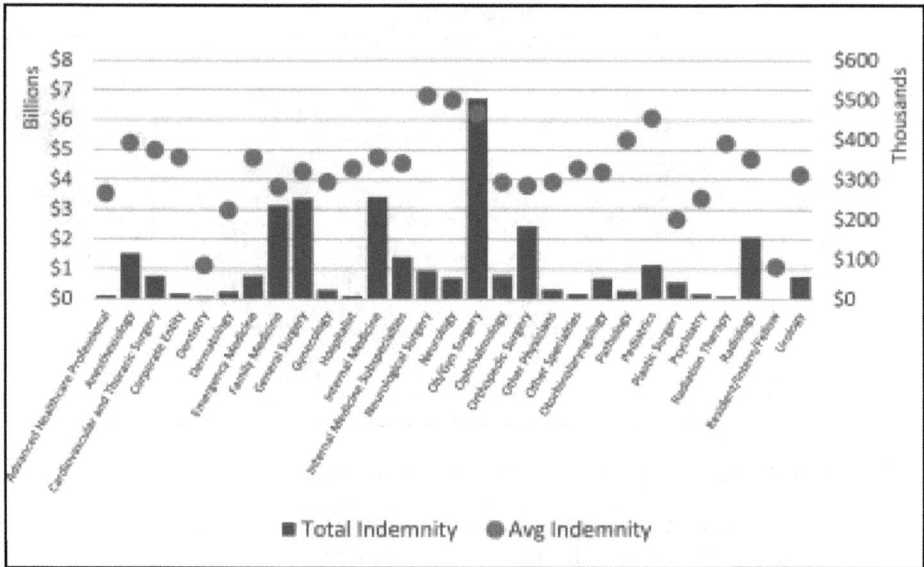

When looking at individual specialties, one will see that obstetric and gynecologic (Ob/Gyn) surgery had the most paid claims reported in the cumulative data (roughly 14,400 since 1985). This is evidenced in Figure 3, where total Ob/Gyn surgery payments exceeding $6.7 billion, substantially outpacing its nearest "competitor," internal medicine , which came in at just over $3.4 billion in payouts (on approximately two-thirds the number of paid claims as Ob/Gyn surgery).

Neurological surgery reported the highest average indemnity over the course of reporting—$510,226 in 2019 dollars—but barely outpaced neurology ($498,932). Rounding out the top five in the average payment category were Ob/Gyn surgery ($466,097), pediatrics ($454,047), and pathology ($399,912).

At the other end of the spectrum are residents/interns, who have a low average indemnity ($80,212). Joining residents/interns at the lower end of the total payment spectrum are dentists (and oral surgeons), who also have an average indemnity of less than $85,000 per paid claim, but for whom the ratio of payment to claims is relatively large (41 percent).

Figure 4 graphs the percentage of paid claims for large-loss claims by medical specialty for the 1985-2019 period. Dentistry and oral surgery accounted for the fewest large payouts, with more than 81 percent of paid claims for the combined specialties resulting in indemnity payments of

**Figure 4. Percentage of Paid Claims by Indemnity Payment Threshold
by Medical Specialties (1985-2019)
2019 Dollars**

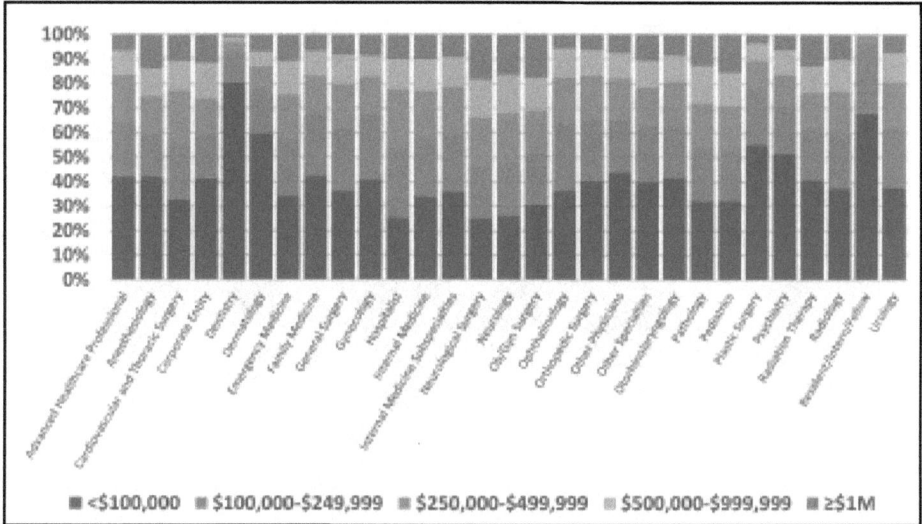

less than $100,000. Hospitalists and neurological surgeons had the lowest percentage of claim payments falling below $100,000—both specialties came in at 25 percent of claims. The most expensive claims to pay were from neurological surgery, neurology, and Ob/Gyn surgery, where more than 30 percent of paid claims in each of those specialties resulted in indemnity payments of $500,000 or more.

Comparative Total Expense Payments by Specialty

Reviewing the expense payments for each specialty gives one an idea of the different overall expenses involved in defending a given specialty.

With regard to total expenses, the costliest specialty for MPL insurers to defend has been Ob/Gyn surgery with more than $1.92 billion in expense payments since 1985 (in 2019 dollars). The next most expensive specialties have been internal medicine ($1.53 billion), general surgery ($1.25 billion), and family medicine ($1.17 billion).

**Figure 5. Total and Average Expenses by Medical Specialty (1985-2019)
2019 Dollars**

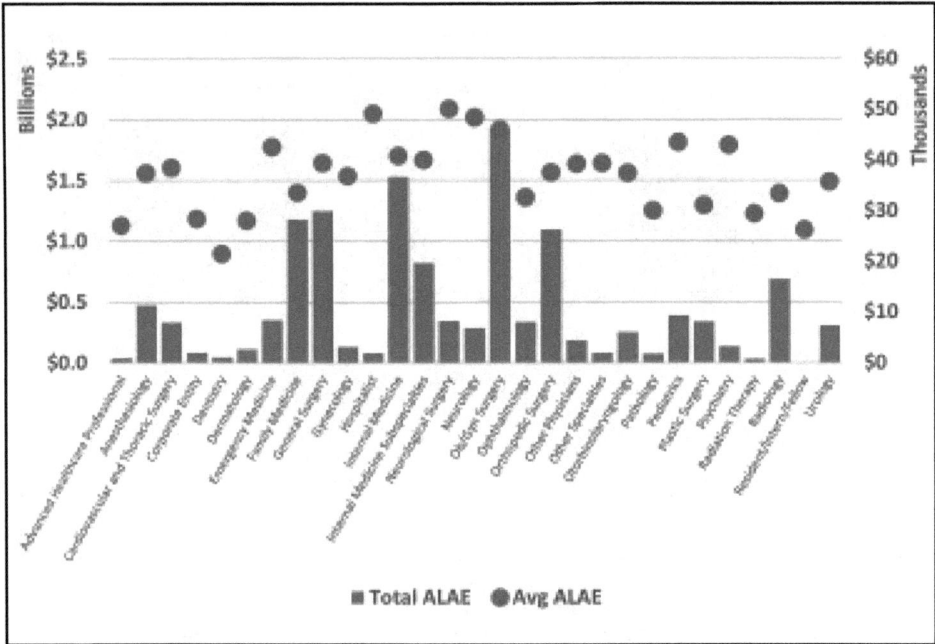

Differing slightly from that list, the three specialties with highest average expenses are neurological surgery, weighing in at $50,146 per claim, hospitalist at $49,205, and neurology at $48,433. It is interesting to note that none of the three aforementioned specialties crack the list of highest total expenses, indicating that each has a smaller number of total claims, which helps offset the fact that such claims are exceptionally costly to defend (Figure 5).

Claims by Adjudication Status

Of the approximately 331,500 closed claims that have been reported to the DSP between 1985 and 2019, the vast majority (more than 307,000 or almost 93 percent) were resolved *not as the result of a verdict*. In other words, these claims did not make it to trial. Conversely, there were roughly 24,000 (7 percent) that did end up in the courts (insufficient information exists to appropriately classify the remaining closed claims), and were resolved as a *result of a verdict* for either the *plaintiff* or the *defendant*.

Figure 6. Percentage of Closed Claims
By Adjudication Status (1985-2019)

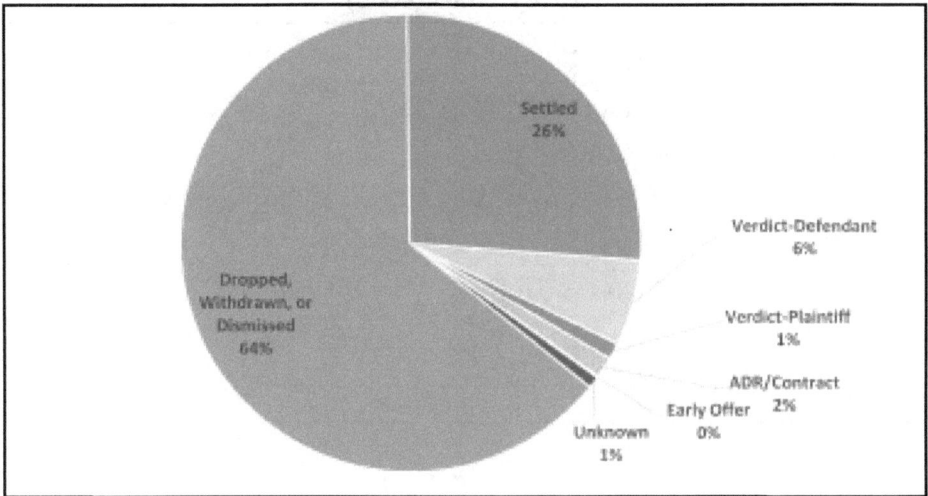

When a decision about negligence was left up to a jury, the process resulted in a finding in favor of the *defendant* 84 percent of the time. Figure 6 displays the percentage of closed claims by adjudication status. When a claim does go to trial it results, on average, in $116,300 in expenses when a defendant wins, and nearly $150,000 in expenses when a plaintiff proves negligence. Indemnity payments in the latter claims exceed an average value of $639,000.

Approximately 64 percent of all claims filed against healthcare providers were eventually *dropped, withdrawn, or dismissed* because they lacked merit. Thus, nearly two-thirds of all claims filed each year eat up valuable resources that could be used to compensate truly injured patients, but instead were simply wasted. On average, each of these cases consumes approximately $22,000 in expenses.

A claim is resolved via an out-of-court *settlement* approximately 26 percent of the time with an average expense exceeding $54,000 and an average indemnity payment of nearly $336,000. When dropped/with-drawn/dismissed cases (i.e. those that are shown to have no merit) are removed from the equation, in nearly three-quarters of legitimate claims the insurer agrees to a prompt, out-of-court settlement. The remaining claims that go on to actual litigation tend to be those that are so complex it is difficult to tell if any negligence actually occurred. Again, however, in

Figure 7. Average Indemnity and Expenses
By Adjudication Status (1985-2019)
2019 Dollars (000s)

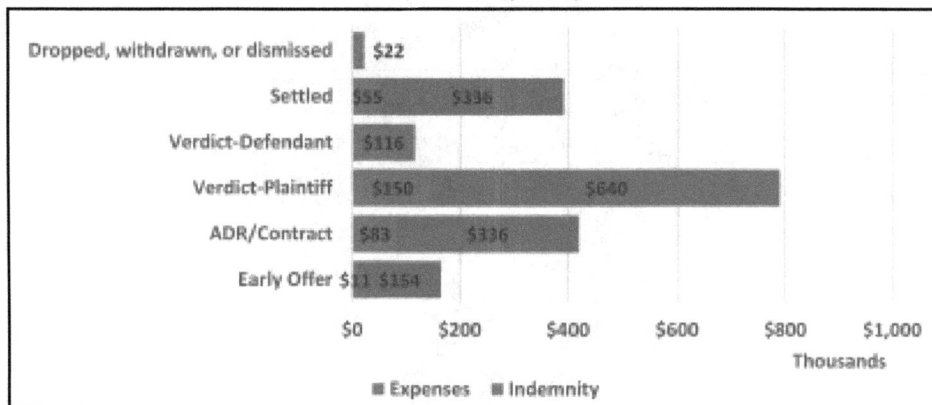

these cases which may have a degree of merit, it is demonstrated that no negligence occurred more than 84 percent of the time.

A small percentage of closed claims were resolved through some type of *alternative dispute resolution (ADR) or contract liability agreement.* Since 1985, 1.5 percent of all claims were resolved by this method. The average payment over that timespan was $336,200 with an average expense of $83,016. More recently, early offer programs have become established as a method for resolving adverse medical outcomes (the DSP began tracking them in 2016). The average indemnity payment under that approach was $154,200, while expenses averaged a mere $10,500 (Figures 6 and 7).

Summary

While the data reveals a brief drop in indemnity payments, the long-term trend has been for both payments and total expenses associated with MPL claims to continue upward. Over the last 35 years, both of these categories have seen increases that have significantly outpaced inflation. At times this increase has been sharper than others, but it has been trending upward overall. As a result, governments have occasionally stepped in to address the ramifications of such increases.

Part B—Medical Professional Liability Legislative Trends[5]

Between 1969 and 1975, the number of medical liability claims filed against doctors in the United States tripled, triggering a medical liability crisis.[6] Since that time the U.S. has experienced two more nationwide crises (in the 1980s and early 2000s) and numerous efforts have been made to find legislative fixes to the problems beleaguering the MPL system.

Advocates for MPL reform have touted numerous benefits from any number of legislative reforms, including reduced or stabilized MPL premiums, and increased access to care.[7,8] Conversely, they note that a failure to implement such reforms results in less access to healthcare providers and certain healthcare services.[9] Opponents of these reforms make several arguments, including that no liability crisis has ever existed, and that the constant threat of lawsuits is necessary to keep healthcare providers from harming their patients.[10] Opponents also claim that reforms do not affect MPL premiums, which they say are adjusted solely on economic cycles.[11]

 Neither side has been able to gain an upper hand in the debate, thus interested parties in the states and the U.S. Congress continue to seek reforms, or bolster reforms already in place, to aid both the patient and healthcare provider, while others continue to oppose enacted reforms as well as those that have only been proposed. Below are some of the reform efforts that have taken place within the states, a review of their successes and failures, and what the future may hold in store for state reform advocates. The chapter will conclude with a similar analysis of federal MPL reforms.

---

5. Legislative information from MPL Association documentation. Policy analysis of this documentation is solely the opinion of the author.

6. A medical liability crisis is defined as a period in which the affordability and/or availability of MPL insurance declines due to significantly increased premiums and/or a sharp decrease in the number of insurers.

7. Californians Allied for Patient Protection, *Why MICRA* (4/5/2021) *available at* http://https://micra.org//micra/.

8. Texas Alliance for Patient Access, *Improving Access to Care* (4/5/2021) *available at* http://tapa.info/improving-access-to-care.html.

9. American Medical Association, *Medical Liability Reform NOW!* (2021) *available at* https://www.ama-assn.org/system/files/2020-05/mlr-now.pdf.

10. American Association of Justice, *Medical Negligence: The Role of America's Civil Justice System in Protecting Patients' Rights* (February 2011) *available at* https://www.justice.org/-/media/files/research-reports/medical-negligence-2011.pdf

11. Robert J. Hunter, et al, *True Risk: Medical Liability, Malpractice Insurance and Health Care* (Jul 22, 2009) *available at* http://www.insurance-reform.org/studies/TrueRiskF.pdf.

State Reforms

The Medical Insurance Compensation Reform Act and Traditional State Reform Efforts

The beginning of effective MPL reforms can be traced back to California in the mid-1970s. At the time, MPL insurance premiums were skyrocketing in the wake of rising liability payouts, threatening to force healthcare providers to flee the state. In response, Governor Jerry Brown (D) called an emergency session of the legislature to develop a solution that would ensure that access to care was not harmed. That solution was the Medical Insurance Compensation Reform Act (MICRA).[12] MICRA provides for a cap of $250,000 on noneconomic damages (but does not cap economic damages, such as medical expenses and lost wages); a sliding fee-scale for plaintiffs' attorneys, to ensure the majority of any award goes to the patient, not the lawyer; collateral source reform, so that juries are informed about other sources of payments received by a plaintiff; statute of limitations reform, to ensure that cases are filed in a timely manner; and periodic payment of damages, to ensure that patients get funds as they are needed. More than 40 years later, the success of these efforts is clear. MPL insurance rates stabilized and have remained relatively stable for decades. Claims resolution quickened and remains significantly faster than in many other states. Access to healthcare remains available.

Despite numerous legal challenges, and a 2014 ballot initiative that would have gutted the law's limits on noneconomic damages,[13,14] MICRA has withstood the test of time and been the model for many subsequent MPL reform efforts.[15] Since MICRA's enactment, other states undertook MPL reform initiatives to varying degrees of success.

---

12. The key provisions of MICRA are scattered throughout several of California's codes: CAL. CIV. CODE § 3333.2 (limitations on noneconomic damages); CAL. CIV. CODE § 3333.1 (evidence of collateral source payments and ban on subrogation); CAL. BUS. & PROF. CODE § 6146 (sliding scale for attorney contingency fees); CAL. CODE OF CIV. PROC. § 667.7 (periodic payment of future damages); and CAL. CODE OF CIV. PROC. § 340.5 (statute of limitations).

13. Proposition 46, which would have raised the cap to approximately $1.1 million, and then indexed it to annual inflation, was defeated by California voters by a 67%-33% margin on Nov. 4, 2014.

14. In 2021, a new ballot initiative to alter MICRA is being pursued. It aims to not only dramatically increase the noneconomic damage cap but also to weaken every element of the current statute. The initiative is scheduled to appear on the California ballot in 2022.

15. MPL Association, *State Enactments of Selected Health Care Liability Reforms* (3/6/2020), *available at* https://www.mplassociation.org/docs/GR/State_Enactments_Citations_3-2021.pdf.

A handful of states enacted reforms in the 1980s and 1990s, primarily spurred on by later MPL crises. The early part of this century, however, saw a more dramatic crisis that resulted in numerous legislative initiatives, many of which mirrored California's MICRA program. As of today, 28 states have caps on damages of one sort or another. While most cap only noneconomic damages (i.e. subjective damages such as "pain and suffering"), some have chosen to enact total damage caps. In most cases, including Indiana, Louisiana, Nebraska, and New Mexico, these total damage caps are supplemented by state Patient Compensation Funds. Virginia stands out as the sole state with a hard cap on total damages, currently set at $2.45 million and scheduled to increase incrementally to $3 million over the next 10 years. Of the remaining states with noneconomic damage caps, these, too, have a degree of variety. California and Montana have the only hard caps of $250,000, while others have enacted higher caps, indexed their caps to inflation, or provided exceptions to the damage limit. The most recent change occurred in Iowa, where a $250,000 cap (with exceptions for "serious" injuries) was enacted in 2017.[16] Of states with any damage limitations, Maryland claims the highest noneconomic cap with its annually increased cap now sitting at $845,000.[17]

While many, if not all, of these states saw improvements in their liability environments after enacting caps,[18] the latest "model" is Texas, which enacted a unique cap in 2003.[19] This cap limits noneconomic damages to $250,000, but, unlike California, contains three tiers that allow for separate limits for a healthcare provider and up to two separate healthcare institutions. Thanks to simultaneous passage of a constitutional amendment allowing caps to be enacted,[20] Texas saw a rapid improvement in not only its MPL environment, but also in its overall healthcare environment with a rapid influx of healthcare practitioners. These improvements remain today, nearly two decades after the law's original passage.

While caps on damages get the lion's share of attention when MPL reforms are discussed, it should be noted that MICRA's other reforms were also very important in creating the current liability environment. Like the noneconomic damage cap, these additional reforms were also widely copied by other states.

---

16. *Id.*
17. *Id.*
18. Robert Lowes, *Malpractice Premiums Drop for 6th Straight Year,* Medscape (Oct. 10, 2013) *available at* http://www.medscape.com/viewarticle/812451.
19. Tex. Civ. Prac. & Rem. Code Ann. § 74.301 (2003).
20. Tex. Const. Art. III § 66.

A wide variation exists amongst statutes of limitations in the states. While every state has a statute of limitations in place for MPL cases, the lengths can vary substantially. The most common time is two years from the date of discovery of the injury, with a wide variety of upper limits as to when a claim may be filed.[21]

Periodic payment of future damages is a tremendously helpful reform allowing payments to be made to a victim of an adverse medical outcome on a timescale more closely aligned to the accrual of ongoing expenses, rather than in a lump sum at the time of settlement or verdict. A total of 31 states have enacted some type of this reform, although some leave its application up to the discretion of the courts rather than making the spreading of such payments mandatory above a certain dollar threshold.[22]

Limitations on attorney fees are not as popular, with only 16 states legislating a payment scale for contingency fees in MPL cases.[23] Other states allow for limits to be put in place, but leave the exact nature of the limit, if one is applied at all, to the courts' discretion.

Perhaps the most divergent of all the MICRA reforms is reform of the collateral source rule, i.e. the common law rule preventing evidence that a third party has paid a portion of the expenses incurred by the alleged victim. Eleven states, like California, have adopted an evidentiary rule allowing juries to be informed that some or all of a claimant's expenses have been paid by a third party. Of these, only four have adopted California's ban on the subrogation of an MPL claim by a collateral source. A total of 19 states mandate offsets to an MPL award by at least some amount of collateral source benefits. Of these, only four ban the subrogation of a subsequent award, while six specifically prohibit the offset if a subrogation claim exists.[24]

Supplemental Reforms

In more recent times, some states have sought (to varying degrees of success) reforms that differ from all of the MICRA reforms, but that nonetheless may have a positive effect on the medical liability

---

21. For example, in Louisiana a claim must be filed within one year of the alleged incident, or one year of the discovery of the injury (LA. REV. STAT. ANN. § 9:5628 (West Supp. 1997), while in Maryland a claim must only be filed within five years of the alleged incident, or within three years of discovering the injury (MD. CODE ANN., Cts. & Jud. Proc. § 5-109 (1995)).

22. MPL Association, *supra* note 17.

23. *Id.*

24. *Id.*

system. These may work in conjunction with the aforementioned reforms, or as stand-alone reforms. Among these are:

- Certificates of merit: Pre-litigation requirement to provide documented substantiation that an MPL claim is sufficiently valid to be pursued. The benefits of these laws depend largely on the qualifications required of the medical professional signing the certificate. Where enacted, certificates of merit help weed out those cases that otherwise are eventually dropped, withdrawn, or dismissed, but without having to go through the initial, and expensive, stages of litigation.

- Provider communication protections: Prohibition on the use of a healthcare provider's expression of sympathy as evidence of negligence. Anecdotal evidence indicates this reform is more effective if it is sufficiently broad so as to include actual admissions of fault. Otherwise, the "apology" is subject to being misinterpreted as a declaration of fault and therefore admitted into evidence anyway. These laws are designed to improve provider-patient communication, which helps resolve MPL questions without resorting to litigation.

- Litigation waiting periods: Requires advance notice of an intent to file a medical liability claim and a set time period before litigation may commence. Also known as "cooling off" periods, the intent is to ensure that patient and physician will have a final opportunity to resolve a negligence claim before resorting to expensive and time-consuming court proceedings.

- Expert witness reforms: Requirements that anyone serving as an expert witness have certain minimum qualifications, usually along the lines of expertise in the same medical specialty as the defendant or specific knowledge of the treatments for the illness/injury in question. Such reforms ensure that "experts for hire" are less likely to be used, and that experts for either side actually have a true understanding of the underlying medical issues.

- Pre-litigation screening panels: States that have adopted this reform usually require a combination of individuals with legal or medical backgrounds to review a MPL claim before it may be taken to litigation. Some states allow evidence of the screening panel's decision to be entered into evidence in court, while others do not. Proponents believe the panels weed out meritless cases, not unlike certificate of merit requirements. It has been suggested by others, however, that such panels rarely prevent claims from being litigated, and thus frequently add to the costs of resolving such claims.

- Truth in Damages: A variant of collateral source rule reform. This reform allows the actual amount paid (or necessary to be paid) to cover the plaintiff's medical expenses to be admitted into evidence. The idea is to prevent damage awards from being inflated by basing them on medical expenses billed, since those amounts are frequently substantially higher than the amounts medical providers/facilities have agreed to accept in compensation.

Alternative Reforms

As efforts to enact MICRA-like reforms have slowed dramatically in the states (likely due to two reasons—1. The state has a solid anti-MPL reform majority in the legislature (such as in New York State), or 2. Legislators are constitutionally prohibited from enacting reforms, such as caps on damages (such as in Wyoming[25])), some have begun turning to other possible options in an attempt to address ongoing MPL issues. These "alternative" reforms are largely, if not wholly, untested and frequently carry more questions than answers. Despite this, they have appeal, especially to those who may be frustrated over the lack of success in implementing proven reforms like MICRA in their own states. Perhaps the most prominent of these reforms are health courts, early offers programs, safe harbors, and early disclosure and resolution.

The idea of health courts is quite simple—specialized courts overseen by judges with some degree of medical knowledge/training would handle all MPL cases and juries would not be used. The details of how such a court would operate vary from plan to plan. Some have suggested using expert witnesses called by the court instead of those provided by the claimant or defendant. Others have recommended incorporating a specific damage scale for various injuries in order to ensure that all like claims receive like awards. One of the biggest problems with the health court approach, however, is that it focuses solely on the litigation side of the equation. As noted in the previous section, healthcare providers win the vast majority of claims that end up in court. Establishing a new court structure to deal with these claims may bring a level of efficiency to the process, but it would do little to cut down on the expense of trying such claims and nothing to address the numerous meritless claims that continue to consume vast resources in terms of both time and money. This may be the reason why no states, to date, have enacted health courts.

---

25. Wyo. Const. Art. 10 §4.

Early offers programs, a variation of which was enacted in New Hampshire in 2013,[26] use a stick and carrot approach in order to promote more prompt resolution of claims. Under such a system, if a negligence claim is filed, the defendant (and his/her insurer), would be given a specific time period in which to offer compensation for full economic damages and attorney fees. If no offer is made, the matter may proceed to court. If an offer is made and agreement is reached, the matter would be resolved and no further court action would be allowed. If the offer is made but the plaintiff rejects it, he or she may proceed to court but would do so facing a higher burden of proof and an increased standard of negligence than normally applies in an MPL claim. This incentivizes defendants to make legitimate offers (since they will be guaranteed not to have to pay noneconomic damages), and plaintiffs to accept, as winning a trial would be substantially more difficult than under the present system. Both sides, however, have found objections with this concept. Defendants are concerned that the narrow time frame in which to respond to a claim would "force" them to make offers on non-meritorious claims in order to avoid going to court. Plaintiff attorneys have vigorously opposed such programs on the grounds that they fail to adequately compensate victims because they do not allow for large noneconomic damage awards.[27]

The idea of creating medical "safe harbors" gained popularity after passage of the Patient Protection and Affordable Care Act, spurred in part by the likes of Peter Orszag, former director of the Office of Management and Budget in the Obama administration. In fact, Mr. Orszag noted the lack of a safe harbors provision in the Patient Protection and Affordable Care Act as one of the great failings of the law.[28] Under this concept, treatment protocols (developed by government entities or medical specialty societies, depending on one's preference) would create "best practices" for healthcare services, and providers would be able to use proof that they abided by said "best practices" as evidence that they were not negligent in their care of a patient. While very appealing on the surface, this concept could create significant problems. For starters, the adoption of best practices could result in "cookbook" medicine, in which healthcare providers were encouraged to follow a given treatment plan, without regard to whether that plan was in their patient's best interest, because doing so

---

26. N.H. Rev. Stat. Ann. § 519-C (2013).

27. *See* NH Early Offer Exposed (4/5/2021) *available at* http://www.nhearlyofferexposed.org/.

28. Peter Orszag, *Malpractice Methodology*, N.Y. Times, Oct 20, 2010, *available at* http://www.nytimes.com/2010/10/21/opinion/21orszag.html.

would guarantee protection from a liability suit. In addition, medicine is a rapidly changing field and it would be difficult for any entity to approve new safe harbors quickly enough to keep up with medical advances. Thus, doctors could actually be discouraged from using new, effective treatments and technologies because doing so would not provide adequate legal protections. Finally, the implementation of "safe harbor" protections could lead to new medical liability claims as personal injury lawyers could cite the failure to follow a given safe harbor as evidence of de facto negligence—regardless of the legitimacy of the provider's rationale for seeking an alternative course of treatment. Safe harbors have as much potential to serve as a sword against the provider's interest as they do to be a shield.

The most recent proposal to come forward in the alternative reform market is the "early disclosure and resolution" concept. Distinct from the "early offers" model in that it is far less structured, this proposal calls on healthcare providers and entities to communicate promptly with a patient and/or the patient's family following a suboptimal outcome, and then offer compensation if appropriate. It is believed that such programs may substantially reduce litigation by addressing two key factors that lead to lawsuits—the patient's need to understand what happened and to know that efforts are being made to correct the situation. Similar programs have been tested in selected health systems throughout the country,[29] and several states have enacted laws to encourage early resolution programs.[30]

The Future of State Reforms

Going forward, it appears unlikely that a dramatic uptick in traditional reform efforts will sweep the states barring one or both of the following events—a new, severe MPL crisis arises in which premiums rise substantially or insurers drop out of the market, or a sudden and dramatic political swing occurs in states that currently lack effective reforms. Most of the states that have a political environment favorable to true tort reforms already have such legislation (or have had it nullified by the courts).[31] Those states on the other end of the spec-

---

29. Stanford Health Care's Process for Early Assessment and Resolution of Loss (PEARL) program and Ascension Care Management's Communicate Openly Resolve Early (CORE) program have both been noted for their innovative early disclosure activities.

30. Massachusetts (Chapter 224 of the Acts of 2012), Oregon (Chapter 5, 2013 laws), Iowa (Iowa Code Chapter 135P), and Colorado (CRS §§ 25-51-101 et seq.).

31. AL, FL, GA, IL, KS, NH, OK, OR, and WA have all had duly enacted caps on damages ruled unconstitutional by their state supreme courts (see MPL Association, *supra* note 17).

trum are unlikely to enact such reforms as they have already neglected to do so through no less than three major crises.

More likely is legislative tinkering around the edges as states with reforms already in place seek additional ways to further improve their liability environment, and states without such reforms seek to improve their MPL systems without risking the political wrath of the personal injury bar. Thus, some of the supplemental reforms discussed earlier, especially "early disclosure and resolution" laws, which have not raised the ire of the personal injury bar, may prove to be the most appealing to state legislators in the years ahead.

Federal Reforms

Traditional Reforms

For many years, federal MPL reform meant one thing—the Help, Efficient, Accessible, Low-cost, Timely Healthcare (HEALTH) Act. First introduced in 2002 (although variations on many of its reforms had been introduced in earlier years), it quickly became the standard for federal MPL reform. Containing all the major MICRA reforms previously mentioned (a cap on noneconomic damages, limitations on contingency fees, periodic payment of future damages, collateral source rule reform with a ban on subrogation, and a statute of limitations), the bill deviated from MICRA, as well. Its damage cap was adjustable, allowing a state to establish a cap at any level. The bill also contained provisions addressing punitive damages and joint and several liability, and applied to a broader section of the healthcare community, including prescription drug manufacturers and health insurers. It has enjoyed a high level of backing over the years, passing the U.S. House of Representatives six times since its introduction— most recently in 2017 under a new name, the Protecting Access to Care Act, [32] and with a variety of modifications to narrow its focus to healthcare providers only and to address states' rights concerns. A new version of the bill, dubbed the Accessible Care by Curbing Excessive lawSuitS Act of 2017 or the ACCESS Act of 2019 also expands its reform focus by including some of the aforementioned state supplemental reforms. [33]

Despite the strong support for the bill in the House, efforts to pass the bill in the Senate have not been successful. As a result, numerous other proposals have been introduced, especially over the last few years. While some attempt new variations on comprehensive MPL

---

32. H.R. 1215, 115th Cong. (2017).
33. H.R. 3656 116th Cong. (2019).

reform, others are more targeted, addressing only a small portion of the MPL community.

Additional Reforms

While some of the proposals pursued within the states never caught on at the federal level, health courts appeared to have bucked that trend. Numerous federal bills have been introduced in both the House and Senate to move forward with this concept.[34] In general, these bills have not sought to create federal health courts but instead have focused on providing seed money to allow states to create their own health courts. As such, the bills have left a great deal of the details up to the states thus leaving interested parties with little idea of what form such courts might actually take in practice. In recent years interest appears to have waned as such legislation has failed to be introduced in Congress

The "safe harbors" concept has attracted federal attention and briefly gained some followers. Legislation was introduced in 2014 to create federal standards of care based upon guidelines developed by organizations representing the various medical specialties, and re-introduced in 2015.[35] The most recent iteration, however, did not alleviate the previously discussed concerns with these proposals, so more work remains to be done. While the issue may generate more discussion in the future, partisan opposition to the proposal suggests it would be difficult to pass in the current political environment, likely explaining why the bill has not be introduced in the most recent sessions of Congress.

Many of the MPL bills introduced in Congress over the years were variants on the provisions of MICRA. Tiered caps like those found in Texas have been introduced, as have caps indexed to inflation or simply set at a different dollar value. Variations on collateral source rule reform and periodic payment of damages have also been proposed. Numerous bills have been introduced to promote other options for bringing claims to a close, such as arbitration, mediation, and other forms of ADR. None of them, however, have come any closer to enactment than the HEALTH Act/Protecting Access to Care Act.

---

34. For examples, see H.R. 1546, 109th Cong. (2005); S. 1377, 109th Cong. (2005); H.R. 1372, 111th Cong. §4 (2009); S. 1851, 113th Cong. §502 (2013); H.R. 2300/S. 2519, 114th Cong. §402 (2015); H.R. 3777, 114th Cong. §328 (2015).

35. H.R. 4106, 113th Cong. (2014); H.R. 2603/S. 1475, 114th Cong. (2015); H.R. 1565, 115th Cong. (2017).

Targeted Reforms

Most recently, there has been an increased interest in reforms that are not intended to improve the medical liability system as a whole, but instead to make the system work better through more modest fixes. These reforms avoid some of the most controversial elements of other reform models such as caps on damages and strict timelines for resolving claims. Instead, they focus on isolated circumstances where reforms may simply make the healthcare system function a bit better.

The Good Samaritan Health Professionals Act is one such proposal. First introduced in the 112th Congress, it is a specific response to some of the problems that arose after Hurricane Katrina struck the Gulf Coast. In brief, the bill proposes to grant immunity from liability for any healthcare provider who treats victims of a federally declared disaster on a volunteer basis. Exclusions are included in the bill for situations involving gross negligence or criminal misconduct. The intent is to ensure that an adequate number of healthcare providers are available in the event of a widespread calamity, something current programs that require advanced registration in order for a provider to participate have been unable to achieve.[36] When offered as an amendment to other healthcare legislation in 2012, the proposal secured bipartisan support and passed the House by a vote of 251-157. The underlying bill, however, was never considered by the U.S. Senate. Proponents of the bill are undeterred, however, and the bill was re-introduced in both the 115th Congress[37] (where it was ap-proved by the House Energy & Commerce by a unanimous, bipartisan vote), and 116th Congress.[38] A variant of the proposal was enacted, however, in response to the COVID-19 pandemic. Section 3215 of the Coronavirus Aid, Relief, and Economic Security (CARES) Act (Public Law 116-136) established liability protections for volunteer health professionals providing care in response to "an actual or suspected case of COVID-19."

Another targeted area of focus is on emergency medicine. Several bills have been introduced in recent years that would provide increased protections for those who provide care in emergency departments,

---

36. For example, the Emergency System for Advance Registration of Volunteer Health Professionals (ESAR-VHP), operated by the U.S. Department of Health & Human Services requires advance registration of volunteers, thus not providing for the outpouring of spontane-ous volunteerism that often follows a disaster. For more information on the ESAR-VHP, see http://www.phe.gov/esarvhp/Pages/home.aspx.

37. H.R. 1876, 115th Cong. (2017).

38. S. 1350, 116th Cong. (2019).

recognizing that these providers often serve in difficult circumstances with little time to react and often limited knowledge of a patient's medical background. One approach has been to raise the burden of proof in MPL lawsuits against emergency department personnel. Another approach is to provide federal liability coverage under the Federal Tort Claims Act to these healthcare providers. This would put them on the same footing as providers in community health centers. This latter proposal, known as the Health Care Safety Net Enhancement Act, was also offered as an amendment on the House floor in 2012, and passed by voice vote. While the bill was never considered by the Senate, it was reintroduced in the House in 2019.[39]

One targeted reform that has already succeeded was the Standard of Care Protection Act, which was enacted with bipartisan support as part of the Medicare Access and CHIP Reauthorization Act of 2015.[40] This law makes no changes to the medical liability environment in any state but instead simply ensures the status quo. The statute[41] says that no provision of federal healthcare law may be used as the standard of care in an MPL lawsuit. Specifically, it prevents federal payment methodologies and guidelines, which were never intended to establish a standard of care, from being misused as such in court. The law does not prevent federal standards from being enacted in the future, but merely requires that if a federal standard of care is to be enacted at some point, it will have to be done explicitly rather than via the interpretation of a federal regulation which was designed for a wholly different purpose.

The Future of Federal Reforms

Despite the difficult political environment facing them, MPL reform proponents are not likely to abandon their support for traditional tort reforms. These reforms have a significant track record of success where they have been implemented. It is impossible to ignore the fact, however, that as we move further away from the last MPL crisis, interest in Congress in enacting such reforms grows weaker. Absent a new crisis, it is unlikely that this will change in the foreseeable future.

As such, pragmatists are taking a second look at what might be achievable in Congress. The previously mentioned targeted reforms appear to draw less vigorous opposition than traditional reforms, making them potential candidates for legislative action. In addition,

39. H.R. 3984, 116th Cong. (2019).
40. H.R. 2, 114th Cong. (2015)/Public Law No: 114-10.
41. 42 USC 18122.

as new technologies continue to become increasingly important to the healthcare system (e.g. telemedicine), new liability exposures may also develop and thus give birth to new efforts to reform targeted aspects of our medical liability system.

Furthermore, just as MPL leaders looked to the success of MICRA's reforms when crafting a federal proposal, they will likely look at other successful state reforms when putting together new federal legislation in the future. Early disclosure proposals may become of particular interest, given the relatively recent release of the Communication and Optimal Resolution (CANDOR)[42] toolkit by the federal Agency for Healthcare Quality and Research (AHRQ). Based on federal demonstration projects that employed aspects of the early disclosure and resolution concept, voluntary adoption of this toolkit by healthcare systems may encourage Congress to further promote this idea. Issues such as apology protections, certificates of merit, and other reforms designed to head off lawsuits before they are filed may well gain in popularity in Washington, D.C., if they can be drafted in a way to limit opposition from states' rights activists. Efforts to enact any of these concepts will not be easy, but may pose the best opportunities to enact nationwide reforms in the foreseeable future.

Summary

Early MPL crises were met with a call for comprehensive medical liability reform legislation. This continued through the crisis in the early 2000s, which saw numerous state level reforms enacted, in addition to a more significant push for such reforms at the federal level. While the easing of the most recent crisis slowed the call for reform, advances in the healthcare system may give rise to new theories of liability, which will increase the desire to address flaws within our medical liability system.

Conclusion

The MPL system continues to be a concern for many stakeholders, as it should be given the evident trends in both the underlying data (which demonstrates the inefficiency and high cost of the current system) and the legislative efforts initiated in response to that data. The extent of that concern, however, fluctuates with changes in the liability environment. Likewise, the proposed legislative response also fluctuates correspondingly. While the latest systemic trends have been more favorable in more recent years, resulting in a shift toward more targeted reforms, it is not clear how much longer those trends can hold. If the trend continues, the

---

42. AHRQ Communication and Optimal Resolution toolkit (4/5/2021), *available at* http://www.ahrq.gov/professionals/quality-patient-safety/patient-safety-resources/resources/candor/introduction.html

emphasis on "supplemental" reforms will likely increase as the need for comprehensive reforms appears less evident and legislators' attention focuses on simple, more achievable fixes. Should the trend reverse, however, and crisis conditions arise yet again, it is likely that the demand for comprehensive reforms, like MICRA, will increase substantially wherever the political environment makes such reforms feasible. In either event, it is incumbent upon advocates for MPL reform to prepare themselves for both options. The current MPL system is flawed (as evidenced, for example, by the nearly 70 percent of claims that result in no payment due to either a lack of merit or a legal finding that no negligence occurred[43]), and thus inefficient. Change must come—the only question is whether that change will be dramatic or gradual.

---

43. See figure 6.

Chapter 4

TELEMEDICINE

BY: *JEREMY SHERER, J.D., LL.M. AND AMY JOSEPH, J.D.*

I. Introduction: What Is Telehealth? Is It Different from Telemedicine?

This chapter introduces the range of legal issues that providing clinical services via telehealth may implicate. The purpose of this chapter is to set forth a non-exhaustive framework for analysis of the practice of medicine through telehealth modalities in the United States.

This chapter is organized into five sections, including this introduction. Section II explores the state-specific regulatory and scope of practice issues that clinicians need to consider when providing services in various jurisdictions. Section III addresses coverage and reimbursement of clinical services delivered via telehealth, and the differences involved depending on who is paying for such services. Section IV discusses how federal and state fraud and abuse laws apply in the telehealth context. Finally, Section V includes a number of important, miscellaneous issues that arise in this context.

Please note that this chapter is meant to function as a guide to key issues, and does not attempt to comprehensively address all applicable telehealth laws for each state across the U.S.

A. COVID-19

The rapid evolution of the telehealth landscape as a result of the COVID-19 pandemic cannot be overstated. Telehealth in 2021 and beyond is simply a different creature than telehealth pre-COVID-19, and the paradigm-shifting changes we have seen are innumerable, from the ways in which clinicians are comfortable using digital health technology, to patient expectations regarding convenience in clinical care, to regulators' perceptions of how telehealth can be utilized to promote a higher quality of care.

Without the aid of a crystal ball, predicting the state of telehealth after the pandemic is a fool's errand. Fortunately, healthcare lawyers and their clients are already accustomed to a rapidly changing landscape, which will be as critical as ever as we (eventually) emerge from the COVID-19 pandemic. Because the pandemic's regulatory landscape is temporary, the challenge for healthcare lawyers and their clients in the years to come will be navigating telehealth's "new normal" as it unfolds. That task undoubtedly requires a working knowledge of waivers and new laws introduced during the pandemic, but it is equally important to understand the pre-pandemic landscape, which will supersede the non-permanent changes introduced during the pandemic and be restored when federal and state public health emergencies are lifted, unless legislatively changed. The 2021 edition of this chapter therefore endeavors to guide the reader through the concepts that stakeholders will need to understand during, and in the period immediately following, the COVID-19 pandemic.

B. Telehealth vs. Telemedicine

As the utilization of "telemedicine" or "telehealth" has increased in recent years, universal definitions of these terms reference remain elusive, and they are used somewhat interchangeably. "Telemedicine" is traditionally used to reference the clinical services that are delivered via telehealth technology, while "telehealth" is a more expansive term that describes the range of healthcare services that can be delivered through this technology, including diagnosis and management, education, monitoring, and other services. Because it is more expansive, we use "telehealth" in this chapter instead of "telemedicine."

Certain terms are used throughout this chapter, and we introduce them here. An "originating site" references the site where the patient is located during a telehealth encounter, while a "distant site" references the location of the clinician while they treat the patient. Under the "hub" and "spoke" model, an arrangement that describes a healthcare facility's clinicians rendering services to patients at other facilities, the physician is located at the "hub" facility, while the patient is located at the "spoke" facility.

C. Telehealth Modalities

What constitutes "telehealth" varies, as we will discuss in this chapter. Generally, however, telehealth encompasses three primary clinical modalities, or ways of delivering healthcare services to patients. "Synchronous audio-video" references a live, two-way, audio-video communication between a practitioner and a patient. In everyday terms, this looks like a "video chat" one might have through services like Zoom, or the FaceTime feature on an iPhone. This most closely replicates the face-to-face interaction that is normally involved in establishing a practitioner-patient relationship. The Centers for Medicare & Medicaid Services (CMS), within the U.S. Department of Health and Human Services, limits telehealth to such two-way, real-time, interactive communication between a patient at an "originating site" and a physician at a "distant site," and specifically excludes communication through telephones, fax machines, and email.[1] Many states' definitions follow CMS's lead in this definition of telehealth by explicitly including synchronous audio-video communication and excluding other, less interactive forms of communication.[2]

In addition to synchronous, or live, communication, telehealth often includes "store and forward" communication, a type of "asynchronous" interaction where a patient captures—or "stores"—clinical data, and then transmits—or "forwards"—such data to a practitioner to evaluate it remotely. Clinical services that commonly utilize "store and forward" technology include x-ray or CT image analysis, and prerecorded photographs or videos highlighting a patient's symptoms. From a clinical perspective, this type of communication is most widely utilized in disciplines like dermatology and ophthalmology, where an image may provide sufficient data to enable a practitioner to competently treat a patient.

A third type of telehealth technology is remote patient monitoring, or "RPM." RPM involves using digital technology to collect medical and other forms of data from individuals in one location and electronically transmit that information securely to healthcare providers in a different location for assessment and recommendations. Often, this involves monitoring data like a patient's vital signs, blood pressure, weight, blood sugar, oxygen levels, or heart rate, and enables a clinician (or team of clinicians) to monitor a patient's progress over an extended period of time.

D. Online Questionnaires

At the moment, one of the more pressing topics in telehealth for providers, medical boards and other regulators is the use of asynchronous online questionnaires to gather information about a patient's symptoms for a clinician to review, make a diagnosis and, if clinically appropriate, prescribe medication. Some online questionnaires are "smart" or "adaptive" questionnaires, meaning that the tools are interactive, and the questions presented to the patient are determined using algorithm-driven workflows designed by clinicians to gather the information that a practitioner requires to treat the patient consistent with the applicable standard of care. Proponents of these tools argue that regulators should focus on the quality of care that is furnished, rather than the particular form that it takes; critics question the clinical efficacy of this technology.

---

1. 42 U.S.C. § 1395m(m)(1); 42 C.F.R. § 410.78(a)(3). As discussed in Section III, CMS *does* cover a number of services that do not use synchronous audio-video communication, and are within the scope of telehealth as the term is used colloquially. However, CMS does *not* consider those services to be "telehealth."

2. *E.g.*, CAL. BUS. & PROF. CODE § 2290.5(a).

Some state laws and regulatory guidance criticize treating patients through use of a questionnaire alone. For example, the Oregon Medical Board's Telemedicine Policy states, in relevant part, "[t]reatment based solely on an online questionnaire without individualized review and assessment does not constitute an acceptable standard of care."[3] New Jersey law implements a similar approach, but distinguishes based upon whether there is a pre-existing practitioner-patient relationship, stating, "[u]nless the provider has established a proper provider-patient relationship with the patient, a provider shall not issue a prescription to a patient based solely on the responses provided in an online questionnaire."[4] Such definitions beg the question of whether utilizing an online questionnaire together with other tools, such as an audio-only telephone interaction or review of a patient's history and medical records, is sufficient to satisfy the applicable standard of care.

Advances in the clinical sophistication and thoroughness of online questionnaires have spurred some changing views in this area. Indeed, as states update their telehealth frameworks to accommodate, and in some cases encourage, the increased utilization of telehealth during the COVID-19 pandemic, some states are introducing telehealth definitions that are agnostic concerning clinical modalities.[5] Massachusetts, for example, introduced a new definition of telehealth in early 2021: "synchronous or asynchronous audio, video, electronic media or other telecommunications technology, including, but not limited to: (i) interactive audio-video technology; (ii) remote patient monitoring devices; (iii) audio-only telephone; and (iv) online adaptive interviews, for the purpose of evaluating, diagnosing, consulting, prescribing, treating, or monitoring of a patient's physical health, oral health, mental health or substance use disorder condition."[6] This definition expressly permits the use of online questionnaires, but may suggest a distinction between static questionnaires and those that are responsive to the information that the patient presents. Other states are less specific.

---

3. Oregon Medical Board Statement of Philosophy, Telemedicine (as amended Oct. 2, 2020) (emphasis added).

4. N.J. Stat. § 45:1-62(d)(2).

5. *See, e.g.,* Ga. Code § 360-3-.07 (permitting providers to furnish treatment via telehealth without an in-person examination if the practitioner is "able to examine the patient using technology or peripherals that are equal or superior to an examination done personally by a provider within that provider's standard of care.").

6. MGL ch. 112 § 5O(a) (emphasis added).

Georgia, for example, permits the use of telehealth technology if the treating provider can satisfy the applicable standard of care.[7]

Several principles guide the less-proscriptive approach seen in Massachusetts and Georgia regarding the clinical technology that providers can use to furnish professional services via telehealth. Two of the more important principles are the recognition that broad definitions can withstand the introduction of new clinical technology, deferring to healthcare providers to determine what forms of technology are appropriate to furnish professional services, and emphasizing the quality of care that is furnished, rather than the technology that is utilized.

Ultimately, this is an important area to watch, and one which requires careful state-by-state analysis.

II.   State-specific Regulatory Issues

The practice of medicine is regulated on a state-by-state basis, by a combination of state medical board standards and state law. As such, while a practitioner's clinical practices likely will not vary from state to state, the rules surrounding such practices almost certainly will, and in some situations quite materially. This is perhaps the most ubiquitous challenge facing providers delivering services to patients across state lines via telehealth and their counsel. This section outlines the primary issues that must be considered when crossing state lines to provide professional services.

A.   Licensure

When providing services via telehealth, a clinician generally needs to be licensed in the state in which the patient is located. There are exceptions to this statement, which we discuss below. However, as a general matter, for reasons related to states' consumer protection interests, a state or territory has an interest in maintaining oversight when a practitioner is providing services to residents of that state, via telehealth or otherwise.

Licensure requirements and the issues they address vary among the states. Some states explicitly address telehealth in their state medical-licensing laws and define the practice of medicine to include telehealth that reaches into their state.[8] Some states indirectly address telehealth by deeming the act of diagnosing or recommending treatment through any "electronic"

---

7. GA. COMP. R. & REGS. § 360-3-.07. (Permitting providers to furnish treatment via telehealth without an in-person examination if the practitioner is "able to examine the patient using technology or peripherals that are equal or superior to an examination done personally by a provider within that provider's standard of care.").

8. *E.g.*, TEX. OCC. CODE § 151.056(a).

means to constitute practicing medicine in their state.[9] Other states use broader language, such as "by any means or instrumentality," to implicitly subject out-of-state physicians to their medical licensing laws.[10] Still other states do not address telehealth, directly or indirectly, in their state physician licensing statutes or regulations.

Most importantly, as a general rule, all state medical boards require a license or some other form of permission granted by the board to practice medicine in their state. Therefore, in the absence of licensure exceptions for telehealth or special telehealth licensure requirements, all states' medical boards require a physician to obtain a license to practice medicine in their state before allowing the physician to provide services via telehealth to a patient physically located in their state. Some of the exceptions to this general rule are addressed below.

CMS normally requires practitioners to be licensed in the state in which a Medicare beneficiary is located, and waived that requirement early in the pandemic.[11] However, that change was temporary in nature and will not remain in place after the COVID-19 pandemic. Moreover, that waiver did not alter underlying licensure requirements existing under applicable state law, which is of course beyond the jurisdiction of an executive agency.

B. Licensure Exceptions

There are at least eleven state medical or osteopathic boards that issue special licenses or certificates permitting clinicians to provide services via telehealth: Alabama, Indiana, Louisiana, Maine, Minnesota, New Mexico, Ohio, Oregon, Tennessee (osteopathic board only), Georgia, and Texas.[12] Some states waive licensure requirements for practitioners in neighboring states, such as New York and Maryland.[13] Other states create exceptions for specific circumstances. Ohio, for instance, allows clinicians who have treated patients outside of Ohio to provide follow-up treatment when the patient returns to Ohio, as long as such treatment is for the same condition for which the physician last treated the patient outside of Ohio and the physician outside of Ohio does not receive compensation for the services at issue.[14] Many states have exceptions for professional consults between

---

9. *See, e.g.*, Ga. Comp. R. & Regs. § 360-3-.07.

10. *See, e.g.*, Wis. Stat. § 448.01(9)(a).

11. Centers for Medicare & Medicaid Services, COVID-19 Emergency Declaration Blanket Waivers for Health Care Providers, at 33.

12. Ala. Code § 34-24-502-507; In. code 25-1-9.5-9; La. Rev. Stat. 37:1276.1; Me. Reg. §. 02-373 Ch. 1; Minn. Stat. § 147.38; N.M. Stat. Ann. § 61-6-11.1; Ohio Rev. Code § 4731.296; Or. Admin. Rules § 847-025-0000 et seq.; 22 TAC § 172.12.

13. *See, e.g.*, Md. Code Health Occ. § 14-302.

14. Ohio Rev. Code § 4731.41.

clinicians, colloquially known as "curbside consults." Such states generally require each physician to be licensed in the state in which they are
physically located, and that the services provided be along the lines of a
second opinion.[15] Still other states exempt physicians from licensure
requirements only when the services they provide are infrequent,[16] and
prohibit out-of-state physicians providing services to residents of the state
from taking certain steps suggesting a more permanent presence within the
state.[17]

C. Interstate Licensure Compacts

The Interstate Medical Licensure Compact (IMLC) provides an expedited
pathway to licensure for qualified physicians who wish to practice in
multiple states. If they satisfy certain requirements for eligibility for IMLC
licensure, physicians who are licensed in one of the 31 states to have
joined the IMLC, the District of Columbia or Guam (which have also
joined the IMLC) may be able to obtain a license to practice in another
IMLC state faster than a physician from a non-IMLC state.[18] Importantly,
physicians in IMLC states do not automatically have licensure in other
IMLC states. To be eligible for expedited licensure through the IMLC,
physicians must:

- possess a full and unrestricted license to practice medicine in an
  IMLC state;
- either hold primary residence in one's State of Principal Licensure
  (SPL), conduct at least 25 percent of one's practice of medicine in
  the SPL, be employed by an entity in the SPL, or use the SPL as
  one's state of residence for U.S. federal income tax purposes;
- have graduated from an accredited medical school, or a school
  listed in the *International Medical Education Directory*;
- have successfully passed each component of the USMLE,
  COMPLEX-USA, or equivalent in no more than three attempts;

---

15. *See, e.g.*, Mass. Gen. Laws ch. 112, § 7 (providing that state licensure and registration
requirements "shall not apply … to a physician or surgeon resident in another state who is a
legal practitioner therein, when in actual consultation with a legal practitioner of the common-
wealth").

16. *See, e.g.*, Conn. Gen. Stat. § 20-9(d).

17. *See, e.g.*, Cal. Bus. & Prof. Code § 2060 (stating that practitioners eligible for limited
licensure exceptions "shall not open an office, appoint a place to meet patients, receive calls
from patients within the limits of this state, give orders, or have ultimate authority over the
care or primary diagnosis of a patient who is located within this state.").

18. In addition to the 31 states that have joined the IMLC, Oregon, Texas, Missouri,
Ohio, New York, and New Jersey lawmakers have also introduced IMLC legislation.

- hold a current specialty certification or time-unlimited certification by an ABMS or AOABOS board;
- have no history of disciplinary actions toward one's medical license;
- have no criminal history;
- have no history of controlled substance actions toward one's license; and
- not currently be under investigation.[19]

The IMLC is not the only professional compact in place. The Nurse Licensure Compact is in place in 34 states, and unlike the IMLC, nurses who hold an NLC license are automatically licensed to practice in other NLC states.[20] The PT Compact, meanwhile, allows physical therapists licensed in member states to practice across at least 21 states.[21]

The Federation of State Medical Boards (FSMB) also introduced a new platform to mobilize volunteer healthcare professionals during the COVID-19 pandemic in early 2021.[22] Provider Bridge supports license portability for physicians and physician assistants, with a stated goal of "making it easier to connect volunteer healthcare professionals with state agencies and healthcare entities in order to quickly increase access to care for patients in rural and underserved communities."[23] Notably, Provider Bridge was built with HHS grant funding made available under the CARES Act, which may suggest that the agency is interested in playing a role in licensure portability. However, like so many other developments involving telehealth during the COVID-19 crisis, the nature of that interest–and whether it is limited to circumstances surrounding the pandemic or more broad in nature–will not be clear until the country emerges from the public health emergency.

---

19. Interstate Medical Licensure Compact Eligibility Requirements, https://imlcc.org/do-i-qualify/.

20. National Council of State Boards of Nursing NLC FAQs, https://www.ncsbn.org/nlc-faqs.htm.

21. PT Compact, http://ptcompact.org/ptc-states.

22. Federation of State Medical Boards Provider Bridge Press Release, https://www.fsmb.org/advocacy/news-releases/new-platform-to-mobilize-volunteer-health-care-professionals-during-covid-19-launches/

23. *Id.*

D. Establishing a Physician-Patient Relationship

After licensure, the next question that a physician should ask before providing clinical services in another state is what that state requires to establish a physician-patient relationship. Treating a patient without successfully establishing a physician-patient relationship as required by state law leaves physicians at risk of engaging in the unauthorized practice of medicine.

Historically, the question for physicians utilizing telehealth was whether a physician-patient relationship could be established via telehealth, or if such a relationship could only be established through an in-person consultation. This issue was litigated to great effect by the Texas Medical Board and telehealth services provider Teladoc, which ultimately resulted in the Texas Medical Board updating its telehealth regulations to enable providers to establish a physician-patient relationship via telehealth in late 2017.[24] Today, a physician-patient relationship can be established via telehealth in all 50 states, when the encounter involves synchronous audio-video communication. However, it is often less clear whether a physician-patient relationship can be established, for instance, via asynchronous store-and-forward communication, text message, or audio-only interactions. Many states specifically delineate the types of communication that are *not* sufficient to establish a physician-patient relationship. Arkansas, for instance, states that a professional relationship cannot be established through an internet questionnaire, email message, patient-generated medical history, audio-only communication (including interactive audio), text messaging, facsimile alone, or any combination thereof.[25] Maryland, meanwhile, allows a physician-patient relationship to be established via interactive audio *or* audio-video communication.[26] Other states, such as Missouri, defer to the applicable standard of clinical care, providing that a physician-patient relationship can be established via telehealth if the standard of care does not require an in-person encounter (while also stating that an online questionnaire is not an acceptable interview and examination sufficient to establish such a relationship).[27] Maine allows a physician-patient relationship to be established via telehealth, but specifically states that such a relationship cannot be established through use of a static online questionnaire "in contrast to an adaptive interactive and responsive online interview," to meet the applicable standard of care.[28]

---

24. 22 TAC § 174.2; *see* Teladoc, Inc. v. Texas Medical Board, 112 F. Supp. 3d 529, 533 (W.D. Tex. 2015).
25. ARK. CODE § 17-80-403.
26. CODE OF MD. ADMIN. REGS. § 10.32.05.05.
27. MO. REV. STAT. Ch. 191 § 191.1146.
28. 02-373-006 ME. CODE R. § 3(2016).

Finally, providers and counsel should note that establishing a physician-patient relationship involves more than the telecommunication modality utilized, and may implicate other regulatory requirements discussed herein. For instance, under New Jersey law, a physician-patient relationship can be established only if the provider verifies the patient's identity, the provider informs the patient about their clinical qualifications, and the provider reviews the patient's medical records before the interaction begins (with exceptions).[29] These rules can also be discipline-specific, reflecting differences in the information and patient interaction required to meet the standard of care across clinical disciplines. In Delaware, for example, while a physician-patient relationship typically requires interactive communication, the regulations specifically state that such standards do not apply to radiology or pathology.[30]

E. Informed Consent

Some states require clinicians to educate their patients about the benefits, risks, costs, and limitations of a particular course of treatment furnished via telehealth. At least 42 states currently have telehealth informed-consent requirements set forth in statute, regulation, or applicable Medicaid policies,[31] and both the FSMB and the American Medical Association (AMA) have outlined guidelines for providers obtaining informed consent from patients before providing treatment via telehealth, focusing on a patient's right to refuse services via telehealth without impacting their ability to receive other healthcare services and to validate and identify the provider's credentials. The guidelines also address provider obligations, including identifying the patient's location, disclosing financial interests they might have, informing the patient about how to obtain follow-up care, describing how the patient can obtain his or her medical records, disclosing privacy risks that may exist, highlighting the limitations that exist when providing treatment via telehealth, explaining fees and other payment matters, and obtaining the patient's express informed consent.[32]

The rights of patients and obligations of providers are ultimately informed by applicable state law, which varies state by state, but often incorporates many of the concepts outlined in the FSMB and AMA guidelines. Many states specify whether informed consent must be in writing or can be obtained verbally, but the act of obtaining informed consent should

---

29. N.J. STAT. C.45:1-63(a).
30. DEL. CODE tit. 24, § 1769D.
31. Center for Connected Health Policy, State Telehealth Laws and Reimbursement Policies: 2020; *see, e.g.*, LA ADMIN. CODE 46:XLV.7511 (2009).
32. AM. MED. ASS'N, Code of Medical Ethics Opinion 1.2.12. 1.1.3, Fed. St. Med. Boards, Model Policy for the Appropriate Use of Telemedicine Technologies (2014).

always be documented, regardless of state.[33] Other states, such as Mississippi, have specific requirements for informed consent when treatment is provided via telehealth, including that the patient must be informed about the risks and benefits of telehealth and how they can obtain follow-up care, and must receive information about the treatment they will receive.[34] Providers and their counsel should note, however, that there is considerable variance among the states in how they approach this issue. Indiana, for instance, explicitly prohibits requiring healthcare providers to obtain a separate, written consent before providing services via telehealth.[35]

F. Patient and Provider Verification/Validation

Telehealth technology advances seemingly by the day, yet there are still limitations involved with this technology when compared with in-person treatment. During in-person consultations, patients can fairly easily verify their provider's qualifications, providers can verify the patient's identity, and there are no questions about where the patient and the provider are located. In this sense, telehealth complicates matters; where the provider and the patient are located matters for purposes of state law, and telehealth increases the risk of unlicensed or under-credentialed individuals misrepresenting their qualifications. For these reasons, states such as South Carolina require providers to disclose their name, location, and credentials to patients when providing services via telehealth.[36] Some states, including Mississippi, Louisiana, and South Carolina, also require clinicians to verify the patient's identity and/or location before providing services via telehealth.[37]

G. Medical Records and Patient Privacy

Numerous states expressly require that any electronic records or other documents created during or as a result of a telehealth encounter become part of the patient's permanent medical record and are subject to all other general requirements of patient medical records.[38] Similarly, numerous states have taken care to ensure that any electronic records or other documents created during or as a result of a telehealth encounter are subject to all other medical record privacy and confidentiality require-

---

33. *See, e.g.*, CAL. BUS. & PROF. CODE § 2290.5(b).
34. MISS. ADMIN. CODE tit. 30, § 2635, Rule 5.3.
35. IND. CODE § 16-36-1-15.
36. S.C. CODE ANN. § 40-47-37.
37. *See* S.C. CODE 40-47-37(C); LA. ADMIN. CODE 46:XLV.7503; MISS. ADMIN. CODE tit. 30, § 2635, Rule 5.4 & 5.5.
38. *E.g.*, ARIZ. REV. STAT. § 36-3602(C); CAL. HEALTH & SAFETY CODE § 123149.5(a); COLO. REV. STAT. §§ 25-1-801, 25-1-802; 22 TEX. ADMIN. CODE § 174.1 *et seq.*

ments.[39] As a general matter, healthcare providers and their counsel should assume that all federal and state privacy and security obligations, as well as medical record retention obligations, that apply to in-person encounters in the state in which the patient is located also apply to services provided via telehealth.

For example, when contracting with a telehealth vendor to provide the technology with which to connect with patients, physicians that are "covered entities" as defined under the Health Insurance Portability and Accountability Act of 1996 (HIPAA) should require that the vendor sign a business associate agreement, and others should perform due diligence as needed to confirm that the vendor employs reasonable and appropriate technical, administrative, and physical safeguards to protect the information.

H. Remote Prescribing

Federal Law. In addition to state statutes and regulations governing medical services provided via telehealth, providers and their counsel must consult state pharmacy and prescribing laws to ensure that their remote-prescribing practices are legal. Historically, the regulation of controlled-substance prescribing practices is within the jurisdiction of the federal Drug Enforcement Administration (DEA), leaving states to primarily focus on regulating the prescribing of non-controlled substances. In recent years, however, states have begun to enact their own restrictions regarding practices in prescribing controlled substances, adding requirements beyond those imposed by the DEA. This intersection between state and federal law is one of the most complicated features of the telehealth regulatory landscape and requires significant attention from providers and their counsel. While the requirements outlined below are largely waived for the duration of the COVID-19 public health emergency, there is presently no indication that such waivers will remain in place post-pandemic.[40] As such, healthcare counsel should be prepared to operate under the regulatory framework discussed below.

In 2008, Congress enacted the Ryan Haight Online Pharmacy Consumer Protection Act (the Ryan Haight Act) following the death of Ryan Haight, an 18-year-old who overdosed on Vicodin that he obtained through an

---

39. *E.g.,* Ariz. Rev. Stat. § 36-3602(B), (D); Ky. Rev. Stat. § 311.5975(1)(B); (5); Tex. Occ. Code § 111.003.

40. U.S. Drug Enforcement Administration Guidance Document DEA067, issued by William T. McDermott, Assistant Administrator, Diversion Control Division (March 25, 2020) https://www.deadiversion.usdoj.gov/GDP/(DEA-DC-018) (DEA067)%20DEA%20state%20reciprocity%20(final)(Signed).pdf.

online pharmacy from a clinician he never met.[41] In response to a growing number of rogue online pharmacies engaging in dangerous prescribing practices, Congress passed this law to prohibit any person from dispensing a controlled substance through the internet without a "valid prescription."[42] A "valid prescription" requires the prescribing practitioner to conduct at least one in-person evaluation of the patient, unless the prescribing provider is a "covering practitioner" who conducts a medical evaluation remotely at the request of a provider who is temporarily unavailable and has previously examined the patient in person.[43]

The Ryan Haight Act does not apply to the "practice of telemedicine."[44] However, the scope of the telemedicine exception is significantly limited, such that in most cases it will not allow a provider to prescribe controlled substances without performing a prior in-person examination. The practice of telemedicine exception allows a provider to prescribe controlled substances to a patient without personally performing an in-person physical exam of the patient if the following three conditions are met:

- the patient is being treated by, and physically located in, a DEA-registered hospital or clinic during the telemedicine encounter;

- the remote telemedicine provider is registered with the DEA in the state in which the patient is physically located during the telemedicine encounter; and

- the telemedicine physician interacts with the patient using a two-way, real-time interactive audio and video communications system during the telemedicine encounter.[45]

Further complicating matters, one of the main elements of the Ryan Haight Act telemedicine exception—a special registration process through which clinicians could obtain training and permission from the DEA to prescribe controlled substances via telehealth without performing an in-person evaluation—was never promulgated by the DEA, despite first receiving explicit instruction from Congress more than ten years ago (and, as noted below, again as recently as 2018).[46]

In recent years, as the opioid epidemic has swept across the United States, lawmakers have become increasingly aware that many of the regions most

---

41. Pub. L. No. 110-425, 122 Stat. 4820 (Oct. 15, 2008); 21 U.S.C. §§ 802(54)(A), 829(e)(3); 42 U.S.C. § 1395m(m)(1); 42 C.F.R. § 410.78(a)(3).
42. 21 U.S.C. § 841(h).
43. 21 U.S.C. § 829(e).
44. 21 U.S.C. § 829(e)(3).
45. *Id.*
46. *See* 21 U.S.C. § 831(h)(2).

impacted by this epidemic are rural, and that patients struggling with substance use disorder (SUD) have not been able to obtain necessary medication because of the Ryan Haight Act prohibition on prescribing controlled substances via telehealth without a prior in-person evaluation amidst nationwide physician shortages, particularly in behavioral health. In 2018, the SUPPORT for Patients and Communities Act was signed into law, introducing several reforms in this area.[47] First, it added the home as an approved "originating site" for Medicare beneficiaries receiving treatment for SUD, thereby enabling physicians to provide SUD treatment to Medicare beneficiaries, including by prescribing controlled substances, when such patients are located in the home, as of July 1, 2019.[48] Second, it instructed state Medicaid programs to develop guidance setting forth how they would allow for controlled substances to be prescribed to patients for purposes of SUD treatment via telehealth.[49] Third, it reinforced the DEA's obligation to develop the telemedicine registration process discussed above by October 2019.[50] As of early 2021, the DEA special registration has not been established, though the agency had indicated that it hoped to publish a proposed rule in 2020, before the onset of the COVID-19 pandemic.

State Law. Federal law aside, it is important to note that many states have enacted their own restrictions on prescribing controlled substances, in addition to the limitations set forth under applicable federal law. For instance, in 2018, Connecticut passed a law allowing clinicians to engage in medication-assisted treatment via telehealth, but prohibiting them from prescribing opioids in the process.[51] Many states have waived these authorities temporarily during the COVID-19 pandemic consistent with the federal waivers discussed above.[52] However, like the federal waivers they mirror, these changes are not expected to remain in place beyond the public health emergency. Thus, it is critical to consider both federal and state law when determining what practices are acceptable in a particular state concerning controlled substances and remote prescribing.

---

47. H.R. 6 (2018).

48. SUPPORT for Patients and Communities Act (H.R. 6), § 2001; 42 U.S.C. § 1395m(7). The concept of an "originating site" is discussed in the Medicare reimbursement portion of this chapter.

49. SUPPORT for Patients and Communities Act (H.R. 6), § 1009; 42 U.S.C. § 1396a.

50. SUPPORT for Patients and Communities Act (H.R. 6), § 3232; 21 U.S.C. § 831(h)(2).

51. Conn. Gen. Stat. § 19a-906(c).

52. *See, e.g.,* Massachusetts Executive Office of Health and Human Services, Department of Public Health, Bureau of Substance Addiction Services, "Alert Regarding Use of Telemedicine during Public Health Emergency – COVID-19," April 10, 2020, https://www.mass.gov/doc/alert-regarding-use-of-telemedicine-during-public-health-emergency-covid-19/download

More broadly, state regulation of remote prescribing generally includes professional licensing rules for clinicians, as well as requirements imposed upon pharmacies and pharmacists regarding dispensing medication. In response to the "pill mills" that gave rise to the Ryan Haight Act at the federal level, many states enacted laws to curb the practices of rogue online pharmacies. As a result, many states, including without limitation Arkansas, Colorado, Delaware, Hawaii, Idaho, Iowa, Kansas, Kentucky, Mississippi, and Wisconsin, continue to restrict prescribing medication pursuant to an online questionnaire alone.[53] Some states go further, prohibiting prescribing if a provider has not treated the patient in person. Arkansas law governing the practices of pharmacies and pharmacists states that a "proper physician-patient relationship" must exist before a prescription is issued, and requires an in-person evaluation to establish a "proper physician-patient relationship."[54]

Importantly, however, the fact that a state does not explicitly prohibit such conduct does not necessarily mean that it is permitted. In fact, even states which explicitly *permit* prescribing pursuant to an online questionnaire prohibit doing so in certain situations. California requires a practitioner to perform an "appropriate prior examination" before prescribing medication, and expressly states that a prior examination does not require the use of synchronous technology, and "can be achieved through the use of telehealth, including, but not limited to, a self-screening tool or a questionnaire, *provided that the licensee complies with the appropriate standard of care.*"[55] California's deference to the prescribing clinician to determine the appropriate standard of care, rather than requiring the utilization of specific types of technology, is another example of the emerging modality-agnostic approach described above in Section I. The Medical Board of California (MBC) has implemented that approach by disciplining medical professionals for prescribing medication pursuant to an online questionnaire in a manner which, in the MBC's view, has not satisfied the applicable standard of care.

With such laws in place, there may be risk in prescribing medication pursuant to these types of communication, even when a clinician feels that she has gathered enough information to satisfy the applicable standard of care. As direct-to-consumer (DTC) platforms grow, prescribing medication pursuant to online questionnaires, interactions with artificial intelligence

---

53. Ark. Code Ann. § 17-92-1003, 3 Colo. Code Reg. 719-1, Del. Code, tit. 16 § 4744, Haw. Rev. Stat. § 453-1.3, Idaho Code § 54-1733, Kan. Admin. Regs., § 68-2-20, Ky. Rev. Stat. § 311.597, Miss. Code § 41-29-137, Wis. Adm. Code Med 24.02.

54. Ark. Code. 17-92-1003(14)-(15).

55. Cal. Bus. & Prof. Code § 2242 (emphasis added).

tools, and text-message communication raise potential legal issues that an increasing number of clinicians and attorneys must navigate.

III. Reimbursement

Coverage and reimbursement for telehealth services (or the lack thereof) is one of the most complex and frustrating areas of telehealth law to navigate for providers and their counsel. Controlling legal authority and coverage policies vary significantly depending on how the services at issue are being financed, i.e., whether a third-party payer is paying for the services and, if so, what that payer requires for claims to be paid. This section contains a high-level overview of the issues that providers should understand when submitting claims for telehealth services to Medicare, state Medicaid programs, and commercial insurers.

A. Medicare Reimbursement

Medicare coverage of telehealth services is historically restrictive, in part because CMS initially perceived telehealth as a way to help rural beneficiaries access care, but not necessarily as a clinical tool to be used more broadly. Congress amended the Social Security Act to cover telehealth services in 1997, and established the present definition of "Medicare telehealth services" at that time.[56] At a baseline level, in order for Medicare fee-for-service to cover services delivered via telehealth, those services must satisfy the following requirements (with certain exceptions): the originating site (i.e., where the patient is located) must be in a qualifying rural area, the beneficiary must be located at a qualifying originating site, the provider involve an eligible "distant site practitioner," the interaction must be an interactive, real-time, audio-video communication, and the service must be included on the current year's list of covered telehealth services.

Each of the core requirements for "Medicare telehealth services" outlined below was waived or relaxed in some capacity during the COVID-19 pandemic, and those waivers are briefly noted in the appropriate sections below accordingly. While the telehealth landscape in place during the pandemic is drastically different than the pre-pandemic telehealth framework, with a few exceptions, most of the flexibilities that CMS introduced in 2020 will only last until the later of the end of calendar year 2020, or the end of the COVID-19 public health emergency.[57] The explosion of telehealth utilization among Medicare beneficiaries during the pandemic has pushed scores of hospitals, skilled nursing facilities, and other participating providers to build out their telehealth programs, and the role of counsel will be critical in helping these less experienced providers

---

56. *See* 42 U.S.C. § 1395m(m); 42 C.F.R. § 410.78.
57. 85 Fed. Reg. 84472 (Dec. 28, 2020) *et seq.*

understand how their telehealth offerings will need to change when the COVID-19 public health emergency ends.

As discussed elsewhere in this chapter, CMS normally does not have the authority to fundamentally alter Medicare's telehealth restrictions, and did so during the COVID-19 pandemic under authority specifically granted by Congress through the CARES Act. Thus, for any of these changes to become permanent, legislative action will be necessary to amend the Social Security Act.

What is a qualifying rural area? Qualifying areas must be health professional shortage areas, or HPSAs, with certain exceptions, including being outside of a "Metropolitan Statistical Area" but in a rural census tract, or in a county outside of a Metropolitan Statistical Area.[58] Conceptually, designation as a HPSA indicates that that there are healthcare provider shortages in primary care, mental health, or dental health.[59] Geographic areas that qualify as HPSAs typically experience a shortage of a particular type of provider in the entire service area. In practice, this means that a patient located in an area sufficiently populated with behavioral health clinicians is unlikely to be eligible to receive behavioral health services via telehealth. It also makes it virtually impossible for facilities in urban areas to obtain reimbursement for telehealth services. Providers can determine whether or not they practice in a qualifying area by using the Medicare Telehealth Payment Eligibility Analyzer on the Health Resources and Services Administration (HRSA) website.[60]

What is a qualifying originating site? For the most part, qualifying originating sites are limited to the following:

- physician or practitioner's office;
- critical access hospital;
- rural health clinic;
- federally qualified health center;
- inpatient or outpatient hospital;
- a hospital-based or critical-access hospital-based renal dialysis center (including satellites);
- skilled nursing facility;

---

58. 42 C.F.R. § 410.78(b)(4).

59. *See, e.g.*, Health Resources and Services Admin., "Health Professional Shortage Areas," *available at* https://bhw.hrsa.gov/shortage-designation/hpsas.

60. *Available at* https://data.hrsa.gov/tools/medicare/telehealth.

- a renal dialysis facility (for the purposes of certain monthly clinical assessments related to treatment for end-stage renal disease);

- the patient's home (for the purposes of certain monthly clinical assessments related to treatment for end-stage renal disease or treatment of substance use disorder or a co-occurring mental health disorder);

- a mobile stroke unit (for purposes of diagnosis, evaluation, or treatment of symptoms of an acute stroke); or a

- community mental health center.[61]

Notably, Congress recently added several approved originating sites to this list through the Balanced Budget Act of 2018, including mobile stroke units, renal dialysis facilities, and the patient's home for purposes of monthly assessments in the context of home dialysis. There have also been a series of waivers under which Medicare's traditional telehealth reimbursement requirements have been waived for patients participating in certain value-based demonstrations, such as the Next Generation ACO telehealth waiver, and Medicare Advantage plans have had flexibility to offer additional telehealth services as "supplemental" benefits, which we discuss in part B of this section.[62] Except under these very narrow circumstances, Medicare does not cover telehealth services rendered to patients in their homes as fee-for-service benefits. In addition to the reimbursement of the physician at the distant site, qualifying originating sites may also bill Medicare for a facility fee related to the provision of the telemedicine service using CPT code Q3014. CMS waived the originating site requirement for the duration of the COVID-19 pandemic, however that change was not made permanent through the 2021 Physician Fee Schedule.[63] Medicare does not pay a distant site facility fee to cover administrative costs when physicians furnish services from a distant site facility.

Who is a qualifying distant-site practitioner? In addition to requiring practitioners to be licensed to provide the services at issue, CMS only covers telehealth services delivered by the following types of practitioners: physicians; physician assistants; nurse practitioners; clinical nurse specialists; nurse-midwives; clinical psychologists; clinical social workers; registered dietitians or nutrition professionals; and certified nurse

---

61. 42 C.F.R. § 410.78(b)(3). Note that renal dialysis facilities, the patient's home, and mobile stroke units, in the particular instances described here, are also exempt from the geographic requirements. 42 C.F.R. § 410.78(b)(4)(iv).

62. *See, e.g.,* 42 C.F.R. § 510.605 (waiving certain telehealth requirements for patients participating in the Combined Joint Replacement ("CJR") model).

63. 85 Fed. Reg. 85003 (Dec. 28, 2020).

anesthetists.[64] During the COVID-19 pandemic, CMS expanded the categories of practitioners eligible to bill Medicare for professional services to include physical therapists, occupational therapists, speech language pathologists, and others.[65]

What constitutes qualifying technology? Generally speaking, "Medicare telehealth services" must be provided using an "interactive telecommunications system."[66] Interactive telecommunications system means "multimedia communications equipment that includes, at a minimum, audio and video equipment permitting two-way, real-time, interactive communication between the patient and distant-site physician or practitioner. Telephones, facsimile machines, and electronic mail systems do not meet the definition of an interactive telecommunications system."[67] In other words, CMS requires these services to be provided via synchronous, audio-video communication between the practitioner and the patient, and explicitly excludes certain devices and methods of communication: telephones, facsimile machines, and e-mail communications.

During the COVID-19 Public Health Emergency (PHE), CMS added the CPT codes for audio-only (*i.e.*, telephone) services to the list of Medicare telehealth services, and reimbursed those services at the same level as corresponding audio-video services.[68] However, audio-only services will not be covered as Medicare telehealth services after the COVID-19 PHE.[69]

What is a qualifying service? To be covered by CMS, a clinical service must be included on that year's "telehealth list," which is available on the CMS website and includes the codes required to submit claims for such services.[70] CMS typically adds a few new services each year. There were 97 for calendar year 2019, including newly added coverage for prolonged preventive services through HCPCS codes G0513 and G0514.[71] CMS

---

64. 42 C.F.R. § 410.78(b)(2).

65. *See* CMS, COVID-19 Emergency Declaration Blanket Waivers for Health Care Providers.

66. 42 C.F.R. § 410.78(b).

67. *Id.*

68. CMS, Physicians and Other Clinicians: CMS Flexibilities to Fight COVID-19 at 5. ("Medicare payment for telephone evaluation and management visits ... is equivalent to the Medicare payment for office/outpatient visits with established patients effective March 1, 2020.")

69. 85 Fed. Reg. 85433.

70. 42 C.F.R. § 410.78(b); https://www.cms.gov/medicare/medicare-general-information/telehealth/telehealth-codes.html.

71. CMS's MLN Matters MM11063, *available at* https://www.cms.gov/Outreach-and-Education/Medicare-Learning-Network-MLN/MLNMattersArticles/Downloads/MM11063.pdf.

nearly doubled the list of qualifying services by adding 89 new codes during the COVID-19 PHE, however with a few exceptions, these services will not be covered as "Medicare telehealth services" after the end of the pandemic.[72] New telehealth services added effective in 2021 including group psychotherapy services (CPT code 90853), psychological and neurological testing (CPT code 96121), and cognitive assessment and care planning services (CPT code 99483).[73]

B. Telehealth Beyond "Medicare Telehealth Services"

Most services provided utilizing digital health technology must satisfy the reimbursement standards outlined above to be covered by CMS (COVID-19 waivers aside). However, there are certain services that, despite being colloquially known as telehealth, are *not* considered "Medicare telehealth services" by CMS. As a result, these services do not need to satisfy the statutory reimbursement requirements for "Medicare telehealth services." This means that, among other things, Medicare covers these services when they are provided to patients in the home, and regardless of whether the patient is located in a rural area.

Remote Patient Monitoring. CMS has covered RPM for years.[74] Officially called "Chronic Care Remote Physiological Monitoring," CMS expanded RPM coverage in 2018 by implementing coverage of CPT Codes 99453, 99454, and 99457.[75] CMS now provides broader coverage for the "remote monitoring of physiologic parameters" (e.g., weight, blood pressure, pulse oximetry, respiratory flow rate) including initial patient set up and education on using the equipment (CPT 99453), data transmissions reviewed on a monthly basis (CPT 99454), and 20 minutes or more of a clinician's professional time requiring interactive communication with the patient or caregiver each month (CPT 99547).[76]

Communication Technology Based and Remote Evaluation Services. Effective in 2019, CMS distinguished a number of services, which it calls "communication technology based and remote evaluation services," from Medicare telehealth services.[77] CMS explained that it has come to view Medicare telehealth services as specifically referencing the physician

---

72. 85 Fed. Reg. 84506.
73. *Id.*
74. *See* 82 Fed. Reg. 52,976, 53,014 (Nov. 15, 2017).
75. 83 Fed. Reg. 59,452, 59,492 (Nov. 23, 2018).
76. *Id.*
77. 83 Fed. Reg. 59,452, 59,482 (Nov. 23, 2018).

services listed on the "telehealth list" on the CMS website.[78] Thus, CMS covers "virtual check-ins," "store-and-forward" communication, and interprofessional consults, regardless of where the patient is located geographically or whether the patient is at an approved originating site.

Virtual check-ins are "brief check-in services furnished using communication technology that are used to evaluate whether or not an office visit or other service is warranted."[79] Clinicians only receive separate payment for virtual check-ins if the patient does *not* have an office visit shortly after the virtual check-in, and the patient has not had an in-person visit for the same issue in the preceding week. If the patient does have an office visit shortly after (or before) the virtual check-in, the clinician's payment is wrapped into payment for the in-office visit. Patient consent is required, and coverage is available only for existing patients.[80] As of 2020, patients do not need to provide their informed consent for every encounter. Instead, CMS has opted for an annual informed consent requirement.

CMS describes store-and-forward services as "the remote professional evaluation of patient-transmitted information conducted via pre-recorded 'store and forward' video or image technology."[81] The same requirements regarding consent, pre-existing relationships, and reimbursement also apply. "Interprofessional consults" provide a method of paying clinicians who consult with originating-site clinicians from a distant site, but do not assume responsibility for the patient's care, instead providing technical expertise to the originating-site physician.[82]

CMS expanded the categories of providers who can furnish communication technology based and remote evaluation services during the COVID-19 pandemic, and has made those changes permanent beginning in 2021. As such, licensed clinical social workers (LCSWs), clinical psychologists, physical therapists (PTs), occupational therapists (OTs), speech language pathologists (SLPs), and other non-physician providers can bill Medicare directly for these services.[83]

---

78. "We have come to believe that section 1834(m) of the Act does not apply to all kinds of physicians' services whereby a medical professional interacts with a patient via remote communication technology. Instead, we believe that section 1834(m) of the Act applies to a discrete set of physicians' services . . . . For CY 2019, we are aiming to increase access for Medicare beneficiaries to physicians' services that are routinely furnished via communication technology by clearly recognizing a discrete set of services that are defined by and inherently involve the use of communication technology." 83 Fed. Reg. 59483 (Nov. 23, 2018).

79. *Id.*

80. *Id.*

81. 83 Fed. Reg. 59,482, 59,487.

82. 83 Fed. Reg. 59,489.

83. 85 Fed. Reg. 84,532.

Additional telehealth services and Medicare Advantage. Beginning in 2020, Medicare Advantage plans were authorized to cover "additional telehealth services" for their beneficiaries.[84] "Additional telehealth services" are services that 1) do not meet the requirements for "Medicare telehealth services" and 2) the Medicare Advantage plan has determined can be provided in a clinically competent manner via telehealth.[85] Importantly, "additional telehealth benefits" are covered as basic, not supplemental, benefits. While a detailed discussion is beyond the scope of this chapter, the importance of this distinction is that basic benefits are factored into the capitated payments that CMS makes to Medicare Advantage plans, while supplemental benefits are not. As a result, providers should note that certain Medicare beneficiaries are eligible to receive additional treatment via telehealth, though the exact details of what those services are will vary from one Medicare Advantage plan to another. Additionally, providers should note that all Medicare Advantage requirements, such as provider credentialing and the coverage appeals process, will apply. As a result, even providers with deep experience in obtaining reimbursement from Medicare for telehealth services may face new requirements in obtaining coverage for "additional telehealth services" provided to Medicare Advantage beneficiaries.

C. Medicaid Reimbursement

All 50 state Medicaid programs cover live, synchronous, audio-video interactions of some type; at least 18 states cover services provided via store-and-forward communication; and at least 20 state Medicaid programs cover RPM.[86] MassHealth, the Massachusetts Medicaid program, was the last state to adopt reimbursement of telehealth encounters utilizing live audio-video technology when it expanded coverage of certain behavioral health services to include those delivered via telehealth in January 2019.[87] As a federal-state partnership, there are certain requirements that the federal government imposes upon all state Medicaid programs regarding telehealth, including that states satisfy federal requirements of "efficiency, economy and quality of care."[88] States are free

---

84. 42 C.F.R. § 422.135.

85. *Id.*.

86. Center for Connected Health Policy, *State Telehealth Laws and Reimbursement Policies*, Fall 2020, *available at* https://www.cchpca.org/sites/default/files/2020-10/CCHP%2050%20STATE%20REPORT%20FALL%202020%20FINAL.pdf?fbclid=IwAR0IqFoT4aUUENd8_k_zvXZqTOBUwwZINSAyNiZj1d1EpnTIeUPXh94R3ww.

87. *See* MassHealth All Provider Bull. 281, January 2019, *available at* https://www.mass.gov/files/documents/2019/01/23/all-provider-bulletin-281.pdf.

88. *See* Medicaid.gov, *Telemedicine*, https://www.medicaid.gov/medicaid/benefits/telemed/index.html.

to select from a variety of HCPCS codes, CPT codes, and modifiers to identify, track, and reimburse providers for services delivered via telehealth. Coverage policies and the coding required to obtain reimbursement vary considerably by state. Some state Medicaid programs limit the providers eligible to receive payment for services delivered via telehealth, and whether a state Medicaid program will pay a "facility fee" to the originating site varies state-by-state. The differences can be quite drastic, so it is critical to examine a state Medicaid program's telehealth landscape before making any major decisions involving Medicaid patients. As a reminder, this means reviewing the law in every state where a *patient* will be located, not just where providers will be located. Like Medicare, many state Medicaid programs drastically expanded their coverage of telehealth services during the COVID-19 pandemic, but those changes may not last beyond the end of the public health emergency.

D. Private Payers

Private-payer reimbursement for telehealth must be determined on a patient-by-patient, plan-by-plan basis. There are, however, state-level legal requirements concerning reimbursement for telehealth services that apply to private payers in a majority of states. Generally known as "parity" laws, these authorities address two questions: whether payers need to cover services when they are delivered via telehealth if the service is covered when provided in-person (known as "coverage parity" laws), and whether payers need to pay the same amount for a service when it is delivered via telehealth and when it is delivered in person (known as "payment parity" laws). More than 40 states currently have coverage parity laws of some sort in place, while approximately half that many have payment parity laws.

Importantly, determining that a state has parity laws in place does not necessarily mean one is "out of the woods." Indeed, some states have parity laws that defer to the terms of contracts between payers and providers. Other state parity laws, meanwhile, prohibit applying a higher patient co-pay to a service delivered via telehealth, as compared to the applicable co-pay when the same service is delivered in-person.[89] Other state parity laws only apply when the patient is located at a qualified category of originating site facility when treatment is furnished, while others prohibit charging a patient coinsurance that exceeds what would be charged if the service were furnished in-person.[90] When structuring or expanding a telehealth program, counsel should review the laws of every state in which program patients will be located, determine whether those states have payment and/or coverage parity laws in place, and consider whether there

---

89. *See, e.g.,* S.D. Codified Laws § 58-17-168(3).
90. *See, e.g.,* FLA. STAT. § 627.42396; COLO. REV. STAT. § 10-16-123(f).

are any limitations on such laws (to the extent that they exist) in addition to reviewing the specific provisions of the payer contracts.

A number of states passed legislation introducing coverage and/or payment parity laws for telehealth services in 2020.[91] As telehealth utilization continues to soar during the COVID-19 pandemic, it is clear that this landscape will continue to evolve as federal and state public health emergencies expire, and patients expect continued access to the many benefits of telehealth services.

E. Cash Pay

Many start-up companies offering telehealth services structure their businesses around a DTC model, which seeks to bypass payers, reimbursement restrictions, and the administrative complexity of the American healthcare system. The concept is simple: provide care directly to patients, who pay for the services out-of-pocket. This allows telehealth platforms, and the providers rendering services through them, to avoid some of the headaches associated with the Section IV of this chapter, which focuses on fraud and abuse, as well as the reimbursement restrictions discussed above in this Section III.

However, there is a common misconception that DTC operations are not subject to regulatory oversight. As we discuss later, DTC operations, and the providers treating patients through them, remain subject to applicable state law, even if certain federal authorities that only apply to claims submitted for services billed to Medicare, Medicaid, and other public payers (with exceptions)—*e.g.,* the physician self-referral prohibition (the Stark law) and the federal anti-kickback statute (the AKS) —do not.

State scope of practice laws also apply, regardless of the source of payment for the services at issue. This can create tension between risk-tolerant companies seeking to spur progress through innovation, including by pushing the bounds of what practices fit within the applicable standard of care, particularly where applicable laws lag behind the ways that digital tools are utilized in the field, and the clinicians implementing those practices, who may be less risk tolerant. Innovation is, of course, necessary to continue advancing the ways in which digital health technology can improve patient care. The Teladoc example noted in Section II is a case in point. However, a clinician's professional licensure is in many cases the single asset most critical to her career, even more so for physicians holding licensure in many jurisdictions to optimize their value to national platforms. Thus, for physicians and their counsel, understanding the regula-

---

91. *See, e.g.,* Tennessee HB 8002, West Virginia HB 4003.

tory risk that a cutting-edge model presents, and the distribution of that risk between a digital health company and the providers furnishing professional services through such models, is critically important.

IV.   Fraud and Abuse Issues Unique to Telehealth

As with any delivery method for the practice of medicine in the United States, a physician undertaking a telehealth endeavor is subject to a multitude of complex federal and state healthcare fraud and abuse statutes, regulations, and case law. In general, the fraud and abuse laws applicable to other forms of healthcare delivery equally apply in the case of telehealth. In addition, fraud and abuse issues that arise specific to telehealth relate to the infrastructure, equipment, and support necessary to implement any effective telehealth endeavor. This section provides an overview of the key issues and arrangements that could arise in the telehealth context that pose particular healthcare fraud and abuse risks, but a discussion of the full range of possible fraud and abuse risks presented by telehealth arrangements is beyond the scope of this chapter.

A.   Federal Kickback and Beneficiary Inducement Restrictions

The AKS prohibits the knowing or willful offer, payment, solicitation, or receipt of remuneration (including any kickback, bribe, or rebate), directly or indirectly, overtly or covertly, in cash or in kind, as inducement for the referral of patients or arranging for the referral of patients to receive services for which payment may be made in whole or in part under a "federal health care program" (defined to include Medicare, Medicaid and TRICARE, and State healthcare programs).[92] However, the statute's prohibition is not limited to payments for referrals; the statute also prohibits payments to induce the purchasing, leasing, or ordering of any good, facility, service, or item for which payment may be made under a federal healthcare program, or recommending or arranging for the purchasing, leasing, or ordering of any such item or service.[93] Voluntary safe harbors apply, so if an arrangement meets the requirements of an applicable safe harbor, then the arrangement will not be prosecuted under the statute.[94] Notably, meeting all components of a safe harbor is not required, as ultimately whether or not the AKS is implicated turns on intent.

There are two safe harbors to the AKS that specifically relate to healthcare technology, including technology used in the telehealth context. These safe harbors apply to situations in which a physician receives items and services necessary to engage in electronic prescribing (including hard-

---

92. 42 U.S.C. § 1320a-7b(b).
93. *Id.*
94. 42 C.F.R. § 1001.952.

ware, software, information technology, and training), as well as situations in which a physician receives items and services necessary to create, transmit, and receive electronic health records (including software, information technology and training), all subject to a number of conditions.[95] Such arrangements between providers on the one hand, and hospitals or other healthcare facilities or technology providers on the other hand, where the provider receives such items or services for free or a discounted cost, could potentially implicate the AKS, depending on the intent of the parties in entering into the arrangements. Structuring such arrangements to comply with the applicable safe harbors provides some certainty regarding avoidance of a finding of a violation. In addition, other safe harbors frequently looked to in the context of relationships with physicians or other referral sources, including the personal services and management contracts safe harbor and employee safe harbor, could equally apply in the telehealth context depending on the arrangement in question (e.g., where a health system contracts with a physician to provide services via telehealth).[96]

It is important to note that whether or not the services in question are reimbursed by a federal healthcare program do not necessarily impact risk of violation of the AKS. A telehealth arrangement could implicate the AKS by inducing other referrals for which governmental payor reimbursement is available. For example, the AKS could be implicated if a cardiologist provided free telehealth equipment to a general practitioner and offered free telehealth consultations to the general practitioner's patients in return for the general practitioner's referral of patients to the cardiologist for Medicare-covered cardiology services. In addition, various state anti-kickback laws may be implicated when private-payor reimbursement is available, or regardless of source of payment.

A provision under the Civil Monetary Penalties statute (CMP) addressing beneficiary inducement often goes hand-in-hand with analysis under the AKS when items or services of value are provided to Medicare and Medicaid beneficiaries.[97] In particular, the applicable provision prohibits the offer or transfer of remuneration that a person knows or should know is likely to influence a beneficiary's selection of a particular provider for the provision of items or services payable under the Medicare or Medicaid program. The beneficiary inducement CMP could be implicated in the telehealth context when, for example, a Medicare patient is provided with

---

95. 42 C.F.R. § 1001.952(x), (y). A new safe harbor, effective January 19, 2021, also protects nonmonetary remuneration in the form of cybersecurity technology and related services. 42 C.F.R. § 1001.952(jj).

96. 42 C.F.R. § 1001.952(d),(i).

97. 42 U.S.C. § 1320a-7a(a)(5).

a tablet or other device to facilitate consultations with a practitioner or to gather and transmit data for the purpose of RPM.

One exception frequently relied upon is an exception for items or services that improve a beneficiary's ability to obtain items or services payable by Medicare or Medicaid (i.e., promoting access to care), and that pose a low risk of harm to both Medicare and Medicaid beneficiaries and the Medicare and Medicaid programs.[98] In particular, the items or services offered pose a low risk of harm if: (1) they are unlikely to interfere with, or skew, clinical decision making; (2) they are unlikely to increase costs to federal healthcare programs or beneficiaries through overutilization or inappropriate utilization; and (3) they do not raise patient safety or quality-of-care concerns.[99] Although broad in concept, commentary and guidance from the Office of the Inspector General (OIG) of the U.S. Department of Health and Human Services should be reviewed and analyzed closely to determine the scope of this exception and applicability to any particular scenario.

The OIG has also stated that there is no violation of the CMP statute where the items or services provided to beneficiaries have a retail value of no more than $15 per item or $75 in the aggregate, per person on an annual basis, if such items are not cash or cash equivalents.[100]

Lastly, a new exception effective as of January 19, 2021, applies to the provision of "telehealth technologies" by a provider, physician, or renal dialysis facility to an individual with end-stage renal disease who receives home dialysis reimbursable under Medicare Part B, if certain conditions are met (including that the telehealth technologies are not offered in an advertisement or solicitation, and are provided for the purpose of furnishing services related to the individual's end stage renal disease).[101]

The OIG is responsible for publishing advisory opinions interpreting the AKS and the beneficiary inducement CMP. The OIG has published multiple advisory opinions addressing telehealth-related issues.

Advisory Opinion 98-18 addressed a proposed arrangement between an ophthalmologist and an optometrist for the sublease of certain telehealth imaging equipment, whereby the ophthalmologist leased the equipment pursuant to a written lease with a fair market value rental amount to the

98. 42 U.S.C. § 1320a-7a(i)(6)(F).

99. 42 C.F.R. § 1003.110.

100. *See* Office of Inspector General, Policy Statement Regarding Gifts of Nominal Value to Medicare and Medicaid Beneficiaries (Dec. 7, 2016), *available at* https://oig.hhs.gov/fraud/docs/alertsandbulletins/OIG-Policy-Statement-Gifts-of-Nominal-Value.pdf.

101. 42 C.F.R. § 1003.110.

optometrist, and provided free telehealth consultations for the optometrist's patients as to whether the patient required ophthalmology services. The optometrist also could use the equipment to provide other services to the patients independent of the telehealth consultations. The OIG determined that the arrangement did not implicate the AKS for the following reasons: (1) the lease agreement for the equipment complied with the equipment lease safe harbor requirements; (2) patients referred for ophthalmology services after the free telehealth consultation were allowed to choose any ophthalmologist to provide the recommended services; and (3) the ophthalmologist's free telehealth consultations only resulted in minimal and incidental business benefits for the optometrist.

Advisory Opinion 99-14 involved a health system that operated a rural telehealth network under a federal grant and wanted to fund and continue to administer the network after the grant expired, including compensation for practitioners and certain costs of equipment. The OIG found that although the health system's ongoing financial support could implicate the AKS, since it would confer benefits on both the practitioners and the "spoke" facilities, the OIG would not impose sanctions based on a number of factors, including the clear congressional intent favoring the study and development of rural telehealth networks and community benefit to rural citizens through increased access to care.

Advisory Opinion 04-07 analyzed an arrangement between a health system and school-based clinics in rural areas, where physicians at one of the health system's "hub" facilities would consult with nurses at school-based clinics on appropriate follow-up care resulting from screening tests, including potential consultation via telehealth. Students who required a referral to another physician would be referred to their primary care provider. Those who did not have a primary care provider would be provided a list of primary care providers in their town. The health system paid for the telehealth equipment and the services of the physicians. The OIG concluded that although the health system conferred benefits on potential referral sources, and the AKS could be implicated, the OIG would not impose sanctions because the screening services were non-reimbursable services for purposes of federal healthcare programs, there were otherwise sufficient safeguards in place, and the OIG acknowledged the "obvious public benefit in facilitating better access to screening services for low-income children in rural areas."

Advisory Opinion 11-12 addressed a nonprofit health system's proposal to provide neuro-emergency clinical protocols, technological devices, and services to community hospitals to facilitate immediate consultations with stroke neurologists, and where the parties could use one another's trademarks and service marks for some marketing activities, and each community hospital agreed not to participate in other neuro-emergency telehealth services without the health system's approval for the duration of the agreement. Under the arrangement, participation was based on access to care considerations, not volume or value of any actual or anticipated referrals. On its face, the arrangement implicated the AKS and did not satisfy any safe harbor because it involved the free provision of valuable items and services among hospitals, all of which had previously referred Medicare business to and from each other. However, the OIG concluded that the facts and circumstances adequately reduced the risk under the AKS. This opinion highlighted a common impediment to increased use of telehealth. Telehealth projects inherently require a large upfront investment to develop the technology infrastructure necessary to realize the much larger cost-reduction, efficiency, and quality of care benefits of telehealth for Medicare patients and private-pay patients alike. The OIG took a progressive step in this opinion by recognizing the AKS as a potential barrier to telehealth projects across the country. As such, the OIG permitted the proposed arrangement for the following reasons:

- The objective of the telehealth project was to *reduce* the number of transfers of stroke patients to the funding hospital in circumstances where those patients can be managed at the local hospital if telehealth resources are available.

- Neither the volume nor value of a hospital's previous or anticipated referrals, nor the volume nor value of any other business generated between the parties, would be a condition of participation in the telehealth project.

- The primary beneficiaries of the telehealth project would be the stroke patients who, with the funding hospital's support, could be treated at the local hospital emergency departments, when treatment is most effective. It would also benefit the patients who need the more advanced level of care that the funding hospital can provide, but who might not otherwise have been able to receive it due to capacity issues.

- The timely treatment of stroke patients would likely decrease the incidence of stroke-related disabilities, which, in turn, would likely decrease the costs associated with treating and supporting such patients.

Advisory Opinion 18-03 addressed a proposal by a federally qualified health center (FQHC) look-alike to provide telehealth equipment at no cost to a rural health clinic to help provide HIV treatment services to patients. The FQHC look-alike proposed to use funds from a state grant dedicated to HIV treatment to fund the purchases involved in the proposed arrangement. The OIG concluded that the arrangement posed a low risk under the AKS for a few reasons. First, OIG noted that there were anti-steering safeguards in place, since the rural health clinic advised its patients that they could use any provider for HIV treatment or consultation, and the FQHC look-alike permitted the rural health clinic to use the telehealth equipment to connect patients with other providers. Second, the risk of over-utilization was mitigated, since the rural health clinic would have performed preliminary tests and referred patients for consultations otherwise. Third, OIG emphasized the benefit of increased access to preventive HIV treatment, which could "reduce the prevalence of HIV and promote public health." Fourth, OIG emphasized that although the FQHC look-alike could benefit from the arrangement, the primary beneficiaries would be the clinic patients who could receive HIV prevention services more conveniently and efficiently.

Most recently, OIG Advisory Opinion 19-02 addressed a proposed arrangement whereby a pharmaceutical company sought to loan a smartphone to low-income patients which would be stripped of all functionality except for an app that tracks data regarding use of a drug and other related data, as well as the ability to make domestic calls for purposes of reaching customer support with questions. The offer of the phone would not be advertised, would not have independent value since essentially all other functionality was removed, and would be loaned for 8-12 weeks for the duration of the drug therapy to patients who met financial need criteria and did not otherwise own a smart phone. The OIG found that this arrangement could potentially implicate the AKS as well as the beneficiary inducement CMP, because by taking the device the patient would believe they needed to continue to work with the pharmacy in question. However, the OIG found that the arrangement met the access-to-care exception under the beneficiary inducement CMP, and the OIG would not impose sanctions under the AKS under the circumstances. The device promoted access to care because it was necessary in order to receive the full scope of benefits of the drug therapy, which is payable by Medicare. The provision of the device for free posed a low risk of harm because it did not affect prescribing decisions, only certain eligible patients would receive the device, the offer would not be advertised, the use of the device was time-limited, and the device did not have real independent value (OIG stated that if the phone had access to an internet browser or other functionality, the conclusion likely would be different). This opinion is noteworthy in that it addresses the RPM modality, as opposed to real-time audiovisual consultations between a patient and practitioner. As RPM grows in popularity, it is helpful to have an advisory opinion supportive of providing free or discounted technology to foster increased adoption of the modality, where certain safeguards are in place.

In summary, telehealth arrangements in which free telehealth equipment or services are provided should be analyzed for possible anti-kickback and beneficiary inducement risks. However, there has been steadily increased recognition of the value of telehealth in increasing access to medically necessary care, including in the RPM context, and if structured thoughtfully with appropriate safeguards in place, such arrangements may be permissible.

Another common anti-kickback potential issue that can arise relates to the scenario where a telehealth services vendor enters into arrangements with medical groups or individual physicians. Depending on certain factors, such as how the services are marketed, how the physicians are featured, and how the funds flow generally works, the AKS could potentially be implicated if federal healthcare program reimbursement is involved (for further discussion regarding such arrangements, see Section IV.E).

B. Federal Self-Referral Prohibition

The federal physician self-referral law (the Stark law) prohibits physicians from referring Medicare beneficiaries for certain "designated health services" (DHS) reimbursable by Medicare to an entity with which the physician (or an immediate family member) has a financial relationship.[102] Although the Stark law applies directly only to referrals of (and claims submitted for) Medicare beneficiaries, some federal courts in False Claims Act ("FCA") cases have interpreted another federal provision, 42 U.S.C. Section 1396(b)(s), as creating potential FCA liability for a person submitting Medicaid claims, in cases where the Stark law would have been violated had the individuals receiving items or services been Medicare beneficiaries.[103] The Stark law definition of a financial relationship includes almost any arrangement in which a physician receives something of value from an entity to which he or she makes referrals, including direct and indirect compensation and ownership interests.[104]

---

102. 42 U.S.C. § 1395nn.

103. The arguments raised in these cases is that 42 U.S.C. § 1396b(s), which prohibits federal financial participation payments to state Medicaid programs for items or services that would have been provided in violation of the Stark law if the patients had been Medicare beneficiaries, creates potential provider liability, either because the provider is indirectly submitting a claim to the federal government in violation of such statute, or causing the state to do so. *See, e.g., U.S. ex rel. Parikh v. Citizens Med. Ctr.,* 977 F. Supp.2d 654 (S.D. Tex. 2013) (denying a motion to dismiss, in part, by finding that a hospital could be "liable for causing Texas to submit a claim in violation of Stark"). Notably, although beyond the scope of this chapter (which provides only a high-level overview of the Stark law), strong counterarguments apply that this position, and the reasoning in *Parikh* and other similar cases, is flawed.

104. 42 C.F.R. § 411.354.

The Stark law is narrower in its scope than the AKS in certain respects, since it is limited to DHS (which includes, without limitation, lab, radiology and certain other imaging, and inpatient and outpatient hospital services), and since a physician (or his or her immediate family member) must have a financial relationship with the entity performing DHS. However, in other ways it is potentially broader, or is at least easier to run afoul of, because it is a strict liability offense (i.e., it does not require a threshold level of intent), and it is notoriously difficult to navigate and maintain all agreements in compliance with the requirements at all times. Similar to the safe harbors under the AKS, compliance with one of the exceptions to the Stark law protects a physician from liability under the self-referral prohibition.[105] However, a critical difference is that while the AKS safe harbors are voluntary, meeting all requirements to a Stark law is mandatory to avoid violation, if the Stark law otherwise applies.

Applicability of the Stark law to various arrangements is nuanced and complex, and an in-depth summary is outside the scope of this chapter. However, as with the AKS, telehealth arrangements that involve free telehealth equipment or services, volume discounts, "per-click" payments, or advertisements on physician websites should be analyzed for possible self-referral risks and self-referral exceptions (in addition to analysis under the Stark law as applicable for all physician relationships, whether involving telehealth or not).

Similar to the AKS safe harbors discussed above, two exceptions under the Stark self-referral prohibition are relevant in the context of healthcare technology, including telehealth services. These exceptions apply specifically to financial arrangements in which a physician receives free electronic prescribing technology or training or free electronic health records software, information technology, or training.[106] In addition, other exceptions frequently looked to, including the personal services and fair market value exceptions, could equally apply in the telehealth context depending on the circumstances.[107]

C. Value-Based AKS Safe Harbors and Stark Exceptions

Effective on January 19, 2021, CMS and OIG have respectively issued new safe harbors and exceptions applicable to value-based enterprises.[108]

---

105. *Id.*; 42 C.F.R. §§ 411.351 et seq. (setting forth relevant definitions, exceptions, and other applicable regulations).
106. *Id.* at § 411.357(v), (w). A new exception, effective January 19, 2021, also protects nonmonetary remuneration in the form of cybersecurity technology and related services. 42 C.F.R. § 411.357.(bb).
107. 42 C.F.R. § 411.357.
108. 42 C.F.R. §§ 1001.952(ee), (ff), (gg); 42 C.F.R. § 411.357(aa).

While the details regarding these new safe harbors and exceptions are beyond the scope of this chapter, it is worth noting that they signal a recognition of the importance of telehealth, and technology innovation more generally, as a critical part of the promotion of coordinated care.[109] These rules provide additional flexibility related to utilization of telehealth by both patients and providers, under those circumstances where two or more individuals or entities have formed a value-based enterprise. For example, participants in value-based enterprises would have a safe harbor that would expressly permit the provision of patient engagement tools and supports, which could include items to assist with access to services via telehealth.[110] As another example, although certain companies are not eligible for protection under the new "care coordination arrangements" AKS safe harbor as a value-based enterprise participant as a general rule (such as medical supply or device manufacturers), such entities may fall within the safe harbor when exchanging digital health technology as a "limited technology participant" when certain conditions are met. [111]

D. False Claims Act and Civil Monetary Penalties

Specific healthcare fraud and abuse violations, such as violations of the AKS and the Stark law, are often coupled with more general federal sanctions under the federal False Claims Act (FCA) and the CMP authority of the OIG. The FCA prohibits, among other things, knowingly submitting or causing to be submitted false or fraudulent claims for payment or false statements or certifications to the federal government.[112] CMPs are applicable if a person knowingly presents, or causes to be presented, to a state or federal government employee or agent any false or improper claims.[113] Consequences under the FCA and CMP can be steep. For example, violations of the FCA are subject to treble damages and penalties.[114]

As adoption of telehealth continues to grow, there has been a correspond-ing uptick in attention by regulators. Some of this activity has focused on regulatory compliance and billing practices. In April 2018, the OIG published a report on a post-payment audit of telehealth claims that CMS

---

109. 85 Fed. Reg. 77891 (Dec. 2, 2020); 85 Fed. Reg. 77492 (Dec. 2, 2020) (the pre-ambles to both rules provide examples involving digital health in discussions of the new safe harbors and exceptions).

110. 42 C.F.R. § 1001.952(hh).

111. 42 C.F.R. § 1001.952(ee).

112. 31 U.S.C. § 3729.

113. 42 U.S.C. § 1320a-7a(a).

114. 31 U.S.C. § 3729(a); 28 C.F.R. § 85.5.

processed in 2014 and 2015.[115] Using a 100-claim sample, OIG determined
that 31 of the claims that CMS paid did not satisfy the "Medicare
telehealth services" requirements discussed in Section III.[116] Most frequently, the claims failed to satisfy the "originating site" requirement,
because the beneficiaries received services in nonrural originating sites. In
the report, OIG recommended that CMS continue to engage in postpayment audits of telehealth claims, a recommendation that OIG had
already made in its 2017 Work Plan, which called for further review of
payments for telehealth services. This underscores the importance of
ensuring that a telehealth program is in compliance with applicable
regulatory and fraud and abuse authorities.

There has also been a corresponding increase in enforcement activity.
Beginning in late 2018 and continuing into 2019, the Department of
Justice (DOJ) issued several indictments targeting allegedly fraudulent
telehealth endeavors. In October 2018, for instance, the DOJ took action in
United States v. Roix, a case based on an alleged scheme involving
improperly solicited prescriptions for pain creams resulting in almost $1
billion in false claims (defendants subsequently pleaded guilty, and a
related qui tam case settled for $2.5 million).[117] Then, in April 2019, the
DOJ cracked down on an allegedly fraudulent arrangement involving
dozens of durable medical equipment (DME) companies and practitioners
delivering services via telehealth resulting in more than $1.2 billion in
false claims, which the DOJ called "one of the largest health care fraud
schemes investigated by the FBI and HHS-OIG and prosecuted by the
DOJ."[118]A similar takedown occurred in September 2020, which involved
telemedicine executives, DME companies, genetic testing laboratories,
and medical practitioners.[119]

Notably, the OIG issued a statement in February 2021 expressly recognizing the positive role of telehealth and other digital health tools in improv-

---

115. Dep't of Health and Human Services Office of Inspector General, CMS Paid
Practitioners for Telehealth Services That Did Not Meet Medicare Requirements, A-05-16-
00058 (April 2018), *available at* https://oig.hhs.gov/oas/reports/region5/51600058.pdf.
    116. *Id.*
    117. No. 2:18-cr-00133 (E.D. Tenn. filed Sept. 14, 2018); U.S. Dep't of Justice, Press
Release, Telemarketer and His Companies Agree to Pay $2.5 Million To Settle Allegations
That They Operated Telemedicine Schemes Involving Illegal Kickbacks and Unnecessary
Prescriptions (Aug. 1, 2019), https://www.justice.gov/usao-mdfl/pr/telemarketer-and-his-
companies-agree-pay-25-million-settle-allegations-they-operated.
    118. U.S. Dep't of Justice Press Release 19-341 (Apr. 9, 2019), https://www.justice.gov/
opa/pr/federal-indictments-and-law-enforcement-actions-one-largest-health-care-fraud-
schemes.
    119. *See, e.g.,* OIG's 2020 National Health Care Fraud Takedown Fact Sheet, *available at*
https://oig.hhs.gov/documents/root/230/2020HealthCareTakedown_FactSheet_9dtIhW4.pdf.

ing care coordination and outcomes, and distinguishing these so-called "telefraud" schemes (involving billing fraudulently for other items or services through "sham remote visits") from "telehealth fraud" (i.e., fraudulent billing for telehealth services).[120] Nothing about these "telefraud" enforcement actions indicates any inherent issue or higher level of risk when billing for the provision of services via telehealth in the ordinary course.

E. State Fraud and Abuse Laws

The federal Stark law and AKS are only the starting point for a telehealth program fraud and abuse analysis. Indeed, given the limited reimbursement available under Medicare, Medicaid, or other federal healthcare programs (although, as referenced earlier in this chapter, the reimbursement landscape is changing), many providers that provide services via telehealth do so on a cash-pay basis only, or by possibly contracting with private third-party payors as well. Such services may be subject to any self-referral and anti-kickback laws of the states into which the telehealth program may reach, depending on the specific state law.

State statutes and regulations can vary significantly in how they address fraud and abuse concerns. Certain states have chosen to integrate the federal fraud and abuse statutes into their state Medicaid statutes.[121] Some apply where reimbursement for the item or service is payable by a healthcare insurer,[122] and others apply regardless of reimbursement source.[123] In addition, a state may create telehealth-specific fraud and abuse laws. For example, Texas specifically requires physicians practicing telehealth to establish certain protocols to reduce the additional fraud and abuse risks presented by telehealth activities.[124]

Thus, physicians should be aware that a federally compliant telehealth arrangement may still be subject to state fraud and abuse sanctions if the applicable state telehealth laws and fraud and abuse laws are not independently identified and addressed.

---

120. *See* Principal Deputy Inspector General Grimm on Telehealth, available at https://oig.hhs.gov/coronavirus/letter-grimm-02262021.asp?utm_source=oig-home&utm_medium=oig-hero&utm_campaign=oig-grimm-letter-02262021 (Feb. 26, 2021).
121. *See, e.g.,* ALA. CODE. § 22-1-11(c); ALA. ADMIN. CODE r. § 560-x-4.04.
122. *See, e.g.,* MASS. GEN. LAWS Ch. 175H § 3.
123. *See, e.g.,* CAL. BUS. & PROF. CODE § 650.
124. 22 TEX. ADMIN. CODE § 174.3.

F. Corporate Practice of Medicine and Fee-Splitting

Successful telehealth ventures are often composed of the three following players—technology experts, venture capitalists, and physicians or other practitioners. Whenever business ventures include the close alignment of licensed healthcare professionals and non-licensed individuals or entities, the arrangement should be reviewed carefully to identify any potential violation of a state's fee-splitting rules or corporate practice restrictions, in addition to potential kickback and self-referral issues. A common scenario where this arises is where a technology vendor, backed by venture capital, develops a telehealth platform and otherwise provides related administrative services so that providers can utilize the technology platform to provide services.

Many states expressly prohibit the "corporate practice of medicine," meaning an unlicensed individual or entity is prohibited from engaging in the practice of medicine.[125] This means that, in some states, only licensed physicians or other healthcare providers may contract with other licensed physicians to provide healthcare services, unless an exception applies. Similarly, in many states, only licensed healthcare providers are allowed to own or control a company that is "practicing medicine."[126] The criminal act of aiding and abetting the unlicensed practice of medicine is potentially a concern that should be considered for all involved in a telehealth venture, depending on the state(s) of operation.[127] Whether there is a violation may be a nuanced analysis, as the distinction between what is and is not the practice of medicine by a person (or corporation) varies from state to state, and often is not clearly defined. Prior to engaging in a telehealth venture, to the extent unlicensed individuals or entities are involved, a close review of the applicable state laws where patients will receive the services should be undertaken to determine if there is a corporate practice of medicine prohibition, and if so the scope of such prohibition, including any medical board guidance or prior enforcement actions.[128]

---

125. *See, e.g.*, CAL. BUS. & PROF. CODE §§ 2052, 2400.

126. *See, e.g.*, CAL. CORP. CODE § 13400 et seq.

127. By analogy, in the context of dentistry, a large dental management company entered into a significant settlement upon a finding by the New York attorney general that it was engaged in the unauthorized practice of dentistry and illegal fee-splitting. *See* https://ag.ny.gov/press-release/ag-schneiderman-announces-settlement-aspen-dental-management-bars-company-making.

128. *See, e.g.*, California Medical Board guidance, http://www.mbc.ca.gov/Licensees/Corporate_Practice.aspx.

In addition to the corporate practice of medicine, many states prohibit physicians from "splitting" their fees with non-physicians.[129] Therefore, although a "lay entity" technology company or venture capitalist may wish to receive a portion of the profits of the venture, either as an owner in the venture or by receiving a percentage of profits from the professional entity, in many states such arrangements could raise potential issues under applicable fee-splitting statutes (as well as potentially under corporate practice of medicine and/or anti-kickback statutes).

The variety in state laws and enforcement on these issues requires legal counsel to thoughtfully consider how best to structure the arrangement on a state-by-state basis. For example, if a patient pays for an online consultation by a physician, who is permitted to share in a portion of that payment and under what terms? Are there payments between the various parties to an arrangement that could be viewed as illegal kickbacks for generating healthcare business? Analyzing the applicable legal landscape and compliant structures by which the relevant parties can affiliate and receive compensation for their involvement should occur early in the planning process for any new telehealth venture.

V. Miscellaneous

A. Proxy Credentialing

CMS requires Medicare-participating hospitals to have an organized medical staff that operates under bylaws that are approved by the hospital's governing body, and that is responsible for the quality of clinical care provided to hospital patients.[130] The medical staff needs to examine the credentials of candidates for medical staff membership, and make recommendations regarding their candidacy in compliance with applicable state law.[131] This presents operational challenges for originating site, or "spoke," hospitals, whose patients are receiving treatment from clinicians located at other facilities. The credentialing process can be very labor-intensive, particularly if a clinician is simply providing coverage and not intending to be a long-term contributor to the originating site facility. Recognizing these difficulties, CMS and the Joint Commission have developed options for facilities to credential their providers. Specifically, the Joint Commission provides three options for credentialing providers treating patients via telehealth:

---

129. *See, e.g.*, N.Y. Educ. Law § 6509-a; 8 NYCRR § 29.1(b)(4).
130. 42 C.F.R. § 482.22.
131. 42 C.F.R. § 482.22(a)(2).

- originating site fully privileges and credentials the practitioner;

- originating site uses credentialing information from the distant site (if the distant site is Joint Commission-accredited); and

- originating site uses the credentialing and privileging decision from the distant site to make a final privileging decision pursuant to specific conditions being satisfied (i.e., "credentialing by proxy").[132]

Credentialing by proxy is permitted only if the originating site hospital's governing body establishes an agreement with the distant site hospital, or distant site telemedicine entity,[133] ensuring that the distant site hospital is a Medicare-participating hospital; that the clinician providing services is privileged at the distant site hospital, and included on a list of the distant site clinician's privileges to the originating site hospital; the distant site clinician is licensed to practice in the state in which the originating site hospital is located; and the originating site documents its internal review of the distant site clinician's performance of clinical privileges and sends such information to the originating site to use in reviewing the performance of the distant site clinician, which must at least include reviewing all adverse events that result from the telehealth services provided by the distant site clinician to the originating site hospital's patients, and complaints the originating site has received about the distant site clinician.[134] Importantly, hospitals utilizing proxy credentialing must ensure that their hospital bylaws allow for this practice to avoid a scenario where non-credentialed clinicians are providing services via telehealth.

B. Malpractice Insurance

When providing services via telehealth, providers must ensure that their medical malpractice coverage is effective. In particular, it is important to verify that the malpractice policy at issue applies to services provided via telehealth, and that it applies to services rendered in every state where a patient of the practitioner may be located.

---

132. Joint Commission, MS 13.01.01.
133. An originating site can rely upon the credentialing of another Medicare-accredited hospital or a "distant site telemedicine entity," per 42 C.F.R. § 482.12(a)(9).
134. 42 C.F.R. § 482.22(a)(3).

Chapter 5

HIPAA COMPLIANCE: PRIVACY, SECURITY AND BREACH OBLIGATIONS

BY: TAMMY WARD WOFFENDEN

Maintaining robust Health Insurance Portability and Accountability Act of 1996 (HIPAA) compliance practices is a significant challenge for physicians whose practices, which now primarily rely on electronic health records, are becoming more frequent targets in cybersecurity incidents. They are also facing increased enforcement activity by the U.S. Department of Health and Human Services (HHS), Office for Civil Rights (OCR), for privacy and security violations. In the past few years, physician groups have paid settlement amounts ranging from $31,000 to $500,000 for HIPAA violations such as those involving loss of unencrypted laptops, failure to enter into business associate agreements (BAA), breaches resulting from cyberattacks, inappropriate public disclosure of protected health information, and failure to perform comprehensive risk assessments to ensure compliance with HIPAA. These settlements demonstrate the importance of developing and implementing effective HIPAA compliance policies and procedures. In order to do so, physicians and their compliance staff must navigate HIPAA's privacy and security requirements and be able to effectively identify, address, and mitigate HIPAA risks and breaches.

Evolution of HIPAA

Until the implementation of HIPAA, the privacy of health and medical information was regulated by state law and varied greatly on a state-by-state basis. However, in light of the concerns regarding the protection of personally identifiable health information and the uneven application of state law, the U.S. Congress, in 1996, passed HIPAA.[1] In particular, HIPAA called for what at that time were sweeping changes to the manner in which the healthcare industry uses an individual's health information and the manner in which such information is handled and transmitted. The intent of these requirements was and is to safeguard the privacy of individuals' health information.

Following passage of HIPAA, HHS issued Standards for Privacy of Individually Identifiable Health Information (the Privacy Rule), Security Standards (the Security Rule), and the HIPAA Enforcement Rule.[2] The intent of these regulations

---

1. Pub. L. 104-191.
2. 42 U.S.C. § 201 *et seq.* (HIPAA), 45 C.F.R. pt. 160 and subparts A and E of pt. 164 (Privacy Rule); 45 C.F.R. pts. 160 and 164 subparts A and C (the Security Rule); 45 C.F.R. pt. 160, subparts C, D, and E (the Enforcement Rule).

was and is to protect the privacy of individually identifiable health information that is maintained or transmitted in any form, whether electronic or not, and that relates to: (1) a past, present, or future physical or mental health condition; (2) the provision of healthcare; or (3) the past, present, or future payment for the provision of healthcare to an individual.[3] The Privacy Rule regulates information that is generally categorized as protected health information (PHI).[4] The Security Rule applies to PHI that is maintained in electronic form (EPHI).[5]

On February 17, 2009, the Health Information Technology or Economic and Clinical Health Act, under Title XIII of the American Recovery and Reinvestment Act of 2009, Public Law 111-5 (HITECH Act), was signed into law and contained numerous provisions affecting the privacy and security requirements for PHI. The final rule implementing most of the amendments mandated by the HITECH Act was issued on January 25, 2013 (the Omnibus Final Rule).[6] In addition to changes to the Privacy and Security Rules, the Omnibus Final Rule updated the penalty structure and enforcement scheme of HIPAA's Enforcement Rule and finalized breach notification requirements established by the HITECH Act (the HIPAA Breach Notification Rule).[7]

Application of HIPAA to Physicians

HIPAA and its implementing regulations apply to health plans, healthcare clearing-houses, and healthcare providers who engage in electronic data interchange using one or more of the "standard transactions," as defined by HIPAA regulations governing electronic data interchange (collectively referred to as "covered enti-ties").[8] Pursuant to the HITECH Act and Final Omnibus Rule, "business associates" are also directly regulated by HIPAA and certain implementing regulations, including the HIPAA Security Rule.[9] "Business associates" perform functions or activities on behalf of covered entities and create, maintain, receive, or transmit PHI in relation to such functions or activities. This business associate relationship is also governed by contractual obligations, typically outlined in a business associate agreement (BAA) between a covered entity and its business associate that seeks to ensure the privacy and security of PHI created, maintained, received, or transmitted on behalf of the covered entity.

---

3. 45 C.F.R. § 160.103.
4. *Id.*
5. 45 C.F.R. § 164.302.
6. 78 Fed. Reg. 5566 (Jan. 25, 2013).
7. 45 C.F.R. pt. 164, subpart D (the Breach Notification Rule).
8. 45 C.F.R. § 160.103.
9. *Id.*

The HIPAA Privacy Rule

The Privacy Rule governs the use and disclosure of an individual's PHI by covered entities and their business associates and sets standards for an individual's right to understand and control some aspects of how his or her PHI is used and disclosed.[10]

Individual Rights Established by the Privacy Rule

The Privacy Rule establishes the following rights for individuals with regard to their PHI:

- *Access.* An individual has the right to access his or her PHI.[11] Under the Privacy Rule, a covered entity must allow the individual to inspect or obtain a copy of his or her PHI contained in a designated record set.[12] Further, if the individual request is made in the appropriate manner and form, PHI must be provided to a designated third person.[13] The covered entity generally must provide the records requested within 30 days.[14] Certain exceptions to the provision of access to PHI apply.[15] For example, a covered entity may deny access to psychotherapy notes; information compiled in reasonable anticipation of or use in a civil, criminal, or administrative action or proceeding; PHI subject to the Clinical Laboratory Improvements Amendments of 1988 to the extent access would be prohibited by law; or PHI exempt from the Clinical Laboratory Improvements Amendments of 1988.[16] The individual is entitled to have an independent licensed healthcare professional review a denial for access, if the denial was made pursuant to one of the following situations: (1) a licensed healthcare professional has determined that the access requested is reasonably likely to endanger the life or physical safety of the individual or another person; (2) the PHI makes reference to another person (who is not a healthcare provider) and a licensed healthcare professional has determined that the access

---

10. *See* 45 C.F.R. §§ 164.520–164.528.

11. 45 C.F.R. § 164.524.

12. A designated record set means a group of records maintained by or for a Covered Entity that satisfies one of the following: (1) the medical and billing records about individuals maintained for or by a healthcare provider; (2) the enrollment, payment, claims adjudication, and case or medical management records systems maintained by or for a health plan; or (3) used, in whole or in part, by or for the Covered Entity to make decisions about individuals. 45 C.F.R. § 164.501.

13. 45 C.F.R. § 164.524.

14. *Id.* § 164.524(b).

15. *Id.*

16. *Id.* § 164.524(a)(1).

request is likely to cause substantial harm to such other person; or (3) the request for access is made by the individual's personal representative and a licensed healthcare professional has determined that the provision of access is reasonably likely to cause substantial harm to the individual or another person.[17] If no review is required or if access continues to be denied following the review, the covered entity must provide instructions to the individual regarding how to file a complaint with the covered entity or HHS.[18] If access is granted, the covered entity may charge reasonable copying costs.[19] It should be noted that an individual may request a summary of the records, in lieu of a copy, and the covered entity may charge a reasonable fee to prepare the summary.[20] Some state laws govern how much a physician can charge a patient for copies of his or her medical records.

- *Amendment.* An individual has the right to request that a covered entity amend PHI for as long as the PHI is maintained in a designated record set.[21] The request for amendment can be denied for the following reasons: (1) the PHI was not created by the covered entity (unless the individual provides a reasonable basis to believe that the originator of the PHI is no longer available to act on the requested amendment); (2) the PHI is not part of the designated record set; (3) the PHI would not be available for access under the right to access; or (4) the PHI is accurate and complete.[22] A covered entity must act on a request for amendment within 60 days of receipt.[23] If the covered entity needs additional time to respond, it is required to provide the individual with a statement of the reasons for the delay and the date by which it can respond (which cannot be longer than a 30-day extension).[24] If the covered entity denies the amendment, the individual must be offered an opportunity to submit a written statement disagreeing with the denial and the covered entity must file this statement in the designated records set.[25] The covered entity can file a rebuttal

---

17. *Id.* § 164.524(a)(3) & (4).
18. *Id.* § 164.524(d).
19. *Id.* § 164.524(c)(4).
20. *Id.* § 164.524(c)(2).
21. *Id.* § 164.526.
22. *Id.* § 164.526(a).
23. *Id.* §164.526(b).
24. *Id.*
25. *Id.* § 164.526(d).

statement for the record as well.[26] The individual also has the right to complain about the denial to the covered entity or HHS.[27]

- *Accounting.* The HIPAA Privacy Rule provides individuals with the right to obtain an accounting of certain PHI disclosures made by the covered entity for up to six years prior to the date on which the accounting is requested.[28] However, certain disclosures are excluded from HIPAA accounting requirements.[29] Most notably, individuals do not have a right under HIPAA to obtain an accounting of disclosures made to carry out treatment, payment, or healthcare operations (TPO).[30] The covered entity generally must act on the request for the accounting within 60 days.[31] The HITECH Act expands certain accounting responsibilities to include TPO if the covered entity uses or maintains an electronic health record (EHR).[32] When records are maintained in an EHR, the HITECH Act provides individuals with the right to receive an accounting of disclosures relating to their PHI for up to the previous three years. The accounting shall include any reason the PHI is used, even for purposes of TPO.[33] However, at this time, final regulations implementing this requirement have not been adopted.[34]

- *Restrictions and Confidential Communications.* The Privacy Rule requires covered entities to permit an individual to request, and the covered entity, in certain situations, must approve, an individual's request to restrict access to PHI.[35] In addition, a covered entity must permit individuals to request and, in specific situations, accommodate the individual's request for confidential communications. This means that the individual would receive communications by an alternative means or at alternative locations.

To communicate these rights to individuals, the Privacy Rule requires a covered entity to disseminate to its patients or members a Notice of Privacy Practices, which explains how the covered entity will use an

---

26. *Id.*
27. *Id.*
28. *Id.* § 164.528.
29. *Id.* § 164.528(a)(1).
30. *Id.*
31. *Id.*
32. *Id.*
33. *Id.*
34. *Id.*
35. *Id.* § 164.522.

individual's PHI and the individual's rights to control the uses, disclosures of, and access to that information.[36] The Notice of Privacy Practice must also provide information regarding how to file complaints and contact information for the covered entity.[37]

Use and Disclosure of PHI—Individual Authorizations

The Privacy Rule restricts the use and disclosure of PHI. Unless certain exceptions apply, a covered entity must obtain an individual's authorization before using or disclosing that individual's PHI.[38] The authorization must contain specific requirements and be signed by the individual or his or her personal representative.[39] The authorization may be revoked at any time, except that the revocation cannot be retroactive and does not apply to PHI disclosed by the covered entity in reliance on the authorization.[40] A revocation also does not apply if the authorization was obtained as a condition of obtaining insurance coverage.[41] In addition, other obligations apply to the use of psychotherapy notes, as well as the use or disclosure of PHI for research and marketing. However, with certain exceptions, an authorization is required for all other uses and disclosures.

The HITECH Act and Omnibus Final Rule included additional requirements relating to disclosures for sale of PHI and use or disclosure of PHI for fundraising and marketing. Even if an individual signs an authorization, additional steps must be taken by the covered entity before engaging in these activities:

- *Sale of PHI*: Sale of PHI without prior authorization is prohibited under the Privacy Rule, which generally defines "sale of PHI" to mean disclosure of PHI by a covered entity or business associate in exchange for direct or indirect remuneration.[42] "Remuneration" can apply to the receipt of nonfinancial as well as financial benefits.[43] In the HIPAA Omnibus Rule, HHS clarified that "sale of PHI" does not include the following: (1) payments to a covered entity in the form of grants, contracts, or other arrangements to perform certain programs or activities, such as a research study or

---

36. *Id.* § 164.520.

37. *Id.*

38. *Id.* §§ 164.508, 164.512.

39. The HIPAA Privacy Regulations contain specific guidance on personal representatives, including for minors and other individuals who lack decision-making ability. 45 C.F.R. § 164.502(g).

40. 45 C.F.R. § 164.508.

41. *Id.*

42. 45 C.F.R. § 164.502(a)(5)(ii).

43. *Id.*

(2) payments received for the exchange of PHI through a health information exchange. There are also limited exceptions to the sale prohibition, such as disclosures for public health.[44] An individual's authorization for the sale of PHI must specifically state that the sale will result in remuneration.

- *Use or Disclosure of PHI for Marketing Purposes*: The Privacy Rule defines "marketing" to mean making a communication about a product or service that encourages recipients of the communication to purchase or use the product or service.[45] While a covered entity can still communicate with patients regarding treatment and for its own healthcare operations without authorization, prior authorization is required when a covered entity (or its business associate) receives "financial remuneration" from a third party for making a marketing communication on the third party's behalf. "Financial remuneration" for this purpose means direct or indirect payment but does not include nonfinancial benefits. The authorization form must explain that PHI is being used for marketing purposes and disclose that the covered entity (or business associate) is receiving financial remuneration from a third party for such communications.

- *Use of PHI for Fundraising*: HIPAA's definition of healthcare operations includes fundraising activities.[46] Despite early efforts under implementation of the HITECH Act to eliminate fundraising activities from this definition, the Privacy Rule still permits fundraising activities by a covered entity using an individual's PHI, as long as any written fundraising communication provides individuals with an opportunity to opt out of future fundraising communications. Covered entities have discretion to decide what opt-out method to use, but the chosen methods cannot impose an undue burden or more than a nominal cost on individuals.[47]

Uses and Disclosures—Without Authorization

A covered entity may generally use or disclose PHI for treatment, payment, or healthcare operations without authorization, which may include disclosure to a business associate.[48] For these purposes, "treatment" means the provision, coordination, or management of healthcare and related

---

44. *Id.*
45. 45 C.F.R. § 164.501.
46. 45 C.F.R. § 164.501.
47. 45 C.F.R. § 164.514(f).
48. 45 C.F.R. § 164.506.

services by one or more healthcare providers, including coordination or management of healthcare by a healthcare provider with a third party; consultation between healthcare providers relating to a patient; or the referral of a patient for healthcare from one healthcare provider to another.[49] "Payment" includes activities relating to obtaining reimbursement for the provision of healthcare, such as billing, claims management, collection activities, obtaining payment under contract, and related healthcare data processing.[50] "Healthcare operations" is a broader category of use, which can include conducting quality assessment and improvement activities (e.g., outcomes evaluation and development of clinical guidelines; patient safety activities; population-based activities relating to improving health or reducing healthcare costs; protocol development; case management and care coordination; and contacting of healthcare providers and patients with information about treatment alternatives and related functions that do not include treatment) reviewing the competence or qualification of healthcare professionals; evaluating practitioner and provider performance and health plan performance; conducting training programs, accreditation, certification, licensing, or credentialing activities; conducting or arranging for medical review, legal services, and auditing functions; business planning and development; and business management and general administrative activities.[51]

A covered entity may also disclose PHI without authorization for treatment activities of another healthcare provider, to the individual whose PHI is being disclosed, and to another covered entity for payment activities of the covered entity that receives the information. A covered entity may also disclose PHI to another covered entity for healthcare operations activities of the entity that receives the information if each entity either has or had a relationship with the individual who is subject to the PHI being requested and the PHI pertains to such relationship.[52] An example of such disclosure is when a provider discloses its patients' health information to the patients' insurance plan for the plan's care coordination or case management services.

The HIPAA Privacy Rule also contains additional situations in which patient authorization is not required, but other obligations must be met before information may be disclosed. For example, if certain specified requirements are met, a covered entity may disclose PHI without an authorization under the following circumstances: when required by law; for public health activities; to assist victims of abuse, neglect, or domestic violence; for health oversight activities; for judicial and administrative

49. 45 C.F.R. § 164.501.
50. *Id.*
51. *Id.*
52. 45 C.F.R. §§ 164.501, 164.502; 164.506.

proceedings; for law enforcement purposes; about decedents to coroners, medical examiners, or funeral directors; for cadaveric organ, eye, or tissue donation purposes; for research purposes; to avert a serious threat to health or safety; for specialized government functions, such as military and veterans' activities; disclosures for worker's compensation; and in certain situations if an opportunity to agree or object is provided.[53]

Disclosures to Business Associates

The requirements of the Privacy Rule also affect the practices of a covered entity's business associates that perform functions for the covered entity involving the use or disclosure of protected health information, such as legal or accounting work, administrative or financial activities, billing and payment, or management and consulting services. A covered entity must enter into an agreement with each of its business associates requiring business associates to also safeguard the privacy of individuals' health information.[54] The HIPAA Privacy Rule outlines minimum elements that must be addressed in a BAA. A BAA should be carefully reviewed to confirm that the agreement meets the Privacy Rule, and the agreement should be negotiated to address other contractual obligations the parties may want (but are not required under HIPAA), such as indemnification and cyber insurance coverage requirements. To assist covered entities and business associates with these obligations, HHS has posted a sample BAA on its website for reference.[55]

Prior to the HITECH Act, violations of HIPAA were generally not directly enforceable against business associates, and covered entities were not generally liable for, or required to monitor, the actions of their business associates unless the covered entity discovered a material breach or violation of the business associate's contract. The HITECH Act expanded HHS HIPAA enforcement capabilities to include violations by business associates.[56] The HIPAA Omnibus Rule extended this enforcement authority and liability to subcontractors of business associates.[57] Thus, a subcontractor receiving access to PHI from a covered entity's business associate is considered a business associate, despite how far "down the chain" the subcontractor provides services.[58] This regulation also modifies

---

53. 45 C.F.R. § 164.512.
54. 45 C.F.R. § 164.54(e).
55. U.S. DEPT. OF HEALTH & HUMAN SERVS., BUSINESS ASSOCIATE CONTRACTS (published Jan. 25, 2013), *available at* https://www.hhs.gov/hipaa/for-professionals/covered-entities/sample-business-associate-agreement-provisions/index.html.
56. 42 U.S.C. § 17,938.
57. 78 Fed. Reg. 5566, 5692-5702 (Jan. 25, 2013).
58. *Id.;* 45 C.F.R. § 164.314.

the definition of "business associate" to include an entity, such as a data storage company, that maintains PHI, even if the entity does not actually view the PHI.[59] Health information organizations, E-prescribing gateways, and personal health records vendors are also now classified as business associates.[60]

Minimum Necessary Requirement and Limited Data Sets

While a covered entity may have legitimate reasons to use and disclose an individual's PHI, such uses and disclosures—whether performed directly by covered entities or their business associates—should be the minimum amount of PHI necessary to carry out the particular function for which the information is needed.[61] This requirement applies to most disclosures except for disclosures by a healthcare provider for treatment purposes, disclosure made to the individual, uses and disclosures made pursuant to an authorization, disclosures made to the Secretary of HHS, and disclosures required by law.[62] Furthermore, even within a covered entity's organization, only the personnel who need particular health information to perform their jobs should have access to that information.[63] The rule permits the disclosure of a "limited data set" for certain specified purposes, such as research.[64] A limited data set is considered by HHS to pose a low privacy risk because most of the patient's identifying information has been removed.[65]

Other Administrative Requirements

The HIPAA Privacy Rule includes a number of administrative requirements for a covered entity to meet. These include:

- Implementation and maintenance of policies and procedures on how PHI is handled and safeguarded within the covered entity's own organization, and on how such information will be used and disclosed to others.[66]

- Designation of a privacy officer who is responsible for the development and implementation of the privacy policies and procedures.[67]

---

59. 78 Fed. Reg. 5566, 5692-5702; 45 C.F.R. § 164.103.
60. *Id.*
61. 45 C.F.R. § 164.514(d) and 164.502(b).
62. 45 C.F.R. § 164.502(b)(2).
63. *Id.*
64. 45 C.F.R § 164.514(e).
65. *Id.*
66. 45 C.F.R. § 164.530(i)(1).
67. 45 C.F.R. § 164.530(a)(i).

- Designation of a contact person for receiving complaints and development of a process for individuals to make complaints.[68]

- Conducting training of employees regarding policies and procedures created to safeguard protected health information.[69]

- Establishing disciplinary and sanctions policies relating to workforce violations of the Privacy Rule and the covered entity's policies and procedures.[70]

- Documenting activities with respect to PHI, including activities related to obtaining authorizations, dissemination of the Notice of Privacy Practices, BAAs, requests relating to individual rights, certifications of training, complaints, breach response, and other documentation evidencing implementation of policies and procedures to safeguard PHI.[71] This documentation must be retained for a minimum of six years.[72]

The HIPAA Security Rule

The HIPAA Security Rule requires covered entities and their business associates to adopt specified standards for protecting electronically stored and transmitted PHI. These security standards are written to be flexible and scalable to covered entities' and business associates' size, complexity, capabilities, technical infrastructure, hardware, and software security capabilities.[73] Nevertheless, it is important for covered entities and business associates to adopt practices that meet all required standards set forth in the Security Rule and, unless otherwise justified in writing, the "addressable" standards as well. The Security Rule implementation standards are:

- *Administrative Safeguards*: The Security Rule defines administrative safeguards as "administrative actions, and policies and procedures, to manage the selection, development, implementation, and maintenance of security measures to protect EPHI and to manage the conduct of workforce in relation to the protection of that information."[74] Examples of administrative safeguards include: (1) developing plans, policies, and procedures for assessing the capabilities and vulnerabilities of the electronic information system, including conducting a risk analysis; (2) establishing sanctions policies to apply when workforce members fail to comply with the security policies and procedures; (3) information system activity review; (4)

---

68. 45 C.F.R. § 164.530(a)(ii), (d)(1).
69. 45 C.F.R. § 164.530(b)(1).
70. 45 C.F.R. § 164.530(e)(1).
71. 45 C.F.R. § 164.530(j).
72. 45 C.F.R. § 164.530(j)(2).
73. 45 C.F.R. § 164.306(b).
74. 45 C.F.R. § 164.308.

designating a security official to be responsible for the development and implementation of the entity's policies and procedures required under the Security Rule; (5) workforce security and access controls; (6) security awareness training; (7) security incident procedures; (8) contingency planning, including formulating plans for data backup, data restoration, and continued operation of electronic data systems in the event of an emergency; and (9) ensuring that BAAs are obtained when needed.[75]

One critical aspect of complying with these administrative safeguards is the requirement for a HIPAA security risk analysis and risk management review, which require a covered entity or business associate to conduct accurate and thorough assessments of potential risks and vulnerabilities to the confidentiality, integrity, and availability of EPHI held by the entity.[76] The results of this analysis should become the baseline for security processes within the entity. Failure to conduct a comprehensive risk assessment has been a common deficiency cited by OCR in recent enforcement actions. To assist covered entities and business associates with conducting their security risk assessment, in March 2014, HHS released an online security risk assessment (SRA) tool. An updated version of the SRA tool was released in October 2018 with the goal of making it easier to use and apply more broadly to risks of health information. The tool is designed for use by small to medium-sized health practices and business associates to help them identify risks and vulnerabilities to EPHI.[77]

- *Physical Safeguards.* The Security Rule requires covered entities and business associates to give attention to physically securing the media by and through which EPHI is stored, transmitted, received, and disposed. Among the requirements are facility access controls (implementing policies to limit physical access to systems that contain or can access PHI only to those who need access), workforce use and security policies and procedures to ensure proper use of workstations and how they are physically secured, and device media controls that include policies on how devices will be disposed of or reused in order to reasonably protect PHI. Other addressable requirements include having a contingency operation plan (for facility), facility security plan, facility access controls, and documentation of maintenance records.

- *Technical Safeguards.* The Security Rule requires covered entities and business associates to consider the technical aspects of the systems and processes that are used to store and transmit PHI electronically. Requirements include use of login IDs and unique passwords for each user and an

---

75. *Id.*

76. 45 C.F.R. § 164.308(a)(1)(ii).

77. This tool is available at http://www.healthit.gov/providers-professionals/security-risk-assessment.

emergency access procedure to obtain access to PHI in an emergency, audit controls that can examine activity on systems that contain PHI, policies and procedures to prevent improper alteration or destruction, verification, and technical security measures to guard against unauthorized access to PHI during transmission. Addressable controls include capabilities such as automatic logoff and encryption controls.[78]

Breach Notification Rule

The HIPAA Breach Notification Rule outlines the requirements for covered entities and business associates to follow when a breach of unsecured PHI occurs.[79] When investigating a potential breach of unsecured PHI, conducting and documenting a thorough assessment of the incident and confirming that the incident falls within the definition of a breach is critical. A breach under the HIPAA Breach Notification Rule is defined as the acquisition, access, use, or disclosure of unsecure PHI that is impermissible under the Privacy Rule and that compromises the security or privacy of the PHI.[80] A covered entity or business associate must conduct the following four-prong inquiry to determine if a breach has occurred:

- *Does the potential "breach" involve unsecured PHI?* PHI is unsecured if it is not rendered unusable, unreadable, or indecipherable to unauthorized individuals through the use of a technology or methodology specified in guidance published by HHS.[81]

- *Has there been an impermissible acquisition, access, use, or disclosure?* Did the alleged impermissible acquisition, access, use, or disclosure violate the HIPAA Privacy Rule?

- *Is the probability low that the PHI was compromised?* An impermissible acquisition, access, use, or disclosure of PHI is presumed to be a breach unless there is a low probability that the PHI has been compromised based on a risk assessment of at least the following factors: (1) the nature and extent of the PHI involved, including the types of identifiers and the likelihood of re-identification; (2) the unauthorized person who used the PHI or to whom the disclosure was made; (3) whether the PHI was actually acquired or viewed; and (4) the extent to which the risk to the PHI has been mitigated.[82]

---

78. 45 C.F.R. § 164.312.

79. 45 C.F.R. pt. 164, subpart D.

80. 45 C.F.R. § 164.402.

81. *Id.*; *see* Dept. of Health and Hum. Serv., *Guidance Specifying the Technologies and Methodologies that Render Protected Health Information Unusable, Unreadable, or Indecipherable to Unauthorized Individuals for the Purposes of the Breach Notification Requirements under the HITECH Act* (April 17, 2009), *available at* http://www.hhs.gov/ocr/privacy/hipaa/administrative/breachnotificationrule/brguidance.html.

82. 45 C.F.R. § 164.402(2).

- *Does an exception apply?* There are three exceptions to the definition of "breach." Two of these exceptions generally capture benign incidents of unintentional acquisition, access, use or disclosure of PHI by or to a workforce member or person acting under the authority of a covered entity or business associate. To meet these exceptions, the PHI cannot be further used or disclosed in a manner not permitted by the Privacy Rule. The final exception applies if the covered entity or business associate has a good-faith belief that the unauthorized person to whom the impermissible disclosure was made would not have been able to retain the information.[83]

Upon discovering a breach of unsecured PHI, covered entities must notify affected individuals, HHS and, if more than 500 residents of a state or jurisdiction are affected, the media. These notifications must be reported without unreasonable delay but no later than 60 days from discovery, unless otherwise directed by law enforcement.[84] If the breach is discovered by a business associate, the business associate must notify the covered entity of such breach without unreasonable delay but no later than 60 days following discovery, unless otherwise directed by law enforcement. To the extent possible, the business associate should provide the covered entity with the identification of each individual affected by the breach as well as any other available information required to be provided by the covered entity in its notification to affected individuals.[85] In addition to the Breach Notification Rule, business associates may be subject to contractual requirements relating to a breach as outlined in the BAA with the affected covered entity.[86]

The Breach Notification Rule includes specific direction regarding what information must be reported to individuals, HHS, and the media:

- *Notice to Individuals.* Notification to an individual should be written in plain language and include, to the extent possible, the following: (1) a brief description of what happened, including the date of the breach and the date of the discovery of the breach, if known; (2) a description of the types of unsecured PHI that were involved in the breach; (3) any steps individuals should take to protect themselves from potential harm resulting from the breach; (4) a brief description of what is being done to investigate the breach, to mitigate harm to individuals, and to protect against any further breaches; and (5) contact procedures for individuals to ask questions or learn additional information, which shall include a toll-free telephone number, an email address, website, or postal address.

- *Notice to the Media.* If a breach of unsecured PHI involves more than 500 residents of a state or jurisdiction, notification shall be provided to

---

83. 45 C.F.R. § 164.402(1).
84. 45 C.F.R. §§ 164.404, 164.406, 164.408.
85. 45 C.F.R. § 164.410.
86. 45 C.F.R. §§ 164.404, 164.406, 164.408.

prominent media outlet(s) serving the state or jurisdiction (such as a newspaper). This notice should be written in plain language and include, to the extent possible, the same information provided to individuals.

- *Notice to the Secretary of HHS.* Every breach of unsecured PHI must be reported to the Secretary. If 500 or more individuals are affected, written notification must be provided to the Secretary in the manner specified on the HHS website.[87] If fewer than 500 individuals are affected, the covered entity shall maintain a log of such breaches and shall submit notification to HHS within 60 days of the close of each calendar year. Notification must be provided in the manner specified on the HHS website.[88]

HIPAA violations, including those related to the HIPAA Breach Notification Rule, may result in significant civil money penalties, with maximum penalties for violations of the same HIPAA provision of $1.5 million per year.[89] A breach reported to HHS may lead to a full investigation by OCR or trigger an OCR audit.

HIPAA Enforcement

Since passage of the HITECH Act, new developments relating to both the compliance and enforcement environment surrounding HIPAA continue to emerge. Fines for violations of the HIPAA Privacy, Security, and HIPAA Breach Notification Rules have significantly increased due to a tiered penalty structure adopted under the Omnibus Final Rule that generally ranges from $100 per violation to $1.5 million.[90] Along with its audit activity, OCR continues to investigate complaints and reports of breaches. The single largest individual HIPAA settlement in history was announced in 2019 and involved a $16 million settlement with Anthem, Inc. In the Anthem case, it was reported that cyber-attackers gained access to Anthem, Inc.'s IT system and stole nearly 79 million people's EPHI, including the individuals' names, Social Security numbers, medical identification numbers, addresses, and dates of birth. According to its press release, OCR found that Anthem failed to implement appropriate measures for detecting hackers, failed to conduct an enterprise-wide risk analysis, had insufficient procedures to regularly review information system activity, failed to identify and respond to suspected or known security incidents, and failed to implement adequate minimum access controls to prevent cyber-attackers from accessing sensitive EPHI.[91]

---

87. *See also* http://www.hhs.gov/ocr/privacy/hipaa/administrative/breachnotificationrule/brinstruction.html.

88. *See also id.*

89. 45 C.F.R. § 160.404.

90. *Id.*

91. U.S. Dept. of Health & Human Servs., *Anthem Pays OCR $16 Million in Record HIPAA Settlement Following Largest U.S. Health Data Breach in History* (Oct. 15, 2018), *available at* https://www.hhs.gov/about/news/2018/10/15/anthem-pays-ocr-16-million-record-hipaa-settlement-following-largest-health-data-breach-history.html.

On January 31, 2021, OCR reported the following enforcement highlights and statistics:

- Since the compliance date of the Privacy Rule in April 2003, OCR has received over 254,940 HIPAA complaints and has initiated over 1,067 compliance reviews. OCR has resolved 98 percent of these cases (approximately 250,987 cases). The most common types of complaints OCR receives are impermissible uses and disclosures of PHI, lack of safeguards of PHI, lack of patient access to their PHI, lack of administrative safeguards of EPHI, and use and disclosure of more than the minimum necessary PHI.

- OCR has investigated and resolved over 28,594 cases by requiring changes in privacy practices and corrective actions by, or providing technical assistance to, HIPAA covered entities and their business associates.

- OCR has settled or imposed a civil money penalty in 95 cases resulting in a total dollar amount of $135,058,482.[92]

- The most common types of covered entities that are alleged to have committed violations are, in order of frequency: (1) general hospitals; (2) private practices and physicians; (3) outpatient facilities; (4) pharmacies; and (5) health plans.

In 2016, OCR announced its first settlement with a business associate after investigating the theft of the business associate's mobile device, resulting in the compromise of nursing home residents' PHI.[93] The business associate provided management and information technology services to six skilled nursing facilities. The total number of individuals affected by the combined breaches was 412, and the settlement included a monetary payment of $650,000 and a corrective action plan.

While most enforcement actions have involved underlying HIPAA violations that have resulted in reported breaches, in 2017, OCR announced its first HIPAA settlement for the untimely reporting of a breach of unsecured PHI. The nonprofit health system that sustained a data breach in October 2013 but took 101 days for the system to report the breach (rather than the 60 days required by the Breach

---

92. U.S. Dept. of Health & Human Servs., *Health Information Privacy Enforcement Highlights* (Feb. 29, 2020), *available at* https://www.hhs.gov/hipaa/for-professionals/compliance-enforcement/data/enforcement-highlights/index.html.

93. U.S. Dept. of Health & Human Servs., *Business Associate's Failure to Safeguard Nursing Home Residents' PHI Leads to $650,000 HIPAA Settlement* (June 29, 2016), *available at* http://www.hhs.gov/hipaa/for-professionals/compliance-enforcement/agreements/catholic-health-care-services/index.html.

Notification Rule) paid $475,000 for the violation.[94] Importantly, this settlement signals OCR's intention to enforce breach notification deadlines, and covered entities and business associates must be mindful of reporting timelines. In November 2019, OCR announced a $2.175 million settlement after a hospital failed to notify HHS of breaches involving 577 patients.[95]

A number of enforcement actions have targeted physician practices. In March 2020, a gastroenterological medical practice agreed to pay a $100,000 settlement to OCR for failing to implement HIPAA security rule requirements. OCR began investigating the practice after it filed a breach report with OCR related to a dispute with a business associate. OCR's investigation concluded that the physician who owned the practice had never conducted a risk analysis and failed to implement sufficient security measures. When announcing the settlement, OCR's director emphasized that "all health care providers, large and small, need to take their HIPAA obligations seriously . . . [and] . . . [t]he failure to implement basic HIPAA requirements, such as an accurate and thorough risk analysis and risk management plan, continues to be an unacceptable and disturbing trend within the health care industry."[96]

Another current enforcement trend important to physicians focuses on OCR's initiative to vigorously enforce rights of patients to get access to their medical records promptly, without being charged and in the readily producible format of their choice. In February of 2021, OCR announced its sixteenth settlement of an enforcement action to support individuals' right to timely access to their health records under the HIPAA Privacy Rule. This action involved a settlement of $70,000 when a health system failed to provide a patient with timely access to requested medical records.[97]

Although facts vary from one settlement to another, a number of consistent compliance issues have resulted in significant settlements with OCR over the past several

---

94. U.S. Dept. of Health & Human Servs., *First HIPAA Enforcement Action for Lack of Timely Breach Notification Settles for $475,000* (Jan. 9, 2017), *available at* http://wayback.archive-it.org/3926/20170127111957/https://www.hhs.gov/about/news/2017/01/09/first-hipaa-enforcement-action-lack-timely-breach-notification-settles-475000.html.

95. U.S. Dept. of Health & Human Servs., *OCR Secures $2.175 Million HIPAA Settlement after Hospitals Failed to Properly Notify HHS of a Breach of Unsecured Protected Health Information* (Nov. 27, 2019), *available at* https://www.hhs.gov/about/news/2019/11/27/ocr-secures-2.175-million-dollars-hipaa-settlement-breach-notification-and-privacy-rules.html.

96. U.S. Dept. of Health & Human Servs., *Health Care Provider Pays $100,000 Settlement to OCR for Failing to Implement HIPAA Security Rule Requirements* (March 3, 2020), *available at* https://www.hhs.gov/about/news/2020/03/03/health-care-provider-pays-100000-settlement-ocr-failing-implement-hipaa.html.

97. U.S. Dept. of Health & Human Servs., *OCR Settles Second Case in HIPAA Right of Access Initiative* (Dec. 12, 2019), *available at* https://www.hhs.gov/about/news/2019/12/12/ocr-settles-second-case-in-hipaa-right-of-access-initiative.html.

years. Physicians should understand these trends and adopt compliance measures to prevent making compliance mistakes that consistently result in OCR settlements. Common violations resulting in penalties have included:

- *Failure to Enter into BAAs.* In recent years, OCR has reported several settlements, ranging from $5.5 million to $31,000, involving the failure to enter into BAAs. In August 2016, OCR entered into a $5.5 million settlement with Advocate Healthcare after a three-year investigation of multiple breach reports filed with HHS. One of the bases for the settlement was failure to obtain satisfactory assurances in the form of a written business associate contract that its business associate would appropriately safeguard all EPHI in its possession.[98] In March 2016, OCR announced a $1.55 million settlement with a Minnesota healthcare system following investigation of a breach report that indicated that an unencrypted, password-protected laptop was stolen from a business associate's workforce member's locked vehicle, impacting the electronic PHI of 9,497 individuals.[99] OCR expressed concern that the system failed to enter into a BAA with a major contractor and failed to institute an organization-wide risk analysis to address the risks and vulnerabilities to its patient information. OCR concluded that a risk assessment should have covered all applications, software, databases, servers, workstations, mobile devices and electronic media, network administration and security devices, and associated business processes. In December 2018, OCR announced a $500,000 settlement with a hospitalist group that contracted with hospitals and nursing homes to provide internal medicine physicians in west central Florida. Between November 2011 and June 2012, the group engaged the services of a third-party billing company but failed to obtain a BAA. The billing agency experienced a breach that exposed 400 individuals' names, Social Security numbers, and dates of birth on a publicly available website. OCR's investigation of this breach revealed that the group failed to regularly conduct risk analysis or implement security measures or written HIPAA policies and procedures.[100] The settlement resulting from this investigation reveals that, although business associates are now directly liable for compliance with certain aspects of

98. U.S. Dept. of Health & Human Servs., *Advocate Healthcare Settles Potential HIPAA Penalties for $5.5 Million* (Aug. 4, 2016), *available at* https://www.hhs.gov/hipaa/for-professionals/compliance-enforcement/agreements/ahcn/index.html.

99. U.S. Dept. of Health & Human Servs., *$1.55 million settlement underscores the importance of executing HIPAA business associate agreements* (March 16, 2016), *available at* https://www.hhs.gov/hipaa/for-professionals/compliance-enforcement/agreements/north-memorial-health-care/index.html.

100. U.S. Dept. of Health & Human Servs., *Florida Contractor Physicians' Group Shares Protected Health Information with Unknown Vendor without a Business Associate Agreement* (Dec. 4, 2018), *available at* https://www.hhs.gov/about/news/2018/12/04/florida-contractor-physicians-group-shares-protected-health-information-unknown-vendor-without.html.

HIPAA, maintaining BAAs remains an important component of a covered entity's HIPAA compliance obligations.

- *Lack of Access Controls and Monitoring.* In order to comply with the HIPAA Privacy and Security Rules, internal access rights must be monitored and regularly updated in order to meet the Minimum Necessary Rule. Upon termination of workforce, access rights should be immediately terminated. In February 2017, OCR announced a $5.5 million settlement with Memorial Healthcare System in relation to the system's inaction, which allowed unauthorized users to access the PHI of 115,143 individuals through use of login credentials belonging to a former employee of a physician practice affiliated with the health system. According to OCR's press release, the health system had workforce access policies and procedures in place but failed to implement procedures with respect to reviewing, modifying, and/or terminating users' right of access. OCR also found that the system had failed to regularly review records of information system activity on applications that maintain PHI by workforce users and users at affiliated physician practices. When announcing the settlement, OCR emphasized that "organizations must implement audit controls and review audit logs regularly."[101] More recently, in December 2018, OCR announced a $111,400 settlement with a critical access hospital resulting from a complaint that a former employee continued to have remote access to the medical center's web-based scheduling calendar, which contained EPHI. As a result, OCR determined that 557 individuals' information was impermissibly disclosed to the former employee and coincidentally also determined that the medical center failed to enter into a BAA with its web-based scheduling calendar vendor.[102]

- *Unauthorized Disclosures on Websites and Social Media.* Entities with a presence on social media should consider adopting a social media policy along with a specific HIPAA-compliant authorization form relating to the use of individual images and videos. In February 2016, a small physical therapy practice entered into a $25,000 settlement with OCR following an investigation of a complaint that the practice posted patient testimonials, including full names and full face photographic images, to its website without obtaining valid, HIPAA-compliant authorizations. In addition to finding that the practice failed to reasonably safeguard PHI and made

---

101. U.S. Dept. of Health & Human Servs., *$5.5 Million HIPAA Settlement Shines Light on Importance of Audit Controls* (Feb. 16, 2017), *available at* https://www.hhs.gov/about/news/2017/02/16/hipaa-settlement-shines-light-on-the-importance-of-audit-controls.html.

102. U.S. Dept. of Health & Human Servs., *Colorado Hospital Failed to Terminate Former Employee's Access to Electronic Protected Health Information* (Dec. 11, 2018), *available at* https://www.hhs.gov/about/news/2018/12/11/colorado-hospital-failed-to-terminate-former-employees-access-to-electronic-protected-health-information.html.

impermissible disclosures on its website, OCR found that the practice failed to implement policies and procedures with respect to PHI that were designed to comply with HIPAA's requirements regarding authorization.[103] In October 2019, a dental practice paid $10,000 to settle social media disclosures of PHI in response to a patient's negative Yelp review.[104]

- *Media Exposure.* Some more recent settlements have involved the inappropriate exposure of PHI by covered entities in various media outlets. In November 2018, OCR announced a $125,000 settlement with an allergy practice composed of just three physicians. OCR reported that the practice contacted a local television station to speak about a dispute that had occurred between a patient and a doctor in the practice. When the reporter subsequently contacted the doctor involved, the doctor impermissibly disclosed the patient's PHI to the reporter. OCR found that the doctor's discussion demonstrated a reckless disregard for the patient's privacy rights. Further, OCR found that the practice failed to take disciplinary actions against the doctor or take any corrective action.[105] Also in 2018, OCR announced settlements with three different hospitals in the Boston, Massachusetts, area totaling $999,000 for allowing film crews on premises for an ABC television network documentary series without first obtaining patients' consent.[106] In 2017, OCR announced a $2.4 million Resolution Agreement in connection with a hospital press release that impermissibly identified a patient by name.[107]

103. U.S. Dept. of Health & Human Servs., *Physical therapy provider settles violations that it impermissibly disclosed patient information* (Feb. 16, 2016), *available at* http://www.hhs.gov/hipaa/for-professionals/compliance-enforcement/agreements/complete-pt/index.html.

104. U.S. Dept. of Health & Human Servs., *Dental Practice Pays $10,000 to Settle Social Media Disclosures of Patients' Protected Health Information* (Oct. 2, 2019), *available at* https://www.hhs.gov/about/news/2019/10/02/dental-practice-pays-10000-settle-social-media-disclosures-of-patients-phi.html.

105. U.S. Dept. of Health & Human Servs., *Allergy Practice Pays $125,000 to Settle Doctor's Disclosure of Patient Information to a Reporter* (Nov. 26, 2018), *available at* https://www.hhs.gov/about/news/2018/11/26/allergy-practice-pays-125000-to-settle-doctors-disclosure-of-patient-information-to-a-reporter.html.

106. .S. Dept. of Health & Human Servs., *Unauthorized Disclosure of Patients' Protected Health Information During ABC Television Filming Results in Multiple HIPAA Settlements Totaling $999,000* (Sept. 20, 2018), *available at* https://www.hhs.gov/about/news/2018/09/20/unauthorized-disclosure-patients-protected-health-information-during-abc-filming.html.

107. U.S. Dept. of Health & Human Servs., *Texas Health System Settles Potential HIPAA Disclosure Violations* (May 10, 2017), *available at* https://www.hhs.gov/about/news/2017/05/10/texas-health-system-settles-potential-hipaa-disclosure-violations.html.

In May 2020, OCR issued guidance on covered healthcare providers' restrictions on media access to PHI about individuals in their facilities.[108] The guidance explains that covered health care providers are still required to obtain a valid HIPAA authorization from each patient whose PHI will be accessible to the media **before** the media is given access to that PHI. Masking or obscuring patients' faces or identifying information before broadcasting a recording of a patient is not sufficient, and a HIPAA authorization is still required. Additionally, the guidance provides reasonable safeguards that should be used to protect the privacy of patients whenever the media is granted access to facilities.

- *Loss or Theft of Unencrypted Laptops and Other Devices.* Covered entities and business associates that permit workforce members to use and travel with laptops containing PHI should address risks associated with such laptop use in policies and procedures, ongoing security risk assessments, and workforce training. Some of OCR's largest settlements have been from lost or stolen portable devices. As recently as July 2020, OCR entered into a $1,040,000 settlement with a nonprofit health system related to the theft of an unencrypted laptop.[109] OCR entered a $3 million settlement with a health system in November 2019 after the system reported breaches resulting from the loss of an unencrypted flash drive and theft of an unencrypted laptop.[110] In December 2019, OCR announced that an ambulance company paid $65,000 to settle allegations of longstanding HIPAA noncompliance, brought to light upon reporting a breach concerning loss of an unencrypted laptop containing the PHI of 500 individuals.[111] Although encryption of EPHI is an "addressable" standard under the HIPAA Security Rule, OCR has consistently taken the position that "[c]overed entities and business associates must understand that mobile device security is their obligation, . . . [and OCR's] message to these organizations is simple: encryption is your best defense against these

---

108. U.S. Dept. of Health & Human Servs., Guidance on Covered Health Care Providers and Restrictions on Media Access to Protected Health Information about Individuals in Their Facilities (May 5, 2020), *available at* https://www.hhs.gov/sites/default/files/guidance-on-media-and-file-crews-access-to-phi.pdf.

109. U.S. Dept. of Health & Human Servs., *Lifespan Pays $1,040,000 to OCR to Settle Unencrypted Stolen Laptop Breach* (July 27, 2020), *available at* https://www.hhs.gov/about/news/2020/07/27/lifespan-pays-1040000-ocr-settle-unencrypted-stolen-laptop-breach.html.

110. U.S. Dept. of Health & Human Servs., *Failure to Encrypt Mobile Devices Leads to $3 Million HIPAA Settlement* (Nov. 5, 2019), *available at* https://www.hhs.gov/about/news/2019/11/05/failure-to-encrypt-mobile-devices-leads-to-3-million-dollar-hipaa-settlement.html.

111. U.S. Dept. of Health & Human Servs., *Ambulance Company Pays $65,000 to Settle Allegations of Longstanding HIPAA Noncompliance* (Dec. 30, 2019), *available at* https://www.hhs.gov/about/news/2019/12/30/ambulance-company-pays-65000-settle-allegations-longstanding-hipaa-noncompliance.html.

incidents."[112] Covered entities and business associates should maintain an inventory of any mobile devices that contain PHI and all such mobile devices should be encrypted.

- *Losing PHI.* Over the years, OCR has fined covered entities for losing records in public, having records stolen, and failing to ensure that records are properly returned after an employee's termination. In October 2019, OCR imposed a $2.15 million civil money penalty against Jackson Health System, a nonprofit academic medical system, following submission of a breach report stating that its Health Information Management Department had lost paper records containing patients' PHI in January 2013.[113]

- *Improper Disposal of PHI.* OCR has also sought enforcement against entities that fail to properly discard PHI.[114] Covered entities and business associates should have document destruction policies and procedures requiring secure disposal of PHI and should train workforce on its proper disposal.[115] With regard to EPHI, entities should confirm that practices are in place for secure disposal or recycling of equipment—including servers, laptops, and photocopiers—containing PHI.

- *Use of Insecure Applications and Software.* OCR has expressed concern and pursued enforcement actions against covered entities for using unsecured, internet-based document storage and share sites;[116] failing to update IT resources with available patches and running outdated, unsupported software;[117] disabling firewalls;[118] and inadvertently

---

112. U.S. Dept. of Health &Human Servs., *Stolen laptops lead to important HIPAA settlements* (April 22, 2014), *available at* https://www.hhs.gov/hipaa/for-professionals/compliance-enforcement/examples/concentra-health-services/index.html.

113. U.S. Dept. of Health & Human Servs., *OCR Imposes a $2.15 Million Civil Money Penalty against Jackson Health System for HIPAA Violations* (Oct. 23, 2019), *available at* https://www.hhs.gov/about/news/2019/10/23/ocr-imposes-a-2.15-million-civil-money-penalty-against-jhs-for-hipaa-violations.html.

114. U.S. Dept. of Health & Human Servs., *HIPAA Settlement Highlights the Continuing Importance of Secure Disposal of Paper Medical Records* (April 30, 2015), *available at* http://www.hhs.gov/hipaa/for-professionals/compliance-enforcement/examples/cornell/index.html.

115. U.S. Dept. of Health & Human Servs., *$800,000 HIPAA Settlement in Medical Records Dumping Case* (June 23, 2014), *available at* http://www.hhs.gov/hipaa/for-professionals/compliance-enforcement/examples/parkview-health-system/index.html.

116. U.S. Dept. of Health & Human Servs., *HIPAA Settlement Highlights Importance of Safeguards When Using Internet Applications* (July 10, 2015), *available at* http://www.hhs.gov/hipaa/for-professionals/compliance-enforcement/examples/semc/index.html.

117. U.S. Dept. of Health & Human Servs., *HIPAA Settlement Underscores the Vulnerability of Unpatched and Unsupported Software* (Dec. 2, 2014), *available at* http://www.hhs.gov/hipaa/for-professionals/compliance-enforcement/agreements/acmhs/index.html.

118. U.S. Dept. of Health & Human Servs., *Data breach results in $4.8 million HIPAA settlements* (May 7, 2014), *available at* https://www.hhs.gov/hipaa/for-professionals/compliance-enforcement/examples/new-york-and-presbyterian-hospital/index.html; *Idaho State*

permitting public online access to PHI or not having proper controls securing online access to PHI.[119] In December 2018, a nonprofit health system agreed to pay $3 million to OCR as a result of two breach reports of unsecured EPHI affecting more than 62,500 individuals. The breaches, exposed over the internet, included patient names, addresses, dates of birth, Social Security numbers, diagnoses, conditions, lab results, and other treatment information.[120]

- *Cybersecurity.* Cybersecurity remains a top security concern for HHS due to its high risk for large-scale breaches. In September 2020, a health insurer agreed to pay $6,850,000 when cyber-attackers gained access to the insurer's IT system using a phishing e-mail that installed undetected malware for nearly nine months. The undetected cyberattack resulted in the disclosure of more than 10.4 million individuals' PHI.[121] In April 2017, OCR entered into a $400,000 settlement with a healthcare provider following an investigation of a breach caused by a phishing incident from which a hacker accessed employee email accounts and obtained the PHI of 3,200 individuals.[122] OCR has consistently communicated that covered entities and business associates must carefully consider the security of IT resources, ensure that PHI available through online access is secured through access controls, and that an enterprise-wide security risk assessment is conducted routinely.

University Settles HIPAA Security Case for $400,000 (May 21, 2013), *available at* http://www.hhs.gov/hipaa/for-professionals/compliance-enforcement/agreements/idaho-state-university/isu-agreement/index.html.

119. *U.S. Dept. of Health & Human Servs., County Government Settles Potential HIPAA Violations* (March 7, 2014), *available at* http://www.hhs.gov/hipaa/for-professionals/compliance-enforcement/examples/skagit-county/index.html; *WellPoint pays HHS $1.7 million for leaving information accessible over Internet* (July 11, 2013), *available at* http://www.hhs.gov/hipaa/for-professionals/compliance-enforcement/examples/wellpoint/index.html; *HHS settles case with Phoenix Cardiac Surgery for lack of HIPAA safeguards* (April 7, 2012), *available at* https://www.hhs.gov/hipaa/for-professionals/compliance-enforcement/examples/phoenix-cardiac-surgery/index.html.

120. U.S. Dept. of Health & Human Servs., *OCR Concludes All-Time Record Year for HIPAA Enforcement with $3 Million Cottage Health Settlement* (Feb. 7, 2019), *available at* https://www.hhs.gov/about/news/2019/02/07/ocr-concludes-all-time-record-year-for-hipaa-enforcement-with-3-million-cottage-health-settlement.html.

121. U.S. Dept. of Health & Human Servs., *Health Insurer Pays $6.85 Million to Settle Data Breach Affecting Over 10.4 Million People, available at* https://www.hhs.gov/about/news/2020/09/25/health-insurer-pays-6-85-million-settle-data-breach-affecting-over-10-4-million-people.html.

122. U.S. Dept. of Health & Human Servs., *Overlooking Risks Leads to Breach, $400,000 Settlement* (April 12, 2017), *available at* https://www.hhs.gov/about/news/2017/04/12/overlooking-risks-leads-to-breach-settlement.html.

HHS and OCR have issued a significant amount of guidance on cybersecurity risks and HIPAA compliance, including a Fact Sheet on Ransomware[123] and HIPAA and quarterly cyber-security newsletters, which aim to help HIPAA covered entities and business associates remain in compliance with the HIPAA Security Rule by identifying emerging or prevalent issues, and highlighting best practices to safeguard PHI. These newsletters have addressed hot topics in cybersecurity, such as cyber extortion, phishing, cloud computing and file sharing, and advanced persistent threats. These newsletters are available on the HHS website.

In 2017, OCR released a simple Quick Response Cyber Attack Checklist and Infographic, which outlines the steps for a HIPAA covered entity or business associate to take in response to a cyber-related security incident.[124] In 2016, OCR released guidance to help covered entities and business associates better understand and respond to the threat of ransomware.[125] On December 28, 2018, HHS released the *Health Industry Cybersecurity Practices (HICP): Managing Threats and Protecting Patients* publication. The four-volume publication aims to provide voluntary cybersecurity practices to healthcare organizations of all types and sizes, ranging from local clinics to large hospital systems. The publication resulted from an industry-led effort to develop practical cybersecurity guidelines to cost-effectively reduce cybersecurity risks for the healthcare industry. The main document of the publication explores the five most relevant and current threats to the industry.[126]

Based on the number of settlement agreements in this area and OCR expectations that are consistently communicated regarding cybersecurity, entities must also adopt—and follow—HIPAA security policies and procedures and risk management policies that effectively identify and mitigate risks related to EPHI.

- *Failure to Perform Complete and Accurate Security Risk Assessments.* The HIPAA Security Rule requires all covered entities and business associates to conduct accurate and thorough risk assessments to help prevent, detect, contain, and correct security violations.[127] An overarching theme seen in

---

123. U.S. Dept. of Health & Hum. Servs., *Ransomware Guidance, available at* https://www.hhs.gov/sites/default/files/RansomwareFactSheet.pdf?language=es.

124. U.S. Department of Health & Human Servs., Cyber Security Guidance Material, *available at* https://www.hhs.gov/hipaa/for-professionals/security/guidance/cybersecurity/index.html.

125. *Id.*

126. U.S. Dept. of Health & Human Servs., *HHS, in Partnership with Industry, Releases Voluntary Cybersecurity Practices for Health Industry* (Dec. 28, 2018), *available at* https://www.hhs.gov/about/news/2018/12/28/hhs-in-partnership-with-industry-releases-voluntary-cybersecurity-practices-for-the-health-industry.html.

127. 45 C.F.R. § 164.308.

most OCR enforcement actions is the failure to conduct ongoing and routine risk assessments or conducting incomplete, inadequate, or infrequent risk assessments that fail to address or identify common vulnerabilities such as laptop security, maintenance of proper IT resources, and facility and access controls.[128] In 2017, OCR's investigation of Children's Medical Center of Dallas, following reports of stolen portable devices and laptops containing unprotected PHI, determined that in 2007 and 2008, Children's had conducted HIPAA security risk assessments that identified vulnerabilities relating to laptop encryption. OCR concluded that despite Children's awareness of the risks involved with maintaining unencrypted PHI on mobile devices, it continued to allow its workforce to utilize unencrypted devices for several years. OCR assessed a $3.2 million civil money penalty against Children's for impermissible disclosures of unsecured PHI and prolonged noncompliance with the HIPAA Security Rule.[129] Covered entities and business associates should confirm that they have a current and thorough security risk assessment on file and that any potential vulnerabilities noted in the risk assessment have been addressed with a documented response. If applicable, entities should also confirm that they have documented justification explaining why any safeguards regarded as addressable implementation standards under the Security Rule have not been adopted. The failure to perform a risk assessment is possibly the most common reason for the assessment of penalties.

HIPAA enforcement actions and penalties routinely involve informal settlements and corrective action plans with OCR. However, there have been some cases involving civil monetary penalties (CMPs) assessed against the covered entity. In 2017, OCR assessed CMPs against Children's Medical Center of Dallas (discussed above) to resolve multiple HIPAA violations spanning a number of years. In 2019, OCR imposed a $2.15 million CMP against Jackson Health System (discussed above) to resolve multiple HIPAA violations including the failures to conduct enterprise-wide risk analyses, to manage identified risks to a reasonable and appropriate level, to regularly review information system activity records, and to restrict authorization of its workforce members' access to patient EPHI to the minimum necessary to accomplish their job duties.

In addition to OCR enforcement efforts, the HITECH Act also permits a state attorney general to pursue an action against an entity that is subject to HIPAA when the attorney general "has reason to believe that an interest

---

128. *See* U.S. Dept. of Health & Human Servs., *Advocate Healthcare Settles Potential HIPAA Penalties for $5.5 Million* (Aug. 4, 2016), *available at* https://www.hhs.gov/hipaa/for-professionals/compliance-enforcement/agreements/ahcn/index.html.

129. U.S. Dept. of Health & Human Servs., *Lack of Timely Action Risks Security and Costs Money* (Feb. 1, 2017), *available at* https://www.hhs.gov/about/news/2017/02/01/lack-timely-action-risks-security-and-costs-money.html.

of one or more of the residents of [a] state has been or is threatened or adversely affected by any person who violates a [privacy or security provision under HIPAA].["][130] Such lawsuits can implicate both state and federal law violations. Massachusetts has been the most prolific state with respect to HIPAA enforcement actions, settling at least five cases with covered entities for breaches of federal and state data privacy requirements in recent years.[131] There have also been HIPAA enforcement actions by attorneys general in California,[132]Connecticut,[133] Vermont,[134] Minnesota,[135] New Jersey,[136] and New York.[137]

New Legal Developments

While many OCR investigations end in settlement, 2021 began with a significant ruling from the U.S. Court of Appeals for the Fifth Circuit vacating a penalty imposed by OCR on the University of Texas M.D. Anderson Cancer Center (MD Anderson).[138] The case involved MD Anderson's appeal of a $4,348,000 CMP for alleged HIPAA violations arising from three separate but similar incidents involving the loss of an electronic device containing unencrypted EPHI. In total, information involved in the loss related to approximately 34,000 individuals, and while M.D. Anderson had provided its employees with access to encryption technology, the technology had not been employed in these three instances. An administrative law judge (ALJ) upheld the penalties in 2018, as did the HHS Departmental Appeals Board in 2019. After M.D. Anderson filed its ALJ appeal, OCR on its own initiative reduced the penalty to $450,000.

---

130. 42 U.S.C. § 1320d-5(d).

131. Massachusetts v. South Shore Hosp., No. 12-01925 (Mass. Super. Ct., May 24, 2012); Massachusetts v. Goldthwait Associates, No. 12-4568H (Mass. Super. Ct., Jan. 7, 2013); Massachusetts v. Women & Infants Hosp., No. 13-2332G (Mass. Super. Ct., July 22, 2014); Massachusetts v. Beth Israel Deaconess Med. Ctr., No. 14-3627G (Mass. Super. Ct., Nov. 20, 2014); Massachusetts v. Boston Children's Hosp. Corp., No. 14-3955 (Mass. Super. Ct., Dec. 19, 2014).

132. California v. Anthem Inc., No. RG20075118 (Cal. Super. Ct., Sept. 30, 2020).

133. Connecticut v. Health Net of the Northeast, Inc. (No. 3:10-CV57PCD), D. Conn., July 6, 2010.

134. Vermont v. Health Net, Inc. (No. 2:11-cv-00016-wks), D. Vt., Jan. 14, 2011.

135. Minnesota v. Accretive Health, Inc. (No. 12-145), D. Minn., Jan. 19, 2012.

136. N.J. Office of the Atty. Gen., *Virtua Medical Group Agrees to Pay Nearly $418,000, Tighten Data Security to Settle Allegations of Privacy Lapses Concerning Medical Treatment Files of Patients* (Apr. 4, 2018), *available at* https://nj/gov/oag/newsreleases18/pr20180404b.html.

137. N.Y. State Office of the Atty. Gen., U.R.M.C. Letter Fully Executed (Nov. 20, 2015), *available at* http://www.ag.ny.gov/pdfs/URMC_Letter_Agreement_Fully_Executed_11_30_2015.pdf.

138. Univ. of Texas M.D. Anderson Cancer Ctr. v. United States Dep't of Health & Hum. Servs., 985 F.3d 472 (5th Cir. 2021).

In its ruling on January 14, 2021, the Fifth Circuit determined that even the reduced penalty was improper under the federal Administrative Procedures Act and vacated the ALJ's ruling. The Court made four key findings:

- **M.D. Anderson appropriately implemented a *mechanism* to encrypt electronic protected health information**. While OCR argued that M.D. Anderson's failure to encrypt the lost devices violated the HIPAA Security Rule, the Court disagreed and found that M.D. Anderson complied with the Security Rule by implementing "a mechanism to encrypt electronic protected health information" and providing its employees with access to encryption technology. Notably, the Court pointed out that the Security Rule does not command that the supplied mechanism for encryption be perfectly applied in every situation and that a single failure to encrypt a device in a particular instance, if the technology to encrypt is available, does not amount to a violation of the rule.

- **There was no evidence that protected health information was impermissibly "disclosed."** The Court found that there was no evidence that any unauthorized person had received or viewed protected health information on the lost devices. In contrast, OCR has long taken the position that loss of device with unsecured protected health information is deemed an improper disclosure, regardless of whether there is evidence that an unauthorized person actually accessed the information. The Court disagreed and held that the loss alone cannot be equated with an affirmative disclosure of data. The Court ruled that OCR bears the burden of proving that some unauthorized person received the information. Because OCR could not prove this, the Court concluded that M.D. Anderson did not make an unauthorized disclosure of unsecured protected health information.

- **OCR's penalty was arbitrary and capricious**. The Court found M.D. Anderson's penalty to be arbitrary and capricious compared to the wide variation in penalties and settlements imposed by OCR in similar cases. The ALJ who heard M.D. Anderson's initial appeal ruled that neither he nor OCR were obligated to impose a penalty based on prior enforcement actions and that each case could stand alone without any comparison to prior decisions. The Court emphatically rejected that approach, noting that "it is a bedrock principle of administrative law that an agency must treat like cases alike." The Court noted that in another case, a hospital has lost an encrypted laptop that contained protected information of 33,000 patients and that OCR had not imposed any penalty. The Court stated that such variation in treatment of similar cases is prohibited by the Administrative Procedures Act.

- **OCR's penalties were in excess of amounts authorized by HIPAA.** OCR imposed millions in penalties against M.D. Anderson despite having determined that the alleged violations were due to "reasonable cause" and not willful neglect. The Court read the HITECH Act as capping total annual penalties for a violation of any one requirement or prohibition based on reasonable cause at $100,000. The Court further rendered the penalty ruling arbitrary and capricious and a violation of the Administrative Procedure Act because the lost devices did not cause physical, financial, or reputational harm to any person and did not hinder any person's ability to obtain healthcare.

It remains to be seen whether the Fifth Circuit's reasoning will be adopted by other circuit courts when evaluating HIPAA violations. Nevertheless, this a new development that may benefit covered entities and business associates facing investigations and potential sanctions for alleged HIPAA violations.

Private Enforcement Actions

Issues surrounding compliance with the Privacy and Security Rules may also become a component of third-party lawsuits. Although there is not a private cause of action under HIPAA, lack of compliance with such regulatory safeguards may give rise to state law claims of negligence relating to the security procedures of companies that sustain a breach, defamation in a case involving disclosure of sensitive health information, or breach of a provider's fiduciary duty for failure to protect a patient's health information.[139]

State Laws and HIPAA Preemption

The HIPAA Privacy Rule provides that if a state law imposes privacy requirements that are in conflict with HIPAA, then HIPAA preempts the state law; however, if the state law provides more protection for the privacy of health information, the state law must be followed.[140] Consequently, state laws could potentially impose additional and more stringent requirements on covered entities regarding the protection of health information.

---

139. *See* Amborgy v. Express Scripts, Inc. et al., Civ. Doc. #4:09-VC-00705-FRB, filed in May 2009 in the U.S. District Court, Eastern District of Missouri. This lawsuit was commenced as a class action against an entity that provided pharmacy services and drug formulary management services to member groups, including managed care organizations, insurance carriers, and employer and union-sponsored health plans. It received an extortion demand by persons who had gained access to its customers' confidential Personal Information. The plaintiffs based their complaint on, among other things, the company's alleged failure to comply with HIPAA in a purported breach of assurances of compliance in its Privacy Notice.

140. 45 C.F.R. § 160.202–160.203.

Businesses that handle an individual's health information may be subject to privacy protections under state law as well as HIPAA. As held by the 11th Circuit, HIPAA preempts contrary state laws that impede the purpose and objective of HIPAA in keeping an individual's PHI strictly confidential.[141] However, state laws that create additional or more stringent privacy protections for individuals are not preempted. Thus, state laws that protect health information, including laws governing the disclosure of the results of HIV tests, genetic tests, or other sensitive information, and/or require additional notification in the event of a breach, also must be considered when assessing requirements relating to health information and responding to potential breach incidents. Physicians may also have state licensing laws that must be followed regarding the confidentiality of medical records and providing patients with access to records (including specific requirements to what charges can be applied for copies of records).

---

141. *Opis Mgmt. Resources v. Sec'y Fla. Agency for Healthcare Admin.*, Doc. No. 4:11-cv-00400-RS-CAS, Apr. 9, 2013 (in which the Florida Agency for Healthcare Administration issued citations to nursing facilities for violating Florida law when they refused to release a deceased's medical records to a spouse and certain others on the grounds that they were not "personal representatives" under the relevant provisions of HIPAA).

Chapter 6

ACCOUNTABLE CARE ORGANIZATIONS—OVERVIEW[1]

UPDATED BY: *KENYA S. WOODRUFF*

I.   What Are ACOs?

A.   History and Background

Drs. Elliott Fisher and Glenn Hackbarth first coined the term "accountable care organization" (ACO) at a 2006 Medicare Payment Advisory Committee meeting.[2] Subsequent input, such as Drs. Stephen Shortell and Lawrence Casalino's 2007 paper, "Accountable Care Systems for Comprehensive Health,"[3] and the passage of the Patient Protection and Affordable Care Act of 2010 (ACA),[4] has refined this concept. Generally speaking, the ACA defines an ACO to be an organization of physicians and other healthcare providers held accountable for the overall quality and cost of care delivered to a defined population of traditional fee-for-service (FFS) Medicare beneficiaries who are assigned by the Centers for Medicare and Medicaid Services (CMS) to an ACO.[5] The theory behind the ACO concept is that effective delivery of and coordination of care (and thus cost savings) are difficult to achieve without integration among the providers that deliver patient care. Therefore, ACOs are incentivized, in the form of "shared savings," to manage care in a manner that results in cost savings.[6] The ACO also holds providers accountable for clinical outcomes by

---

1. The original edition of the chapter was written by Sidney Welch; the 2018 edition was updated by Jennifer Rangel; the 2019, 2020 and 2021 editions were updated by Kenya Woodruff of Katten Muchin Rosenman, with special thanks to Ashley Francois and Bernard Miller of Katten Muchin Rosenman for their contributions.

2. Jordon T. Cohen, *A Guide to Accountable Care Organizations, and Their Role in the Senate's Health Reform Bill,* (HEALTH REFORM WATCH, March 11, 2010), *available at* https://pdfs.semanticscholar.org/e9b6/7816493d28182b3c84cf342111589f681d78.pdf.

3. Stephen M. Shortell & Lawrence P. Casalino, *Accountable Care Systems for Comprehensive Health Care Reform* (March 2007), *available at* https://www.rwjf.org/en/library/research/2007/03/accountable-care-systems-for-comprehensive-healthcare-reform.html.

4. Patient Protection and Affordable Care Act, Pub. L. No. 111-148, 124 Stat. 119 (2010) (ACA).

5. ACA at 3022.

6. *Supra* note 3.

required clinical outcomes reporting and other performance measures.[7] While extremely similar to the players in the alphabet soup of managed care players in the 1990s—the independent physician associations (IPAs), the physician-hospital organizations (PHOs), and the healthcare maintenance organizations—ACOs differ significantly in four main areas: (1) the accountability rests with the providers, rather than the health insurers; (2) no health plan intermediary is required to contract with the provider organization; (3) ACOs have great flexibility in their provider composition; and (4) ACOs allow for payment under a FFS arrangement.

The government's support, if not directive, of clinical integration is fairly evident and includes, but is certainly not limited to, ACOs. For example, in 2013 alone, Medicare's Physician Quality Reporting System incentives totaled approximately $215 million for quality reporting.[8] A more recent and dramatic example of the government's support is the enactment of the Medicare Access and CHIP Reauthorization Act of 2015 (MACRA), which represented the most significant change in Medicare physician payment policy in over 25 years. (MACRA is more fully discussed under Section V. Viability). A recent example of this direction has been the Independence at Home Demonstration Project, where CMS tracks a beneficiary's care experience provided by selected participants including primary care practices providing home-based primary care to targeted, chronically ill beneficiaries for a period of three years.[9] Practices that succeed in meeting certain quality measures, while generating Medicare savings, are given the opportunity to share in such savings after meeting a minimum savings rate.[10]

Recent years have been hallmarked by local and national hospital acquisition and employment of physicians. These trends are positioning hospitals, and potentially their affiliated physicians, to take advantage of government directives and incentives encouraging clinical integration and associated quality and cost accountability.

7. *See generally See generally* Fisher, Elliott et al., *Fostering Accountable Health Care: Moving Forward in Medicare,* 28 Health Affairs at 219–231 (2009), *available at* www.dartmouth.edu/~jskinner/documents/FisherESFostering.pdf.

8. CMS Fact Sheet, Participation continues to rise in Medicare Physician Quality Reporting System and Electronic Prescribing Incentive Program (April 23, 2015), *available at* https://www.cms.gov/newsroom/fact-sheets/participation-continues-rise-medicare-physician-quality-reporting-system-and-electronic-prescribing.

9. CMS Fact Sheet, Independence at Home Demonstration Fact Sheet (August 2016), *available at* https://innovation.cms.gov/initiatives/independence-at-home/.

10. *Id.*

B. The Affordable Care Act

The enactment of the ACA on March 23, 2010, codified the ACO concept into federal legislation.[11] Under Section 3022 of the ACA, Congress charged the Secretary of Health and Human Services (HHS) to establish a Shared Savings Program for Medicare no later than January 1, 2012.[12] Congress envisioned a program that would encourage providers of services and suppliers to create a new type of health entity, one where participants would agree to be held accountable for the quality and experience of care for assigned Medicare beneficiaries while also reducing the growth rate of healthcare spending for the assigned population.[13] In addition, Section 3021(a) created the Center for Medicare & Medicaid Innovation (CMMI), the entity responsible for devising many of the ACO types currently in existence.[14] Notably, while the new program established a shared savings model for providers billing Medicare, Section 3022 also authorized the HHS Secretary to give preference to ACOs who participate in similar arrangements with third-party payers. In recent years, third-party payers have created shared savings programs for ACOs interested in extending their reach into the commercial managed care market. As of 2018, 1477 health systems or physician groups have commercial, Medicare, Medicaid ACO contracts.[15]

On November 2, 2011, CMS published its final rule implementing Section 3022 of the ACA.[16] The final rule incorporated several important revisions to the proposed rule to accommodate industry concerns about the pace of implementation.[17] Key changes in the final rule from the proposed rule included: the ability of the ACO to select a one-sided (shared savings only) model for a full three years; a change in the governance participation by ACO participants from proportionate to meaningful; a significant reduction in the number of quality measures that must be reported, i.e., from 65 to 33; change from the requirement that 50 percent of primary care physicians must be electronic health records (EHR) users to a simple requirement of reporting the percent that qualify for an EHR incentive program payment; and elimination of a 25 percent withhold and retrospective patient assignment.[18]

---

11. Patient Protection and Affordable Care Act, 42 U.S.C. § 18001 et seq. (2010).
12. 42 U.S.C.A. § 1395jj (2010).
13. CMS, ICN 907404, Summary of the June 2015 Final Rule Provisions for Accountable Care Organizations (ACOs) under the Medicare Shared Savings Program (2016).
14. 42 U.S.C.A. § 1315a (2010).
15. Emily Rappleye, *Medicare is driving ACO growth: 4 report findings?* BECKER'S HOSPITAL REVIEW, *available at* https://www.beckershospitalreview.com/accountable-care-organizations/medicare-is-driving-aco-growth-4-report-findings.html.
16. 76 Fed. Reg. 67802 (Nov. 2, 2011); *see also* 42 C.F.R. Part 425.
17. Frank Pasquale, *Accountable Care Organizations in the Affordable Care Act*, 42 SETON HALL L. REV. 1371, 1372 (2012).
18. *Id.*

With the end of the first three-year agreement period looming, CMS released a proposed rule recommending changes to the Medicare Shared Savings Program (MSSP) on December 8, 2014.[19] In issuing this proposed rule, CMS intended to codify existing guidance, reduce administrative burden, and improve program function and transparency.[20] The proposed rule contained several major changes to the existing regulatory framework, including: clarifying existing and establishing new definitions, including the definition of an ACO participant; adding a process for ACOs to renew participation agreements for additional agreement periods; updating CPT codes that would be considered primary care services; including claims for primary care services furnished by certain mid-level practitioners; changing governance and leadership requirements; and adding or changing policies to encourage greater participation by offering ACOs the ability to continue participation under a one-sided agreement after the first three-year agreement's expiration, reducing risk under Track 2, and adopting an alternative risk-based model referred to as Track 3.[21]

On June 9, 2015, CMS released a final rule[22] substantively revising parts of the MSSP (the June 2015 Final Rule). The revisions, intended to ensure continued robust participation in the MSSP, permitted Track 1 ACOs (one-sided ACOs that shared savings but not losses generated by ACO participants) to continue in Track 1 for an additional agreement period beyond the first three-year agreement period instead of mandating their transition to Track 2 (a two-sided ACO model in which participants share savings and losses generated).[23] The June 2015 Final Rule also created a new two-sided risk sharing ACO model under the MSSP, called Track 3 ACOs, in which participants share savings and losses generated and revised Track 2 ACOs to enable participants to select from many minimum savings rates and loss rates according to their risk tolerance.[24] These and other changes in the June 2015 Final Rule are intended to incentivize existing Track 1 ACOs to transition away from one-sided models to the two-sided models (Track 2 and Track 3 ACOs).[25] To further incentivize such transition, the June 2015 Final Rule also waived the rule requiring a beneficiary to have a three-day in-patient hospital stay to become eligible for skilled nursing

---

19. 79 Fed. Reg. 72759 (Dec. 8, 2014).

20. *Id.*

21. *Id.*

22. 80 Fed. Reg. 32692 (June 9, 2015).

23. *Id.*

24. *See* CMS finalizes rules for Medicare Shared Savings Program, *available at* https://www.cms.gov/newsroom/press-releases/cms-finalizes-rules-medicare-shared-savings-program.

25. *See* 80 Fed. Reg. at 32692 *stating* CMS was adding or changing policies to encourage greater ACO participation in risk-based models.

facility (SNF) coverage, commonly referred to as the SNF 3-day rule, for participants in Track 3 ACOs.[26] The June 2015 Final Rule revisions further streamline data sharing between CMS and ACOs to allow ACOs to easily and securely access patient information.[27] Furthermore, the rule refined policies for setting benchmarks to better incentivize ACOs to improve patient care and generate cost savings.[28] CMS announced its intent to propose further improvements later in 2015.[29]

On February 3, 2016, CMS followed through with its commitment to revise the MSSP regulations by releasing a new proposed rule.[30] CMS published the final rule on June 10, 2016, and the new regulation took effect on August 9, 2016, (referred to hereafter as the June 2016 Final Rule).[31] Prior to these revisions, critics had lamented the benchmarking system's failure to effectively reward providers who possessed high marks for quality prior to entering into an MSSP ACO and punished those who made drastic improvements in the first year of the three-year agreement.[32] In amending the regulations, CMS sought to address these concerns by modifying the program's benchmarking methodology and increasing flexibility for Track 1 ACOs transitioning into performance-based risk arrangements.[33] Instead of using national trend factors to determine an ACO's rebased historical benchmark, after the June 2016 Final Rule, CMS relies on regional trends when an ACO enters a second or subsequent agreement period.[34] The June 2016 Final Rule also removed the requirement that the adjustment only accounts for savings generated under the ACO's prior agreements and allows for CMS to consider the difference between regional FFS spending and the ACO's historical expenditures.[35] According to CMS, these revisions make the ACO's cost target less dependent on the ACO's past performance and more reflective of the regional market experience.[36] Additionally, under the June 2016 Final

---

26. *Id.* Further, the December 2018 Final Rule expanded the eligibility for the SNF 3-day rule waiver to include ACOs participating in a two-sided model under preliminary prospective assignment with retrospective reconciliation. *See* 83 Fed. Reg. at 67973.

27. *Id.*

28. *Id.*

29. *Supra* note 25.

30. 81 Fed. Reg. 5824 (Feb. 3, 2016).

31. 81 Fed. Reg. 37950 (June 10, 2016).

32. Jennifer Bresnick, *CMS to Update to MSSP Accountable Care Organization Benchmarks*, HEALTH IT ANALYTICS (Jan. 29, 2016), *available at* http://healthitanalytics.com/news/cms-to-update-to-mssp-accountable-care-organization-benchmarks.

33. 81 Fed. Reg. 37950, 37951 (June 10, 2016).

34. *Id.*

35. *Id.*

36. *Id.*

Rule, if CMS approved a Track 1 ACO's renewal request for a second agreement period under a two-sided model, the Track 1 ACO could have requested that its initial participation agreement under Track 1 be extended for an additional year.[37] This allowed the Track 1 ACO to delay the transition to a two-sided model for one year instead of three years had the ACO felt it did not need three years to prepare for a risk-bearing arrangement.[38] Finally, the June 2016 Final Rule established time frames and criteria for ACOs to appeal calculation of bonuses and penalties.[39] As a result of this final rule, CMS projects that the Shared Savings Program for CYs 2017 through 2019 will net the federal government an additional 110 million in savings.[40]

On December 21, 2017, CMS published a Shared Savings Program Interim Final Rule for Extreme and Uncontrollable Circumstances with comment period establishing policies for assessing the quality and financial performance of Shared Savings Program ACOs affected by extreme and uncontrollable circumstances such as hurricanes and wildfires occurring during Performance Year 2017.[41] CMS specifically noted examples including Hurricanes Harvey, Irma, and Maria, and the California wildfires.[42] The interim final rule provides that CMS will use the same determination of an extreme and uncontrollable circumstance as determined under the Quality Payment Program, including the identification of affected geographic areas.[43] Pursuant to the regulation, ACOs in which 20 percent or more of their assigned beneficiaries reside in counties impacted by an extreme and uncontrollable circumstance as defined in the regulation, or an ACO legal entity located in impacted counties, will receive the higher of their ACO reported quality score or the mean Shared Savings Program ACO quality score.[44] CMS will adjust any owed losses of performance-based risk ACOs for the percent of the ACO's assigned beneficiaries residing in impacted counties and the length of the emergency declaration.

On December 31, 2018, CMS released a final rule overhauling the MSSP by introducing the concept of "pathways to success" (the December 2018 Final Rule). Under the December 2018 Final Rule, CMS discontinued Track 1 and Track 2, and rebranding Track 1+ and Track 3.[45] These

---

37. *Id.* at 37994.
38. *Id.*
39. *Id.* at 37997.
40. *Id.* at 38006.
41. 82 Fed. Reg. 60912 (Dec. 26, 2017).
42. *Id.*
43. *Id.* at 60918-60-919.
44. *Id.*
45. 83 Fed. Reg. 67841 (Dec. 31, 2018).

revisions permit an ACO to elect to participate in one of two MSSP "pathways to success:" the BASIC Track or the ENHANCED Track. An ACO may choose to enter the BASIC Track on 1 of 5 levels (A through E), each of which contained distinct levels of shared savings and risks. This system is designed to allow ACOs to glide into risk sharing progressively, with level A being a one-sided model and the final level E being equivalent to the former Track 1+.[46] Under the December 2018 Final Rule, the ENHANCED Track is equivalent to the former Track 3. Further, the December 2018 Final Rule further refined benchmarking regional adjustments by reducing the maximum weight used in calculating the regional adjustment, and capping the adjustment amount for all agreement periods as to not excessively reward or punish an ACO based on the ACO's location.[47] Finally, the December 2018 Final Rule added a new section to the Shared Savings Program regulation to govern the payment for certain telehealth services furnished in accordance with § 1899(l) of the Social Security Act as added by the Bipartisan Budget Act of 2018 for ACOs participating under a two-sided model with prospective assignment.[48]

C. American Medical Association ACO policy

At its 2010 Interim Annual Meeting held on November 11, 2010, the American Medical Association's (AMA) House of Delegates adopted principles for ACOs, which include the following:

1. the guiding principle that the goal of an ACO is to increase access to care, improve the quality of care and ensure the efficient delivery of care;

2. ACOs must be physician led (to ensure that medical decisions are based on patients' versus commercial interests) and encourage an environment of collaboration among physicians;

3. physician and patient participation should be voluntary;

4. the ACO's savings and revenues should be retained for patient care services and distributed to the ACO participants;

5. waivers and safe harbors should be created to give flexibility to the patient referral and antitrust laws necessary to allow physicians to form or participate in ACOs without being employed by hospitals or ACOs;

6. additional resources should be provided to encourage ACO development in the form of financing up-front costs of creating an ACO;

---

46. *Id*. at 67820.
47. *Id*. at 67822.
48. *Id*. at 67978.

7.   ACO spending benchmarking should be adjusted for difference in geographic practice costs and risk adjusted for individual patient risk factors, and ACOs spending less than the national average per Medicare beneficiary should be provided an additional bonus payment so that organizations that have already achieved significant efficiencies are incented to participate;

8.   the quality performance standards established by the HHS Secretary must be consistent with the AMA's principles for quality reporting;

9.   an ACO must be afforded due process before it is terminated from Medicare for failing to meet quality performance standards;

10.   the ACO should be allowed to use different payment models, and any capitation payments must be risk-adjusted;

11.   the Consumer Assessment of Healthcare Providers and Systems Patient Satisfaction Survey should be used to determine whether an ACO meets the required patient-centeredness criteria;

12.   Medicare must ensure that electronic health record systems are interoperable; and

13.   If an ACO bears risk, it must abide by financial solvency standards for risk-bearing organizations.

II.   The Center for Medicare and Medicaid Innovation and Current ACO Models

A.   The Center for Medicare and Medicaid Innovation.

The CMMI was established, pursuant to Section 3021 of the ACA, for purposes of testing various proposed innovative payment and service delivery models to identify effective methods to reduce program expenditures, while preserving or enhancing the quality of care given to beneficiaries.[49] In selecting models to test under CMMI, HHS is charged with giving preference to models that not only reduce cost but also improve the coordination, quality, and efficiency of healthcare services furnished to Medicare or Medicaid beneficiaries or beneficiaries of both programs. Since its inception, CMMI has implemented various ACO initiatives, leading to the creation of many of the ACO models detailed below.

B.   ACO Models

Medicare offers several ACO models, including: (i) the MSSP ACO Models (BASIC track and ENHANCED track); (ii) the Pioneer ACO Model; (iii) the ACO Investment Model; (iv) the Next Generation ACO Model; (v) the

---

49. *See* ACA at § 3021.

Comprehensive ESRD Care (CEC) Model; and (vi) the Medicare-Medicaid ACO Model. While the Pioneer ACO Model is no longer accepting applicants, certain other models permit dual participation. Specifically, participants in the ACO Investment Model may simultaneously participate in the MSSP. However, participants in the Next Generation ACO Model may not simultaneously participate in the MSSP or the Pioneer ACO Model.

1. *Medicare Shared Savings Program (MSSP) ACO Models (BASIC and ENHANCED Tracks)*

The MSSP is a voluntary program for Medicare providers that is intended to facilitate coordination and cooperation among providers to improve the quality of care extended to Medicare FFS beneficiaries while simultaneously lowering Medicare's total program expenditures. The MSSP encouraged the development of ACOs to achieve these dual objectives.[50] The MSSP has been operating since 2011, was revised in the June 2015 and the June 2016 Final Rules,[51] and again revised in the December 2018 Final Rule.

Under the MSSP, CMS has provided various incentives to ACOs to assist them in obtaining the dual objectives, including: (1) incentives to promote accountability for an entire patient population's health; (2) incentives to coordinate the provision of items and services under Medicare parts A and B; and (3) incentives to encourage investment in infrastructure and redesigning care processes to promote high-quality and efficient service delivery.[52] Under the MSSP, ACOs (as opposed to individual participating providers) that successfully meet the established quality of care and cost-savings targets are eligible to share a percentage of the achieved savings with Medicare, in the form of additional payments.[53] The additional payment is calculated as a percentage of the "shared savings" or a percentage of the difference between the estimated per-capita Medicare expenditure for patients assigned to the ACO and the per-capita cost-savings threshold established for that type of ACO. The percentage of shared savings is defined by the type of ACO in its initial agreement with CMS. CMS distributes the payments to the ACO. Applicable regulations do not specify the method that ACOs are to use in distributing the payments to their participating providers; rather, this is left to each ACO.

---

50. CMS, *Shared Savings Program, available at* http://www.cms.gov/Medicare/Medicare-Fee-for-Service-Payment/sharedsavingsprogram/index.html?redirect=/sharedsavingsprogram/.

51. 81 Fed. Reg. 37950 79 Fed. Reg. at 62356 and 62357 (Oct. 17, 2014).

52. *Id.*

53. *Supra* notes 44 and 45.

Consequently, the terms negotiated in the participation agreement entered between the ACO and ACO participants—particularly those terms addressing compensation and any shared savings distributions—are critical to ACO participants.

The ACA initially set forth the following specific requirements for ACOs to serve under the MSSP. To be eligible for MSSP participation, an ACO must: (1) have a sufficient number of primary care physicians to serve at least 5,000 Medicare beneficiaries; (2) agree to three years of participation in the program; (3) have a formal legal structure; (4) have defined processes to promote evidence-based medicine and patient centeredness; (5) have a mechanism of shared governance among ACO participants; and (6) have a health information infrastructure to enable community-wide care assessment and coordination, including functional, integrated EHR.[54] Additionally, an ACO is precluded from participating in the MSSP if the ACO includes an ACO participant that is participating in any other Medicare initiative that involves shared savings payments.[55] These requirements were revised, in part, by the June 2015 Final Rule, as discussed further below.

Generally, ACOs that participate in the MSSP are measured by performance standards, which are aligned with the standards in other CMS quality reporting requirements of the Medicare Merit-based Incentive Payment System, and with standards approved by the National Quality Forum, the National Committee on Quality Assurance (NCQA), and the Agency for Healthcare Research and Quality.[56] The 2019 publication of the Medicare Shared Savings Program Quality Measure Benchmarks sets forth the measures applicable to the MSSP.[57] As of January 2020, 23 quality measures are included in the MSSP.[58]

The measures are organized around four domains, including (i) the patient/caregiver experience; (ii) care coordination and patient safety; (iii) preventive health; and (iv) clinical care for at-risk populations.[59]

---

54. ACA at § 3022; *see also* 42 C.F.R. §§ 425.10 *et seq.*
55. *Id.*
56. 76 Fed. Reg. at 67871.
57. *See* Medicare Shared Savings Program Quality Measure Benchmarks, *available at* https://edit.cms.gov/files/document/quality-measure-benchmarks-2019-performance-year-update-pdf.
58. *See* 82 Fed Reg. 52976 (Nov. 15, 2017); *see also* Quality Measure Benchmarks for the 2018 and 2019 Reporting Years, *available at* https://www.cms.gov/Medicare/Medicare-Fee-for-Service-Payment/sharedsavingsprogram/Downloads/2018-and-2019-quality-benchmarks-guidance.pdf.
59. *Id.*

The first domain, patient/caregiver experience, includes metrics for getting timely care, appointments, and information; provider communication; patient ratings of providers; access to specialists; health promotion/education; shared decision-making; health/functional status; stewardship of patient resources, courteousness of office staff, and care coordination.[60] The second domain, care coordination/ patient safety, includes performance standards, such as risk standardized, all-conditions readmissions; all-cause unplanned admissions for patients with Multiple Chronic Conditions; Ambulatory Sensitive Condition Acute Composite; and falls screening.[61] The third domain, preventive health measures, includes data for breast cancer and colorectal cancer screening; flu shots; preventive care screening and follow-up for tobacco use or depression; and statin therapy for the prevention of cardiovascular disease.[62] Finally, the fourth domain, clinical care for at-risk population measures, involves efforts to care for patients with diabetes, hypertension, and depression.[63]

The operational time and expense involved in monitoring and reporting these measures is a significant concern and can prevent certain ACOs from achieving savings. In order to be eligible to receive shared savings distributions, an ACO participant needs to meet a minimum attainment level on at least 70 percent of the measures included in each of the four domains.[64] The total points earned for measures in each domain, including any quality improvement points, will be summed and divided by the total points available for that domain to produce an overall domain score of the percentage of points earned relative to points available. The percentage score for each domain will be averaged together to generate a final overall quality score for each ACO that will be used to determine the amount of savings it shares or, if applicable, the amount of losses it owes. In the first performance year, an ACO stands to receive the maximum available score where the entity completely and accurately reports on all quality measures.[65] In the second or subsequent performance years, CMS will phase in quality performance benchmarks that measure an ACO's performance relative to national standards to determine an

---

60. *Id.*
61. *Id.*
62. *Id.*
63. *Id.*
64. *See* 42 CFR § 425.316
65. *See* Medicare Shared Savings Program Quality Measure Benchmarks for the 2016 and 2017 Reporting Years (Dec. 2016), *available at* https://www.cms.gov/Medicare/Medicare-Fee-for-Service-Payment/sharedsavingsprogram/Downloads/MSSP-QM-Benchmarks-2016.pdf.

ACO's final sharing rate.[66] Following the June 2016 Final Rule, CMS will begin using regional FFS spending metrics when calculating an ACO's performance benchmarks.[67]

After consideration of these measures, CMS's payments to ACOs are based on retrospective reconciliation of the ACO's expenses incurred and deducted from any shared savings earned by the ACO. The method, or formula, used to reconcile shared savings and expenses varies by the ACO Track elected. Under the June 2015 Final Rule, an ACO formerly could elect to participate in one of three MSSP Tracks: Track 1, Track 2, or Track 3.[68]

Before Track 1 was retired, ACOs electing Track 1 (a one-sided model) could share in savings but were not at risk for sharing in any of the losses generated by the ACO during its three-year term.[69] Initially, before issuance of the June 2015 Final Rule, an ACO could only participate in Track 1 for an initial three-year agreement period and then was required to convert to a Track 2 ACO.[70] In the 2015 Final Rule, Track 1 ACOs were allowed to continue participating in Track 1 for an additional three-year agreement period following the expiration of their initial three-year term with the same shared savings rate as in the initial term (50 percent of the savings accrued by the ACO).[71] Further, the June 2016 Final Rule provided Track 1 ACOs even greater flexibility because the entity can elect to extend its initial three-year agreement by one year before transitioning to a two-sided model.[72] The December 2018 Final Rule retired Track 1, disallowing any new agreement periods starting in 2019 and subsequent years.[73]

Before Track 2 was retired, ACOs electing to participate under Track 2 (a two-sided model) agreed to share in any losses generated by the ACO in exchange for a greater share of any savings accrued by the ACO (60 percent shared savings rate).[74] Thus, Track 2 ACOs assumed an upside and downside financial risk in conjunction with CMS. The June 2015 Final Rule substantively modified Track 2 ACOs in two ways: (1) it lowered the threshold that Track 2 ACOs must meet before they can begin sharing in any savings or losses accrued by the ACO

---

66. *Id.*
67. *Id.*
68. *See* 42 C.F.R. §§ 425.10 *et seq.*
69. *See* 42 C.F.R. § 425.604.
70. 80 Fed. Reg. at 32694.
71. *See* 80 Fed. Reg. at 32694.
72. 81 Fed. Reg. 37950, 37994 (June 10, 2016).
73. 83 Fed. Reg. at 67817.
74. *See* 42 C.F.R. § 425.606.

and (2) it allowed Track 2 ACOs to choose among several options for their Minimum Savings Rate/Minimum Loss Rate (MSR/MLR), thereby allowing such ACOs to tailor their Track 2 Model to their preferred level of risk-tolerance.[75] The December 2018 Final Rule retired Track 2, disallowing any new agreement periods starting in 2019 and subsequent years.[76]

The December 2018 Final Rule created a new BASIC Track ACO that offers a glide path from a one-sided model to progressively higher increments of risk and potential reward within a single agreement period.[77] With agreement periods beginning on July 1, 2019, ACOs participating under the BASIC Track are engaged in a five-year agreement, and have five levels of risk and potential reward. One-sided models are available only for the first two consecutive performance years, each year of which is a separate level (levels A and B). In performance years three through five, two-sided models are available, each with a progressively higher risk and potential reward (levels C, D, and E).[78]

- An ACO entering into the BASIC Track under levels A or B is eligible for a shared savings rate not to exceed 40 percent, and does not share any risks.

- An ACO entering into the BASIC Track under level C is eligible for a shared savings rate not to exceed 50 percent, while sharing in 30 percent of losses exceeding the ACO's MLR, with losses capped at 2 percent of total Medicare Part A and B FFS revenue for the ACO or 1 percent of the ACO's historical benchmark for the applicable performance year, whichever is less.[79]

- An ACO entering into the BASIC Track under level D is eligible for a shared savings rate not to exceed 50 percent, while sharing in 30 percent of the losses exceeding its MLR, with losses capped at 4 percent of total Medicare Part A and B FFS revenue for the ACO participant or 2 percent of the ACO's historical benchmark for the applicable performance year, whichever is less.[80]

---

75. *Id; see also* 80 Fed. Reg. at 32694.
76. 83 Fed. Reg. at 67817.
77. *Id*. at 67822.
78. *Id*. at 67844.
79. *Id*. at 67850-51.
80. *Id*.

- An ACO entering into the BASIC Track under level E is eligible for a shared savings rate not to exceed 50 percent, while sharing in 30 percent of the losses exceeding its MLR. Under level E, the percentage of total Medicare Part A and B FFS revenue used to limit loss sharing would be set each performance year consistent with the generally applicable nominal amount standard for an Advanced Alternative Payment Model (APM).[81]

ACOs participating in the BASIC Track are automatically advanced to the next level of risk at the start of each participation year.[82] If the ACO does not qualify to move from a one-sided model to a two-sided model, CMS will terminate the ACO's agreement.[83] The level in which an ACO enters the BASIC Track depends on whether the ACO is classified as "high" or "low" revenue and whether the ACO has previous experience with the Shared Savings Program.[84] New legal entities entering the Shared Savings Program who are both "inexperienced" and classified as "low revenue" may enter the BASIC Track at level A, while those with previous experience participating in Track 1, those who are "re-entering," or those who are classified as "high revenue" may only, if eligible, enter into the BASIC Track at level E.[85]

The December 2018 Final Rule rebranded the June 2015 Final Rule's Track 3 ACO (an alternative two-sided risk model based on the successful features of the Pioneer ACO Model) to the ENHANCED Track. The ENHANCED Track ACO Model offers a higher shared savings rate (75 percent of accrued savings), prospective assignment of beneficiaries, and the opportunity to use new care coordination tools.[86] ENHANCED Track will be most appealing to those entities willing to accept increased performance-based risk in exchange for the opportunity to receive a higher proportion of any shared savings (75 percent).[87] As an additional incentive, ENHANCED Track participants may apply for a programmatic waiver of the SNF 3-day rule, which

---

81. *Id.*

82. *Id.* at 67844. Note, however, that ACOs engaging the BASIC Track on July 1, 2019, for its first performance year through December 31, 2019, may elect to remain at the same level for Performance Year 2020, only being compelled to advance to the next level at the start at Performance Year 2021. *Id.*

83. *Id.* at 67851.

84. *Id.*

85. *Id.* Note, however, that certain entities may be unable to participate in the BASIC Track at any level depending on their classification of "high revenue" or previous experience. *See generally, id.* at 67911-12.

86. *Id.*

87. *See* 42 C.F.R. § 425.610.

increases the revenue, and potential shared savings, available to ENHANCED Track ACO participants.[88]

The administrative revisions to the MSSP introduced in the June 2015 Final Rule remain in place under the December 2018 Final Rule. First, the June 2015 Final Rule established a consolidated application review process and clarified CMS's ability to deny applications based on incompleteness or an ACO's failure to timely submit additional information requested by CMS.[89] CMS also introduced procedures, at 42 C.F.R. § 425.224, for ACOs to renew their participation agreements prior to their expiration and established the following criteria for authorizing renewals: (i) the ACO's historical satisfaction of the risk model's operating criteria, (ii) the ACO's current compliance with the MSSP eligibility and other requirements, (iii) whether the ACO met the quality performance standards in one of the first two years of the prior agreement period, and (iv) whether the ACO repaid any losses owed if participating under a two-sided model.[90] ACOs failing these criteria may not renew their participation agreements. Additionally, by 2017, ACOs were required to contract directly with each ACO participant (ACO provider/supplier) rather than indirectly through an IPA or PHO.[91] By 2017, each participation agreement must include terms that: (i) require ACO participants to expressly adhere to MSSP requirements, (ii) set participants' rights and obligations, (iii) describe how the opportunity to receive shared savings encourages participants to adhere to the ACO's guidelines, (iv) require participants to update enrollment information, (v) permit the ACO to take remedial actions against participants, (vi) require participants to take remedial action against providers/suppliers for noncompliance with MSSP guidelines, (vii) are for a term of one year, and (viii) require completion of a closeout process upon termination or expiration of the participation agreement.[92]

The revised requirements for ACO's governing body and legal entity established in the June 2015 Final Rule also remain unaltered by the December 2018 Final Rule. The June 2015 Final Rule specified that

---

88. *See* 80 Fed. Reg. at 32695. (Under the SNF 3-day rule, Medicare will not pay for otherwise covered services provided to a Medicare beneficiary in a SNF if the beneficiary was admitted to the SNF without a prior three-day inpatient hospital stay. The Final Rule waives this rule for Track 3 ACOs so that any such services provided prospectively to assigned beneficiaries will be covered.)

89. *See* 80 Fed. Reg. at 32729 and 42 C.F.R. § 425.206(a)(1).

90. *See* 80 Fed. Reg. at 32730 and 42 C.F.R. § 425.224(b).

91. *Id.*

92. *Id.*

each ACO must have an identifiable governing body with the ultimate authority to execute the functions of an ACO and satisfy three criteria: (i) the ACO's governing body must be the same as the governing body of the legal entity that is the ACO, (ii) if the ACO comprises multiple ACO participants, the governing body must be separate and unique to the ACO (not the governing body of any ACO participant), and (iii) the governing body must satisfy all requirements at 42 C.F.R. § 425.106, including its fiduciary duty of loyalty to participants.[93] Per CMS commentary, the revisions were designed to prevent an ACO from delegating its decision-making authority to a committee of the governing body or assigning it up the chain to a parent company.[94] In its commentary, CMS stated that the governing body must be at an organizational level where it is not responsible for, nor influenced by, any individuals who are not ACO participants.[95] Further, each ACO must have a formal legal structure that will allow it (i) to receive shared savings payments and distribute them among providers and (ii) to institute the processes required by 42 C.F.R. § 425.112, such as evidence-based medicine, patient engagement, reporting on quality and cost measures, coordinated care, and accountability for the ACO's management.[96] Following the June 2015 Final Rule, health systems, which wholly own and control ACOs/clinically integrated networks as separate entities and reserve authority over them to a parent company, no longer comply with this MSSP governance requirement.[97]

Additionally, the June 2015 Final Rule provided guidance for issues that arise when an ACO participant acquires another Medicare-enrolled provider that is not participating in an ACO, by merger or otherwise.[98] Following the rule, ACOs may annually submit a request to CMS that the claims billed pre-merger by an acquired entity be considered in determining if the ACO meets the 5,000 assigned beneficiaries threshold and setting the ACO's historical benchmarks, provided that three criteria are met: (i) the ACO participant subsumed the acquired entity's tax identification number (TIN) in its entirety, (ii) each provider/supplier that reassigned his/her right to receive Medicare payment to the acquired entity's TIN has reassigned it to the ACO participant, and (iii) the acquired entity's TIN is no longer used to bill Medicare.[99] Effectively, this rule permits an ACO to grow or alter the

---

93. *See* 80 Fed. Reg. at 32716.
94. *Id.*
95. *Id.*
96. *Id.*
97. *See* 80 Fed. Reg. 32716-32719.
98. 80 Fed. Reg. at 32715.
99. *Id.*

quality of its beneficiary pool by acquiring Medicare participating providers.

The final rule entitled "Payment Medicare Program; Revisions to Payment Policies Under the Physician Fee Schedule and Other Revisions to Part B for CY 2018; Medicare Shared Savings Program Requirements; and Medicare Diabetes Prevention Program," issued on November 15, 2017, further revised certain of the MSSP ACO regulations to make additional administrative changes.[100] These changes are designed to reduce burden and streamline program operations.[101] For example, the final rule revises the assignment methodology for ACOs that include Federally Qualified Health Centers (FQHCs) and Rural Health Clinics (RHCs) by eliminating the requirement to specifically enumerate each physician working in the FQHC or RHC on the ACO participant list.[102] The final rule further initiates changes to revise the application for an ACO submitting an initial Shared Savings Program application or the application for use of the SNF 3-day rule waiver to reduce the burden on the applicant.[103] In addition, CMS added three new chronic care management codes and four behavioral health integration codes to the definition of primary care services used in the ACO assignment methodology.[104]

Currently over 477 ACOs participate in the MSSP,[105] and 2 ACOs have NCQA accreditation.[106] Further information on the MSSP, including the list of the current ACOs participating in the model, can be accessed on CMS's website.[107] Based on quality and financial results from 2019, the MSSP ACOs generated over $1.19 billion in total net savings to Medicare.[108] According to CMS, these savings are attribut-

---

100. 82 Fed. Reg. 52976 (Nov. 15, 2017).

101. *See* CMS, Fact Sheet, Final Policy, Payment, and Quality Provisions in the Medicare Physician Fee Schedule for Calendar Year 2018 *available at* https://www.cms.gov/Newsroom/MediaReleaseDatabase/Fact-sheets/2017-Fact-Sheet-items/2017-11-02.html?DLPage=1&DLEntries=10&DLSort=0&DLSortDir=descending

102. 82 Fed. Reg. 53370 (to be codified at 42 C.F.R. § 424.404).

103. 82 Fed. Reg.53369-53369.

104. 82 Fed. Reg.53010 and 53078.

105. *See* Medicare Shared Savings Program Fast Facts, *available at* https://www.cms.gov/Medicare/Medicare-Fee-for-Service-Payment/sharedsavingsprogram/Downloads/ssp-2019-fast-facts.pdf.

106. NCQA ACO Report Card, *available at* https://reportcards.ncqa.org/#/other-health-care-organizations/list?program=Accountable%20Care%20Organization.

107. CMS Shared Savings Program Information, *available at* http://www.cms.gov/Medicare/Medicare-Fee-for-Service-Payment/sharedsavingsprogram/index.html?redirect=/sharedsavingsprogram/.

108. https://www.healthaffairs.org/do/10.1377/hblog20200914.598838/full/.

able to more ACOs taking accountability for downside risk, and CMS notes that ACOs that have taken on downside risk continue to perform better than those that do not.[109]

2. *Pioneer ACO Model*

CMMI designed the Pioneer ACO Model for organizations that already had experience coordinating patient care among several different types of settings and providers and allowed such organizations to move more quickly from shared savings payment methodologies to a per-member-per-month (PMPM) payment model. Thirty-two ACOs (Pioneer ACOs) were selected initially to participate in the Pioneer ACO program starting on January 1, 2012 (PY 1).[110] As of January 2020, only nine organizations still participate in the Pioneer Model.[111] In the first two years of their Pioneer ACO contract with CMS, the Pioneer ACOs shared both savings and risk at higher levels than MSSP ACO participants. In the third year of the program, if the Pioneer ACO achieved sufficient savings in the preceding two years, the Pioneer ACO was permitted to transition to a PMPM payment methodology.

In July of 2013, CMS announced the quality and financial performance esults for the Pioneer ACOs for PY 1 (2012). [112] In PY 1, all 32 Pioneer ACOs reported successful quality measures and achieved the maximum reporting rate.[113] Overall, Pioneer ACOs performed better than published rates in FFS Medicare for all 15 clinical quality measures for which there was comparable data.[114] For example, 25 of the 32 Pioneer ACOs generated lower risk-adjusted readmission rates for their aligned beneficiaries than the benchmark rate for all Medicare FFS beneficiaries.[115] With respect to the financial performance of the Pioneer ACOs, CMS reported that in PY 1, 13 out of the 32 Pioneer ACOs produced shared savings and generated a gross savings of $87.6 million equaling nearly a $33 million savings to the Medicare Trust Funds.[116] However, two Pioneer ACOs shared losses totaling approxi-

---

109. *Id.*

110. *See* Actuary Certification of Pioneer ACO Model Savings, *available at* http://www.cms.gov/Research-Statistics-Data-and-Systems/Research/ActuarialStudies/Downloads/Pioneer-Certification-2015-04-10.pdf.

111. *See* Pioneer ACO Model Fact Sheet, *available at* http://innovation.cms.gov/initiatives/Pioneer-ACO-Model/PioneerACO-FactSheet.html.

112. CMS, Press Release, Pioneer Accountable Care Organizations Succeed in Improving Care; Lowering Costs, (July 16, 2013), *available at* https://www.cms.gov/newsroom/press-releases/pioneer-accountable-care-organizations-succeed-improving-care-lowering-costs.

113. *Id.*

114. *Id.*

115. *Id.*

116. *Infra* note 106 and 111.

mately $4 million and seven Pioneer ACOs did not produce any savings.[117] As a result, seven Pioneer ACOs notified CMS of their intent to exit the Pioneer ACO Model and apply to the MSSP[118] and two Pioneer ACOs exited the program completely.[119]

In September of 2014, CMS released the quality and financial performance results for Performance Year 2 (PY 2) (2013) for the remaining 23 Pioneer ACOs. In PY 2, the mean quality score among the Pioneer ACOs increased from 71.8 percent in 2012 to 85.2 percent in 2013, an improvement of 19 percent.[120] The Pioneer ACOs also showed improvements in 28 of the 33 quality measures, and improved an average 14.8 percent across all quality measures.[121] In PY 2, Pioneer ACOs generated an estimated total savings of over $96 million and qualified for shared savings payments of $68 million.[122] The Pioneer ACOs also saved approximately $41 million for the Medicare Trust Funds and achieved lower per capita growth in spending for the Medicare program.[123] At a rate of 1.4 percent, the Pioneer ACO's per capita growth was approximately 0.45 percent lower than Medicare FFS.[124]

CMS released Performance Year 3 (PY 3) results for Pioneer ACOs in August of 2015.[125] The mean quality score increased to 87.2 percent in 2014 from 85.2 percent in 2013.[126] Participants also showed improvements in 28 of 33 quality measures in 2014 and experienced average improvements of 3.6 percent across all measures compared to 2013 performance.[127] The Pioneer ACOs generated savings of $120 million in 2014, a 24 percent increase from 2013 savings.[128] Total model savings for each ACO rose from $2.7 million in 2012 to $4.2 million in 2013 to $6.0 million in 2014.[129]

---

117. *Id.*

118. *See* 79 Fed. Reg. at 72779-72780.

119. *Infra* note 106.

120. CMS, Fact Sheet: Medicare ACOs Continue to Succeed in Improving Care, Lowering Cost Growth, (Sept. 16, 2014), *available at* https://www.cms.gov/newsroom/fact-sheets/medicare-acos-continue-succeed-improving-care-lowering-cost-growth.

121. *Id.*

122. *Id.*

123. *Id.*

124. *Id.*

125. Fact Sheet, CMS, Medicare ACOs Provide Improved Care While Slowing Cost Growth in 2014 (Aug. 8, 2015) *available at* https://www.cms.gov/newsroom/fact-sheets/medicare-acos-provide-improved-care-while-slowing-cost-growth-2014.

126. *Id.*

127. *Id.*

128. *Id.*

129. *Id.*

In August of 2016, CMS released performance results for the Pioneer ACO program that indicate that the Pioneer ACO Model continued to achieve savings in Performance Year 4 (PY 4) (2015).[130] According to the report, several Pioneer ACOs generated greater savings in 2015 and one garnered savings for the first time.[131] While the number of participating Pioneer ACOs decreased by nearly a third between PY 3 and PY 4, the entities collectively generated total model savings of over $37 million.[132] The Pioneer ACOs also continued to show strong performance and improvement across quality measures.[133] According to the same fact sheet, the mean quality score among Pioneer ACOs increased to 92.26 percent in PY 4 from 87.2 percent in PY 3.[134] Additionally, of the 12 Pioneer ACOs, nine had overall quality scores above 90 percent for PY 4 with scores ranging from 92.59 percent to 98.38 percent.[135]

In addition, performance results for Performance Year 5 (2016) for the nine remaining Pioneer ACOs indicate that the ACOs collectively achieved savings of over $60.8 million and reported quality scores ranging from 88.93 percent to 95.74 percent.[136] Please note, however, that the Pioneer ACO Model is no longer active.

3. *ACO Investment Model (AIM)*

The AIM is a model built on the experience gained from the Advance Payment Model ("APM")[137] to (i) encourage new ACOs to form in rural and underserved areas and (ii) encourage current MSSP ACOs to transition to arrangements with greater financial risk.[138] CMS provides ACOs participating in this model with financial support to make

---

130. CMS, Fact Sheet, Medicare Accountable Care Organizations 2015 Performance Year Quality and Financial Results (Aug. 25, 2016), *available at* https://www.cms.gov/newsroom/fact-sheets/medicare-accountable-care-organizations-2015-performance-year-quality-and-financial-results.

131. *Id.*

132. *Id.*

133. *Id.*

134. *Id.*

135. *Id.*

136. *See* https://innovation.cms.gov/initiatives/Pioneer-ACO-Model/.

137. *See* CMMI Advance Payment Model Application Information, *available at* http://innovation.cms.gov/initiatives/Advance-Payment-ACO-Model/Advance-Payment-ACO-Model-Application-Information.html Applications for participation in the Advance Payment Model were initially accepted for ACOs applying to participate beginning on April 1, 2012, or July 1, 2012, and extended to those participating with a start date of Jan. 1, 2013. Applications are no longer being accepted for participation.

138. *See* ACO Investment Model Overview, *available at* http://innovation.cms.gov/initiatives/ACO-Investment-Model/.

infrastructure investments and develop new ways to improve care for Medicare beneficiaries.[139] Through the model, CMS initially provided approximately $95.6 million in upfront and ongoing investments.[140] CMS places some restrictions on using money received through this model. For instance, recipients cannot use the money to augment provider salaries or as bonuses for executives or administrators.[141]

Participation is limited to two distinct groups: (i) those that joined the MSSP in 2016 and (ii) those that joined the MSSP starting in 2012, 2013, and 2014.[142] Those that began participating in the MSSP in 2016 receive three types of payments: (1) upfront, fixed payment; (2) upfront, variable payment based on the number of their preliminarily prospectively assigned beneficiaries; and (3) a monthly payment varying in amount depending on the size of the ACO.[143] Those that began participating in the MSSP in 2012, 2013, and 2014 receive two types of payments: (1) upfront variable payment based on the number of their preliminary prospectively-assigned beneficiaries and (2) a monthly payment varying in amount depending on the size of the ACO.[144]

ACOs participating in the AIM may be required to repay CMS.[145] For AIM ACOs that began participating in the MSSP between April 1, 2012, and January 1, 2014, CMS will recover payments from earned shared savings as long as the ACO remains in the Shared Savings Program.[146] For AIM ACOs that entered the MSSP in 2015 or 2016 (New ACOs), CMS will recover payments from earned shared savings for as long as the New ACO remains in the Shared Savings Program.[147] While CMS will recover all prepayments up to the total shared savings earned by the New ACO, it will not pursue amounts in excess of the earned shared savings.[148] Additionally, if a New ACO fails to earn sufficient shared savings during its first performance period to fully repay the prepayments and also decides not to participate in the MSSP for a subsequent MSSP agreement period, then CMS will not pursue full recovery of the remaining prepayments from that ACO.[149]

---

139. *Id.*
140. CMS, Media External Frequently Asked Questions: Accountable Care Organization Investment Model (AIM) (Mar. 4, 2016), *available at* https://innovation.cms.gov/Files/x/AIM-FAQs.pdf; *see also* https://innovation.cms.gov/Files/reports/aim-second-annrpt.pdf.
141. *Id.*
142. ACO Investment Model Overview, *supra* note 119.
143. *Id.*
144. *Id.*
145. *Supra* note 121.
146. *Id.*
147. *Id.*
148. *Id.*
149. *Id.*

CMS gave ACOs serving rural areas of low ACO penetration and existing ACOs committed to moving to higher risk tracks greater preference in the selection process as well as to those providing high quality of care.[150] Currently, the AIM consists of 45 participating ACOs, including two that had been previously selected and 43 ACOs selected for a 2016 start.[151] Collectively, AIM participants serve a total 487,000 beneficiaries.[152] Further information related to the AIM is available on CMMI's website.[153]

4. *The Next Generation ACO Model*

The Next Generation ACO Model offers financial arrangements to organizations that have experience coordinating patient care and are willing to take higher risks with the potential for higher rewards than other ACO initiatives.[154] Applicants have the opportunity to be reimbursed for expanded telemedicine services for urban and at-home patients.[155] The model prospectively sets benchmarks at the start of each performance year to reward attainment and improvement in efficiency.[156] The model consists of two to three initial performance years and two optional one-year extensions.[157]

Under the Next Generation ACO Model, organizations are offered two risk arrangements, either shared savings and losses of up to 80 percent or up to 100 percent.[158] Providers would be rewarded for the first dollar saved below the benchmark, and accountable for the first dollar above the benchmark.[159] The Next Generation ACO Model also offers the option of four payment mechanisms: (1) normal FFS claims; (2) normal FFS plus an additional per-beneficiary per-month (PBPM) payment recouped against shared savings; (3) population-based payments similar to the Pioneer Model; and (4) capitation, in which the ACO receives monthly PBPM payments and must pay claims for ACO providers.[160]

---

150. *See* ACO Investment Model Overview, *supra* note 119.

151. *Supra* note 121.

152. *Id.*

153. *See* ACO Investment Model Overview, *supra* note 119.

154. *See* Next Generation ACO Model, *available at* http://innovation.cms.gov/initiatives/Next-Generation-ACO-Model/index.html.

155. CMS, Fact Sheet: Pioneer ACO Model and Next Generation ACO Model: Comparison Across Key Design Elements, (Apr. 28, 2015), *available at* http://innovation.cms.gov/Files/fact-sheet/nextgenaco-comparefactsheet.pdf.

156. *Id.*

157. *Id.*

158. *Id.*

159. *Id.*

160. *Id.*

Additionally, all Next Generation beneficiaries will be eligible for CMS's Coordinated Care Reward and will be compensated if a specified percentage of patient encounters are with Next Generation Providers/Suppliers, Preferred Providers, and Affiliates.[161] The Next Generation ACO Model offers the following enhanced benefits: (1) SNF 3-day rule waiver; (2) telehealth originating site expansion; and (3) post-discharge home visits.[162]

Eligibility in the Next Generation ACO program is based on five key domains: (1) organizational structure; (2) leadership and management; (3) financial plan and experience with risk sharing; (4) patient centeredness; and (5) clinical care model. One round of applications was held in 2015, and a second round was held in 2016.[163] Those participants currently enrolled in MSSP or the Pioneer ACO Model may apply for the Next Generation ACO Model but may not simultaneously perform in these programs if selected.[164]

CMS organized two application rounds for prospective participants to apply to the Next Generation ACO Program. Round one closed on June 1, 2015, and round two closed on June 1, 2016. Further information related to the Next Generation ACO Model is available on CMMI's website.[165] Forty-one ACOs are now participating in the Next General ACO Model.[166]

In their third performance year (2018), Next Generation ACOs saved approximately $242.1 million.[167]

5. *The Comprehensive ESRD Care (CEC) Model*

In 2013, CMS announced the CMMI would begin testing a new CEC Model to improve beneficiary health outcomes and reduce per capita Medicare expenditures.[168] Currently, more than 700,000 Americans have end-stage renal disease (ESRD), which requires the provision of weekly dialysis treatments.[169] These treatments represent a significant

---

161. *Id.*
162. *Id.*
163. *Id.*
164. *Id.*
165. *See* Next Generation ACO Model *supra* note 136.
166. https://innovation.cms.gov/initiatives/Next-Generation-ACO-Model/.
167. *See* https://innovation.cms.gov/initiatives/Next-Generation-ACO-Model/.
168. CMS, Fact Sheet, Comprehensive ESRD Care Model (April 15, 2014), available at https://www.cms.gov/newsroom/fact-sheets/comprehensive-esrd-care-model-fact-sheet.
169. CMS, Comprehensive ESRD Care Model, *available at* https://innovation.cms.gov/initiatives/comprehensive-ESRD-care/.

cost for the Medicare Trust Funds. In 2013, beneficiaries with ESRD constituted 1 percent of the Medicare population, yet accounted for an estimated 7.1 percent of the total Medicare spending, totaling over $30.9 billion.[170] Because beneficiaries with ESRD typically exhibit multiple comorbidities, their state of health requires them to visit multiple providers and follow multiple care plans.[171] In testing this new initiative, CMS hopes to incentivize greater coordination between providers as part of an overarching scheme to reduce costs while maintaining or improving upon the quality of care for ESRD beneficiaries.[172]

Through the CEC Model, dialysis clinics, nephrologists, and other providers unite to create an ESRD Seamless Care Organization (ESCO) for the purpose of coordinating care.[173] Significantly, ESCOs assume responsibility for both clinical quality outcomes and financial outcomes measured by Original Medicare spending, including all spending on dialysis services for their matched ESRD beneficiaries.[174] To establish eligibility, ESCOs must be located within a single market, have a minimum of 350 beneficiaries "matched" to their organization, and have at least one dialysis facility or one nephrologist and/or nephrology practice as participant owners.[175] Additionally, the ESCO must be capable of (i) receiving and distributing shared savings payments, (ii) repaying shared losses (if applicable), and (iii) establishing reporting mechanisms and ensuring ESCO participant compliance with program requirements, including quality performance standards.[176]

The model offers two payment tracks depending on the size of the dialysis facility participating in the model.[177] If at least one of the participating dialysis facilities is owned by a large-dialysis organization (defined as an organization with 200 or more dialysis facilities), then the ESCO participates through the large-dialysis organization (LDO) track.[178] ESCOs that do not have a dialysis facility owned by an LDO participate through the non-LDO track.[179] The distinction is

---

170. *Id.*
171. *Id.*
172. *Id.*
173. *Id.*
174 *See* CMS, Request for Applications, *Comprehensive ESRD Care (CEC) Model* (May 18, 2016), *available at* https://innovation.cms.gov/Files/x/cec-py2-rfa.pdf.
175. *Id.*
176. *Id.*
177. *Id.*
178. *Id.*
179. *Id.*

significant because LDO ESCOs must participate in a risk-based payment arrangement over the life of the model whereas the non-LDO ESCOs have the option of participating in a one-sided payment arrangement over the life of the model.[180]

In October of 2015, CMS selected 13 applicants (12 LDO ESCOs, one non-LDO ESCO) to participate in the CEC Model for the program's first year.[181] The initial agreement period for these participants lasts for three years with an optional two-year extension. The second round of ESCO participation began on January 1, 2017.[182] As of January 2020, there are 33 participating ESCOs.[183] More information on the CEC Model can be found on the CMS website.[184]

6. *The Medicare-Medicaid ACO Model*

On December 15, 2016, the CMS announced its intent to partner with states and ACOs to test a new ACO model: the Medicare-Medicaid Accountable Care Organization (Medicare-Medicaid ACO, MMACO).[185] As an MMACO, Shared Savings Program ACOs will assume accountability for both Medicare and Medicaid expenditures for dually eligible beneficiaries (Medicare-Medicaid enrollees) within their assigned population.[186] The MMACO Model will offer ACOs financial arrangements that will align Medicare and Medicaid incentives, as well as facilitate access to Medicare and Medicaid data to promote better care coordination and investment in population health management.

Currently, Medicare ACOs only take on accountability for Original Medicare expenditures.[187] As a result, care for Medicare-Medicaid enrollees is complicated by varying priorities under the two reimbursement schemes.[188] Because Medicare beneficiaries enrolled in both Medicare and Medicaid represent a vulnerable population group

---

180. *Id.*

181. CMS, Frequently Asked Questions, *Comprehensive ESRD Care Initiative, available at* https://innovation.cms.gov/Files/x/cecfaq.pdf.

182. *Id.*

183. *See* CMS, Comprehensive ESRD Care Model (CEC Model) Fact Sheet *available at* https://innovation.cms.gov/Files/fact-sheet/cec-fs.pdf.

184. *See* CMS, *Comprehensive ESRD Care Model, available at* https://innovation.cms.gov/initiatives/comprehensive-ESRD-care/.

185. CMS, Fact Sheet, Medicare-Medicaid Accountable Care Organization (ACO) Model (Dec. 15, 2016), available at https://www.cms.gov/newsroom/fact-sheets/medicare-medicaid-accountable-care-organization-aco-model.

186. *Id.*

187. *Id.*

188. *Id.*

with relatively higher service demands, CMS believes an ACO initiative specifically tailored for these patients could lower costs and improve quality of care.[189]

CMS has issued a Request for Letters of Intent from states wishing to partner with CMS to design state-specific criteria for the MMACO Model, including the Medicaid shared savings/shared losses arrangements, selection of additional quality measures, and additional ACO eligibility requirements.[190] While applications for the MMACO Model are open to all states and the District of Columbia, CMS will only enter into Participation Agreements with up to six states.[191] In making this determination, CMS will give preference to states with relatively fewer Medicare ACOs.[192] Letters of Intent submitted by states will be nonbinding, but must be accompanied by at least one Letter of Intent from a potential ACO partner.[193] Because CMS will contract with states on an individual basis, certain aspects of the MMACO Model will vary from state to state.[194] However, CMS assures prospective participants that the over-arching principles and parameters will be consistent.[195] In the event a MMACO achieves Medicaid savings, CMS may share a portion of those savings with the state where the MMACO is located.[196] To be eligible for the 2020 Performance Year, states were required to submit their Letters of Intent by August 3, 2018.[197]

To participate, states must (i) have a sufficient number of Medicare-Medicaid enrollees in FFS Medicaid; (ii) not be simultaneously participating in a Financial Alignment Initiative that includes the state's MMACO Model target population in its model population; and (iii) have at least one potential ACO partner participating jointly in the state-specific development process.[198]

For an ACO to participate, the potential ACO partner must apply to or renew its Participation Agreement for the MSSP.[199] The potential ACO partner does not need to be a formal legal entity at the time it submits its Letter of Intent, but of course, will need to have become a legal

189. *Id.*
190. *Id.*
191. *Id.*
192. *Id.*
193. *Id.*
194. *Id.*
195. *Id.*
196. *Id.*
197. *Id.*
198. *Id.*
199. *Id.*

entity before participating.[200] Those ACOs that submit a letter of interest and engage in the development stage of the state-specific features of the MMACO Model will not be obligated to participate as a MMACO.[201] Similarly, ACOs that refrain from submitting Letters of Intent and contributing to the development process will still have the opportunity to become a MMACO.[202] ACOs wishing to participate in the MMACO Model must also demonstrate compliance with all applicable state laws and regulations with respect to risk-bearing entities, and produce documentation upon request.[203]

III. Legal Issues

A. Antitrust

The formation and operation of an ACO have antitrust ramifications. On October 28, 2011, the Federal Trade Commission (FTC) and the Department of Justice (DOJ) issued a Statement of Antitrust Enforcement Policy Regarding Accountable Care Organizations Participating in the Medicare Shared Savings Program.[204] On April 10, 2013, the FTC and DOJ issued a joint summary of the ACO Working Group activities between October 2011 and March 31, 2013, which summarized various questions fielded by the group submitted by ACOs, including, for example, questions related to primary service area calculations.[205]

B. Anti-Kickback Statute/Stark/Gainsharing Civil Monetary Penalty Waivers

1. *Brief description of the Anti-Kickback/Stark/Gainsharing Civil Monetary Penalty Laws*

During the process that led up to the development of the November 2, 2011, Final Rule, considerable discussion focused on the extent to which three major federal fraud and abuse laws would apply, and possibly hinder, ACO development. These three laws are the: physician self-referral law,[206] commonly known as "Stark;" the Anti-

---

200. *Id.*
201. *Id.*
202. *Id.*
203. *Id.*
204. 76 Fed. Reg. 67026 (Oct. 28, 2011).
205. Press Release, FTC/DOJ ACO Working Group Issues Summary of Activities Since October 2011 Release of ACO Antitrust Enforcement Policy (April 10, 2013) *available at* http://www.ftc.gov/news-events/press-releases/2013/04/ftcdoj-aco-working-group-issues-summary-activities-october-2011.
206. 42 U.S.C. § 1395nn(a)(1)(A).

Kickback Statute;[207] and the so-called "Gainsharing" civil monetary penalty statute (Gainsharing CMP).[208]

Stark, a civil statute with civil penalties, generally prohibits a physician from making a "referral" to an "entity" for the furnishing of "designated health services" paid for by Medicare or Medicaid if the physician, or his or her immediate family member, has a "financial relationship" with the entity.[209] Stark may be implicated by an ACO arrangement in which the ACO's members include physicians and hospitals and in which the physicians may refer Medicare or Medicaid beneficiaries to the hospital for designated health services, including, for example, inpatient and outpatient hospital services.[210] If the ACO arrangement calls for shared savings or any other payments to be made to participating physicians from the hospital, the "financial relationship" necessary to implicate the statute is present. CMS did propose an exception to Stark in July 2008 for certain shared savings arrangements that met 16 requirements.[211] However, this specific proposed exception was never adopted by CMS.

The Anti-Kickback Statute, a criminal statute with criminal penalties, makes it a crime for anyone to knowingly and willfully induce/pay or solicit/receive remuneration for the referral of patients for items or services reimbursed under a federal healthcare program.[212] Because most ACO arrangements will involve an exchange of remuneration among parties who are in a position to refer patients for items or services reimbursed under a federal healthcare program such as Medicare, Medicaid, or Tricare and no safe harbor currently exists under the Anti-Kickback Statute for ACO arrangements, the arrangement likely will implicate the Anti-Kickback Statute. Unlike Stark, under the Anti-Kickback Statute, if an arrangement does not fall within a safe harbor it will not automatically violate the statute. It will, however, invite scrutiny from the enforcement agencies to examine the parties' intent to determine whether any one purpose of the arrangement was to solicit, receive, induce or pay for the referrals of patients covered under a federal healthcare program. As this scrutiny usually is not desired, participants are hopeful that a safe harbor may be adopted for ACOs under the Anti-Kickback Statute.

---

207. 42 U.S.C. § 1320a-7(b).
208. 42 U.S.C. § 1320a-7a(b)(1).
209. As such terms are defined under 42 C.F.R. § 411.351.
210. 42 C.F.R. § 411.351.
211. 73 Fed. Reg. 38502, 38548 (July 7, 2008).
212. 42 U.S.C. § 1320a-7(b).

Yet another federal law, the Gainsharing CMP statute, imposes financial penalties on hospitals that make payments to physicians as an inducement to reduce or limit services to Medicare or Medicaid beneficiaries. Traditionally, the HHS Office of Inspector General (OIG) interpreted the Gainsharing CMP statute to prohibit such payments even if the services reduced were not medically necessary or appropriate.[213] Consequently, gainsharing programs—programs designed to reward physicians for reducing unnecessary services or unnecessary elements of services—could make a hospital liable for civil money penalties (CMPs). On October 3, 2014, the OIG proposed codifying the Gainsharing CMP statute and interpreting the definition of "reduce or limit services" more narrowly under the Gainsharing CMP.[214] The OIG stated that healthcare payment and delivery systems have begun to impose greater accountability on providers for providing quality of care at lower costs, and pointed to the MSSP as an example of such a program; but, CMS noted that the Gainsharing CMP had not been similarly amended to promote quality of care.[215] CMS noted that the Gainsharing CMP statute's current language could be (and has been) broadly interpreted to trigger CMP liability for hospitals that initiate reductions in care for patients based on objective quality metrics through an ACO.[216] To remedy this issue, the OIG proposed interpreting the Gainsharing CMP statute broadly enough to protect beneficiaries but narrowly enough to allow hospitals and other providers to participate in low risk programs that further the goal of delivering high quality of care at a lower cost (e.g., ACO quality programs) without triggering liability for them under the Gainsharing CMP.[217] In April of 2015, Congress modified the Gainsharing CMP in MACRA.[218] While the previous language prohibited hospitals from knowingly paying physicians to induce them to "reduce or limit services," the new language prohibits hospitals from knowingly paying physicians to induce them to "reduce or limit *medically necessary* services."[219]

213. OIG Special Advisory Bulletin, *Gainsharing Arrangements and CMPs for Hospital Payments to Physicians to Reduce or Limit Services to Beneficiaries* (July 1999), *available at* http://oig.hhs.gov/fraud/docs/alertsandbulletins/gainsh.htm; *but see* 79 Fed. Reg. 59717, 59729 (Oct. 3, 2014) (proposing a narrow interpretation of the Gainsharing CMP).
214. 79 Fed. Reg. 59717, 59729 (Oct. 3, 2014).
215. *Id.*
216. *Id.* at 59730.
217. *Id.*
218. Pub. L. 114-10.
219. 42 U.S.C. 1320a-7a(b)(1) as amended by Sec. 511 of H.R. 5, the Medicare Access and CHIP Reauthorization Act (April 16, 2015).

Although the Gainsharing CMP law applies only to Medicare or Medicaid beneficiaries, the OIG has viewed the law as prohibiting such payments even for commercially insured patients under the assumption that incenting changes in practice for commercial patients would likely also generate changes in practice for Medicare or Medicaid patients, or alternatively, that the payment incentives are substantial enough to incent changes for all patients, even though they are applied only to commercial payments.[220]

2. *The CMS, FTC, and OIG Workshop, and Subsequent Waivers of Applicability of the Anti-Kickback, Stark, and Gainsharing CMP Laws to MSSP ACOs*

At an October 5, 2010, workshop hosted by CMS, participants from the FTC, OIG, private sector, and government engaged in a discussion focused on the implications of the Anti-Kickback Statute, Stark, and Gainsharing CMP laws for ACOs, the scope of any proposed waivers of the Anti-Kickback, Stark and Gainsharing CMP laws for ACOs, and the different types of financial arrangements that may need waiver protection.[221] The participants did not reach a consensus on the form of any such waivers, safeguards, or future actions to encourage ACO innovation other than agreeing that guidance was needed and that the government faced various challenges in drafting the same.[222]

In April 2011, CMS and the OIG issued a proposal addressing how the application of the Anti-Kickback Statute, Stark, and Gainsharing CMP laws might be waived in the context of ACOs.[223] Following this proposal, an interim final rule was issued establishing waivers of certain provisions of Stark, the Anti-Kickback Statute, Gainsharing CMP, and other applicable laws.[224]

In the interim final rule, which applies to MSSP ACOs but not Pioneer ACOs, CMS and OIG established five separate waivers to the Anti-Kickback, Stark, and Gainsharing CMP laws, which ACOs can claim without prior approval from CMS or OIG as long as the ACO meets the waiver requirements.[225] On October 17, 2014, CMS and OIG published a joint notice extending the fraud and abuse waivers for ACOs participating in the MSSP and issued an extension to the timeline for publication

---

220. OIG Advisory Opinion No. 08-16, Oct. 7, 2008.

221. *See generally* OIG Transcript of Workshop, *available at* http://oig.hhs.gov/fraud/docs/workshop/10-5-10ACO-WorkshopAMSessionTranscript.pdf.

222. *Id.*

223. 76 Fed. Reg. 19655 (April 7, 2001).

224. 76 Fed. Reg. 67991 (Nov. 2, 2011).

225. 76 Fed. Reg. 68007.

of the interim final rule.[226] Typically, Medicare has a three-year timeline for publishing final rules after the publication of an interim final rule.[227] CMS extended the timeline for publication of the final rule addressing fraud and abuse waivers for MSSP ACOs through November 2, 2015,[228] and then, on February 17, 2015, CMS again extended the publication deadline by one year.[229] On October 29, 2015, CMS and OIG published the final rule, which includes waivers of certain fraud and abuse laws for specified ACO arrangements.[230]

Some of these waivers are discussed below:[231]

- **The pre-participation waiver.**[232] The ACO pre-participation waiver waives the Stark law and the Anti-Kickback Statue for ACO-related start-up arrangements in anticipation of participating in the MSSP. These start-up arrangements include infrastructure creation and provision; network development and management; care coordination mechanisms; clinical management systems; quality improvement mechanisms; creation of governance and management structure; care utilization management, including chronic disease, hospital readmissions, care protocols and patient education; creation of incentives for performance-based payment systems and the transition from FFS to shared risk; hiring of new staff; information technology; consultant and professional support; organization and staff training costs; primary care physician incentives; and capital investments. To qualify for the waiver, the ACO must meet five requirements, including:

  - The arrangement is undertaken by the party(ies) (excluding drug and device manufacturers, distributors, durable medical equipment suppliers, or home health suppliers) acting with the good faith intent to develop an ACO that will participate in the MSSP and to submit an application to participate in the MSSP for that year.

  - The parties must be taking diligent steps to develop an ACO that would be eligible for participation that would become effective during the target year, including meeting 42 C.F.R. §§ 425.106 and 108 concerning governance, leadership, and management.

---

226. 79 Fed. Reg. 62356 (Oct. 17, 2014).
227. *Id.*
228. *Id.*
229. 80 Fed. Reg. 8247 (Feb. 17, 2015)
230. 80 Fed. Reg. 66726 (Oct. 29. 2015)
231. 80 Fed. Reg. 66728.
232. 80 Fed. Reg. at 66742-66743.

- The governing body has made and duly authorized a bona fide determination that the arrangement is reasonably related to the purposes of the MSSP.

- The arrangement, the authorization, and the diligent steps to develop the ACO are contemporaneously documented, retained for 10 years following the arrangement, and include the following:

  - a description of the arrangement;[233]

  - the date and manner of the authorization, as well as the basis for the determination that the arrangement is reasonably related to the MSSP; and

  - the steps taken to develop the ACO, including their timing and manner.

- If an application for participation agreement is not submitted by the due date, the ACO must submit a statement describing the reason that is unable to do so.

The waiver period runs starting October 20, 2011, for a 2012 target date or, for later target dates, one year preceding an application due date, and ends on:

- the start date of the agreement;

- six months from the denial notice if the application is denied; or

- if the ACO fails to submit an application by the due date, on the earlier of the due date or the date the ACO submits reasons for failing to submit (in the latter case, the ACO may apply for an extension of the waiver).

- **ACO participation waiver.** [234] Similarly, Stark and the Anti-Kickback Statute are waived for any ACO meeting the following requirements: (1) the ACO enters a participation agreement and is in good standing; (2) the ACO meets the requirements of 42 C.F.R. §§ 425.106 and 108 regarding governance, leadership, and management; (3) the governing body has made a bona fide determination that the arrangement is reasonably related to the purposes of the MSSP; (4) the arrangement and the governing body's authorization are documented contemporaneously and

---

233. 80 Fed. Reg. at 66742 (the description must include all parties, the date, the purpose, the items, services, facilities, and/or goods covered, and the financial or economic terms—of the arrangement).

234. 80 Fed. Reg. at 66743.

retained for 10 years, including the same documentation described in the preceding paragraph, excluding the steps taken to develop the ACO; and (5) the arrangement is publicly disclosed as required by the HHS Secretary.

- **Shared savings distribution waiver.**[235] The shared saving distribution waiver, with respect to use or distribution of shared savings earned by an ACO, waives Stark and the Anti-Kickback Statute if the ACO meets five conditions. First, the ACO must enter a participation agreement and be in good standing. Second, the shared savings are earned pursuant to the MSSP. Third, the shared savings are earned during the course of the participation agreement even if distribution or use occurs after the agreement expires. Forth, the shared savings are distributed during the year in which they were earned or used for activities that are reasonably related to the purposes of the MSSP. Finally, payments of the shared savings made from a hospital to a physician are not made knowingly to induce the physician to reduce or limit medically necessary items or services to patients under the direct care of the physician.

- **Compliance with the Stark law waiver**.[236] The waiver for compliance with the Stark law waives the Anti-Kickback Statute for any financial relationship by or among the ACO and its participants if: (1) the ACO has entered a participation agreement and remains in good standing; (2) the financial relationship is reasonably related to the purposes of the MSSP; and (3) the financial relationship fully complies with a Stark exception.[237] To put the Stark law waiver another way, if the relationship satisfies (1) and (2), and also fits into a Stark law exception, then the relationship not only satisfies the Stark law, but the Anti-Kickback Statute also does not apply to the relationship. The application of the Stark law waiver commences on the start date of the participation agreement and ends on the earlier of the expiration of the term of the participation agreement or the date on which the participation agreement is terminated.

- **Waiver for patient incentives**.[238] The fifth waiver, the waiver for patient incentives, waives the Anti-Kickback Statute for items or services provided by the ACO or its participants to beneficiaries for free or below fair market value if:

---

235. *Id.*
236. *Id.*
237. *Id.*
238. *Id.*

- the ACO has entered into a participation agreement and is in good standing;
- there is a reasonable connection between the items or services and the medical care of the beneficiary;
- the items or services are in-kind;
- the items or services are either preventive care or advance one or more of the following clinical goals:
  - adherence to treatment regime;
  - adherence to a drug regime;
  - adherence to a follow-up care plan; and
  - management of a chronic disease or condition.[239]

This waiver runs from the start date of the participation agreement to the earlier of the expiration or termination of the agreement, although the beneficiary may keep items received before expiration or termination and receive the remainder of any service initiated before expiration or termination.[240]

Of note, when the agencies (CMS and OIG) finalized the waivers for ACOs participating in the MSSP, they made a significant change. Previously, in the interim final rule, the agencies had provided waivers for the application of the Gainsharing CMP law.[241] In the final rule, the agencies reasoned that, because the Gainsharing CMP was amended by MACRA on April 16, 2015, to prohibit hospitals from knowingly paying physicians to induce them to reduce or limit *medically necessary* services, the Gainsharing CMP no longer needed to be waived to carry out the MSSP.[242] The agencies asserted that arrangements between hospitals and physicians that incentivize greater efficiency and reduction of waste, which previously may have run afoul of the Gainsharing CMP, would no longer implicate the provision, provided those arrangements do not involve reductions or limitations in medically necessary care.[243]

Additionally, in the final rule, the agencies made clear that an ACO's governing body's documentation of its authorization must provide the

---

239. *Id.*

240. *Id.*

241. *See* 76 Fed. Reg. 67993. The Gainsharing CMP appears at 1128(b)(1) and (2) of the Act.

242. Pub. L. 114-10.

243. 80 Fed. Reg. 66729-66730.

basis for the determination that an arrangement is reasonably related to the purposes of the MSSP.[244]

C. The Anti-Kickback Safe Harbors and Stark Exceptions

Effective January 19, 2021, the OIG and CMS promulgated new regulations intended to provide providers with greater flexibility to effectuate value based activities. These new Anti-Kickback safe harbors and Stark exceptions give providers more certainty when entering into certain provider arrangements meant to support the ACO's activities. In releasing the new regulations, the agencies stated "The Department identified the broad reach of the physician self-referral law, as well as the Federal anti-kickback statute and beneficiary inducements civil monetary penalty (CMP) law, sections 1128B(b) and 1128A(a)(5) of the Act, respectively, as potentially inhibiting beneficial arrangements that would advance the transition to value-based care and the coordination of care among providers in both the Federal and commercial sectors....To address these concerns, and to help accelerate the transformation of the health care system into one that better pays for value and promotes care coordination, HHS launched a Regulatory Sprint to Coordinated Care (the Regulatory Sprint), led by the Deputy Secretary of HHS."[245]

The new Stark and Anti-Kickback regulations both utilize these common terms and definitions:[246]

Target patient population—an identified patient population selected by a value-based enterprise (VBE) or its VBE participants based on legitimate and verifiable criteria that (1) are set out in writing in advance of the commencement of the value-based arrangement; and (2) further the VBE's value-based purpose(s).

Value-based activity—any of the following activities, provided that the activity is reasonably designed to achieve at least one value-based purpose of the VBE: (1) the provision of an item or service; (2) the taking of an action; or (3) the refraining from taking an action.

Value-based arrangement—an arrangement for the provision of at least one value-based activity for a target patient population to which

---

244. 80 Fed. Reg. 66727. In condition 4 of the pre-participation and participation waivers, as modified in the final rule, the agencies changed "should" to "must" consistent with their view that the ACO governing body's documentation of its authorization must provide the basis for the determination that an arrangement is reasonably related to the purposes of the MSSP.
245. 85 Fed. Reg. 77493 (Dec. 2. 2020).
246. 42 C.F.R. § 411.351 and 42 C.F.R. § 1001.952(ee).

the only parties are: (1) the value-based enterprise and one or more of its VBE participants; or (2) VBE participants in the same VBE.

Value-based enterprise (VBE) —two or more VBE participants—(1) collaborating to achieve at least one value-based purpose; (2) each of which is a party to a value-based arrangement with the other or at least one other VBE participant in the VBE; (3) that have an accountable body or person responsible for the financial and operational oversight of the VBE; and (4) that have a governing document that describes the VBE and how the VBE participants intend to achieve its value-based purpose(s).

Value-based purpose—any of the following: (1) coordinating and managing the care of a target patient population; (2) improving the quality of care for a target patient population; (3) appropriately reducing the costs to or growth in expenditures of payors without reducing the quality of care for a target patient population; or (4) transitioning from health care delivery and payment mechanisms based on the volume of items and services provided to mechanisms based on the quality of care and control of costs of care for a target patient population.

VBE participant—a person or entity that engages in at least one value-based activity as part of a VBE.

The new value-based exceptions under Stark and Anti-Kickback laws have many commonalities. They both anticipate that there will be varying types of risk arrangements and exceptions—full financial risk, substantial risk and general care coordination. For all of the value-based exceptions:

- The remuneration is for, or results from, value-based (VB) activities undertaken by the recipient of the remuneration for patients in the target patient population.

- The remuneration is not an inducement to reduce or limit medically necessary items or services to any patient.

- The remuneration is not conditioned on referrals of patients who are not part of the target patient population or business not covered under the VB arrangement.

- If the remuneration paid to the physician is conditioned on the physician's referrals to a particular provider, practitioner, or supplier, the VB arrangement must comply with both of the following conditions:

- The requirement is set out in writing and signed by the parties

- The requirement does not apply if the patient expresses a preference for a different provider, practitioner, or supplier; the patient's insurer determines the provider, practitioner, or supplier; or the referral is not in the patient's best medical interests in the physician's judgment

- Records of the methodology for determining and the actual amount of remuneration paid under the VB arrangement must be maintained for a period of at least six years and made available to the Secretary upon request.

Under the new provisions, the subject VBE is at full financial risk when the enterprise is financially responsible on a prospective basis for the cost of all patient care items and services covered by the applicable payor for each patient in the target patient population for a specified period of time.[247]

The subject VBE is at meaningful downside risk if the physician is responsible to repay or forgo no less than 10 percent of the total value of the remuneration the physician receives from the entity under the VB arrangement during the duration of the VB arrangement.[248]

For all VB arrangements, the arrangement must be set forth in writing and signed by the parties.[249] The writing must include a description of

- the VB activities to be undertaken under the arrangement;
- how the VB activities are expected to further the VB purpose(s) of the VBE;
- the target patient population for the arrangement;
- the type or nature of the remuneration;
- the methodology used to determine the remuneration; and
- the outcome measures against which the recipient of the remuneration is assessed, if any.

The outcome measures against which the recipient of the remuneration is assessed, if any, are objective, measurable, and selected based on clinical evidence or credible medical support.

The VB entities are also given an opportunity to modify the outcome measures, if after a performance year, the VB entity determines that the methodology is not achieving the purposes of the VB arrangement.[250]

---

247. 42 C.F.R. § 411.357 (aa)(1) and 42 C.F.R. § 1001.952(gg).
248. 42 C.F.R. § 411.357 (aa)(2) and 42 C.F.R. § 1001.952(ff).
249. 42 C.F.R. § 411.357 (aa) and 42 C.F.R. § 1001.952(ee).
250. *Id.*

These new safe harbors and exceptions give some additional guidance and assurances for those designing VB arrangements. When addressing the similarities between the principles in the new rules and the ACO waivers, the drafters state "We agree that thivalue-based purpose shares certain aspects of the pre-participation waiver under the Shared Savings Program. In our discussion of the Shared Savings Program pre-participation waiver in our October 29, 2015, Shared Savings Program Final Waivers in Connection with the Shared Savings Program Final Rule (80 FR 66726) (the SSP waivers final rule), we provided examples of start-up arrangements as guideposts for determining whether a particular arrangement may qualify for protection under the pre-participation waiver (80 FR 66733). We believe those examples, to the extent they create a compensation relationship for purposes of the physician self-referral law, may be illustrative for purposes of interpreting the scope of "transitioning from health care delivery and payment mechanisms based on the volume of items and services provided to mechanisms based on the quality of care and control of costs of care for a target patient population."" This statement suggests that it will be helpful when utilizing the value based exceptions to also consult the commentary related to the ACO waivers.[251]

D. Tax-Exempt Status

Tax issues can creep into play for the ACO entity as well as its participants. Should the ACO be a taxable for-profit entity, a taxable nonprofit entity, or a 501(c)(3)?

For tax-exempt entities participating in an ACO, capital contributions can raise issues under the Internal Revenue Code (Code), including private inurement/private benefit issues, excess benefit transaction concerns, and unrelated business income tax liability. The Internal Revenue Service (IRS) suggested that economic benefits and burdens for tax-exempt entities participating in ACOs should be proportionate to their investment, and all related transactions should be at fair market value.[252]

On April 18, 2011, the IRS issued a notice summarizing how the IRS expects existing IRS guidance to apply to 501(c)(3) tax-exempt organizations participating in the MSSP via ACOs.[253] Notice 2011-20 was based on

---

251. 85 Fed. Reg. 77503.

252. IRS Fact Sheet, FS-2011-11, Tax-Exempt Organizations Participating in the Medicare Shared Savings Program through Accountable Care Organizations (Oct. 20, 2011), *available at* http://www.irs.gov/pub/irs-news/fs-2011-11.pdf.

253. Notice 2011-20, *Private Business Use of Tax-Exempt Bond Financing* (April 18, 2011), *available at* http://www.irs.gov/pub/irs-drop/n-11-20.pdf.

proposed regulations issued by CMS on March 31, 2011.[254] The IRS
followed that notice with a fact sheet issued in October 2011 confirming
that the notice continues to reflect IRS expectations regarding the MSSP
and ACOs.[255] From IRS guidance, ACO participants with tax-exempt status
can glean the following:

- An ACO structured as a corporation for federal tax purposes
  generally will be treated as a separate taxable entity from its
  participants.[256]

- A 501(c)(3) organization can participate in the MSSP through an
  ACO as long as it continues to meet the requirements as a tax-
  exempt organization, including that its participation must not
  result in either (1) its net earnings inuring to the benefit of private
  shareholders or individuals, or (2) it being operated for the benefit
  of private parties participating in the ACO.

- IRS Notice 2011-20 described five factors to avoid inurement or
  impermissible private benefit, which are mirrored in IRS Notice
  2014-67 cited below. It clarified that failure to satisfy all five
  factors does not necessarily result in inurement or impermissible
  private benefit but rather depends on all the facts and circumstances. The five factors are as follows: (1) the terms of the tax-
  exempt organization's participation in the MSSP through the
  ACO (including its share of shared savings or losses and expenses) are set forth in advance in a written agreement negotiated
  at arm's length;[257] (2) CMS has accepted the ACO into, and has
  not terminated the ACO from, the MSSP;[258] (3) the tax-exempt
  organization's share of economic benefits derived from the ACO
  (including its share of MSSP payments) is proportional to the
  benefits or contributions the tax-exempt organization provides to
  the ACO (if the tax-exempt organization receives an ownership
  interest in the ACO, the ownership interest received is proportional and equal in value to its capital contributions to the ACO
  and all ACO returns of capital, allocations and distributions are

254. 76 Fed. Reg. 19528 (March 31, 2011).
255. *Supra* note 181.
256. *Moline Properties, Inc. v. Commissioner*, 319 U.S.436 (1943).
257. FS-2011-11 clarified that the written agreement does not need to specify the
organization's precise share or exact amount of any shared savings payments received from the
ACO as long as the written agreement sets forth the *methodology* for determining an ACO's
allocation of shared savings payments.
258. FS-2011-11 clarified that termination of an ACO from the MSSP would not automatically jeopardize the status of a tax-exempt participant but rather it would depend on all the facts
and circumstances, such as whether the ACO's activities after termination further a charitable
purpose and whether the ACO's activities are attributed to the taxexempt participant.

made in proportion to ownership interests);[259] (4) the tax-exempt organization's share of the ACO's losses (including its share of shared losses) does not exceed the share of ACO economic benefits to which the tax-exempt organization is entitled; and (5) all contracts and transactions entered into by the tax-exempt organization with the ACO and the ACO's participants, and by the ACO with the ACO's participants and any other parties, are at fair market value.

- An ACO's conduct or activities that do not further a charitable purpose will not jeopardize the tax-exempt status of one of its participants if the ACO's activities are not attributed to that participant. On the other hand, the presence of a single, nonexempt purpose, if substantial in nature, may jeopardize a participant's tax-exempt status.[260]

- The tax-exempt entity does not have to have control over the ACO to ensure that the ACO's participation furthers a charitable purpose since CMS's regulation and oversight of the ACO will be sufficient to ensure that the ACO's participation in the MSSP furthers the charitable purpose of lessening the burdens of government.

- For MSSP payments, the IRS expects that, absent inurement or impermissible private benefit, any shared savings payments would derive from activities that are substantially related to the performance of the charitable purpose of lessening the burdens of government. For non-MSSP activities, in some circumstances, such activities may not jeopardize tax-exempt status, so long as they: (1) further an exempt purpose described in § 501(c)(3) (charitable purpose); (2) are attributed to the tax-exempt participant; (3) represent an insubstantial part of the participant's total activities; and (4) do not result in inurement of the tax-exempt participant's net earnings or in the participant conferring an impermissible private benefit. For example, an ACO's activities

---

259. FS-2011-11 clarified that ownership interests in the ACO do not have to be directly proportional to capital contribution and, similarly, the ACO does not always have to distribute shared savings payments in proportion to such ownership interests. Rather, the IRS will examine whether, in the totality of circumstances, the tax-exempt participant's share of economic benefits derived from the ACO (including its share of shared savings payments) is proportional to the benefits or contributions the tax-exempt participant provides to the ACO. This factor takes into account all contributions made by the charitable organization and other ACO participants to the ACO, in whatever form (cash, property, services), and all economic benefits received by ACO participants (including shares of shared savings payments and any ownership interests).

260. Better Business Bureau of Washington, D.C. v. United States, 326 U.S. 279 (1945).

related to serving Medicaid or indigent populations might further the charitable purpose of relieving the poor and distressed or the underprivileged.

- A 501(c)(3) entity's participation in an ACO and any MSSP payments to the entity will not generally be subjected to unrelated business income tax (UBI). Generally, non-MSSP activities that are substantially related to a tax-exempt participant's charitable purposes will not generate UBI for that participant. Whether an ACO's activities that are not substantially related to a charitable purpose will generate UBI for its tax-exempt participants will depend on a variety of factors. For example, certain kinds of income from the ACO, including dividends and interest, may be excluded from UBI under one of the modifications described in § 512(b) of the Code.

On October 24, 2014, the IRS issued Notice 2014-67 as additional guidance specifying the conditions a 501(c)(3) organization, which is participating in the MSSP through an ACO, would need to meet in order to avoid causing private business use of its tax-exempt bond financing.[261] IRS Notice 2014-67 also provided notice of two ACO-related modifications to Rev. Proc. 97-13 with respect to a new safe harbor for management contracts and the introduction of a tiered productivity award.[262]

E. State Insurance Laws

Not unlike the issues associated with PHOs and other managed care entities in the 1990s, ACOs may involve state insurance laws and their requirements as a result of the ACO's shared financial risk.[263] This analysis would occur on a state-by-state basis, and federal law could preempt state law.

IV. Practical issues

The ACA gives the participants great discretion in the formation and operation of their ACO, which has benefits and challenges on a practical front.

A. Who Are Members?

Group practices, IPAs or other networks of individual practitioners, and additional groups defined by HHS can participate as certain types of ACOs

---

261. IRS Notice 2014-67 (Oct. 24, 2014), *available at:* http://www.irs.gov/pub/irs-drop/n-14-67.pdf.

262. *Id.*

263. Robert Feightner, *State Regulation of Capitated Reimbursement for Physician-Hospital Organizations,* 7 HEALTH MATRIX 301 (1997) (generally discussing the legal issues with PHOs accepting capitation payments and implication of insurance regulations).

if properly structured. Although the ACA also permits hospitals to form ACOs, and many ACOs are hospital-driven, an ACO need not include a hospital. Yet, because the stated goal for ACOs is to deliver coordinated and efficient care, a hospital is often viewed as a critical component for an ACO. This fact, however, does not preclude physician-only or physician-driven ACOs. According to the first national survey of ACOs conducted from October 2012 to May 2013, at that time, 51 percent of ACOs were headed by physicians; 33 percent were jointly led by physicians and hospitals; 3 percent were led by hospitals alone; and the remaining 13 percent were led by other entities.[264] Further, data indicates that physician-led ACOs have been more successful in achieving results than their hospital counterparts due, in part, to physician-led ACOs' understanding of the importance of filtering all patient interactions through the patient's primary care doctor[265] and to their work to save money by keeping patients out of the hospital versus trying to manage the patient's care once admitted.[266] Regardless of the ACO's structure, physician leadership and participation are keys to an ACO's success since physician decisions contribute greatly to healthcare utilization and cost. Therefore, physician participation is critical to achieve shared savings.

ACO organizers may make membership decisions based on existing structures, networks, and resources in their community. In addition to physician/hospital constituency decisions, organizers should consider the primary care/specialty care physician balance. Primary care physicians clearly play a central role in coordinating care delivery in ACOs.[267] Therefore, these physicians are well-served to take a leadership role in the ACO to ensure their vantage points are incorporated into the ACO's organization and management. Specialists, on the other hand, are not required to be part of an ACO but will continue to play an important role in the coordinated care of assigned patients. Each ACO will need to determine the role for specialists—whether more integrally involved in the coordinated care[268] or, hearkening to managed care days, as argued by

---

264. Megan Brooks, *Physicians Blazing the ACO Trail*, MEDSCAPE MEDICAL NEWS (June 6, 2014), *available at* http://www.medscape.com/viewarticle/826355.

265. See Marty Stempniak, What Physician-Led ACOs Can Teach Hospitals, H&HN (Nov, 11, 2014)

266. *See* 79 Fed. Reg. 59717, 59729 (Oct. 3, 2014).

267. *See* Harold D., Miller, *How to Create Accountable Care Organizations*, CENTER FOR HEALTHCARE QUALITY AND REFORM, p. 5 (Sept, 7, 2009), *available at* www.chqpr.org/downloads/HowtoCreateAccountableCareOrganizations.pdf (recognizing that the "mechanisms to reducing and slowing healthcare expenditures are prevention early diagnosis, chronic disease management, and other tools—tools which are delivered primarily through primary care.").

268. *Accountable Care Organizations: Principles;* American Medical Group Association (May 28, 2010).

some, as a resource to be rationed.[269] All of these decisions will need to be evaluated continually as CMS continues to propose, evaluate, and adopt changes to the requirements related to the leadership, management, and governance structure of ACOs.[270]

B. What Does the Structure Look Like?

Not only in its membership but also in its structure, an ACO is not a one-size-fits-all proposition; the entity's structure must account for the particular community dynamic, resources, and needs. While the ACA requires ACOs to have a formal legal structure in order to participate in the MSSP,[271] the ideal legal structure depends on many factors, including the ACO's goals, the quantity and quality of available participants, cultural differences of participants, and financial resources.[272] For example, in some communities, provider organizations (such as medical groups, IPAs, and PHOs) already exist and have adapted into an ACO context.[273] Others have used existing medical staffs and/or employed physicians to build an ACO. Each ACO will include different participants to meet the goals, needs, and culture of its beneficiaries and communities.

Part of the beauty of the ACA's ACO provisions is that each ACO has great flexibility in establishing its structure. This flexibility gives participants and interested parties the ability to develop models that meet their particular needs, creating a greater likelihood of success. Potential participants and organizers should avail themselves of this flexibility and take the opportunity to assess specific needs, as well as the governance and tax ramifications, that best fit the mission and strategic plan of the ACO.[274]

As a general proposition, five different ACO models have been described: the multi-specialty group practice model; the hospital medical staff organization; the PHO; the interdependent practice organization; and the

---

269. *Id.*

270. *See* 79 Fed. Reg. at 72777 and 80 Fed. Reg. 32692 (June 9, 2015).

271. ACA.

272. *See* 79 Fed. Reg. at 72774-72778 (Proposed Rule to MSSP proposes to modify the legal entity and governance structure requirements for MSSP ACOs to ensure that ACO decision-making is controlled by individuals whose fiduciary duties are exclusively to the ACO and not any particular ACO participant or other person).

273. Kelly Devers & Robert Berenson, *Can Accountable Care Organizations Improve the Value of Health Care by Solving the Cost and Quality Quandaries?* (Urban Institute, October 2009), *available at* https://www.urban.org/sites/default/files/publication/30721/411975-Can-Accountable-Care-Organizations-Improve-the-Value-of-Health-Care-by-Solving-the-Cost-and-Quality-Quandaries-.PDF.

274. *Id.*

health plan-provider organization.[275] The multi-specialty group practice model consists of a multi-specialty group with contractual or other relationships with hospitals and health plans.[276] Examples of these models would include the Mayo, the Marshfield, and the Palo Alto Medical Clinics to name only a few.[277] Perhaps due to its ability to deliver coordinated care to a defined group of patients, greater resources, and economies of scale, this model has advantages in caring for patients and episodes of illness over time, particularly in a bundled payment or capitated arrangement.[278] However, its weaknesses may include size, bureaucracy, expense, and specialists/primary care dissent.[279]

Hospital medical staff organizations (often referred to as the extended medical staff ACO model) utilize a hospital or health system's medical staff as the accountable physician component of the ACO, which gives the potential to manage chronic illnesses and acute episodes of hospitalizations.[280] Downsides to this model include the potential history of medical staff/hospital tension, gainsharing concerns, and the absence of financial incentives for physicians and hospitals to work together, as reflected in current payment mechanisms.[281]

The PHO model can utilize existing PHOs put together in the United States, mostly in the 1990s. This model may offer the benefit of using an existing PHO structure and the possibility to manage care across the continuum of delivery.[282] However, it does not necessarily involve all physicians on the medical staff; but rather, those that want to, or the hospital chooses to have, participate—which may help control costs but may also lead to dissention among the medical staff, including potential challenges under state "any willing provider" and antitrust laws.

The IPA model offers a possible structure for physicians who practice in smaller or more independent practices.[283] Like an IPA, this model allows loosely organized collections of relatively small physician practices with strong leadership and governance and ample patient volume to establish an ACO. However, the looser affiliation may create antitrust challenges and/or make it difficult for the organization to achieve shared savings from coordinated care.

---

275. *Supra* note 3.
276. *Id.*
277. *Id.*
278. *Id.*
279. *Id.*
280. *Id.*
281. *Id.*
282. *Id.*
283. *Id.*

Last of all, the health plan-provider organization is a partnership between a health plan and a physician practice that gives greater access to disease management technologies, electronic technology, and financial resources. Kaiser-Permanente and Intermountain Health Plan are two well-known examples.[284] However, this model is limited by the significant distrust that permeates most health plan-physician relationships.

These examples are just a few that we have seen as participants adapt structures to meet their specific needs.

C. Who Controls/Leads?

Another important issue for an ACO is who will provide leadership for the organization. The ACA requires that ACOs have a leadership and management structure for their clinical and administrative functions.[285] CMS finalized modifications to the legal entity and governance structure requirements for MSSP ACOs to ensure that the ACO decision-making is controlled by individuals who owe fiduciary duties to the ACO exclusively and not to any particular ACO participant, other persons, or nonparticipants.[286] The ACO's operations must be managed by an executive, officer, manager, general partner, or similar party whose appointment and removal are under the control of the ACO's governing body.[287] Further, MSSP ACOs must have an identifiable governing body with the ultimate authority to execute the functions of an ACO and satisfy three criteria: (1) the ACO's governing body must be the same as the governing body of the legal entity that is the ACO, (2) if the ACO comprises multiple ACO participants, the governing body must be separate and unique to the ACO (not the governing body of any ACO participant), and (3) the governing body must satisfy all requirements at 42 C.F.R. § 425.106, including its fiduciary duty of loyalty to participants.[288] Per CMS commentary, these revisions were designed to prevent an ACO from delegating its decision-making authority to a committee of the governing body or assigning it up the chain to a parent company.[289]

With these requirements in mind, the ACO leadership will have to be culled from and work with the often-present, strained dynamic between physicians and hospitals. This interdependent relationship may be

---

284. *Id.*

285. ACA at § 3022.

286. *See* CMS finalizes rules for Medicare Shared Savings Program, *available at* https://www.cms.gov/newsroom/press-releases/cms-finalizes-rules-medicare-shared-savings-program.

287. 42 C.F.R. § 425.108.

288. *See* 80 Fed. Reg. 32716.

289. *Id.*

summed up best by the Kaiser Institute's description: "From the hospital's perspective, physicians exist to work with the hospital to achieve its goals. In contrast, from the physician's perspective, the hospital exists to help the physicians meet the goals for their patients and advance the physician's professional practice."[290] This issue can be difficult to resolve against a backdrop of mistrust and battles over control. Regardless, because one of the major goals of any ACO is accountability of clinical care, physicians *must* take, and hospitals, if involved, *must* offer physicians a leadership role and active participation in the development and operation of the ACO. Hospitals contemplating ACOs should not get too far down the path of development without physician involvement and participation in the planning process. Nor should physicians wait for an invitation from the hospital to get involved. They need to be thinking about opportunities for their practices, how their practice might work in an ACO context, and where they might be best positioned in the changing healthcare market.

Participants in the ACO must have "meaningful" participation, defined as accounting for 75 percent of the governing body,[291] and at least one Medicare beneficiary on the governing board (or an alternate means of ensuring meaningful participation by Medicare beneficiaries).[292] The percentage requirement reflects CMS's belief that the ACO should be operated and directed by Medicare-enrolled entities that directly provide healthcare services to beneficiaries, while at the same time acknowledging that providers often lack the capital and infrastructure to form and run the ACO and could benefit from partnerships with non-Medicare enrolled entities. In an effort to encourage flexibility in the ACO governing body, the final rule eliminated the 75 percent threshold and the requirement of the proposed rule that each participant must choose a representative within the ACO to represent it on the governing body. Instead, MSSP ACOs with governing bodies that fail these requirements may describe, in their application, how their proposed structure would involve ACO participants in innovative ways in ACO governance or provide meaningful opportunities for beneficiaries to participate in ACO governance to seek a waiver of either requirement.[293] CMS noted such modification was required to account for state-specific regulatory issues, such as corporate practice of medicine doctrines.

---

290. Francis J. Crosson, & Laura A. Tollen, Partners In Health: How Physicians and Hospitals Can Be Accountable Together, ch. 3, p. 50 (Kaiser Institute, 2010).

291. *But see supra* note 218 (proposed rule includes the proposal to eliminate the current exception to the general requirement that at least 75% control of the governing body must be vested in ACO participants).

292. 76 Fed. Reg. 67802.

293. 80 Fed. Reg. 32719.

The beneficiary involvement in the governing body is directly reflective of CMS's interest in involving beneficiaries in the ACO.[294] To avoid a conflict of interest and to ensure a "genuine voice" in ACO governance, CMS required that such beneficiaries may not have a conflict of interest and cannot be an ACO provider/supplier.[295]

Although leadership and control decisions will also be unique to each situation, generally, shared governance is critical to building a successful integrated system. Generally, a governing board should (1) be able to provide diversity of experience and opinions, (2) require individual responsibility and interactive discussions, and (3) allow for efficient decision-making. To the extent that both hospitals and physicians are to participate in the governance of the ACO entity, the board should reflect a balanced constituency of participating provider groups and hospital(s).

For those situations in which trust is a potential obstacle to collaboration and the ACO's success, strong physician leadership represented as a majority will be necessary to establish the trust necessary to promote and achieve the ACO's collaborative efforts. ACO leadership must recognize the importance of understanding all ACO constituents' needs and reconciling conflicting interests. The ACO's long-term success is dependent upon collaboration among its participants to achieve its goals.

Finally, leadership, and particularly physician leadership, is a critical issue for ACOs, given their goal of accountability of care. In order to recognize this goal, the ACOs will be focused on developing clinical protocols and guidelines, gathering clinical data, establishing clinical performance indicators and measures, and building reporting mechanisms, all of which will require strong physician participation and leaders. Rather than allowing a few physicians to drive these efforts, the ACO should educate and vest as many participating physicians as feasible with an ownership interest in these deliverables to ensure the future success of the organization.

D. Size

An ACO will need to determine its optimal size and scope. An ACO must have the scale required by the ACA (e.g., the ACO must have a sufficient number of primary care physicians sufficient to treat at least 5,000 Medicare beneficiaries). In addition, ACO size may be dictated by the need to support the administrative and technological infrastructure to satisfy federal ACO performance requirements. The ACO will need to develop protocols, collect quality reporting information, establish mechanisms to

---

294. *See supra* note 218 (proposed rule includes provision to prohibit an ACO provider/supplier from being the required Medicare beneficiary on the ACO governing board).
295. *Id.*

monitor and coordinate utilization and ensure quality and efficiency of care, work with payers, and incentivize providers.[296]

V.   Viability

Not surprisingly, in light of these financial incentives for achieving quality measures, many industry players have recognized that quality is difficult, if not impossible, to achieve without involving all relevant healthcare providers. The result has been a number of collaborative activities between physicians and other providers, usually hospitals. Arguably, ACOs naturally lend themselves to physician-centric organizations since physicians' decisions regarding healthcare resource allocation make up a major portion of healthcare costs and, thus, carry the greatest potential for cost savings in the delivery of healthcare. To date, many of the ACOs in existence or underway are hospital-driven, generally due to capital, financial, organizational, and personnel reasons and a desire by hospitals to retain control over ACOs and their efforts to reduce the costs of inpatient care services via wellness and other preventative care measures.

This latter factor offers great potential for physicians to take the initiative and lead in these organizations.

Critics have made a number of arguments against the long-term viability of ACOs, which arguably have been supported by the quality and financial performance results for the Pioneer ACOs. Critics argue that previous managed care attempts failed miserably because they were poorly executed and employers and patients preferred open panels managed by health insurers rather than closed panels managed by providers.[297] However, these arguments ignore the fact that the ACA's ACO concept involves a shared savings model that does not restrict patient choice or require providers to take financial risks. Others argue that the dynamic between hospitals and physicians will not be adequately incented by the shared savings payment model, particularly in which both parties often benefit from maximizing the volume of services they provide and, therefore, the revenue they receive.[298] Additionally, what incentive do the hospitals have to participate when an ultimately successful ACO will keep patients out of the hospital, meaning less charges and revenues for the hospital?[299] Regardless of the strength of these arguments,

---

296. ACA at § 3022.

297. Jeff Goldsmith, *The Accountable Care Organization: Not Ready for Prime Time*, HEALTH AFFAIR BLOG, Aug. 17, 2009, *available at* http://healthaffairs.org/blog/2009/08/17/the-accountable-care-organization-not-ready-for-prime-time/.

298. Marsha Gold, *Accountable Care Organizations: Will They Deliver?*, Mathematical Policy Research, Inc. MCPP Healthcare Consulting (January 2010), *available at* https://www.mathematica-mpr.com/our-publications-and-findings/publications/accountable-care-organizations-will-they-deliver.

299. Joe Carlson, *ACOs: A mystery of biblical proportion*, MODERN HEALTHCARE (Aug. 9, 2010), *available at* www.modernhealthcare.com/article/20100809/NEWS/308099959#.

physicians certainly need to be well-positioned for future markets; and, as the proliferation of physician-driven ACOs increases, physicians may want to consider joining such organizations.

Additional challenges include issues of control, money, and time investment. Understandably, many physicians are concerned with hospital integration efforts (in the form of practice acquisition and employment) as a means to exert control over physician practices. While the possibility (and reality) of this abuse certainly exists, many hospitals are merely taking the time to position themselves in the marketplace, which has resulted in them taking the lead on the integration front. Physicians can avoid being supplanted in this process if they get involved in the ACO leadership early on and if both parties recognize the need for a collaborative effort.[300] We cannot overemphasize the need to prepare against issues of control, money, and termination disputes through careful drafting of the ACO documents.

The significant financial investment required for an ACO's formation and operation requires deep pockets, significantly more so than is usually available to physician participants, which also explains why it has been more common to see hospitals taking the lead on the ACO front. For example, health information technology is critical to an ACO's success to enable it to accurately report data to CMS. A challenge faced by ACOs is coordinating and managing quality reporting across participants with independent and disparate EHR systems.[301] To a certain degree, CMS has responded to concerns regarding issues of limited access to capital and other resources to fund shared savings activities for small practices through development of, for example, the ACO APM and the ACO Investment Model.[302]

Of equal importance is the time commitment that formation and operation of an ACO will require of its participants. On the clinical side alone, the decision-making, analysis of current systems, and development of protocols, guidelines, and processes, will require a substantial commitment of resources and time. In an environment where time is money and physicians are compensated for medical services they deliver, they may be reluctant to sacrifice this patient care time to work on an ACO. However, despite these challenges, many physician practices have successfully formed and are currently successfully operating their own ACOs.[303] For

---

300. *See* Robert Kocher M.D. & Nikhil Sahni, R. B.S., *Physicians versus Hospitals as Leaders of Accountable Care Organizations*, NEW ENGLAND J OF MED—HEALTH POLICY AND REFORM (Nov. 10, 2010), *available at* http://www.nejm.org/doi/full/10.1056/NEJMp1011712?viewType=Print (for a discussion on physician-controlled ACOs).

301. Amy Fehn, The Importance of Health Information Technology for Accountable Care Organizations, ABA HEALTH ESOURCE (June 2011), *available at* https://www.wachler.com/the-importance-of-health-information-technology-for-accountable.html

302. *See* CMMI Innovation Model information, *available at* http://innovation.cms.gov/initiatives/index.html#views=models.

303. *Supra* note 234.

example, performance data from 2019 suggests that low-revenue ACOs, which are generally led by physicians, generally perform better than high-revenue ACOs, which are generally led by hospitals.[304] Thus, physicians are capable of successfully leading and forming ACOs to achieve better quality of care for their patients and benefit from the resulting cost-savings.

A. Viability of ACOs under MACRA

On October 14, 2016, CMS released a final rule with 60-day comment period to implement the bipartisan MACRA, a new payment system designed to replace the oft-maligned Sustainable Growth Rate formula.[305] The new payment system emphasizes quality, care coordination, and operational efficiency in line with CMS's announced intent to migrate away from the traditional FFS payment system toward a system that incentivizes and rewards quality patient outcomes over the volume of services rendered.[306] The MACRA final rule replaces the multitude of existing Medicare reporting systems with a single Quality Payment Program consisting of two potential tracks for providers to elect: (i) the Merit-based Incentive Payment System (MIPS) and (ii) the Advanced Alternative Payment Models (Advanced APM).[307] Importantly, the rule applies to Medicare Part B payments for professional services that are furnished by the vast majority of all physicians and other individual practitioners who furnish services under Medicare.[308]

Under MACRA, clinicians and groups who participate in an ACO may be able to participate as an Advanced APM.[309] The final rule identifies several ACO arrangements that qualify for this pathway, including Track 2 and Track 3 MSSP ACOs, the CEC Model (LDO and non-LDO Tracks), and Next Generation ACO Models.[310] Notably, this list does not include Track 1 MSSP ACOs because providers do not bear sufficient financial risk. Starting in 2019, providers who participate in an approved ACO may be classified as a Qualified APM Participant (QP).[311] Those entities designated as QPs will be

---

304. https://www.healthaffairs.org/do/10.1377/hblog20200914.598838/full/.

305. HHS, Press Release, *HHS Finalizes Streamlines Medicare Payment System that Rewards Clinicians for Quality Patient Care* (Oct. 14, 2016), *available at* https://wayback.archive-it.org/3926/20170127192642/https://www.hhs.gov/about/news/2016/10/14/hhs-finalizes-streamlined-medicare-payment-system-rewards-clinicians-quality-patient-care.html.

306. 81 Fed. Reg. 77008 (Oct. 14, 2016).

307. *Id.*

308. *Id.*

309. *Id.*

310. *Id.* at 77013.

311. *Id.*

exempted from MIPS and will receive an additional 5 percent Medicare Part B incentive payment.[312] Additionally, clinicians participating in Advanced APMs will also receive 0.75 percent annual fee schedule updates beginning in 2026.[313] However, simply participating in an Advanced APM does not guarantee classification as a QP.[314] To qualify, Advanced APMs must (i) require participants to bear a more than a nominal amount of risk; (ii) base payments on quality measures comparable to those used under the MIPS quality performance category; and (iii) require at least 50 percent of participating clinicians to use certified EHR technology.[315] Additionally, the incentive payment may only be earned where a specified percentage of Medicare patients or payments pass through the Advanced APM.[316]

In the October 2016 final rule, CMS also announced that it had begun development of the Medicare ACO Track 1+ Model—a payment model that would incorporate more limited downside risk than is currently present in either Track 2 or Track 3 of the MSSP, but sufficient risk to be considered an Advanced APM.[317] On December 20, 2016, CMS issued a press release outlining the model's features as well as informing potential participants about likely application deadlines.[318] Like the former MSSP ACO Track 1 Model, the Track 1+ Model had a maximum 50 percent shared savings rate.[319] However, the new Track 1+ Model contained elements of the former Track 3 Model including (i) prospective beneficiary assignment; (ii) choice of symmetrical thresholds from which to start sharing in savings or losses; and (iii) the option to elect the SNF 3-day rule waiver.[320] Additionally, the Track 1+ Model had a fixed 30 percent loss sharing rate with the maximum level of downside risk varying according to the composition of the ACO.[321] In the December 2018 Final Rule, the Track 1+ Model is preserved as level E of the BASIC Track.[322]

---

312. *Id.*

313. *Id.* at 77433.

314. *Id.* at 77013.

315. *Id.*

316. *Id.*

317. *Id.*

318. CMS, Fact Sheet, Advancing Care Coordination Through Episode Payment Models (Cardiac and Orthopedic Bundled Payment Models) Final Rule (CMS-5519-F) and Medicare ACO Track 1+ Model (Dec. 20, 2016), *available at* https://www.cms.gov/medicare/medicare-fee-for-service-payment/sharedsavingsprogram/downloads/new-accountable-care-organization-model-opportunity-fact-sheet.pdf.

319. *Id.*

320. *Id.*

321. *Id.*

322. 83 Fed. Reg. at 67851.

In January of 2017, CMS issued a Request for Applications reopening the Next Generation ACO Model for the 2018 Performance Year to ensure practices and providers did not lose the opportunity to participate as Advanced APMs and applications were due in May of 2017.[323] The participants were announced on January 18, 2018.[324] Similarly, CMS reopened the applications for the Comprehensive Primary Care Plus (CPC+) Model for the 2018 Performance Year in round two as announced in the 2017 Medicare Physician Fee Schedule. [325]

For those providers who participate in an ACO that does not qualify as an Advanced APM, they must participate in MIPS.[326] Under MIPS, eligible clinicians will receive a traditional FFS rate for Medicare Part B items/services, adjusted for their historic quality performance score.[327] CMS determines this figure according to four weighted performance categories, which are then graded on a 100-point composite performance score.[328] For each performance category, clinicians can obtain a certain number of points through adherence to quality measures, efficient use of resources, making clinical practice improvements, and complying with reporting requirements.[329] The points are then aggregated and payments are calculated according to the clinician's placement relative to other providers.[330] Because MACRA requires MIPS to be budget neutral, there will be winners and losers under MIPS. For the initial performance period, CMS authorized up to a 4 percent negative payment adjustment and up to a 4 percent positive payment adjustment.[331] Both positive and negative adjustments will increase for later performance years to the maximum of 9 percent in 2022 and beyond.[332] In the final rule for the fiscal year 2018 Medicare physician fee schedule, CMS reduced the potential negative adjustment for 2018 to negative 2 percent.[333]

---

323. CMS, Fact Sheet, Next Generation Accountable Care Organization Model, *available at* https://innovation.cms.gov/Files/fact-sheet/nextgenaco-fs.pdf.

324. *See* https://innovation.cms.gov/initiatives/Next-Generation-ACO-Model/.

325. 81 Fed. Reg. 77013 (Oct. 14, 2016); *See also* CMS, Comprehensive Primary Care Plus (CPC+) 2018 Payer and Practice Solicitation, *available at* https://www.cms.gov/newsroom/fact-sheets/comprehensive-primary-care-plus-cpc-2018-payer-and-practice-solicitation.

326. *Id.* at 77036.

327. *Id.* at 77014.

328. *Id.* at 77319.

329. *Id.* at 77010.

330. *Id.* at 77339.

331*Id.* at 77332.

332. *Id.*

333. 82 FR 52976, 533230- 53231 (Nov. 15, 2017).

While an ACO that does not qualify as an Advanced ACO must participate in MIPS, it can avoid duplicative reporting as a MIPS APM provided it satisfies the regulatory criteria established by CMS in its October 14 Final Rule.[334] To do so, the ACO must:

1. participate in the APM under an agreement with CMS;

2. include at least one MIPS eligible clinician on a participation list; and

3. base payment incentives on performance (either at the APM entity or eligible clinician level), on cost/utilization, and on quality measures.

VI. Conclusion

The ACOs of today may not be the ACOs of the future. ACOs likely will continue to be modified and redefined, but clearly the modern method of healthcare delivery is changing and will continue to change, particularly as reimbursement models shift away from volume-based payments. Despite challenges with the creation and operation of ACOs, due to the need for strong physician leadership, physician involvement is critical to shaping the future evolution of ACOs and similar models.

---

334. 81 Fed. Reg. 77246 (Nov. 4, 2016).

Chapter 7

DOCTORS' DEFENSE IN MEDICAL STAFF HEARINGS AND APPEALS: AN OVERVIEW FOR ATTORNEYS AND THEIR PHYSICIAN CLIENTS

UPDATED BY: *MERHNAZ HADIAN, M.D.*
PATRICK D. SOUTER, J.D., L.L.M, MBA[1]

I.   Introduction

Hospital medical staff members have much to lose when their membership or clinical privileges are on the line if the practitioner is subject to a peer review. Physicians who are employed or under contract with the hospital are particularly at risk of losing their entire practice, particularly if they are subject to a restrictive covenant such as a non-compete or non-solicitation provision. Independent physicians may find themselves unable to practice because they are prohibited from using the hospital. The loss of privileges and medical staff membership may be reported to the National Practitioner Data Bank (NPDB), disclosed to future employers, licensing bodies and hospitals and other facilities where they render care and be required on subsequent credentialing applications for the remainder of the physician's career. Before the hospital can take away privileges and membership, the physician has a right to a medical staff hearing and appeal. Given the stakes, physicians generally should exercise this right and not waive any rights they possess.

Medical staff hearings and appeals are administrative processes with unique aspects, due not only to the severe consequences for physicians' careers but also to the varying requirements imposed by state and federal law. These requirements are introduced here. In addition to the statutes and regulations, attorneys and physicians need to be aware of basic practice tips and practicalities.

---

1.   The original edition of this chapter was written by Janet L. Pulliam and Elizabeth A. Snelson. Dr. Hadian is an Assistant Professor of Medicine at UCLA, Los Angeles. She is also President of HADIAN, Inc., a consulting firm providing services to healthcare entities. Mr. Souter is Of Counsel with Gray Reed and McGraw, LLP in Dallas, Texas, where the focus of his practice is on regulatory and transactional healthcare matters. He is the Adjunct Professor of Healthcare Studies at Baylor University School of Law in Waco, Texas, and on the Adjunct Faculty of the Robbins Institute for Health Law and Policy at Baylor University Hankamer School of Business.

Until they find themselves in the midst of a medical staff peer review process, most physicians are unfamiliar with its procedures or potential ramifications resulting from an adverse professional review action even though such are usually set forth in the medical staff bylaws. It is indeed the rare medical school that has any curricula related to peer review. For those attorneys who may find themselves in a position of advising a physician client seeking guidance as to a peer review matter, it is likely that the attorney was not exposed to medical staff legal courses in law school or later in practice. Even experienced health lawyers may not be aware of the unique requirements of peer review given the wide range of areas that encompass health law. It is imperative that an attorney representing a physician in a peer review matter have a working knowledge of what constitutes a medical staff peer review, the process and the rights, duties and obligations of all parties associated with it and the immunities granted to those participating in the peer review. The failure to ensure compliance of both the applicable statutory authority and the medical staff bylaws may be disastrous to the physician client. The attorney not recognizing these rights may result in the failure to ensure the physician is provided due process and a fair hearing and may unwittingly waive the rights afforded. This chapter addresses such a gap in knowledge by providing a primer for lawyers and physicians preparing a defense in a medical staff peer review matter.

II. Anatomy of a Medical Staff Hearing and Repercussions Resulting from a Negative Outcome

An adverse finding in a medical staff peer review may have far-reaching implications as previously noted. Not surprisingly, these matters are frequently litigated since an adverse finding may result in negative implications from a licensure, certification and credentialing standpoint. There are limitations on the relief a physician may seek in the event there is a revocation or limitation of medical staff privileges and such may haunt the physician for years to come. Therefore, counsel should be thorough in reviewing the current requirements as interpreted by state and federal courts in preparing to defend physicians in medical staff hearings.[2]

A. The Need for Legal Counsel

Hearing and appeals processes are complicated by nature. Medical staff processes feature additional complications, not least among them the opportunity of federal immunity for those individuals and entities that participate in the peer review process and the threat of federal and state reporting to such organizations such as the NPDB, governmental payers and state licensure boards. An adverse professional review action may also

---

2. A review of the case law and all regulatory aspects of a medical peer review is beyond the scope of this overview. Rather, the intent of this material is to provide insight into the process as an aid in understanding what is necessary to be able, appropriate counsel.

negatively impact credentialing with commercial payers since it may be disclosed to the payer or appear when payers search the NPDB during the credentialing process. No physician should attempt to engage in the process before hiring competent legal counsel familiar with the unique character and elements of medical staff hearings and appeals.

1. *Right to Representation*

   With the enactment of the Federal Health Care Quality Improvement Act of 1986[3] (HCQIA), the physician's right to representation by counsel in hearings has become the standard in medical staff bylaws throughout the country. Some state law, such as that of Arkansas,[4] protect the right to be represented by an attorney in the hearing.

2. *How Lawyers Are Selected*

   The physician requesting the hearing selects his or her attorney, who should be experienced in representing physicians undergoing peer review. Local medical societies or professional liability insurers may be able to identify qualified physician advocates.

3. *Cost*

   The cost of representation is borne by the physician requesting the hearing and appeal. The cost may be substantial depending upon the complexity of the peer review and the resources needed, such as expert witnesses, to effectively participate in the process. It is advisable that the physician who is involved in a professional review activity ascertain from their professional liability insurer whether their coverage includes reimbursement for costs related to professional review activities. Those insurers may be a source for knowledgeable attorneys the insurer will pay for, subject to limitations time of disclosure to the insurer and deductible amount, if the physician has such coverage.

4. *Hospital and Medical Staff Lawyers*

   Whether the hospital or medical staff is represented by counsel in the hearing may depend upon the physician requesting the hearing. Some medical staff bylaws or state law condition the use of counsel in the hearing on the physician's decision to be represented. For example, under California law, the hospital or medical staff cannot be represented in the hearing by an attorney unless the physician is also represented by an attorney.[5] Arkansas encourages, but does not require, that profes-

---

3. 42 U.S.C. 11101 *et seq.* (1986).
4. ARK. CODE § 20-9-1304(b)(2).
5. CAL. BUS. & PROF. CODE § 809.3(c).

sional review bodies use separate legal counsel from the legal counsel used by the hospital, and that medical staff obtain independent legal counsel to review medical staff bylaws to ensure that the bylaws contain provisions that comply with the requirements of Arkansas law. However, these requirements are not mandatory.[6]

If counsel is permitted, the charges brought against the physician may be raised by either the medical staff, via the Medical Executive Committee (MEC), or the hospital, and therefore either the medical staff's or the hospital's counsel may present its case. It is not uncommon for the medical staff to be represented by hospital counsel in a hearing. Even if the physician is represented by counsel, the hospital or medical staff may elect to have a medical staff leader or hospital administrator, rather than a lawyer, present its case to the hearing body. The attorney representing the medical staff or the hospital should recognize the possible conflicts that may arise if serving as legal counsel in this instance if the physician exercises additional rights offered to him or her. The aggrieved physician may in some instances appeal the decision of the peer review hearing to the hospital's board. The attorney who represents the medical staff or the hospital in the proceeding should be cognizant of the possible conflict if he serves in dual capacity of also representing the board. The board should be viewed as an independent body from the peer review hearing and representation of the MEC and the board may create issues in a subsequent review of the proceedings.

5. *Hearing Officer*

Hearing officers are not required, but, given the complexity and reach of the hearing process, are commonly used and usually recommended. Hearing officers may be useful in addressing disputes prior to or during the peer review process since they serve to oversee it. The typical hearing officer is an attorney experienced with administrative proceedings and preferably, with medical staff hearings. Retired judges, or physicians who are veterans of medical staff hearings, may also qualify. For instance, Arkansas law stipulates that the hearing officer ". . . shall be independent of all parties involved; have no conflict of interest; and not: have served as an attorney for the hospital or the physician under review at any time within two years prior to the hearing date; or be affiliated with a law firm that has represented the hospital or the physician under review at any time within two years from the date of the hearing.[7] Hearing officer qualifications should be stipulated in medical staff bylaws.

---

6. ARK. CODE § 20-9-1304(c)(1)-(2).
7. ARK. CODE § 20-9-1310(b)(2)(A)-(C)(i)-(ii).

The hospital or medical staff usually selects and compensates the hearing officer, but the selection process may involve the physician requesting the hearing if medical staff bylaws require that the hearing officer is mutually acceptable to the parties. The HCQIA only requires that the hearing officer "… is not in direct economic competition with the physician involved…."[8] State law may address the qualifications and authority of the hearing officer. For example, California statutes state that "the hearing officer shall gain no direct financial benefit from the outcome, shall not act as a prosecuting officer or advocate, and shall not be entitled to vote."[9]

The only duty specifically demanded of the hearing officer under the HCQIA is to determine the relevance of the evidence presented.[10] However, medical staff bylaws usually provide for additional duties, including preserving the efficiency and dignity of the process, and writing up the decision of the hearing committee.

B. Governing Law

1. Federal Health Care Quality Improvement Act[11]

The HCQIA was passed prior to the Supreme Court's decision in *Patrick v Burgett*,[12] which held competitors liable for bad faith peer review.[13] The HCQIA, which was not in effect at the time of the acts at

---

8. 42 U.S.C. § 11112 (b)(3)(A)(ii).
9. CAL. BUS. & PROF. CODE § 809.2(b).
10. 42 U.S.C. § 11112 (b)(3)(C)(iv).
11. 42 U.S.C. § 11101 *et seq.* (1986).
12. 108 S. Ct. 1658 (1988). The *Patrick* case involved a surgeon who sued several physicians who were partners in a private medical clinic that were also participants in a medical peer review hearing initiated against the surgeon. The surgeon asserted causes of action pertaining to alleged violations of Sherman Act and interference with prospective economic advantage under Oregon law. The U.S. Supreme Court held that the state-action doctrine did not protect Oregon physicians who are participants in hospital peer-review committees from liability under the federal antitrust laws. The HCQIA was passed in response to this case so as to allow state law protections to extend to federal antitrust actions if it involves those participating in a peer review process.
13. When passing the HCQIA, Congress recognized the need to create national standards and protections to provide for an effective peer review system to ensure the effective delivery of quality healthcare. To incentivize those to participate in peer review functions, it was necessary to establish a framework of protections that included certain immunities. *See* U.S.C. § 11101 that states: " The Congress finds the following:

(1) The increasing occurrence of medical malpractice and the need to improve the quality of medical care have become nationwide problems that warrant greater efforts than those that can be undertaken by any individual State.

issue in *Patrick v. Burgett*, creates a rebuttal presumption that results in conditional immunity for a peer review action meeting if taken:

(1) in the reasonable belief that the action was in the furtherance of quality healthcare;

(2) after a reasonable effort to obtain the facts of the matter;

(3) after adequate notice and hearing procedures are afforded to the physician involved or after such other procedures as are fair to the physician under the circumstances; and

(4) in the reasonable belief that the action was warranted by the facts known after such reasonable effort to obtain facts and after meeting the requirement of paragraph (3).[14]

"Adequate notice and hearing procedures" are stipulated by the HCQIA[15] (although a procedure can be otherwise proved fair), summarized below, and discussed in detail in subsequent sections:

(a) notice of action;

(b) notice of hearing, including a list of the witnesses expected to testify;

(c) impartial hearing officer, hearing body or arbitrator;

(d) representation in the hearing by an attorney or other person of the physician's choice;

(e) a record made of the proceeding;

(f) the ability to call, examine and cross-examine witnesses;

(g) the ability to present relevant evidence;

(h) submission of a written statement at the close of the hearing;

(i) a written recommendation of the hearing body, including a statement of the basis for the recommendation; and

(j) a written final decision of the hospital.

---

(2) There is a national need to restrict the ability of incompetent physicians to move from State to State without disclosure or discovery of the physician's previous damaging or incompetent performance.

(3) This nationwide problem can be remedied through effective professional peer review.

(4) The threat of private money damage liability under Federal laws, including treble damage liability under Federal antitrust law, unreasonably discourages physicians from participating in effective professional peer review.

(5) There is an overriding national need to provide incentive and protection for physicians engaging in effective professional peer review.

14. 42 U.S.C. § 11112(a).

15. 42 U.S.C. § 11112(b).

Hospitals are presumed to have met these "safe harbor" elements,[16] but that presumption can be successfully challenged. Well-drafted medical staff bylaws extend physicians at least these rights, to meet these safe harbor elements. To ensure that aggrieved physician is able to identify these rights, many hospitals include a Fair Hearing Plan in the medical staff bylaws that succinctly sets forth these rights. If the medical staff procedure as described in medical staff bylaws falls short of these elements, the physician should tender a written request for them, in compliance with the HCQIA, so as not to waive the physician's rights as provided to them by law.

2. *State Immunities and Confidentiality Law*

In addition to the federal protection under the HCQIA, most, if not all, states provide some level of legal protections for peer review and peer reviewers. Generally, state law provides immunity from liability to those conducting good faith peer review, including investigating, charging, and enforcing adverse peer review actions. While the federal immunity is conditioned on providing fair procedures, state law may or may not place such conditions on immunity.

Confidentiality and privilege protections vary from state to state, and must be considered at every phase of peer review activity. Generally, the minutes and actions of medical staff committees, and the credentials files of medical staff members, are privileged, not subject to subpoena and not discoverable or usable in litigation. Typical state confidentiality statutes provide an exception for physicians challenging an adverse peer review action to enable a physician to access the records needed to make their case.[17] State law might limit that access to challenges in court, rather than at the medical staff hearing level.

Releases of information may be required in medical staff bylaws. Further, medical staff applications, or attestation or other forms, may have been executed as part of the credentialing process that govern access and use of privileged information. It is important for the sharing of such information in limited circumstances to have an effective credentialing process. However, access to this information is not unfettered and subject to protections from various legal and contractual sources.

---

16. 42 U.S.C. § 11112(a).

17. Alabama is an exception; physicians have no rights to confidential peer review information with which to challenge an adverse action. ALA. CODE § 6-5-333(d).

3. State Procedural Law

Some states have established requirements for medical staff hearings rather than relying solely on the HCQIA. For example, California's fairly comprehensive peer review statute addresses notice content and timing, trier of fact, voir dire, access to confidential information, continuances, hearing record, witnesses and burden of proof.[18] Illinois codified detailed requirements for medical staff hearings in its hospital licensing act.[19]

Note that states may also have exemptions to procedural rights. Pennsylvania requires the establishment of fair hearing and appellate review mechanisms to be available upon request, but recognizes that the procedures for initial applicants may differ from those extended to medical staff members.[20] California and Illinois are among states that exclude from procedural protections members of medical staffs of certain hospitals, such as those owned or operated by or licensed to the University of California as a primary teaching facility[21] or those requiring faculty status.[22]

4. Reporting Requirements

Reporting negative decisions to the authorities listed below may be a condition of immunities or licensure, or otherwise required. Because these reports are accessed by hospitals and medical staffs and health plans in credentialing, they have a lasting impact on a physician's future employability and privileging. Attorneys and physicians must become familiar with the reporting ramifications of peer review actions and any decision, including any relinquishment of privileges, while peer review is ongoing.

a. National Practitioner Data Bank

The HCQIA established the NPDB.[23] All adverse peer review actions based on professional conduct or competence and lasting more than 30 days, and any surrender of privileges during any medical staff investigation, are to be reported by the healthcare

---

18. CAL. BUS. & PROF. CODE § 809 *et seq.*
19. 210 ILCS 85/10.4.
20. 28 PA. CODE § 107.12.(4).
21. CAL. BUS. & PROF. CODE § 809.7.
22. 210 ILCS 85/10.4(b).
23. 42 U.S.C. § 11133.

entity[24] where the adverse action occurred or by the state medical board where the healthcare entity is located if the entity failed to report the adverse action. Failure to report can disqualify the healthcare entity from the federal immunity offered under the HCQIA, so those entities are highly motivated to report.

b. State Reporting

States may require reporting not only final adverse actions but also varying activities involving physicians who have not, or not yet, been subject to hearing. For example, Iowa requires reporting to the state board of medicine "any voluntary surrender or limitation of privileges for reasons relating to professional competence. . . ."[25]

c. Settlement of Disputes to Avoid the Reporting of an Adverse Action

Many times a physician will believe that if there is a pending peer review action, it may be avoided, and an adverse action not reported, if there is a settlement through the voluntary resignation of privileges or some other type of agreed upon resolution that directly or indirectly impacts the physician's privileges. This act may result in an adverse finding being reported just as if the physician had continued through the peer review process. The *National Practitioner Data Bank Guidebook* establishes reporting requirements, including mandatory reporting in some instances, where there is a resignation of privileges while a physician is under investigation.[26] Also, it may result in a reportable event if the physician allows for the expiration of privileges, or fails to attempt to renew the privileges, while under investigation.

---

24. According to 42 U.S.C. § 11151(4), a "healthcare entity" is defined as (i) a hospital that is licensed to provide healthcare services by the State in which it is located, (ii) an entity (including a health maintenance organization or group medical practice) that provides healthcare services and that follows a formal peer review process for the purpose of furthering quality healthcare (as determined under regulations of the Secretary), and (iii) subject to subparagraph (B), a professional society (or committee thereof) of physicians or other licensed healthcare practitioners that follows a formal peer review process for the purpose of furthering quality healthcare.

25. Iowa Code 147.135.3.a.

26. National Practitioner Data Bank, Chapter E (October 2018).

C. Medical Staff Bylaws

Medical staff bylaws are required by state law,[27] Federal Medicare Conditions of Participation,[28] and accrediting entities, such as The Joint Commission (TJC),[29] which accredits the majority of American hospitals.

1. Accreditation Requirements

TJC standard MS 10.01.01., Elements of Performance 1 through 5 provides that a fair hearing process be designed to address quality of care issues and has a mechanism to allow for the scheduling of a hearing, sets forth procedures for the process, allows for impartial panel of peers to hear the matter and allows for an opportunity to appeal an adverse decision.[30]

2. State Law Requirements

State statutes may go beyond merely requiring that the medical staff have bylaws and to require specific provisions to be included in the bylaws. State law should be carefully compared to medical staff bylaws provisions to maximize procedural protections where the bylaws may not have been updated or otherwise fail to meet such state-mandated requirements due to the use of a standard set of bylaws utilized by a health system or hospital corporation.

3. Enforceability as Contract

Medical staff bylaws have been construed as contractual in nature by the majority of jurisdictions that have considered the question.[31] It is generally reasoned that the bylaws would be meaningless if a hospital were not bound to them as if it was a contract.[32] However, it has been recognized that it may be contrary to public interest to deem bylaws

---

27. *See* MINN. R. 4640.0800, subp.2.

28. 42 C.F.R. 482.12(a)(3), 482.22(b)(4)(ii).

29. *See* the Joint Commission, Comprehensive Accreditation Manual for Hospitals (2021).

30. TJC states the rationale for these requirements in MS 10.01.01: "Mechanisms for fair hearing and appeal processes are designed to allow the affected individual a fair opportunity to defend herself or himself regarding the adverse decision to an unbiased hearing body of the medical staff, and an opportunity to appeal the decision of the hearing body to the governing body. The purpose of a fair hearing and appeal is to assure full consideration and reconsideration of quality and safety issues and, under the current structure of reporting to the National Practitioner Data Bank (NPDB), allow practitioners an opportunity to defend themselves."

31. Most recently, *Avera Marshall Medical Staff v. Avera Marshall Regional Medical Center,* 857 N.W.2d 695 (Minn. 2014), 836 N.W.2d 549 (MN. Ct. App. 2013).

32. Bouquett v. St. Elizabeth Corp., 538 N.E2d 113, 115 (Ohio 1989).

as a contract since it could limit a hospital's latitude in addressing an issue of substandard care.[33]

While these authorities greatly influence the content of medical staff bylaws, there is nonetheless considerable variety in medical staff bylaws generally and medical staff bylaws hearing and appeal provisions specifically. Some medical staffs may extend hearing rights for admonitions and other non-reportable actions, others restrict access to hearings. Medical staff bylaws can allow limited discovery or call for considerable transparency. Burdens of proof and other key procedures vary from medical staff to medical staff.

D. Hearing Procedural Roadmap

Attorneys for physicians in hearings should be familiar with each of the following hearing elements:

1. *Notice of Proposed Action*

Under the HCQIA, the physician is to be given notice of the proposed action, stating:

- that a professional review action has been proposed to be taken against the physician;

- reasons for the proposed action;

- that the physician has the right to request a hearing on the proposed action;

- any time limit (of not less than 30 days) within which to request such a hearing; and

- a summary of rights in the hearing.[34]

The medical staff bylaws may stipulate additional requirements, such as where and to whom the request for hearing has to be sent. Failure to comply with the requirements for requesting the hearing within the time stipulated is typically deemed a waiver of hearing and appeal rights. Provision of a summary of rights is commonly met by providing the full hearing and appeals section of the medical staff bylaws. The physician and the physician's attorney should obtain the entire current bylaws, as useful provisions may be in sections other than the hearing and appeals section.

---

33. *See* Zipper v. Health Midwest, 978 S.W.2d 398, 417 (Mo. Ct. App. 1998).
34. 42 U.S.C. § 11112(b)(1).

2. *Notice of Hearing*

If a hearing is requested, the HCQIA provides that the physician is to be given notice stating:

- the place, time, and date of the hearing, which date shall not be less than 30 days after the date of the notice; and

- a list of the witnesses (if any) expected to testify at the hearing on behalf of the professional review body.[35]

The bylaws may demand that the physician provide a list of witnesses expected to testify on the physician's behalf. Circumstances may dictate that the physician may require more time to prepare for the hearing. In that instance, it is advisable to consult with the hospital or medical staff counsel to arrive at a time for the hearing and reduce the agreement in writing so as not to waive the right to a timely hearing.

3. *Discovery*

The HCQIA does not address discovery rights. State laws play an important role in filling this void. For example, California's peer review law not only establishes the physician's right to copy any relevant information, but also makes the right reciprocal to the medical staff or hospital,[36] which may occur in medical staff bylaws but is unusual in state statute. Relevancy is determined according to specific parameters set in the peer review law, specifically.

The arbitrator or presiding officer shall consider and rule upon any request for access to information, and may impose any safeguards the protection of the peer review process and justice requires.

When ruling upon requests for access to information and determining the relevancy thereof, the arbitrator or presiding officer shall, among other factors, consider the following:

(1) whether the information sought may be introduced to support or defend the charges;

(2) the exculpatory or inculpatory nature of the information sought, if any;

(3) the burden imposed on the party in possession of the information sought, if access is granted; and

(4) any previous requests for access to information submitted or resisted by the parties to the same proceedings.[37]

---

35. 42 U.S.C. § 11112(b)(2).
36. Cal. Bus. & Prof. Code § 809.2(d).
37. Cal. Bus. & Prof. Code § 809.2(e).

Arkansas law similarly provides for transparency through discovery, requiring that prior to the hearing the hospital administration, professional review body, and the physician under review shall disclose all relevant information to each other including a list of any witnesses expected to testify and copies of any documents expected to be introduced at the hearing."[38]

If state law is silent, medical staff bylaws may or may not fill the vacuum. Bylaws can extend physicians the opportunity to request and receive exculpatory or even comparative information. Medical staff bylaws provisions may also make discovery rights reciprocal, authorizing sharing of information in response to requests by the medical staff's MEC or the hospital's governing board, whichever is presenting and recommending the adverse action.

4. *Evidence*

The HCQIA includes among the physician's hearing rights "to present evidence determined to be relevant by the hearing officer, regardless of its admissibility in a court of law...."[39]

5. *Witnesses*

The physician has the right under the HCQIA to a list of witnesses anticipated to testify against him/her, as mentioned in the HCQIA requirements found in Section 2a above. Medical staff bylaws may make the obligation to provide witness lists reciprocal. Witnesses providing information in good faith to the peer review process, including the hearing and appeals, are protected under the HCQIA.[40]

In the hearing, the physician has the right to call, examine, and cross-examine witnesses, under the HCQIA;[41] this right is typically extended to permit examination and cross-examination of the witnesses the physician calls to support the physician's case. In some cases, the hearing panel is afforded the opportunity to ask the witnesses their own questions to further delve into the facts they deem necessary for the proceeding.

6. *Hearing Body Composition and Voir Dire*

The trier of fact in medical staff hearings is typically an appointed group, referred to as a hearing panel, judicial review committee,

---

38. Ark. Code § 20-9-1310(c)(1)-(2).
39. 42 U.S.C. § 11112(b)(3)(C)(4).
40. 42 U.S.C. § 11111 (a)(2).
41. 42 U.S.C. § 11112 (b)(3)(C)(iii).

hearing committee, or other variant thereof. The HCQIA provides options for the trier to take the form of an individual hearing officer, a mutually acceptable arbitrator, or hearing committee. Some medical staff bylaws extend all three options, to be selected on a case by case basis, while others provide for a hearing committee in all cases, chaired by a medical staff member and/or assisted by a professional hearing officer.

Where a hearing panel is used, the medical staff bylaws should describe the qualifications and application process for selection of members. Typically, given the nature of the issues to be heard, the committee is required to be comprised of actual peers who by education, experience, and licensure are competent to assess whether there is clinical rationale to support restricting the physician's practice. However, some bylaws permit nonmedical staff members and even non-clinicians to be appointed.

The HCQIA states that the hearing panel and hearing officer are not to be "in direct economic competition with the physician involved,"[42] but does not directly provide the physician the right of voir dire. Statutes address this omission in some states, permitting voir dire,[43] or, as in Illinois, requiring that the medical staff and hospital mutually determine the membership of the hearing panel.[44]

7. *Pre-Hearing Conference*

Pre-hearing conferences can be invaluable to the mutual goal of a fair and efficient hearing process. The experienced hearing officer may of the officer's own volition, at the request of either or both parties, or as specifically authorized by the medical staff bylaws, call for the participation of the parties and their counsel in a meeting or meetings to explain the procedure and resolve any procedural questions or problems before the hearing. Unless otherwise stipulated in state law or medical staff bylaws, however, pre-hearing conferences are discretionary, to be determined by the hearing officer.

8. *Hearing Record*

A record of the hearing is called for under the HCQIA.[45] No mode of creating the record is stipulated, only that copies of the record are to be available to the physician "upon payment of any reasonable

---

42. 42 U.S.C. § 11112 (b)(3)(A)(ii)-(iii).
43. *See* CAL. BUS. & PROF. CODE §809.2(c).
44. 210 ILCS 85/10.4(b)(2)(C).
45. 42 U.S.C. § 11112 (b)(3)(C)(ii).

charges associated with the preparation thereof."[46] Medical staff bylaws may identify that the record will be produced by court reporter.

9. *Counsel/Representative in the Hearing*

Physicians have the right to representation as discussed in section 1, above. The HCQIA's standards include representation by counsel or other representative of the physician's choice. Prior to the HCQIA, medical staff procedures commonly limited the physician's choice of representative to another member of the profession, even specifying that the representative had to be a member of the medical staff or possibly of the local medical society. One should not presume that the medical staff bylaws provide the protections mandated by federal law. Not all bylaws may have been timely updated to HCQIA standards such as permitting representation by counsel or any other representative. The medical staff bylaws should be reviewed to ensure they have incorporated the protections afforded by law. Failure to provide the procedures afforded by the HCQIA will prohibit the healthcare entity from being able to take advantage of the immunities afforded by it.[47]

Some medical staff bylaws purport to limit the physician's use of counsel or other representative in the hearing and appeal by limiting physician counsel to a certain number of questions or length of time, or even prohibiting counsel from speaking during the hearing.

10. *Burden of Proof*

The HCQIA does not provide guidance regarding the burden of proof in peer review hearings. Some states address the matter in detail. Consider California statutory requirements, which mandate:

(1) The peer review body shall have the initial duty to present evidence which supports the charge or recommended action.

(2) Initial applicants shall bear the burden of persuading the trier of fact by a preponderance of the evidence of their qualifications by producing information which allows for adequate evaluation and resolution of reasonable doubts concerning their current qualifications for staff privileges, membership, or employment. Initial applicants shall not be permitted to introduce information not produced upon request of the peer review body during the application process, unless the initial applicant establishes that

---

46. *Id.*
47. Granger v. Christus Health Central Louisiana et al., 144 So.3d 736 (La. 2013).

the information could not have been produced previously in the exercise of reasonable diligence.

(3) Except as provided above for initial applicants, the peer review body shall bear the burden of persuading the trier of fact by a preponderance of the evidence that the action or recommendation is reasonable and warranted.[48]

Particularly where state law is silent, burden of proof should be stipulated in medical staff bylaws. "Preponderance of the evidence" is common, although less current bylaws may stipulate that the physician has to prove the adverse recommendations to be arbitrary, capricious or unreasonable. Often, however, medical staff bylaws fail to stipulate any burden of proof parameters, in which situation the parties may wish to approach the hearing officer in pre-trial conference to propose setting the burden of proof. In this event, it is common for the MEC to provide sufficient evidence to support its case which then shifts the burden to the physician to submit the necessary evidence to counter the MEC's case.

11. Written Memoranda

Although frequently omitted in medical staff bylaws, the HCQIA calls for the physician to be permitted to submit a written memorandum to the hearing officer or hearing body at the close of the hearing.[49] Bylaws may extend this right to the medical staff also, to provide the hearing body with memoranda arguing both sides. Because the hearing body deliberates outside the presence of the parties, the opportunity to provide written memoranda for review during the deliberations should not be overlooked.

12. Decision

The hearing body's decision takes the form of a recommendation to the hospital board, because all final actions must be taken by the board.[50] The hearing body's decision must be given to the physician in writing, stating the basis for its recommendation, under the HCQIA.[51] The final decision by the board, including the basis therefor, must also be provided the physician under the HCQIA.[52] However, most medical staff processes permit an appeal of the hearing committee recommendation before the board takes its final action. The same

---

48. CAL. BUS. & PROF. CODE § 809.3(b).
49. 42 U.S.C. § 11112 (b)(3)(C)(v).
50. Joint Commission standard MS 06.01.07, Element of Performance 8.
51. 42 U.S.C. § 11112 (b)(3)(D)(i).
52. 42 U.S.C. § 11112 (b)(3)(D)(ii).

legal counsel representing the MEC during the hearing and the hospital board in the appeal may result in an inherent conflict since the appeal is supposed to be an independent action available to the aggrieved practitioner.

E. Summary Suspension

Hospital medical staff disciplinary procedures provide for summary suspension,[53] by which a physician is immediately barred from practice in whole or in part before a hearing can be held. HCQIA protections are available for such summary actions only if failure to suspend could result in imminent danger to the health of a person.[54] Nonetheless, medical staff bylaws may call for summary suspension for a myriad of alleged infractions, ranging from so-called disruptive behavior to actual substandard performance clinically.

If the physician is under summary suspension, the hearing and appeal process may be modified to accelerate the process and thereby lessen the damages to the physician's practice. The physician's consent to shorter notice periods and other waivers to vary deadlines may be required. Accelerated procedures may be provided for in state statute; for example, in Illinois, the hearing must begin within 15 days of the summary suspension.[55] If there are no state or medical staff bylaws procedures for speeding the process, accommodation may be sought from the hearing officer.

F. Appeals

The decision of the hearing body is generally not the final action, which must be taken by the hospital board;[56] although some medical staff bylaws may deem hearing body decisions to be final actions. An appeals process is not called for by the HCQIA, but is by TJC standards.[57] Consequently, appeals processes are commonly included in medical staff bylaws. Arguably, a process for appealing a hearing body's recommendation has become the industry standard.

---

53. Joint Commission standard MS 01.01.01, Elements of Performance 29 and 32 call for medical staff bylaws to include provisions for indications of and procedures governing summary suspension.

54. 42 U.S.C. § 11112 (c)(2).

55. 210 ILCS 85/10.4(b)(2)(C)(ii).

56. Joint Commission standard MS 06.01.07, Element of Performance 8.

57. Joint Commission standard MS 10.01.01, Element of Performance 5, states, "The organized medical staff has developed a fair hearing and appeal process addressing quality of care issues that has the following characteristics: With the governing body, provides a mechanism to appeal adverse decisions as provided in the medical staff bylaws." *See also,* Joint Commission standard MS 06.01.09, Element of Performance 5.

State law may address appeals. California's peer review statute takes the unique approach of not mandating appeals, but requiring certain elements if appeals are provided, as follows:

> If an appellate mechanism is provided, it need not provide for de novo review, but it shall include the following minimum rights for both parties:
>
> (1) the right to appear and respond;
>
> (2) the right to be represented by an attorney or any other representative designated by the party; and
>
> (3) the right to receive the written decision of the appellate body.[58]

Appeals procedures in medical staff bylaws tend to be minimalistic, particularly compared to hearing procedures. Typically, medical staff bylaws prohibit the introduction of new information which could have been provided at the hearing level. Some processes block oral argument or even representation by counsel in the appellate process, limiting the physician's appeal to a written submission.

G. Alternative Dispute Resolution

Alternate dispute resolution may be a reasonable option in lieu of traditional peer review procedures for some matters, such as actions based on business activities occurring in the context of clinical relationships. Medical staff bylaws may provide options medical staff members can select to address matters more efficiently resolved at the direction of a mediator.

Texas has adopted mediation as an alternative to traditional peer review hearing and appeals procedures, at the behest of the physician, to be conducted under general mediation procedures established under state law, as follows:

> If a hospital's credentials committee has failed to take action on a completed application as required by subclause VIII of this clause, or a physician, podiatrist, or dentist is subject to a professional review action that may adversely affect his medical staff membership or privileges, and the physician, podiatrist, or dentist believes that mediation of the dispute is desirable, the physician, podiatrist, or dentist may require the hospital to participate in mediation as provided in Civil Practice and Remedies Code (CPRC), Chapter 154. The media-

---

58. Cal. Bus. & Prof. Code § 809.4(b)(3).

tion shall be conducted by a person meeting the qualifications required and within a reasonable period of time.[59]

H. Effect of Employment or other Hospital Contracts

If the physician has entered into a contract with the hospital or hospital-related entity for employment or provision of services, the agreement may include terms that negatively affect the physician and his or her employment status. It may include provisions that constitute a waiver of hearing and appeal rights or the termination provisions may conflict with the fair hearing rights. Furthermore, a loss or restriction of hospital privileges may serve as just cause for termination of the agreement with no appeal rights under the medical staff bylaws. The contract is not the only document to be considered in determining the physician's rights in peer review. Medical staff bylaws may be silent as to the effect of any hospital contract or may subrogate the bylaws' hearing provisions to the contract's terms. However, medical staff bylaws terms could provide the basis to challenge contractual provisions.

III. Advice for Those Participating in a Medical Peer Review

A. Preventive Medicine for Avoiding Peer Review

For those who are representing physicians in a peer review proceeding, the physician should be aware of the following:

a. Do not allow yourself the luxury of believing that peer review is what happens to bad doctors.

b. Operate under the assumption that high admissions will not protect you from peer review or corrective actions.

c. Be curious about how the peer review process works, and pay attention to what goes on with physicians outside your specialty.

d. Know who is on the committee and develop relationships with its members. Pay attention to whether you have competitors on the committee.

e. Serve on hospital committees and pay attention to hospital politics without participating in it.

f. When objecting to hospital protocols, do so in a nonthreatening manner and search for colleagues in agreement.

g. Regularly assess whether you and the hospital have a healthy relationship and, if possible, keep your privileges at more than one hospital.

---

59. 25 TAC § 133.41(f)(4)(F)(i)(I).

h. Continually assess whether the hospital conducts its peer review in good faith and take actions that support good faith peer review.

i. Read the bylaws and know what your rights are.

j. Be attentive to complaints of hospital staff and actively manage the conflict.

B. Prescriptions for the Target of Peer Review

1. Physicians Should be Proactive in Their Defense

1. Upon receipt of the notice, carefully read it. Determine if the allegations are presented with enough specificity for you to understand what the alleged wrongdoing is.

2. Draft a written response to the allegations with detailed medical facts and explanation supporting your position, and supplement with peer reviewed articles. However, do not submit that to the MEC. This material will be needed by your counsel who should be the person who presents it after reviewing and ensuring that the information presented is helpful in the peer review process.

3. Immediately obtain competent counsel with experience in the area. Be aggressive in the selection process. You are not selecting a friend. Rather, you are selecting a professional that you respect and trust to understand that your career and reputation are at stake. Most often, for strategic reasons, experienced counsel in these matters will provide "shadow advice" behind the scenes to assist you in preparation for your appearance, preparation of your written submissions, and expert selection.

4. Never manifest anger to those who work for the healthcare entity where the peer review process will be held or to those in hearing process.

5. Attend every scheduled meeting on the matter and appear on time.

6. Work diligently with your attorney and spend the time and money to make certain that the presentation of your case compares with that of the hospital.

7. Be attentive and responsive to questions of the committee and be sensitive that most members will not be familiar with many facts and protocols relating to your sub-specialty. This is your opportunity to educate them.

8. If you have a competitor on the committee, or a member with whom you have had conflict in the past for any reason, notify your legal counsel so the chair may be put on notice and respect-

fully request that a substitute be appointed.

9. Take the time away from your practice to prepare. This is not doctor conversation in the breakroom or cafeteria.

10. If the administration offers you a consent decree as a resolution, do not sign it without review by your counsel.

2. *Legal Counsel Should Be Proactive not just during the Hearing Stage but Early in the Process:*

1. Upon reviewing the notice, examine the facts serving as the underpinning for the inquiry. Request clarification in writing immediately if such facts are not clearly stated with sufficient specificity for you to be aware of the allegations.

2. Get a copy of the most recent medical staff bylaws. Read and pay particular attention to deadlines, due process rights, and when you may have counsel present.

3. If the allegations are not patient safety, but rather disruptive or unethical behavior, inquire whether the hospital medical staff has adopted an alternative dispute resolution process that could take the matter away from peer review.[60]

4. If patient care or safety form the basis of the inquiry, request in writing all medical records that have been reviewed by the hospital staff or outside third party, and any reports that have been provided to hospital staff and/or the committee.

5. Submit a formal written response to the allegations from the written statement provided by the physician who included detailed medical facts and explanation supporting your position along with supporting peer reviewed articles (preferably from recognized medical periodicals).

6. If the MEC has used the service of expert review, consider selection of an expert for rebuttal and provide affidavits supporting the defense. It is advisable to analyze your expert and his/her previous positions espoused on the topic that is the subject of their testimony. A review of their professional credentials and published speeches and periodicals will ensure that you have chosen the best expert to provide the most credible testimony and opinions on the subject matter.

7. Make certain that all communication, whether written or verbal, is in a rational and professional tone emphasizing facts.

8. As soon as the hearing is scheduled, request the names of the

---

60. The HCQIA may not require the reporting of an action.

hearing officer and the hearing panel and consult with your client as to whether objections should be made.[61]

9. Prior to the hearing, request in writing that the meeting be transcribed by a court reporter. If that request is denied, offer to pay for one. A transcript of the proceedings may be a valuable resource in the event there is an issue of whether the hearing conforms with the physician's rights under the law and the medical staff bylaws and that sufficient objections have been made to demonstrate that a waiver of those rights has not occurred.

10. Personally request a commitment from the committee that it will keep an open mind and will be guided in its decision making by substantive and procedural fairness.

11. If you believe you have a reasonable solution, even if it is "out of the box," offer it at the hearing stage but recognize that such a solution may still be reportable to the NPDB.

12. Make certain that you know what your litigation options are although they are usually limited. Be prepared to use them when advantageous.

13. When you receive the report and recommendation of the committee provide it to your client and discuss it in detail.

14. If you are told by the hospital that the proposed corrective actions are not reportable to either federal or state agencies, request that in writing.

15. If an adverse action does result in a reportable event to the NPDB, work with the hospital and its counsel in drafting language that will be included in the report. It is possible to craft language to limit the damage to the physician. Furthermore, if the report is incorrect or does not include all pertinent information, it is possible to legally challenge the submission and have it corrected or voided.[62]

---

61. Understanding the makeup of those in the hearing is of vital importance since those individuals may have personality conflicts or perceived bias against your client. If this occurs take immediate steps to seek their removal from the peer review process.

62. *See* Walker v. Memorial Health System of East Texas, 231 F.Supp.3d 210 (E.D. Tex. 2017).

IV.   Conclusion

A peer review process, from the initiation of the investigation through the hearing process, can have a long-term, career-changing impact on a physician and the physician's career. The physician and his or her counsel should approach it recognizing the need to understand the process and the rights afforded to both the healthcare entity and the physician. Identify the allegations, understand the process, and address the peer review process with such vigor that one would any litigation. It is just as important to recognize the need to ensure that what is reported to the NPDB and the state's licensure board where the events occurred meets the facts and ultimate decision. This approach allows for the protection of the physician's rights and establishes the necessary record in the event post-hearing action is needed.

Chapter 8

PHYSICIAN WELL-BEING: HEALING THE HEALER— ASSISTING PHYSICIANS WITH SUBSTANCE USE DISORDERS AND OTHER HEALTH ISSUES

By: *DANIEL H. ANGRES, M.D.*[1]

I.   Introduction

Medicine has always been a high-reward, high-stress occupation. But with the currently challenging healthcare climate, physicians are placed under even greater burdens. From mounting fears of malpractice suits, and financial concerns— including pressure to treat more patients and the need to adapt to technological advances, physicians are under more stress than ever. This stress takes a tremendous toll on physicians' well-being, all the while increasing their risk of psychiatric disorders, addiction, and stress-related medical illnesses. In addition, physicians are working longer hours, a situation that only compounds these issues.

The American Medical Association (AMA) defines physician impairment as "any physical, mental or behavioral disorder that interferes with ability to engage safely in professional activities...."[2] Recognition of the impaired physician began to emerge as a concern only in the 1970s, and led to the development of physician health programs (PHPs) (Gastfriend 2005).[3] And for decades, these PHPs, such as those sponsored by state medical societies and others at the hospital level, have been vital in the identification, triage, treatment, and monitoring of physicians who may suffer from a number of maladies. Greater support and cooperation from licensing boards and hospital medical disciplinary entities have greatly assisted in this process, while a "tough love" approach that helps physicians but holds them accountable has brought these issues into the foreground where they can be openly addressed. Physicians and patients alike have been positively impacted by these efforts, as physicians' professional engagement, the quality of care they provide, and their ability to prevent becoming overwhelmed depend, in large part, on the

1.   The author acknowledges the contributions of Terri Keville, Esq.; Martin Guerrero, MD, JD; and Beth Ann Middlebrook, Esq., leadership members of the Task Force on Substance Use Disorders and Mental Health of the ABA Health Law Section in the preparation of the 2015 edition of this chapter, in particular the discussion of legal concerns related to this topic.
2.   *See* AMA policy H-95.955 Physician Impairment, *available at* https://policysearch.ama-assn.org/policyfinder/detail/H-95.955?uri=%2FAMADoc%2FHOD.xml-0-5334.xml.
3.   David Gastfriend, *Physician substance abuse and recovery: What Does It Mean for Physicians—and Everyone Else?* JAMA. 2005; 293(12): 1513-1515.

fulfillment they find in work (Gunderman and Brown 2006).[4] In the past, these entities focused on the addiction itself. However, over the years the focus has expanded to providing comprehensive addiction programs specializing in treating physicians and other healthcare professionals in order to achieve higher abstinence rates and successful, responsible transition back to the workplace.[5]

This chapter will focus on the various mechanisms involved with helping the distressed physician, as well as related legal issues. Addiction will be highlighted, but attention will also be given to other areas of potential impairment.

There are some recent disturbing trends involving some licensing boards being more punitive in their approach to addicted physicians who have been appropriately treated and are in comprehensive monitoring with their state PHP. I have had reports from various parts of the country describing some licensing boards offering decreased utilization of a care and counseling agreements, instead, relying on probationary license status instead. One of the problems that stems from this is that a probationary license interferes with one's ability to get on insurance panels and this greatly prohibits the ability to practice. I see this as unnecessary since the same effective process in holding the physician accountable can be accomplished with a care and counseling agreement.

More recently, here in Illinois, we have seen an even more extreme situation where, on appeal, a probationary license recommendation shifted to a suspended license in a physician compliant with all aspects of her treatment and monitoring programs. This case is illustrated by Lillian Walanka, Esq., in vignette form in section VI.C. What seems to be a pattern of members of some medical licensing boards to demonstrate "toughness," ostensibly in the service of protecting the public, will have the opposite effect—that is, a greater reluctance for the physician in need to come forward and get the help he or she needs. If this trend increases, it would be a major step backward and greatly risk driving the problem of physician addiction further underground where all involved will suffer. This would be tragic in the face of the well-documented superior outcomes that result from the properly treated and monitored physician, as highlighted in this chapter, especially at a time of high burnout within our physician population.

II. Unique Features of Physicians in General

The environmental factors that can impede physician well-being include the stress of high expectations, the need to make life-and-death decisions, sometimes with limited experience, and disruptive lifestyles due to demanding and inconsistent schedules.

---

4. Brown S, Gunderman RB, *Viewpoint: Enhancing the professional fulfillment of physicians.* ACAD MED. 2006 Jun; 81(6): 577-82.

5. DANIEL ANGRES, G. DOUGLAS TALBOTT, & KATHY BETTINARDI-ANGRES, HEALING THE HEALER, Psychosocial Press, 1998.

Studies suggest that physicians tend to be compulsive perfectionists, a particular personality trait that has been shown to increase the risk for anxiety and depressive disorders, both of which are linked to addiction.[6] Along with this insight, Glen Gabbard, M.D. from Menninger Clinic describes maladaptive tendencies that include difficulty engaging in leisure activities or taking vacations from work activities, a tendency to be satisfied with a low level of intimacy, such as the type between physician and patient, and a need to assume control of uncontrollable events.

Difficulty setting limits was also noted, along with guilty feelings relative to the pursuit of personal pleasure. Physicians also demonstrate a tendency to seek marital partners who are skilled at maintaining family relationships and household responsibilities, yet may have difficulty connecting on a deep emotional level with their partners because they are satisfied with the low level of intimacy they typically feel at the workplace.

With regard to the medical marriage, social status and financial stability are the rewards, but the bond often feels empty and delayed gratification is common. Future studies may explore the proposition that the combination of high levels of stress, without a commensurate level of emotional intimacy and connection, enhance the physician's vulnerability to substance use. Moreover, it has been established that increased accessibility to drugs does increase the likelihood of abuse or addiction in physicians.

III. Physicians and Personality Styles

Knowledge of the common traits of professionals with addictive disorders helps to facilitate the clinician's formulation of effective individualized treatment plans. In terms of healthcare professionals, as noted above, research studies suggest that physicians tend to be compulsive perfectionists. Gabbard used observations from a workshop setting on the role of compulsiveness in the normal physician and related case examples to illustrate the impact of these behaviors on the professional, personal and family life of the typical physician. Maladaptive implications include difficulty engaging in leisure activities or taking vacations from work activities, problems allocating appropriate time for family functions, and a desire to assume control of uncontrollable events. Difficulties in setting limits were also noted, along with guilty feelings relative to the pursuit of personal pleasure which set up a lifestyle of "delayed gratification." Participation in a competitive and high-profile profession may serve to mitigate long-term feelings of poor self-esteem and to please or impress an internalized parent; similarly, the "impostor phenomenon," "which occurs when high-achieving individuals chronically question their abilities

---

6. K. Henning, S. Ey, D. Shaw, *Perfectionism, the impostor phenomenon and psychological adjustment in medical, dental, nursing and pharmacy students.* MEDICAL EDUCATION.1998; 32(5): 456–464.

and fear that others will discover them to be intellectual frauds," also factors in the road to physicians' addictions.[7]

Certain specialties among healthcare professionals have demonstrated increased risk of addiction and drug of choice (Angres, *Healing the Healer*). In addition to anesthesia, emergency medicine and psychiatry may have higher rates of drug abuse that may be impacted by the baseline personalities of these physicians.

There are any number of personality styles, features, traits, and disorders in addicted professionals. Career choice, drug of choice, gender, age of addiction onset, trauma, and a host of other factors can influence personality. In addition to obsessive tendencies and the minimizing or indirect seeking of dependency needs in professional populations, one study published in the *Journal of Affective Disorders* suggests that physicians and lawyers have higher rates of dysthymic temperament and obsessive-compulsive personality traits when compared with the control group of outpatients in various other professions. Needless to say, the causes of practitioners' distress are numerous, and range from a loss of control over their work spaces to unmanageable workloads and frequent experiences with human suffering and death. (Shanafelt and West, 2007).

In ongoing outcomes research at the Positive Sobriety Institute, an addictions treatment program in Chicago that works with addicted professionals including physicians, we have been looking at personality testing as predictors of abstinence. We have noted that several facets in the NEO five factor personality inventory appear to be predictive of better outcomes in all of our patients. Lower scores in neuroticism and higher scores in conscientiousness, especially the subfactor of dutifulness, correlates with higher levels of participation in continuing care which is a major predictor of good outcome.[8] Physicians tend to be high in conscientiousness overall including higher in the factor of dutifulness which we believe facilitates their participation in state PHP monitoring programs. Participation in these PHP monitoring programs following specialized treatment is critical for the outstanding outcomes as discussed later in this article.

IV. Physician Addiction in the Workplace: Identification, Intervention and Assessment

Many studies suggest physicians are not at greater risk than the general population for substance use disorders—approximately 10 percent to 12 percent will develop chemical addictions during their careers (Berge, Seppala, and Schipper 2006). They tend to use prescription drugs more often than the general public and are more likely to have access to drugs in the workplace or through personal prescription. A

---

7. *Id.*

8. Werby J, Lui P, J. Caldeugh, Angres D. "Personality Predicting Relapse: An Individual Subfactor Analysis of the NEO," NAADAC National Conference, Sept 28-Oct 3rd, 2019 Orlando, FL.

survey conducted by DuPont, et al., found that the most common drugs of abuse were alcohol (50 percent) and opioids (3 percent). The other 15 percent included stimulants, sedatives, marijuana, and other substances. Across PHPs, 31 percent of physicians had problems with both drugs and alcohol, with nearly half (48 percent) also qualified for psychiatric disorders and/or pain problems. (DuPont, McLellan, Carr, et al, 2009).

A. Identification of Addiction in the Workplace

The addicted professional has unique features and tendencies as compared to the general population. Proper identification is essential for the treatment of addiction in the professional. The workplace is often the last place addiction is exposed, so if there are signs at work, the disease is usually progressed. There is increasing emphasis on educating professionals about the course of addiction in themselves and their colleagues. This has been driven in part by addiction being given a disease status—chemical dependency falls under the category of a disability with legal ramifications for employers—and due to the high prevalence of substance use disorders and addiction in our society. Proper identification results from adequately educating those around the addicted professional about the disease of addiction and its manifestations. Education in the workplace is critical in determining whether a colleague is addicted, and should include discussions about the potential liability and legal ramifications of drug diversion and drug abuse.

There are a number of signs that typify addiction in the workplace, and gaining some knowledge of the disease signs can facilitate proper identification. These include:

1) chaotic personal and professional life;

2) frequent tardiness and absenteeism;

3) poorly explained accidents and injuries;

4) relationship discord: martial, family, professional;

5) deterioration in personal appearance;

6) significant weight loss or gain;

7) long sleeves and tinted glasses inappropriate for the setting;

8) overuse of cologne and breath fresheners;

9) legal problems—e.g., DUIs or arrests for possession, disorderly conduct or, in the case of healthcare professionals, inappropriate prescribing of controlled substances;

10) severe mood swings unrelated to situations or exaggerated mood responses, dramatic change in personality;

11) increased isolation (often due to shame and fear);

12) withdrawal from family, friends and coworkers—e.g., always refuses social invitations;

13) frequent disappearances during work hours;

14) overt evidence of addiction at work, such as the smell of alcohol on the individual's breath during working hours;

15) cognitive impairment;

16) excessive time spent with narcotics, missing/unaccounted-for narcotics, excessive "wasting" of narcotics, medical records discrepancies involving narcotics (e.g., record shows patient received half the amount that was drawn, or twice the amount actually given based upon observation), avoidance of medication reconciliation procedures (specific for healthcare);

17) dilated or pinpoint pupils;

18) drug-seeking—e.g., asking other physicians for prescriptions for mood altering substances at a healthcare workplace;

19) increase in physical complaints;

20) financial strain;

21) a negative or apathetic attitude; and

22) working extra shifts (in order to obtain substances).

These changes can be gradual or sudden, and an individual usually exhibits several signs from the above list.

The professional usually takes care to conceal the addiction from the workplace because he or she prioritizes his or her professional identity and thus, as noted above, the workplace is often the last place that addiction is noticed—by which point the condition is progressed. Moreover, the workplace is oftentimes the source for the health professional's substances. Protecting his or her drug source becomes paramount to the addicted professional.

Simply stated, addiction can be detected by observing the professional's work performance. Often, regularly scheduled performance evaluations will illustrate a decline in productivity and quality of work. Performance evaluations and other policies and procedures for handling discovery of addiction problems are badly needed, as addiction has become increasingly common. A lack of pre-existing policies may result in medical or legal liabilities, and also perpetuates the ongoing addiction, which can have catastrophic consequences for the addicted physician and the innocent people with whom that professional comes into contact within the workplace.

Whatever the means of identification, it is imperative to verbalize suspicions in an appropriate manner. When overt evidence of addiction in the workplace is apparent, this often represents a progressed condition. Employers or colleagues often feel the need to avoid confrontation or question their observations. This can create a "conspiracy of silence" that will only allow the addiction to progress with possible adverse effects on the addict and the workplace. If employers and colleagues could think of an intervention as a compassionate and necessary step for the addict, it would benefit everyone. An intervention is often implemented by intervention professionals under an employee assistance program (EAP) or an outside consultant trained in professional interventions. A planned intervention has the greatest success.

Points to Remember

- Identification of an addicted peer requires knowledge of signs and symptoms of addiction and the ability to compassionately and effectively implement an intervention or other assistance measures. Healthcare workplaces can arrange for continuing medical education programs to inform physicians on this subject.

- A "conspiracy of silence" is common in professions, but ineffective and reckless for the safety of the addict and others.

- There are compassionate and effective ways to intervene, such as referral for treatment and supervision under the auspices of a physician "Well-Being Committee" in a hospital, or the use of an EAP within the organization. As discussed further below, hospitals accredited by the Joint Commission are required to have such committees.

B. Intervention

If chemical dependency is suspected, an intervention is the next appropriate step. An intervention occurs when the professional suspected of abusing drugs and/or alcohol is initially confronted, and it is usually an extremely stressful event for both the suspected professional and the individual(s) intervening.[9] Therefore, it is helpful to have a policy in place for these types of scenarios that will facilitate a successful approach.

It is important to discern whether the practitioner's impairment is the result of mood altering substances or some other stressful event in his or her life. The presence of an addiction problem can be elucidated with an effective intervention.

---

9. K.H. Berge, M.D. Seppala, A.M. Schipper, *Chemical dependency and the physician.* MAYO CLINIC PROC. 2009 Jul; 84(7):625-31.

There are a number of ways to intervene with an addict, from informal confrontations to formal professionally facilitated interventions. However, the author cautions employers and colleagues regarding informal confrontations because of the strength of denial in the addict and the risk of an unsuccessful outcome; as Cicala notes, "a hallmark of substance abuse is a remarkable denial on the part of the abuser that there is no problem, even as they go to great lengths to hide the symptoms of the problem."[10]

An informal intervention can be effective in circumstances where there is a high degree of trust and a receptive attitude on the part of the individual suspected of being an addict toward a colleague or supervisor. More likely though, this individual will feel embarrassed, defensive and even betrayed in these circumstances and refuse help. It is crucial that the professional not be directly accused of diverting drugs or asked to stop using drugs. This is an inefficient means of intervening which will most likely result in the denial of drug use, and could result in the occurrence of a desperate act such as suicide.[11]

A formal intervention involves a trained interventionist. A trained interventionist understands the disease of addiction, knows referrals for treatment, and employs a judgment-free attitude of compassion. An employer or colleague may consult with an interventionist, then proceed with the process on his or her own as well. However, please note that this may not be a viable option in the medical staff context, particularly if the physician is not employed, as it may conflict with the physician's fair procedure rights.

Utilizing an EAP human resource department, or ideally, a non-disciplinary process within the work setting like a hospital physician wellness committee, will reap the most successful results in interventions. It is important to note the advantages of a workplace-initiated intervention over family interventions, including the influence of potential workplace consequences, which are important for the financial and professional survival of most individuals. It is the potential or actual consequences of addiction that initially convince an addict to get help.

A compassionate intervention is the ideal situation, but this author is well aware that many addicted professionals are terminated in lieu of any intervention. There are consequences to this action, such as passing on an unfit individual to another workplace, losing the possibility of a grateful and loyal employee in recovery, and becoming part of the "conspiracy of silence" that threatens our society with active addiction.

---

10. R. Cicala, *Substance abuse among physicians: what you need to know.* Hosp Physician. 2005; 39-46.

11. Berge *supra* note 8.

Points to Remember

- There are informal and formal interventions. The most effective approach is a formal intervention via EAP or Well-Being Committee personnel or a trained interventionist.

- The advantages of workplace interventions are the influence and consequences that are important to most professionals; they often have more success in implementing and maintaining sobriety in an individual.

C. **Assessment**

The assessment typically is done upon admission to a program for the treatment of addictions. An initial and brief assessment can be provided or obtained by the Well-Being Committee, EAP, or PHP and thereby give the individual a choice of treatment options based on certain criteria mentioned below. In cases where there is resistance, lack of clarity about the problem, or continued denial on the part of the professional, a mandatory, comprehensive assessment is often necessary and can be instituted by the employer or medical staff with the possible consequence of termination if the individual does not comply. As noted above, procedural rights may apply in the medical staff context.

D. **The Role of the Well-Being Committee**

The Joint Commission requires that each hospital it accredits have an independently functioning wellness committee that can work with physicians who struggle with addiction or other types of impairment. Although these committees, which often are referred to as "Well-Being Committees," can have responsibilities to general medical staff and disciplinary committees, they operate to some degree autonomously and exercise a more supportive role for the struggling physician. These committees are typically composed of members who have an interest in and experience working with physicians, and tend to be individuals interested in the identification, appropriate assessment, rehabilitation, and reentry of these physicians back into the workplace and practice of medicine in a way that is firm yet caring.

In addition, these committees often institute well-being strategies in the hospital for all physicians, such as "fun runs" or other activities that can promote wellness and work-life balance amongst the physician population in that hospital setting.

These committees are critical in identifying possible impairment in their medical staffs and making the necessary referrals for assessment. It is imperative that these committees do not actually assess the suspected individual themselves, but are simply available to intervene and make necessary referrals, including for disciplinary action by the medical staff if the impaired physician does not cooperate. Where the physician does follow the recommendations, the medical staff office can be made aware of the situation and the referral to the Well-Being Committee. The Well-Being Committee also is a necessary element for the continued monitoring of the physician upon his or her return to the medical staff, along with the treatment program and in many instances, the state PHP.

V.   Comprehensive Evaluation

Comprehensive evaluation routinely entails a team of trained professionals with differing areas of expertise. This is sometimes described as a multidisciplinary assessment program (MAP) in one setting and is generally 48 hours or more in duration. A typical MAP team includes:

- MAP clinician/administrator: Responsible for scheduling and organizing the MAP, as well as collecting collateral data after obtaining informed consent. Obtaining collateral data is essential for this type of evaluation. The MAP is generally required because there is significant resistance and/or confusion about the source of any suspected impairment. This collateral data is obtained with written consent from the individual being assessed. There are typically multiple personal and professional sources that are contacted for collateral data. This clinician/administrator is also responsible for organizing and summarizing the final report.

- Psychiatrist: Responsible for performing a comprehensive psychiatric evaluation. This psychiatrist has expertise in addictions and fitness-for-duty issues. At times, a forensic psychiatrist is necessary, especially where legal issues predominate. These legal issues may include multiple DUI offenses, prescribing offenses including suspicion of, or allegations related to, trafficking of controlled substances, or even allegations of boundary violations (e.g. sexual harassment). All legal issues, past and present, must be revealed to determine the appropriate treatment for the individual. A neuro-psychiatrist should be included in a case involving suspected cognitive impairment.

- Psychologist: Responsible for administering and interpreting psychological testing, such as the Millon (MCMI-III) and the Minnesota Multiphasic Personality Inventory (MMPI). Screening with an instrument such as the Wechsler Aptitude Screening Instrument (WASI) is often necessary to rule out deficits in cognition that can occur with substance use disorders or for other reasons, such as dementia. In cases where cognitive deficits are identified or suspected, neuropsychological treatment is performed by an additional neuropsychologist. In these cases, consultation with a neurologist and imaging studies like magnetic resonance imaging are required to rule out a neurologic disorder such as a tumor or degenerative disease (i.e.

multiple sclerosis) or degeneration from alcohol or other substances. This component is obviously important in assessing the high accountability professional and his or her ability to safely do his or her job.

- Addictions Specialist: Responsible for performing an in-depth substance use and abuse evaluation.

- Internist: Responsible for a thorough history and physical including necessary lab work to fully assess medical health.

- Neurologist: Responsible for clinical evaluation in a case involving issues such as impairment of motor skills in a late-career practitioner.

- Senior Supervising Psychiatrist: Responsible for reviewing the report and recommending any necessary changes to ensure completeness of any final report.

Other specialists should be included as appropriate to the specific issues. The MAP is, by far, the most thorough way to evaluate a professional with impairment from addiction or for any other reason.

Points to Remember

- Identification of the professional with addiction or other impairment in the workplace is important for several reasons. It provides the opportunity for an addicted individual to recover and for otherwise impaired physicians to seek appropriate evaluation and treatment, may allow the workplace to retain a valuable member of the team, recognizes addiction as a disease so as to avoid related legal missteps in the workplace (see further discussion below), and reinforces the need for compassionate and early intervention in fighting addiction.

- The natural inclination for employers and colleagues is to avoid the situation and resolve the problem by terminating the addict, so professionals must be educated and encouraged to participate in the identification, intervention, and assessment of the addicted or otherwise impaired colleague.

- There is a formal process for intervention and assessment that increases the accuracy of diagnosis and appropriate referral for help. It reduces the risks involved in the "conspiracy of silence" that drives addiction underground and increases the dire consequences of active addiction on others in the workplace and society.

A. Vignette

1. *Simply More Depressed than Usual*

Dr. Jones was a promising young single general surgeon. Dr. Jones was highly regarded by his peers and the hospital in which he practiced.

It therefore came as a shock when, after about six years of solid practice, he began to change dramatically. He started missing work and when he did show up, he looked disheveled and sad. When friends and office staff asked if he was alright, he would be dismissive and curt, saying he had a cold or was working too hard. Eventually he escalated to the point where his staff was concerned about him and his patients. After he was missing for two consecutive clinic days, and unreachable by phone, two of his staff went to his apartment and had to get security to let them in. Dr. Jones was in bed and difficult to arouse. He eventually agreed to go to the emergency room to be evaluated and it was determined he was under the influence of hydrocodone and antidepressants. Dr. Jones explained to the ER staff that he had injured his back a year ago and became depressed. He assured them that he was taking his medications as prescribed and was simply more depressed than usual. He was reported by the ER staff to the Physician Well-Being Committee of the hospital.[12] The committee in turn required Dr. Jones to receive a comprehensive evaluation despite his insistence to see a psychiatrist in the community. Since there were potential patient safety issues, the committee had the authority to require an independent comprehensive evaluation. The evaluation determined that Dr. Jones had an addiction problem, and he was referred to a professional's treatment program for addiction and depression.

2. Intervening

This was a difficult situation for Dr. Jones' coworkers. He was such a competent and caring doctor, and he was valued by the hospital. His reputation made it particularly difficult to accept the change in behavior and potential harm he posed to himself and his patients. However, when he missed two clinic days without any communication, his staff became worried. They insisted he go to an emergency room, which gave all of his coworkers an opportunity to intervene. In

---

12. Dr. Jones sought treatment at the hospital where he practiced, and was treated in the ER by medical staff colleagues. Under the federal Health Insurance Portability and Accountability Act of 1996 (HIPAA) and the implementing Department of Health and Human Services regulations known as the Privacy Rule (45 CFR §§ 164.500, *et seq.*), the Definitions section found at 45 CFR § 164.501 defines "Healthcare operations" to include "[r]eviewing the competence or qualifications of healthcare professionals, [and] evaluating practitioner and provider performance,. . . ." HIPAA Covered Entities such as hospitals are expressly permitted by the Privacy Rule to use and disclose protected health information, without an authorization, for healthcare operations. *See* 45 CFR §§ 164.502(a)(1)(ii) and 164.506(a). Thus, it would appear that under the circumstances, the ER physicians' report to the Well-Being Committee could be characterized as a permissible part of the hospital's healthcare operations.

this case a formal intervention was avoided but the recommendation was still difficult for the hospital. This was an acute, potentially dangerous situation and his caring staff did the right thing by going to his apartment. In other cases, a family member can be contacted and assist in the process. This was not possible for Dr. Jones, who was single and lived alone. The ER staff was also correct in letting the Well-Being Committee know about Dr. Jones' situation.

B. Potential Reporting Requirements

In cases where there are reportable events, such as diversion of narcotics from the hospital or summary suspension of clinical privileges for more than a very brief period, the hospital may need to report the incident and/or the response to the incident to the state licensing board, the state pharmacy board, the National Practitioner Data Bank (NPDB), and/or the federal Drug Enforcement Administration. The state licensing board usually conducts its own investigation, and typically supports re-entry to practice under certain conditions, such as a consent order or probationary license. If there is noncompliance, for example, if Dr. Jones had refused to be assessed, he would be subject to disciplinary action taken by the hospital and the licensing board. Even in these cases, the hospital and the licensing board will attempt to direct the individual to assessment, treatment and recovery.

C. The Comprehensive Assessment

In the case of Dr. Jones, a comprehensive assessment was necessary. He did not initially admit to addiction, and rationalized his drug use by reporting his problems with pain and depression. He pushed for a less comprehensive evaluation by a psychiatrist in the community. The comprehensive evaluation is valuable to rule out addiction in a formal setting that utilizes professional input, collateral data and a hair analysis. These are examples of elements that are typically part of a comprehensive evaluation such as a MAP. In addition to identifying or ruling out addiction problems, often these comprehensive assessments are also used to evaluate behavior problems like sexual harassment, other improper interpersonal conduct, chronic charting problems or excessive tardiness or absences. These other behaviors fall under the rubric of the "disruptive physician or professional" where addiction may or may not be a source of the difficulties, but if so, it is not the only problem. In these cases, a psychiatric diagnosis, such as a personality disorder or major depression, may be the underlying issue. In certain cases, a cognitive deficit from a neurological condition or medical problem may be the core issue. In any case, the comprehensive evaluation is best suited to identify the problems and give appropriate recommendations for the necessary follow-up. The evaluators must have input from colleagues who are familiar with the physician's behavior in the workplace.

Points to Remember

- Hospitals, like many businesses, are required to have intervention and support mechanisms within their organizations.

- A comprehensive multidisciplinary assessment is of great value in cases where the individual in question is not forthcoming and/or there are serious behavioral concerns.

- Disciplinary action should be used as a backup plan when needed to facilitate necessary treatment.

- In most cases, licensing entities will support successful rehabilitation and re-entry.

VI.   Physician Health Programs

Most states in the country have PHPs that generally operate as part of the state medical society in that particular state. Some of these programs have a direct relationship with the licensing board in that state while others have total independence and autonomy. In either case, PHPs, act as "diversion" programs. That is, they are able to take responsibility for helping to educate, identify, refer, and facilitate reentry and monitoring for the affected physician. They are able to do so with some degree of autonomy and still hold the physicians accountable for their recovery. They are a critical component in the process of the identified excellent outcomes in this population.

Typically, PHPs monitor physicians for a minimum of five years, in some states even longer. They interface with treatment programs, wellness committees at the hospitals, sometimes the licensing board if necessary, as well as other entities that may be involved with the treatment, aftercare and monitoring of the physician. They are the point program to facilitate all of the various elements that are involved in the ongoing support monitoring of the physician; often including treating psychiatrists, individual therapists, and even family support. They are also instrumental in the urine monitoring or hair analysis that is critical to both document ongoing abstinence and to identify relapse. The PHPs are a critical component of the superior outcomes of addicted physicians completing professionals' programs.

A.   Caduceus Groups

These groups were started by G. Douglas Talbott in the 1970s. Dr. Talbott, a pioneer in the field of treating the addicted physician, identified the Caduceus emblem for medicine as a way to create a peer group for physicians. Although there have been many types of Caduceus groups, today they mostly describe the specific aftercare that is specialized for the addicted physician in recovery, and have come to include other addicted professionals. The importance of a peer group is not only evident in the treatment process, but also in the ongoing aftercare support and monitoring for the healthcare professional.

B. The American Medical Association Physician Wellness Program

The AMA has been active in supporting the health and wellness of all physicians, including the appropriate identification, rehabilitation, and reentry of all physicians, whether or not they are AMA members. The AMA has sponsored physician wellness conferences over the last several decades to actively support this initiative.

C. State Licensing Boards

State licensing boards are entrusted to maintain public safety relating to physician practice. Over the years, licensing boards have adopted the approach that it is better to identify and work openly with impairment, rather than to be purely disciplinarian or punitive. The latter stance has historically driven the problem underground, which actually is more risky for the addicted individual and the public. This is known as "the conspiracy of silence" and only exacerbates the problem. The addicted individual continues to use and has more opportunity to hurt him/herself or others when the problem of addiction is not addressed. Licensing boards are responsible for ensuring public safety by monitoring licensed professionals. They do not necessarily become involved in cases of impairment unless there are disciplinary actions taken at the hospital, or there is a complaint filed, or public evidence of impairment such as a driving-under-the-influence arrest and/or charges.

Licensing boards, in many states, will defer to the PHPs, treatment providers, and monitors in regards to managing cases. However, they do investigate cases and hold hearings on licensure status when necessary. A number of licensure status conditions may be imposed, including consent agreements (less formal), consent orders, probations, suspensions, and even revocations. Licensing boards have generally been supportive of those physicians who have followed up responsibly with the various treatment recommendations of the entities involved with their recovery.

The approach of a medical board toward a physician who suffers from alcohol or substance addiction has far-reaching consequences not only to the individual physician but also to the medical community. In Illinois, for example, the Medical Practice Act provides an option allowing the Medical Disciplinary Board (Board) to recommend a non-disciplinary Agreement of Care, Counseling and Treatment in lieu of a public, reportable discipline (225 ILCS 60/22). This type of confidential, non-disciplinary agreement between the physician and the Board allows the physician to continue treatment and aftercare with a high level of accountability to the Board while at the same time enabling the physician to work without the stigma of a public discipline. If the physician fails to comply, the confidential agreement would be terminated and a public discipline may result. Thus, the physician is afforded a chance to demonstrate compliance with a recovery program before a punitive action is taken.

Vignette:

Dr. Smith is a highly respected anesthesiologist who diverted waste from the workplace. He was terminated and reported to the state licensing agency. Immediately upon being terminated, he voluntarily sought in-patient treatment followed by intensive outpatient treatment, which he successfully completed. He entered into a PHP contract, underwent random toxicology screens, attended Caduceus and Alcoholics Anonymous, had almost daily contact with his sponsor, and saw a therapist and a psychiatrist. He self-reported the addiction, termination, and his recovery to the licensing agency. He has been in solid, documented recovery for over two years. The licensing agency compelled Dr. Smith to undergo an evaluation that resulted in a recommendation that he is fit to practice medicine, and specifically anesthesiology, with certain conditions. Dr. Smith's PHP, treatment provider, therapist, and psychiatrist supported the recommendation. Initially, the licensing agency and the Board offered Dr. Smith an Agreement of Care, Counseling, and Treatment, which was later rejected by an administrative supervisor of the agency. The agency proposed a new offer of a public discipline, including the loss of Dr. Smith's controlled substance license thereby precluding Dr. Smith from returning to practice of anesthesiology for an indeterminate period and possibly from the practice of medicine. By taking this punitive position, the licensing agency focused on the initial conduct and ignored the over-two years of recovery Dr. Smith completed and his commitment to continued recovery. The consequence of punishing the recovering physician is that the medical community and patients are deprived of a skilled anesthesiologist. This is a self-defeating and short-sighted position for the licensing agency because the unintended effect of imposing a public, reportable discipline against the recovering physician rather than a non-disciplinary agreement with monitoring conditions is that other impaired physicians may not seek help in fear of jeopardizing their medical careers.

D. Employee Assistance Programs

EAPs are essential in cases where hospitals utilize EAP services. EAPs are composed of staff well-versed in understanding addiction and other impairments, along with the clinical and reentry issues. EAPs can act as intermediaries, much like the PHPs, and often work in conjunction with the other treatment entities for the physician.

E. Physician Impairment Independent of Addiction

Physicians who struggle with conditions other than addiction that can cause impairment, such as mental health conditions, psychiatric disorders, cognitive impairment, chronic pain, or other physical conditions, can benefit from many of the same intervention, assessment, and monitoring entities and activities discussed in this chapter. Whereas specific treatments may substantially differ, such as individual therapy for a depressed physician, some of the support and monitoring strategies mentioned above may need to be accessed if the physician's condition has manifested itself in the workplace. Prevention, assessment, treatment, and monitoring are critical in these instances, especially with conditions such as major depressive disorder that can increase an already higher risk of suicide in physicians as a whole.[13]

VII. Legal Concerns

This section is intended to alert readers to a range of legal issues that may be associated with assisting impaired physicians. It is by no means an exhaustive discussion, and we encourage readers to analyze carefully how federal and/or particular state laws may apply in each case.

A. Fair Procedure

As mentioned above, physicians may be entitled to certain procedural rights in connection with actions taken by healthcare organizations in response to identified or suspected physician impairment.

The federal Health Care Quality Improvement Act of 1986 (HCQIA) resulted in the creation of a national repository for certain information about healthcare practitioners (the NPDB), to help prevent problem physicians from simply relocating to avoid adverse action.[14] HCQIA also provides immunity to peer review participants if they report adverse actions to the NPDB, as required by HCQIA, and they comply with HCQIA's fair procedure requirements. To qualify for immunity, a peer review action must be taken: (1) with the reasonable belief that it is in furtherance of quality healthcare; (2) after a reasonable effort to obtain the facts; (3) after notice and hearing procedures that are reasonable under the

---

13. E. Schernhammer, *Taking Their Own Lives—The high rate of physician suicide*. N ENGL J MED. 2005. 352;2473.

14. *See* 42 USC §§11101, 11134-11136.

circumstances (see below); and (4) with the reasonable belief that the action was warranted by the facts known after a reasonable effort to obtain them and appropriate process. HCQIA specifies various procedures to be followed prior to and during a hearing, such as adequate notice of the action, including the reasons for it; a summary of the applicable hearing rights; deadline for requesting a hearing, etc.; the right to a mutually acceptable arbitrator or a hearing officer and/or hearing panel not in direct economic competition with the physician; the right to representation at the hearing; the right to call, examine, and cross-examine witnesses; the right to a written recommendation of the trier of fact and written decision of the healthcare entity, etc.[15] However, strict compliance with all of the enumerated rights is not required for immunity;[16] in other words, substantial compliance is sufficient.

Some states also have their own fair procedure requirements. For example, California Business and Professions Code sections 809.1 through 809.5 establish minimum procedural requirements (similar but not identical to HCQIA's) that must be met with respect to any adverse action—such as a restriction, suspension, or termination of clinical privileges—that a peer review body must report to the Medical Board of California under Business and Professions Code section 805. In addition, section 809.6 mandates that hospitals comply with any additional procedural rights provided in medical staff bylaws or physician contracts, and prohibits any waiver of the rights established by sections 809.1 through 809.4. Examples of particular statutorily required procedures include notices with specified timing and elements—such as a list of the "acts or omissions with which the licentiate is charged"; the right to *voir dire* of the hearing panel members and hearing officer; the right to prehearing exchange of exhibits and witness lists; the right to call, examine, and cross-examine witnesses; the right to have a record made of the proceedings; the right to submit a written statement at the close of the hearing; and the right to receive a written decision of the trier of fact. Thus, if a hospital or other healthcare provider subject to such laws finds it necessary to restrict or terminate a physician's participation due to impairment issues, the organization must consider whether such rights apply to that action—and if so, the organization must ensure compliance.

Apart from the hospital peer review context, various state laws provide for due process rights with respect to actions that may be taken against the impaired physician. For example, Florida Statutes, section 458.331(1)(s), provides for action to be taken by the Department of Health (DOH) or

---

15. 42 USC § 11112.
16. 42 USC § 11112(b).

applicable board when a physician is unable to practice medicine with reasonable skill and safety to patients by reason of illness or use of alcohol, drugs, narcotics, chemicals, etc., or as a result of any mental or physical condition. Prior to any disciplinary measures, the state surgeon general (or his/her designee) must find that probable cause exists to believe that the physician is unable to practice medicine because of these reasons. Upon a finding of probable cause, the DOH has the authority to issue an order to compel the physician to submit to a mental or physical examination. A physician may refuse to comply and require the DOH to seek enforcement of its order in civil court, placing the burden of proof on the DOH. If the order is enforced, and if the examination results in a finding that the physician is unable to practice medicine with reasonable skill and safety, the physician may choose to self-refer to the impaired practitioner program (professionals resource network (PRN)) as provided for in Florida Statutes section 456.076 (which may likely prevent disciplinary proceedings if impairment is the only issue). The DOH may also pursue disciplinary proceedings as provided for in section 456.073 and chapter 120, which delineate procedural and due process requirements, and/or it may pursue emergency suspension pursuant to section 120.60 and Florida Administrative Code 28-106.501, which also set forth the physician's procedural rights.

B. The Americans with Disabilities Act and the Rehabilitation Act

The federal Americans with Disabilities Act (ADA) and Rehabilitation Act (Rehab Act) generally protect employees from discrimination on the basis of disability.[17] Although these laws clearly apply to employed physicians, courts in different jurisdictions around the country have disagreed about whether the Rehab Act applies to physicians who are **not** employees. For example, the Ninth Circuit decided in 2010 that an independent contractor physician could pursue a Rehab Act claim,[18] and in doing so expressly disagreed with a Third Circuit decision to the contrary. It is also important to note that under the ADA, an individual who is currently engaging in the illegal use of drugs does not have a protected disability.[19] A physician who is in recovery from substance abuse—e.g., participating in a supervised rehabilitation program and no longer engaging in illicit use, is protected[20]—but an employer can prohibit the use of alcohol and the illegal use of drugs by all employees in the workplace, and can hold an active

---

17. Americans with Disabilities Act of 1990, Pub. L. No. 101-336, 104 Stat. 328 (1990), 42 U.S.C. §12101 *et seq.*; Rehabilitation Act of 1973, Pub.L.No.93-112, 87 Stat. 355 (1973), 29 U.S.C. §701 *et seq.*

18. Fleming v. Yuma Regional Medical Center, 587 F.3d 938 (2009).

19. 42 USC §12114(a); 12210(a).

20. 42 USC §12114(b); 12210(b).

alcoholic or a current user of illegal drugs to the same standards of performance as other employees.[21]

Accordingly, it is essential for healthcare organizations dealing with physicians with addiction and other health issues, such as performance limitations resulting from a stroke or injury, to be mindful of disability discrimination laws. As with fair procedure and privacy, rights under state disability laws may apply as well.[22]

C. The Age Discrimination in Employment Act

As the general United States population ages, more Americans are living longer, and medical science is recognizing an increasing number of disorders due to age-related mental and physical processes. In addition, there is a documented increase in the number of Alzheimer's dementia cases; in 2011, the estimated number of Americans with Alzheimer's disease was about 5.4 million, with a projected increase to 7.7 million by the year 2030.[23] Accordingly, as the "baby boomer" cohort of physician's ages, hospitals and other physician workplaces increasingly encounter health-related issues involving late-career practitioners, such as significant decline in cognitive function or motor skills that can potentially affect patient care.[24] Studies have observed that older physicians cannot perform some tasks as well as their younger colleagues,[25] although there is evi-

---

21. 42 USC § 12114(c); *see also* http://www.eeoc.gov/facts/performance-conduct.html#alcohol (EEOC Q&A on application of the ADA to alcoholism and illegal use of drugs). According to the EEOC, "[r]egardless of coverage under the ADA, an individual's alcoholism or drug addiction cannot be used to shield the employee from the consequences of poor performance or conduct that result from these conditions." *Id.* at n.84. *See, e.g.,* Bekker v. Humana Health Plan, Inc., 229 F.3d 662, 672 (7th Cir. 2000) (upholding termination of a physician for treating patients while under the influence of alcohol).

22. Florida Civil Rights Act of 1992, FL Stat. Ch. 760.

23. Journal of the Alzheimer's Association, March 2011; 7(2): 208-244.

24. *See* Jonathan H. Burroughs, James B. Hogan, & Jennifer H. Richter, *The Aging Physician: Balancing Safety, Respect, and Compliance,* MEDSTAFF NEWS, March 2013, http://www.hallrender.com/health_care_law/library/articles/1465/MedStaff_News_AHLA_March_2013.pdf; Sarah Boodman, *Aging Doctors Face Greater Scrutiny,* KAISER HEALTH NEWS, Dec. 10, 2012 *available at* http:www.kaiserhealthnews.org/stories/2012/december/11/aging-doctors-face-greater-scrutiny.aspx.

25. *See, e.g.,* Jennifer F. Waljee, M.D., M.P.H., Lazar J. Greenfield, M.D., Justin B. Dimick, M.D., M.P.H., & John D. Birkmeyer, M.D., *Surgeon Age and Operative Mortality in the United States,* ANNALS OF SURGERY, vol. 244. no. 3, September 2006 (patient mortality rates in complex procedures were higher for surgeons over 60); Douglass H. Powell, M.D., *Profiles in Cognitive Aging,* HARVARD U. PRESS, December 1994 (after age 55 there was "a consistent and more precipitous decline" in physicians' cognitive function, inductive reasoning, verbal memory, and overall reasoning").

dence of variability in the effect of age on different cognitive domains,[26] and some medical specialties will be impacted more greatly by age-related issues than others. Therefore, the cognitive assessment of physicians in different specialties may require task-specific testing to evaluate full practice competence, but general cognitive screening may still serve as a first step to evaluating possible medical practice deficiencies.

In addition to the ADA, the federal *Age Discrimination in Employment Act of 1967, as amended* (ADEA),[27] may apply to such situations. The ADEA declares, in pertinent part, that it is "unlawful for an employer to fail or refuse to hire or to discharge any individual or otherwise discriminate against any individual with respect to his compensation terms, conditions or privileges of employment, because of such individual's age."[28] Although by its terms the ADEA applies only to employees, as noted above, the courts are split on whether non-employed physicians are nevertheless protected by such antidiscrimination laws—and the recent trend seems to be in the direction of broad application. States have similar laws, although both federal and state laws include some exceptions, such as allowable mandatory retirement ages for specified occupations, e.g., airline pilots. For example, California Government Code section 12942(c)(2) allows medical professional corporations to require physician retirement at age 70. These laws must be taken into account when considering adoption of policies such as a mandatory requirement for evaluation at a specified age, and also when contemplating adverse action based on age-related performance issues.

D. Federal and State Reporting Laws

The AMA reminds physicians of their ethical duty to report impaired colleagues, and to comply with applicable state laws in doing so.[29] A survey of over 1,100 United States physicians indicated that although the majority acknowledged the urgency of reporting significantly impaired colleagues, 15 percent believed that nothing would happen as a result of such reports, and 12 percent feared retaliation for reporting. Physicians working in hospitals and medical schools were more likely to report an impaired or incompetent colleague compared to doctors working in other settings.[30]

26. Drag, et al., J. Am. Coll. Surg. 2012; 211 (3): 303-307.
27. *Pub. L. 90-202, 29 USC § 621, et seq.*
28. 29 USC § 623(a)(1).
29. American Medical Association Council on Ethical and Judicial Affairs, Ethics Opinion 9.3.2, https://policysearch.ama-assn.org/policyfinder/detail/ 9.3.2%20Physician%20Responsibilities%20to%20Impaired%20Colleagues?uri=%2FAMADoc%2FEthics.xml-E-9.3.2.xml (accessed May 13, 2019).
30. DesRoches, et al., JAMA, vol. 304 (2): 187-193 (2009).

The *National Practitioner Data Bank Guidebook* specifically addresses the issue of impaired practitioners. According to the *Guidebook*, "The fact that an impaired practitioner voluntarily enters a rehabilitation program should not be reported to the NPDB if no professional review action was taken and the practitioner did not relinquish clinical privileges while under investigation or in return for not conducting an investigation." [31] However, if a practitioner is required to enter a program involuntarily as the result of a professional review action, or by a hospital or medical staff official such as the CEO or a department chair, that is reportable if it is based on competence or professional conduct and lasts longer than 30 days.[32]

State law also may mandate a report to the state licensing agency if a physician enters a rehabilitation program, depending upon the circumstances, although not all states have mandatory reporting requirements, and in many states a report to the state's PHP is sufficient. In Texas, a physician or peer-review committee must report relevant information to the Texas Medical Board (TMB) relating to the acts of a physician practicing in Texas if, in the opinion of the reporting physician or committee, "that physician poses a continuing threat to the public welfare through the practice of medicine."[33] The physician or committee has discretion to determine if the impaired doctor's behavior poses such a threat. If not, the physician or committee may still make the concerns known to the TMB, and/or to the physician Well-Being Committee of the organization where the impaired physician has privileges. Additionally, an individual Texas licensee is required to report to the TMB if he/she is aware that "another licensee … is unable to practice medicine with reasonable skill and safety to patients because of illness; drunkenness; excessive use of drugs, narcotics, chemicals, or another substance; or a mental or physical condition."[34]

New Mexico has no such mandatory reporting of impaired physicians by another physician. New Mexico's Impaired Health Care Provider Act[35] gives the New Mexico Medical Board authority to appoint an examination committee to evaluate a physician who is alleged to be impaired to practice by either mental or physical illness or the habitual or excessive use of alcohol or drugs. The committee is comprised of three licensed physicians who then conduct an examination of the referred physician and report their findings and recommendations to the board. The committee

---

31. https://www.npdb.hrsa.gov/guidebook/EClinicalPrivilegesQA38.jsp.
32. *Id.*
33. TEX. OCCUPATIONS CODE, tit. 3, subtitle B, ch. 160.003.
34. TEX. ADMIN. CODE, tit. 22, pt.9, ch. 179.4 (c)(2).

can also order that the referred physician submit to a separate mental or physical examination for determination of fitness to practice medicine.

Thus, it is important to review all reporting laws that may be applicable in each case.

E. Federal and State Privacy Laws

Matters involving addicted or otherwise impaired physicians are likely to implicate federal and state laws governing the protection of health information—which in these instances may include both health information about the affected practitioner himself or herself, and health information of his or her patients, if the impairment has affected patient care. HIPAA and the Privacy Rule[36] impose substantial restrictions on the use and disclosure of protected health information. In addition, 42 CFR Part 2 (or Part 2) imposes specific federal law restrictions on the disclosure of alcohol and drug abuse patient records of federally assisted programs as defined therein.[37] Under Part 2, the patient consent must include specific elements, and the patient records cannot be re-disclosed. Federally-assisted substance use disorder programs must comply with both the Privacy Rule and Part 2; thus, such programs must ensure that they have cross-referenced both rules.

HIPAA preempts less stringent state laws, but some states have medical privacy laws that are stricter than HIPAA, which may include particular restrictions on use and disclosure of information about substance use disorder and mental health treatment.[38]

---

35. NMSA sections 61-7-1 through 61-7-12, 1978.

36. 45 CFR §§ 164.500, *et seq.*

37. 42 CFR Part 2.

38. *See, e.g.*, CAL. WELF. & INST. CODE §§ 5328-5328.9 (providing stringent protections for the confidentiality of records relating to treatment of mental disorders, and limiting disclosures to specifically listed permissible circumstances only—which are narrower than what HIPAA allows, *e.g.*, there is no provision for using mental health treatment information for general healthcare operations without authorization;); CAL. HEALTH & SAFETY CODE § 11812(c) (applying the protections of WELF. & INST. CODE § 5328 to information and records of alcohol and drug treatment programs funded by county expenditures of state funds); RCW § 70.02.230 (fact of admission to a provider for mental health services, and all related information and records, must be kept confidential except as otherwise specifically permitted by statute); N.M. CODE R. § 16.27.18.17 (counselors and therapists must maintain confidentiality of client information except where the client has given informed written consent to disclosure, or as otherwise mandated by law, or "[w]hen the counselor or therapist judges that disclosure is necessary to protect against a clear and substantial risk of imminent serious harm being inflicted by client on the client or another person(s)," or in the course of a civil, criminal, or disciplinary action arising from the therapy in which the counselor or therapist is a defendant).

VIII. An Integrative Approach to Treatment

There is a growing trend to promote wellness within an integrated mental healthcare paradigm, as well as increasing evidence for its effectiveness. The broad array of alternative treatment modalities includes mind-body interventions such as meditation and spiritual counseling, as well as an emphasis on exercise, diet and lifestyle changes. A current body of research supports the efficacy of these approaches in treating addictions. This integrative mental health paradigm need not diminish the importance of medications and traditional therapeutic approaches, but rather enhances and supplements them. Furthermore, a respect for the benefits and contributions of Alcoholics Anonymous and other 12-step groups must be acknowledged and maintained while increasing efforts to explore other evidence-based approaches to improve outcomes.

A. Use of Mindfulness and Meditation

The technique of mindfulness can facilitate calming the mind, and assist the patient in observing his or her thoughts, thereby enhancing the opportunity for subconscious thoughts to emerge. After the mind is steadied and the patient can practice an observing-ego stance, the result is an increase in self-aware consciousness by simply learning to be present in the moment. Learning how to be present can have significant benefit for addicts. The disease of addiction has neurobiological and psychological underpinnings that can be identified as "the addictive drive," which is quiescent in recovery, but remains ubiquitous. An individual in recovery is often thought of as someone whose disease is in remission. That is why sober addicts are in "recovery," never "recovered." This addictive drive, however, can represent a unique opportunity. When this drive presents itself in recovery in its various forms, such as craving or feelings of deprivation, these feelings can remind one of the need to continue, and even intensify, a meditative practice along with other recovery activities vs. suffering a relapse. Through sublimation, the addictive drive can be fuel for transcendence. The sober addict can achieve and maintain higher states of consciousness and an improved relationship with self, others, and a higher power. For the sober addict, this simple yet profound practice can reduce stress, craving, improve mood, and even create a capacity for experiencing higher and ultimately profoundly rewarding states of consciousness. This helps to perpetuate recovery. For the clinician, incorporating mindfulness in his or her practice can be highly beneficial for both therapist and patient; indeed, researchers in a 2008 study found that when those who meditated heard the sound of human suffering during controlled experiments, there was more activity in their temporal parietal junctures, the part of the brain tied to empathy, than those who did not meditate.[39]

IX. Levels of Care

The treatment of the addict or alcoholic is not a simple recommendation. Treatment has different levels of intensity and recommendations are based on a variety of factors—i.e. legal issues, financial constraints, type of professional, number of previous treatments, etc.

The following summarizes the typical abstinence-based program structures:

A. Day or Evening Intensive Outpatient Program (IOP)

- averages four days or nights a week, three to four hours a day or night and four to six weeks in duration;
- small group therapy plus didactic and experiential groups;
- family involvement;
- 12-step involvement expected during and after treatment; and
- typically three months of weekly continuing care.

B. Partial Hospital Program

- averages five days a week, six to eight hours/day for four to six weeks;
- small group therapy plus didactic and experiential groups;
- family involvement; and
- 12-step involvement and aftercare as above.

An independent (supervised) living program (ILP) can accompany a partial hospitalization program (such a combined program may be referred to as "PHP with ILP" or "boarded partial"). This is common in programs that treat professionals, and allows for more structure, intensity and opportunity for exposure to a therapeutic community as compared with more standard partial hospitalization programs.

C. Inpatient Rehabilitation or Residential Treatment

- Similar elements of partial hospitalization program with ILP except the patient is "under one roof," in a 24-hour supervised, clinical-facility setting.

---

39. A. Lutz, J. Brefczynski-Lewis, T. Johnstone, et al. *Regulation of the neural circuitry of emotion by compassion meditation: Effects of Meditative Expertise.* PLOS ONE. 2008;3(3): e1897.

This level of care provides more structure and may provide a higher level of medical/clinical services for patients with significant co-morbidities, a history of chronic substance abuse, and/or a lack of coping skills to remain sober absent 24-hour supervision. It is often more expensive than a partial hospitalization program with ILP, but oftentimes necessary for those that require a more structured and/or clinically intensive environment.

It is important to note the above-mentioned levels of care may succeed either inpatient or outpatient detoxification when medically necessary, and can vary in structure, length of stay and program emphasis. Also, various levels of care are often combined to provide a continuum of care for some patients. For example, a patient who completes a residential program may step down to a partial hospitalization program or IOP level of care. Also, in many instances the patient's treating providers may recommend that the patient continue the recovery program in a half-way or three quarter-way house following treatment. The disease of addiction is a chronic condition, and usually requires a long-term continuum of care to be treated effectively.

Professional programs often offer more specialized programming, such as Caduceus groups, along with extended aftercare (i.e., two to five years for physicians and nurses).

X.   Specialized Treatment for Professionals

Outcomes for general populations have been anywhere from 40% to 60% recovery following treatment. Extended studies beyond six to 12 months are not well-documented in the general population.

Treatment for professionals has demonstrated a much better outcome than treatment in the general population. Research suggests that factors such as voluntarily seeking treatment and the confidentiality of engagement in treatment have an impact on recovery.

In a recent article by Dr. Tom McLellan, et al., it was noted that addicted physicians (n. 902) demonstrated high rates of complete abstinence over a five-year period. This included 78 percent abstinence over that period and 71 percent remaining in their profession.[40] Similar sobriety rates were noted in *Healing the Healer.*[41] McLellan and his group wanted to discover what the essential ingredients were in these excellent outcomes. They recognized that "physicians enjoy educational, employment, financial, and social benefits that are not typical of the population at large or of the population of addicted individuals in treatment. Some of these

---

40. R.L. DuPont , T. McLellan, G. Carr, et al. *How are addicted physicians treated? A national survey of physician health programs.* J OF SUBSTANCE ABUSE TREATMENT 2009; 37 1–7.
41. Angres, et al. *supra* note 5.

advantages are characteristic of the physicians themselves, but an additional advantage is health insurance and personal resources that make high-quality care possible for extended periods." They also recognized essential elements that could be available to all addicted people. These included extended treatment and monitoring along with clear consequences for non-compliance. They concluded that it was not one of these elements but all of them combined that contributed to these excellent outcomes.[42]

There are some advantages that physicians and other professionals seemingly have. One is that they have a lot to lose, so they have an increased incentive for staying sober. However, in comparison, it has been noted that in the court system, when an individual is monitored and a relapse would result in a return to jail, the prospect of returning to jail does not create a strong deterrent effect. As many as 50 percent or more do return to the jail or prison system, suggesting consequences alone are not a strong enough incentive to remain sober.

One might argue, too, that professionals have a greater degree of access to better treatment. This may be true; however, there are a number of wealthy, nonprofessional individuals who do not have documented good outcomes, despite expensive and extensive treatment programming. Thus, better treatment alone is also not necessarily enough.

It seems logical, then, that better outcomes in physicians, as well as other licensed professionals, have to do with a variety and combination of incentives, treatment and monitoring options. Those include specialized addiction programs, a continuum of inpatient rehabilitation, residential and/or boarded partial programs, and IOP, that are extended; that is, anywhere between two to three months on average. These programs typically have staffs that are conversant with the various risks and problems associated with professionals, including over-identification with career, overwork, and some of the occupational risks associated with reentry. Specialty groups within a treatment setting offer a peer group setting that is essential to minimize the amount of "specialness" that can be associated with the professional, and can offer real empathy. The sense of community and shared experiences are essential in any program, and this is particularly the case for professionals. Extended monitoring following treatment is also critical, and includes urine monitoring. Also essential is the contractual relationship with the addict and the employer and/or medical society that would include potential consequences of relapse or noncompliance in an aftercare program. There are also other important ingredients in long-term success rates of professionals, such as involvement in 12-step recovery meetings and sponsorship, and continuing peer support in aftercare such as Caduceus groups. Typically, individual counseling and monitoring by a primary physician and/or psychiatrist who understands addiction, is part of the aftercare for the recovering professional. If all of these entities and professionals are given

---

42. DuPont et al. *supra* note 39.

permission to communicate with one another by the recovering addict, he or she is able to benefit from the integrated and holistic approach to the recovery process.

The level of treatment can be determined by certain factors. On one hand, a professional can be treated on an outpatient basis if, in particular, his or her disease did not affect the workplace and the professional has appropriate support at home. However, if there is workplace involvement (i.e., evidence of use or impact of use while working, patient care, or legal problems, etc.) and/or there are poor or absent support systems in the home, then a rehabilitation, residential or boarded partial extended program is almost always necessary. All levels of treatment should be followed by extended aftercare and monitoring.

XI.   Monitoring and Support Systems

Aftercare monitoring groups provide ongoing peer support and monitoring following treatment for as long as two years from the treatment program and five years for state-sponsored programs for licensed healthcare professionals. Involvement with peer groups for all recovering professionals following treatment is imperative. Other professionals offer their own support groups, such as the Lawyers' Assistance Programs for attorneys and Peer Assistance Networks for nurses.

Addicted physicians have one of the more elaborate intervention, assessment and reentry systems known today for those who suffer from addiction. As previously mentioned in McLellan's article describing the various "ingredients" that appeared to demonstrate excellent outcomes in this population, physicians are encased in a broad interlocking network of relating elements that both support the physician towards recovery and hold him or her accountable in the reentry monitoring process.

XII.   Stress Management

With all the advances in substance use treatment, mental health, and the science of well-being, we still have some relatively simple and basic time-tested ways to live better, including meditation (as outlined earlier), exercise, and proper diet. The research on the benefits of meditation, exercise, and healthy diet are indisputable. The cost to the individual and society for not living better are also clear. It is estimated that 70 percent of all medical problems are associated with stress, poor diet, substance abuse, or inactivity. The costs of unhealthy living are not only seen in the physical realm, but also reflected in increasing rates of depression and anxiety within our society. These simple activities can make all the difference.

XIII. Summary

The identification, support and monitoring of physicians who suffer from potentially impairment producing conditions have evolved substantially in the past few decades. A climate of openness, compassion and accountability has assisted both the physician and public they serve and it is critical that this trend continue. There has been some backsliding in recent years where political and other pressures have created a somewhat more punitive climate. If we are to continue to benefit from the entities outlined in this chapter, we must move forward not backwards, lest we recreate a dangerous and toxic environment that again drives the problem underground. If this backsliding continues it will not reduce the problems of impairment or make the public safer; quite the opposite will be the result, placing all involved at greater risk.

References

Angres, D., Talbott D. Bettinardi-Angres, K. *Healing the Healer* Psychosocial Press, 1998.

Werby J, Lui P, J. Caldeugh, Angres D. "Personality Predicting Relapse: An individual subfactor Analysis of the NEO" NAADAC National Conference, Sept 28-Oct 3rd, 2019 Orlando, FL

Berge KH, Seppala MD, Schipper AM. *Chemical dependency and the physician.* MAYO CLIN PROC. 2009 Jul;84(7):625-31.

Cicala Roger. *Substance abuse among physicians: what you need to know.* HOSP PHYSICIAN. 2005;39-46.

Lutz Antoine, Brefczynski-Lewis Julie, Johnstone Tom *et al. Regulation of the neural circuitry of emotion by compassion meditation: Effects of Meditative Expertise.* PLoS ONE. 2008;3(3): e1897.

Schernhammer E. Taking Their Own Lives—*The high rate of physician suicide.* N ENGL J MED. 2005. 352;2473.

West Colin, Shanafelt Tait. *Quality of life, burnout, educational debt, and medical knowledge among internal medicine residents.* JAMA.2011; 306(9):952-960.

Chapter 9

THE ALPHABET SOUP OF MEDICARE AND MEDICAID CONTRACTORS

By: QUINN CARLSON
KARA SCHOONOVER, J.D.
EMILY WEBER, J.D.[1]

I. Introduction

Healthcare providers, suppliers, their staff, and attorneys representing healthcare entities are faced regularly with a barrage of private contractors tasked with responsibilities for administering the Medicare and Medicaid programs. These private contractors' responsibilities include claims processing, reimbursement, enrollment, and auditing activities. Given the number of different contractors—and different acronyms, for that matter—it can be difficult to identify the role of the particular contractor with which one is dealing, the focus or goal of the program the contractor is involved in, the responsibilities it is tasked with managing, and the statutory and regulatory scope of its authority. This chapter identifies the various Medicare and Medicaid contractors and outlines each contractor's authority, focus, and responsibilities.

II. Medicare Contractors

Contracting with private entities has been a part of the Medicare program since its inception. Medicare's enactment in 1965 generated concerns over the government's intrusion into Americans' healthcare affairs. As such, Congress provided for the Medicare program's administration primarily by private entities that were already engaged in the health insurance business. Section 1874 of the Social Security Act (SSA) states that "[e]xcept as otherwise provided, the Secretary may perform any of his functions under [Title 18] directly, or by contract providing for payment in advance or by way of reimbursement, and in such installments, as the Secretary may deem necessary."[2] This contracting authority allows the government to task private entities with administering various aspects of the Medicare program.

---

1. The original edition of this chapter was written by Don Romano and Jennifer Colagiovanni; the 2021 edition was updated by the authors listed above.
2. 42 U.S.C. § 1395kk.

III. Claims Processing Contractors

A. Fiscal Intermediaries and Carriers

Prior to the advent of the Medicare Administrative Contractors (MACs), discussed below, Medicare claims were processed by either fiscal intermediaries (FIs) or carriers—a division generally based on whether Medicare Part A or Medicare Part B paid for the services or supplies. FIs administered claims for providers of services, which involved making payments for Medicare Part A, and, in some cases, Part B benefits payable to providers of services on a cost reimbursement basis.[3] FIs also handled claims of dialysis facilities, which are suppliers. Carriers, on the other hand, dealt with suppliers only and made payments for Part B benefits only.[4] The FIs and carriers administered a number of functions, including determining payment amounts, making payments on claims, providing education and assistance to both beneficiaries and providers, communicating with providers and suppliers, and developing local coverage policies.[5]

Local Coverage Determinations (LCDs) are determinations by a Medicare contractor as to whether a particular item or service is covered by Medicare by that type of contractor.[6] MACs are required to follow an administrative process prior to issuing a final LCD, which includes informal requests from stakeholders (beneficiaries, healthcare professionals, suppliers, and other interested parties), research related to the LCD request, publication and allowance or public comment, and open meetings facilitating discussion to review the basis and rationale for the proposed LCD.[7] Effective dates of LCDs are generally the 46th day after the notice period began. Interested parties can request a reconsideration of the final LCD.[8] LCDs are distinct from National Coverage Determinations (NCDs),

---

3. The Medicare statute recognizes two mutually exclusive categories of entities or individuals who deliver healthcare services. A "provider of services" includes "a hospital, critical access hospital, skilled nursing facility, comprehensive outpatient rehabilitation facility, home health agency, [and] hospice program." 42 U.S.C. §1395x(u). A "supplier" is "a physician or other practitioner, a facility, or other entity (other than a provider of services) that furnishes items or services." 42 U.S.C. § 1395x(d). "Provider of service" and "supplier" are also defined at 42 C.F.R. § 400.202.
   4. 42 C.F.R. § 400.202.
   5. 42 U.S.C. § 1395kk-1.
   6. 42 U.S.C. § 1395ff. Local Medical Review Policies (LMRPs) were converted to LCDs as a result of the Benefits Improvement and Protection Act of 2000. LCDs contain only "reasonable and necessary conditions of coverage" as allowed under SSA § 1862(a)(1)(A), whereas LMRPs may have also contained other information such as coding and payment guidelines. Coding and payment guidelines are now published in articles that may accompany a LCD. *See* http://www.cms.gov/Medicare/Coverage/DeterminationProcess/LCDs.html.
   7. MEDICARE PROGRAM INTEGRITY MANUAL (MPIM), ch. 13 § 13.2.
   8. MPIM, ch. 13 § 13.3.

which Centers for Medicare and Medicaid Services (CMS) develops to address Medicare coverage for specific items or services that are applicable across all contractors.[9] Medicare contractors must ensure that LCDs do not restrict or conflict with statutes, rulings, regulations, NCDs, or coverage provisions in interpretive manuals.[10] LCDs, along with local policy articles, NCDs, and proposed NCDs can be accessed through the Medicare Coverage Database.[11]

One notable distinction between an NCD and LCD is the scope of its effect on adjudicators. An NCD is binding on administrative law judges (ALJs) and the Medicare Appeals Council of the Departmental Appeals Board, whereas ALJs and the Medicare Appeals Council are not bound by LCDs or CMS program guidance, such as program memoranda or manual instructions.[12] Despite the fact that they are not bound by this guidance, ALJs and the Medicare Appeals Council are directed to give substantial deference to any applicable policies and explain the reasons why an applicable policy was not followed in a particular case.[13]

FIs and carriers, and now MACs, are also tasked with handling the first level of appeal, known as "redetermination," under the Medicare appeals process.[14] Depending on the circumstances surrounding the claim denial, the contractor responsible for the redetermination may be the same contractor that issued the initial determination denying the claim in whole or in part, but where this is the case, different personnel are required to conduct the redetermination review.[15]

B. Specialty Claims Processing Contractors

In addition to "regular" claims processing contractors, CMS contracted with four specialty contractors, known as Durable Medical Equipment Contractors (DMERCs), effective October 1, 1993. DMERCs are tasked with handling the administration of Medicare claims from durable medical equipment, prosthetics, and orthotics (DMEPOS) suppliers.[16] This change shifted DMEPOS claim processing away from the carrier system in place at

9. 42 C.F.R. § 405.1060.
10. MPIM, 100-08, ch. 13 § 13.5.
11. http://www.cms.gov/medicare-coverage-database.
12. 42 C.F.R. § 405.1060; 42 C.F.R. § 405.1062. There are four levels of appeal within the Medicare administrative appeals process. The ALJ stage is the third level of appeal, followed by a fourth-level appeal to the Medicare Appeals Council.
13. 42 C.F.R. § 405.1062. If the provider or supplier is dissatisfied with the MAC's decision, it may appeal to federal district court.
14. 42 U.S.C. § 1395ff(a)(3) (SSA § 1869(a)(3)).
15. 42 C.F.R § 405.948. (*See also* 42 U.S.C. § 1395ff(a)(3)).
16. 58 Fed. Reg. 60789.

the time to four regional carriers. The move to DMERCs was prompted by increasing complaints over the lack of supplier and beneficiary education on Medicare requirements, a lack of basic data by the contractors for use in fraud prevention, a lack of expertise on DMEPOS claim processing, varying claim forms among the carriers, and concerns over suppliers "carrier-shopping" for more favorable practices.[17] Prior to the shift to DMERCs, the previous workload was handled by thirty-four (34) different carriers, which resulted in local coverage policy variations. In the move to four DMERCs, CMS also called for the establishment of standardized medical review policies for the DMEPOS items with the highest allowable charges.[18]

Effective for claims processed on or after October 1, 1993, CMS also awarded a contract for the Statistical and Analysis Durable Medical Equipment Regional Contractor (SADMERC) to respond to requests for product reviews and to post the results of product review coding decisions on its website.[19] The results of product review coding decisions were posted in the Product Classification List, which allowed suppliers to search for codes or fees for a particular product.[20] The SADMERC was responsible for supporting the four DMERCs contracted by CMS.

In 1988, as it did for the specialty DMERCs contracted to handle DMEPOS claims, CMS then designated four Regional Home Health Intermediaries (RHHIs) to handle claim processing and administration of home health claims.[21]

C. Medicare Contracting Reform—MACs, DME MACs, PDACs, and HH+H MACs

Medicare contracting reform significantly transitioned contractors' responsibilities. The goal of this reform was to improve Medicare's administrative services for beneficiaries, providers, and suppliers by using competitive contracting tools and performance incentives. Section 911 of the Medicare Prescription Drug Improvement and Modernization Act of 2003 required CMS to replace FIs and carriers with MACs.[22] The MACs were designed to cover multi-state regions and process both Medicare Part A and Part B claims, which was intended to reduce the number of contractors with which providers, suppliers, and beneficiaries work with. The geographic assignment of a provider or supplier to a particular MAC was

---

17. https://oig.hhs.gov/oei/reports/oei-04-97-00330.pdf.
18. *Id.*
19. 58 Fed. Reg. 60789.
20. https://www.dmepdac.com
21. 53 Fed. Reg. 17936.
22. 42 U.S.C. § 1395kk-1 (section 911 of the Medicare Modernization Act of 2003).

based on the state in which the provider or supplier was located, which was a departure from the provider nomination provisions applicable to FIs and carriers.[23] CMS currently maintains an interactive map for providers, suppliers, and beneficiaries to use to identify the MACs by their geographic jurisdiction.[24]

CMS began the transition from FIs and carriers to MACs in 2005, utilizing competitively procured contracts. CMS began with fifteen regional Part A/B MAC jurisdictions.[25] In 2010, CMS announced that it would further consolidate the fifteen A/B MAC jurisdictions (1-15) into ten A/B MAC jurisdictions (E-N) over a several-year period. As of March 2014, CMS reported three of the planned contract consolidations, resulting in twelve current A/B MAC contract workloads.[26] CMS announced that further consolidations would not be in the best interest of the MAC program as they could adversely impact competition in the marketplace.[27] CMS also imposed a contract limit that restricts the amount of A/B contract responsibility any single entity or set of affiliated entities can obtain. Often one entity will compete and win multiple A/B MAC jurisdictions.[28] In 2010, CMS issued a request for information setting forth the current contract award limits: 26% of the national Medicare fee-for-service (FFS) claims volume for a single prime contractor and 40% for affiliated A/B MAC contractors.[29]

Durable Medical Equipment (DME) MACs were also designated to replace the DMERCs as a component of contracting reform. The DME MACs are divided into four geographic regions, A-D, and process DMEPOS claims under Medicare Part B.[30] Notably, the DME MACs process claims was based on the Medicare *beneficiary's* principal state of residence, rather than the location of the supplier.[31]

---

23. 42 C.F.R. § 421.404.

24. http://www.cms.gov/Research-Statistics-Data-and-Systems/Monitoring-Programs/Medicare-FFS-Compliance-Programs/Review-Contractor-Directory-Interactive-Map/#mi.

25. https://www.cms.gov/Medicare/Medicare-Contracting/Medicare-Administrative-Contractors/Archives.html.

26. *Id.*

27. https://www.cms.gov/Medicare/Medicare-Contracting/Medicare-Administrative-Contractors/Whats-New-.html.

28. https://www.cms.gov/Medicare/Medicare-Contracting/Medicare-Administrative-Contractors/Who-are-the-MACs.html.

29. Contract Award Limit Policy, https://www.fbo.gov/spg/HHS/HCFA/AGG/CMS-MAC-RFI-20100824/listing.html.

30. https://www.cms.gov/Medicare/Medicare-Contracting/Medicare-Administrative-Contractors/Who-are-the-MACs.html.

31. Medicare Claims Processing Manual (MCPM), Pub. 100-04, ch. 1, § 10.1.5.1.

Medicare contracting reform also resulted in a shift of the SADMERC's responsibilities to a new contractor: the Pricing, Data Analysis, and Coding contractor known as PDAC. The PDAC establishes, maintains, and updates all coding verification decisions on the product classification list available on the Durable Medical Equipment Coding System (known as DMECS);, provides coding guidance for manufacturers and suppliers on proper HCPCS use,[32] and conducts DMEPOS data analysis.[33]

In March 2007, CMS announced four Home Health and Hospice (HH+H) MACs as part of Medicare contracting reform to replace the RHHIs previously designated to handle home health and hospice claims processing.[34] The HH+H workloads were originally awarded separate jurisdictional MAC contracts, but in March 2007 CMS indicated that it would consolidate the HH+H workloads into four of the A/B MAC contracts. Specifically, A/B MAC jurisdictions six, fifteen, K, and M also include an HH+H workload.[35]

D. Medicare Administrative Contractors

The MACs are tasked with claims processing and payment, medical review, beneficiary education and assistance, and provider education on billing requirements.[36] The MACs' claims processing responsibility is significant; collectively, in 2020, the MACs processed more than 1.1 billion Medicare FFS claims.[37] The MACs also handle provider and

---

32. https://www.dmepdac.com/palmetto/providers.nsf/pdac.html. As explained by CMS, the HCPCS or Healthcare Common Procedure Coding System, is the standard code set for items and services furnished in outpatient settings, such as physicians' offices, hospital outpatient departments, and patients' homes. The HCPCS code set is divided into two principal subsystems, referred to as Level I and Level II. Level I consists of the Current Procedural Terminology (CPT), an alpha-numeric coding system maintained by the American Medical Association to identify medical services and procedures furnished by physicians and other healthcare professionals. Level II of the HCPCS is a standardized coding system that is used primarily to identify products, supplies, and services not included in the CPT codes. Because Medicare and other insurers cover a variety of services, supplies, and equipment that are not identified by CPT codes, the Level II HCPCS codes were established for use in submitting claims for these items. Level II codes are maintained and distributed by CMS, taking into consideration input from all insurers including Medicare, Medicaid, and private payor organizations. *See* CMS Innovators Guide 2015 at 22, *available at* https://www.cms.gov/Medicare/Coverage/CouncilonTechInnov/Downloads/Innovators-Guide-Master-7-23-15.pdf.

33. https://www.dmepdac.com.

34. https://www.cms.gov/Medicare/Medicare-Contracting/Medicare-Administrative-Contractors/Archives.html.

35. https://www.cms.gov/Medicare/Medicare-Contracting/Medicare-Administrative-Contractors/Who-are-the-MACs.html#ABandHH+H.

36. 42 U.S.C. § 1395kk-1.

37. https://www.cms.gov/Medicare/Medicare-Contracting/Medicare-Administrative-Contractors/What-is-a-MAC.html.

supplier enrollment, as well as redeterminations-, the first level of the Medicare claims appeals process- as noted above.[38] The MACs are also responsible for processing voluntary refunds received from providers.[39]

E. MAC Medical Review

Another way providers and suppliers may encounter their MAC is in connection with medical review activities. Medical review is defined as "the collection of information and clinical review of medical records ... to ensure that payment is only made for services that meet all Medicare coverage, coding, and medical necessity requirements."[40] The statutory authority for MAC medical review is based on sections 1833(e), 1842(a)(2)(B), and 1862(a)(1) of the SSA and the regulatory authority is based on 42 C.F.R.§§ 421.100, 421.200, and 421.400.

The medical review program is aimed at preventing improper payments and reducing payment error by preventing the payment of claims that do not comply with the applicable coverage, coding, payment, and billing policies.[41] The goal of MAC medical review is to correct behavior and prevent future inappropriate billing, and not necessarily to identify potential fraud or abuse.[42] In cases where the MAC uncovers infractions that are repeated or that indicate potential fraud, the MAC is directed to refer the case to the Program Safeguard Contractor or Zone Program Integrity Contractor (ZPIC), discussed below, for development.[43] The MACs are instructed to develop a problem-focused, outcome-based medical review strategy to target their efforts at error prevention for those services that represent the greatest financial risk to the Medicare program.[44]

The MACs seek to identify patterns of potential billing errors concerning coverage and coding policies through data analysis, evaluation of complaints, enrollment information, and cost report data.[45] Typically, this involves use of Comprehensive Error Rate Testing (CERT) error rates and vulnerabilities identified by the Recovery Audit Contractors (RACs) to focus MAC medical review activities.[46] From here, the MACs analyze their

---

38. *Id.*

39. MPIM, Pub. 100-08, ch. 4 §4.16. Medicare Financial Management Manual (MFMM), Pub. 100-06, ch. 4 § 100.14.

40. https://www.cms.gov/Research-Statistics-Data-and-Systems/Monitoring-Programs/Medicare-FFS-Compliance-Programs/Medical-Review/.

41. MPIM, Pub. 100-08, ch. 1 § 1.3.8.

42. MPIM, Pub. 100-08, ch. 3 § 3.1.

43. MPIM, Pub. 100-08, ch. 1 §§ 1.3.6, 1.3.10.

44. MPIM, Pub. 100-08, ch. 3 § 3.2.1.

45. MPIM, Pub. 100-08, ch. 1 § 1.3.8.

46. MPIM, Pub. 100-08, ch. 1 § 1.3.1(B).

internal claims data to determine what corrective actions can best prevent these vulnerabilities in the future.[47]

MAC medical review activities may involve prepayment and postpayment claim review. Prepayment review requires that the reviewer make the claim determination before payment on the claim is made.[48] Medicare contractors do not perform random prepayment review; that is, prepayment reviews are conducted with a specific reason to substantiate the cause for review. In recent years, regulatory restrictions on how contractors conduct prepayment reviews were lifted.

The Medicare Modernization Act (MMA) of 2003 added a statutory provision that required CMS to establish termination dates for non-random prepayment reviews. CMS issued regulations requiring contractors to terminate non-random prepayment review of a provider or supplier no later than one year following the initiation of the review or when the error rate calculation indicated that the provider reduced its initial error rate by 70% or more.[49]

However, the passage of the Patient Protection and Affordable Care Act in March 2010 (PPACA) resulted in a repeal of the statutory basis for the CMS regulation imposing the prepayment review termination criteria. In response, CMS issued a final rule on November 16, 2012, removing the regulation and, as a result, contractors are not required to terminate non-random prepayment review within a prescribed time but may "terminate each medical review when the provider has met all Medicare billing requirements as evidenced by an acceptable error rate as determined by the contractor."[50]

Postpayment review involves a review of the claim after the claim has been paid.[51] MACs are permitted to conduct postpayment reviews on a claim-by-claim basis or by using statistical sampling to estimate the overpayment for a universe of claims.[52] In order to use a statistical sampling of claims to project an overpayment, the contractor must first determine that there is "a sustained or high level of payment error; or documented educational intervention has failed to correct the payment error."[53]

---

47. *Id.*
48. MPIM, Pub. 100-08, ch. 3 § 3.2.
49. 73 Fed. Reg. 55753.
50. 77 Fed. Reg. 69160.
51. MPIM, Pub. 100-08, ch. 3 §3.2.
52. 42 U.S.C. § 1395ddd(f)(3); MPIM, Pub. 100-08, ch. 3 §3.5.2. Statistical sampling is sometimes used as a means to calculate an overpayment through extrapolating the results of the sampling.
53. 42 U.S.C. § 1395ddd(f)(3).

Notably, the finding of a "sustained or high level of payment error" is not subject to challenge on appeal.[54]

Medical reviews can be provider-specific or service-specific. In cases where data analysis suggests a provider-specific problem, *i.e.*, a potential billing problem that is limited to one or a small number of providers, the MAC is directed to utilize a probe sample of generally twenty to forty claims to validate that there is a billing error before significant medical review resources are dedicated to undertaking a larger audit.[55] In contrast, service-specific medical reviews are utilized when the same issue is widespread and affecting a particular type of service across a jurisdiction.[56] The MACs are directed to notify providers and suppliers of service-specific reviews by posting a review description on their website.[57]

MAC claim review activities can involve non-complex or complex reviews. Non-complex reviews do not involve a review of medical records submitted by the provider or supplier, whereas complex reviews incorporate a clinical review of the medical documentation.[58] In complex claim reviews, the MAC requests the medical documentation supporting the claim through additional documentation requests (ADRs). The *Medicare Program Integrity Manual* sets forth timeframes for providers and suppliers to respond to ADRs in both prepayment and postpayment claim review situations.[59] MACs are directed to apply coverage provisions and policies set forth in the SSA, regulations, CMS Rulings, NCDs, manual guidance, CMS coding policies, Technical Direction Letters (TDL), the relevant MAC's LCDs and articles, and AHA Coding Clinics.[60] In practice, MACs focus much more on sub-regulatory guidance than on the statute and regulations. The MACs are also directed to apply coding guidelines including CPT, ICD, HCPCS, and CMS coding policies.[61] In addition, the MACs have discretion to develop detailed written review guidelines for their staff.[62]

---

54. *Id.*

55. MPIM, Pub. 100-08, ch. 3 § 3.2.2.

56. *Id.*

57. *Id.*.

58. MPIM, Pub. 100-08, ch. 3 § 3.3.1.

59. MPIM, Pub. 100-08, ch. 3 § 3.2.3.2.

60. MPIM, Pub. 100-08, ch. 3 § 3.3. The AHA Coding Clinics are publications issued by the American Hospital Association on various coding issues. *See* http://www.ahacentraloffice.org/codes/products.shtml#CodingClinic.

61. MPIM, Pub. 100-08, ch. 3 §3.3. Currently, CMS uses the International Classification of Diseases, 10th edition, (ICD-10) and HCPCS to process claims. CMS transitioned from International Classification of Diseases, 9th edition, Clinical Modification, to ICD-10 on Oct. 1, 2015. *See* http://www.cms.gov/Medicare/Coding/ICD10/index.html?redirect=/icd10.

62. MPIM, Pub. 100-08, ch. 3 § 3.3.

In evaluating claims under review, the MACs are also tasked with determining if the provider or supplier qualifies for waiver of liability under Section 1870 of the SSA or whether the provider or supplier should receive limitation of liability protection under Section 1879.[63] At the conclusion of the claim review, the MAC sends a review results letter, separately or accompanied by a demand letter, outlining the specific issues involved in the overpayment, and a specific explanation of why any services were determined to be non-covered, as well as any recommended corrective action.[64]

In addition to conducting their own claim reviews, the MACs are responsible for issuing demand letters for overpayments identified through RAC and ZPIC audits. The MACs are also responsible for initiating recoupment of Medicare overpayments where applicable.

CMS published a final rule in November 2016[65] to implement the Quality Payment Program (QPP) mandated by the Medicare and CHIP Reauthorization Act of 2015 (MACRA).[66] Currently CMS performs data validation and auditing functions.

F. MAC Improper Payment Outreach and Education Program

Congress mandated that the Secretary of Health and Human Services (Secretary) implement an improper payment outreach and education program through the MACs.[67] Each MAC is required to furnish providers and suppliers with certain information that the Secretary determines to be appropriate. Such information may relate to the providers and suppliers with the highest rate of improper payments or with the greatest total dollar amounts of improper payments; or items and services furnished in the region that have the highest rates of improper payments or that are responsible for the greatest total dollar amount of improper payments.[68] MACs are required to prioritize activities under the improper payment

---

63. MPIM, Pub. 100-08, ch. 3 § 3.6.2.3. *See also* MFMM, Pub. 100-06, ch. 3 §70. Under the section 1870 waiver of liability provisions, an overpayment made to a provider or supplier will not be recouped if the provider or supplier was without fault in causing the overpayment and recouping the overpayment would defeat the purpose of Title XVIII or would be against equity or good conscience. Under section 1879 limitation of liability, a provider or supplier may receive payment for a claim that is otherwise unallowable for certain reasons (chiefly, lack of medical necessity) if the provider did not know or could not have reasonably been expected to know that the claim was not allowable.

64. MPIM, Pub. 100-08, ch. 3 § 3.6.4.

65. 81Fed. Reg. 77008 (Nov. 4, 2016).

66. Pub. L. No. 114-10.

67. Section 505(a) of MACRA.

68. Section 505(a)(2) of MACRA.

outreach and education program that will reduce improper payments that involve one or more of the following:

(1) items and services that have the highest rate of improper payment;

(2) items and services that have the greatest total dollar amount of improper payments;

(3) due to clear misapplication or misinterpretation of Medicare policies;

(4) clearly due to common and inadvertent clerical or administrative errors; and

(5) due to other types of errors that the Secretary determines could be prevented through activities under the program.[69]

In order to assist MACs in carrying out the improper payment outreach and education programs, the Secretary must provide each MAC with a complete list of the types of improper payments identified by RACs with respect to providers of services and suppliers located in the MAC's jurisdiction.[70]

IV. The Middle Ground: Contractors in Between Claims Processing and Program Integrity

There are several contractors that fall in between claims processing and program integrity contractors: the CERT contractor, the National Supplier Clearinghouse (NSC), Quality Improvement Organizations (QIOs), and the RACs. These contractors have responsibilities related to claims and program integrity, but do not process claims and are not strictly defined as program integrity contractors.

A. Comprehensive Error Rate Testing

The CERT program is used to calculate the Medicare FFS improper payment rate. Historically, the Department of Health and Human Services' (HHS) Office of the Inspector General (OIG) was responsible for estimating the improper payment rate for Medicare FFS from 1996 to 2002.[71] Due to the OIG's small sample size, the improper payment rate calculation could not be broken down further by contractor, contractor type, service type, or provider type.[72]

---

69. *Id.* Other changes made by this section include providing for a ten-year rather than a five-year renewal of MAC contracts, and requiring the Secretary to make available to the public the performance of each MAC.

70. Section 505(a)(2) of MACRA.

71. http://www.cms.gov/Research-Statistics-Data-and-Systems/Monitoring-Programs/Medicare-FFS-Compliance-Programs/CERT/Background.html.

72. *Id.*

In 2001, the OIG and CMS decided to shift responsibility for producing the Medicare FFS improper payment rates to CMS.[73] Shortly thereafter in 2003, the CERT program was created[74] The CERT program was developed to comply with of the Improper Payments Information Act's (IPIA) of 2002, as amended by the Improper Payments Elimination and Recovery Improvement Act of 2012, which requires that federal agencies estimate the amount of improper payments in the programs they administer.[75] HHS publishes the improper payment rate in the Agency Financial Report each November.[76]

Each year, the CERT program evaluates a statistically valid random sample of claims to determine if they were paid properly under Medicare coverage, coding, and billing rules.[77] The CERT improper payment rate is not a measurement of the rate of incidents of fraud, but of payments that did not meet the Medicare requirements. The CERT measurement involves a stratified random sample of approximately 50,000 claims submitted to MACs and DME MACs, which enables the contractors to calculate national improper payment rates, and contractor-specific and service-specific improper payments rates.[78] The CERT program previously used two contractors: the CERT Documentation Contractor (DC), which requested and received the medical record documentation from the provider or supplier, and the CERT Review Contractor (RC), which reviewed the selected claims together with the associated medical record documentation.[79] The CERT Statistical Contractor (SC) is responsible for calculating the improper payment rates and amounts, designing sampling strategy, and maintaining a live data dashboard.[80]

---

73. http://www.cms.gov/Research-Statistics-Data-and-Systems/Monitoring-Programs/Medicare-FFS-Compliance-Programs/CERT/Downloads/FY2003LongReport.pdf. Following the move from OIG to CMS, CMS tasked the CERT Program with determining the percentage of Medicare payments made where the claim did not meet the Medicare coverage, coding and billing rules.

74. http://www.cms.gov/Research-Statistics-Data-and-Systems/Monitoring-Programs/Medicare-FFS-Compliance-Programs/CERT/Background.html.

75. *Id.*

76. MPIM, Pub. 100-08, ch. 12 § 12.3. *See also* http://www.cms.gov/Research-Statistics-Data-and-Systems/Monitoring-Programs/Medicare-FFS-Compliance-Programs/CERT/CERT-Reports.html.

77. MPIM, Pub. 100-08, ch. 12 § 12.3.

78. https://www.cms.gov/Research-Statistics-Data-and-Systems/Monitoring-Programs/Medicare-FFS-Compliance-Programs/CERT/Background.html.

79. https://www.acponline.org/practice-resources/business-resources/payment/medicare-payment-and-regulations-resources/medicare-improper-payment-review-comprehensive-error-ratetesting-cert-contractors.

80. https://certprovider.admedcorp.com/Home/About.

Claims reviewed as part of the CERT improper payment calculation are subject to postpayment denials, payment adjustments, or other administrative or legal actions.[81] Claims reviewed by the CERT contractors may be appealed through the Medicare claims appeals process.[82]

B. National Supplier Clearinghouse (NSC)

The NSC contractor enrolls and disenrolls DMEPOS suppliers.[83] The NSC processes supplier enrollment applications (via the CMS-855S) and verifies the information provided.[84] The NSC may then conduct a site visit to ensure the supplier's compliance with the DMEPOS supplier standards pursuant to 42 C.F.R. § 424.57.[85] DMEPOS suppliers are also required to notify the NSC of changes to their enrollment information.

C. Quality Improvement Organizations (QIOs)

QIOs are tasked with improving the quality of healthcare for Medicare beneficiaries. The QIO program's mission is to "improve the effectiveness, efficiency, economy, and quality of services delivered to Medicare beneficiaries."[86] CMS defines the core functions of the QIO program as improving quality of care for beneficiaries; protecting the integrity of the Medicare Trust Funds by ensuring Medicare pays for only goods and services that are reasonable and medically necessary, allowable, meet professionally recognized standard of care, and provided in the most appropriate setting; and protecting beneficiaries by addressing complaints including individual beneficiary complaints, provider-based notice appeals, and Emergency Medical Treatment and Labor Act (EMTALA) violations.[87] QIOs also perform Diagnosis-Related Group

---

81. MPIM, Pub. 100-08, ch. 12 § 12.5.

82. MPIM, Pub. 100-08, ch. 12 § 12.65.

83. 42 C.F.R § 424.57.

84. https://www.cms.gov/Medicare/Provider-Enrollment-and-Certification/ MedicareProviderSupEnroll/downloads/durablemedicalequip.pdf.

85. *Id.*

86. SSA 1862(g); 42 U.S.C. § 1395y.

87. http://www.cms.gov/Medicare/Quality-Initiatives-Patient-Assessment-Instruments/ QualityImprovementOrgs/index.html?redirect=/qualityimprovementorgs/; *see also* QUALITY IMPROVEMENT ORGANIZATION MANUAL, Pub. 100-10, ch. 1 § 1005. EMTALA is contained at section 1867 of the SSA, 42 U.S.C. § 1395dd. Under EMTALA, where an individual (Medicare beneficiary or otherwise) comes to a hospital emergency department, and a request is made on the individual's behalf for examination or treatment for a medical condition, the hospital must provide for an appropriate medical screening examination within the capability of the hospital's emergency department to determine whether an emergency medical condition exists. If the hospital determines that an emergency condition exists, the hospital must attempt to stabilize the individual's condition or effect an appropriate transfer,

(DRG) validation on hospital Prospective Payment System claims.[88] QIOs are comprised primarily of physicians, nurses, other clinicians, health-quality experts, and consumers. There are two types of QIOs that work under CMS, which include Beneficiary Family Centered Care QIOs and Quality Innovation Network QIOs.

The QIO program, formerly the Utilization and Quality Control Peer Review Program, was originally established in 1982 by sections 142 and 143 of the Tax Equity and Fiscal Responsibility Act.[89] The individual organizations were initially known as Professional Standards Review Organizations—and then Peer Review Organizations—before the regulatory references to these organizations changed to QIOs.[90] Section 261 of the Trade Adjustment Assistance Extension Act of 2011[91] authorized changes to the original QIO Program in an effort to modernize the program and add flexibility to the program's structure. As a result, CMS redesigned the QIO program to incorporate several key changes. First, QIO contracts may now be awarded on a regional basis.[92] Historically, states contracted with a QIO to carry out case review and quality improvement functions on a state-by-state basis. Second, the statutory and regulatory revisions now permit QIOs to perform one or more of the QIO functions rather than requiring one QIO contracted entity to perform all of the functions.[93] For example, one QIO for a particular geographic jurisdiction may be tasked with case review responsibility, whereas another QIO entity for the same jurisdiction may take responsibility for implementing quality improvement initiatives. The scope of entities eligible to be awarded a QIO contract has expanded and now focuses on the functions that the organization would perform under the QIO contract rather than on the structure of the organization.[94] The contract term for QIOs is five years.[95]

---

88. QUALITY IMPROVEMENT ORGANIZATION MANUAL, Pub. 100-10, ch. 4 § 4130. Short-term acute care hospitals are paid under the Inpatient Prospective Payment System (IPPS) under section 1886(d) of the SSA, 42 U.S.C. § 1395ww. Under the IPPS, an inpatient's diagnosis is assigned to a DRG, for which the hospital receives a prospectively determined amount regardless of the resources used (as multiplied by a wage index and subject to certain add-ons, where applicable, and outlier payments for especially high costs incurred in treating the patient).

89. 78 Fed. Reg. 75144 (Dec. 10, 2013).

90. 67 Fed. Reg. 36539 (May 24, 2002).

91. Trade Adjustment Assistance Extension Act of 2011, Pub. L. No. 112-40, § 261, 125 Stat. 401, 423 (2011) (codified as amended at scattered sections of 42 U.S.C.).

92. 78 Fed. Reg. 75148 (Dec. 10, 2013).

93. *Id.*

94. 78 Fed. Reg. 75151 (Dec. 10, 2013).

95. *Id.; see also* https://www.cms.gov/Medicare/Quality-Initiatives-Patient-Assessment-Instruments/QualityImprovementOrgs/index.html?redirect=/qualityimprovementorgs/.

Beginning on October 1, 2015, QIOs assumed responsibility for conducting initial patient status reviews to determine the appropriateness of Part A payment for inpatient hospital short-stay claims–reviews that were previously being conducted by MACs[96] QIOs, specifically BFCC-QIOs, continued conducting initial patient status reviews of inpatient hospital short stay claims in 2016. In the course of these reviews, the BFCC-QIOs referred providers to RACs for further patient status reviews in instances of persistent noncompliance with Medicare payment policy, including high denial rates or consistent failure to adhere to the Two Midnight rule.[97] In May 2016, CMS temporarily stopped the BFCC-QIO initial patient status reviews of short-stay inpatient hospital claims to promote the consistent application of medical review policies and improve standardization in the review process.[98] During the pause of the patient status reviews, BFCC-QIOs were retrained on the Two Midnight rule, re-reviewed claims that were previously denied, and initiated provider outreach and education on the Two Midnight rule.[99] CMS resumed the BFCC-QIO patient status reviews in September 2016.[100]

D. Recovery Audit Contractors (RACs)

RACs, also known as recovery auditors, are probably the most talked about contractor of the last decade. Whereas the RACs audit claims and perform medical reviews as a component of the Medicare Integrity Program, their primary focus is identifying improper payments, not detecting fraud, waste, and abuse. As discussed below, PPACA[101] extended the scope of their audit authority to include Medicare Parts C and D, as well as Medicaid.

E. Medicare RACs

The use of RACs in the Medicare FFS program began as a demonstration program authorized by section 306 of the Medicare Prescription Drug,

---

96. https://www.cms.gov/research-statistics-data-and-systems/monitoring-programs/medicare-ffs-compliance-programs/medical-review/inpatienthospitalreviews.html.

97. In general, the Two Midnight rule provides inpatient admissions will generally be payable under Part A if the admitting practitioner expected the patient to require a hospital stay that crossed two midnights and the medical record supports that reasonable expectation. Medicare Part A payment is generally not appropriate for hospital stays not expected to span at least two midnights. *See* https://www.cms.gov/newsroom/fact-sheets/fact-sheet-two-midnight-rule-0

98. https://www.cms.gov/research-statistics-data-and-systems/monitoring-programs/medicare-ffs-compliance-programs/medical-review/inpatienthospitalreviews.html.

99. *Id.*

100. *Id.*

101. Patient Protection and Affordable Care Act, Pub. L. No. 111-148, § 6411, 124 Stat. 119, 773 (2010) (codified as amended at 42 U.S.C. §1395ddd(h)).

Improvement and Modernization Act of 2003.[102] The demonstration program ran from March 2005 through March 2008 in six states in an effort to evaluate the effectiveness of the RACs at identifying improper payments.[103] The demonstration project established that RACs were successful and, as a result, the RAC program was made permanent and expanded nationwide by section 302 of the Tax Relief and Health Care Act of 2006.[104]

The goal of the RAC program is to identify and correct improper payments, including both overpayments and underpayments.[105] RACs are not claims processing contractors like MACs, although they follow similar regulations and policies as MACs with regard to their medical review activities.[106] The RACs are also required to follow the requirements set forth in the RAC Statement of Work.

There are five Medicare Fee-for-Service RACs. The RACs for Regions 1-4 are each responsible for a geographical area that covers roughly one-quarter of the country.[107] The RACs for Regions 1-4 are responsible for postpayment review of all provider types except DMEPOS and home health and hospice. The Region 5 RAC is dedicated to the postpayment review of DMEPOS and home health and hospice claims nationally.[108]

Given their larger geographical regions, RACs are able to conduct widespread reviews. The Statement of Work authorizes the RACs to audit claims on a postpayment basis.[109] RACs, like MACs, utilize automated (non-complex) and complex reviews, and also engage in a third type of review: semi-automated review.[110] Semi-automated reviews involve identification of a billing aberrancy through an automated analysis of

---

102. Medicare Prescription Drug, Improvement and Modernization Act of 2003, Pub. L. No. 108-173, 117 Stat. 2066, 2256 (2003).

103. Recovery Auditing in Medicare for Fiscal Year 2013, FY 2013 Report to Congress (p. 2).

104. Tax Relief and Health Care Act of 2006, Pub. L. No. 109-432, 120 Stat. 2922, 2991 (2006) (codified as amended at 42 U.S.C. § 1395ddd). *See also* http://www.cms.gov/Research-Statistics-Data-and-Systems/Monitoring-Programs/Medicare-FFS-Compliance-Programs/Recovery-Audit-Program/.

105. 42 U.S.C § 1395ddd(h).

106. MIPM, Pub. 100-08, ch. 3 § 3.3.2.

107. https://www.cms.gov/Research-Statistics-Data-and-Systems/Monitoring-Programs/Medicare-FFS-Compliance-Programs/Recovery-Audit-Program/Downloads/AB-Map-2014-2.pdf.

108. https://www.cms.gov/Research-Statistics-Data-and-Systems/Monitoring-Programs/Medicare-FFS-Compliance-Programs/Recovery-Audit-Program/Recent_Updates.html.

109. RAC Final Statement of Work, Sept. 1, 2011.

110. *Id.*

claims data that suggests a likelihood of an improper payment.[111] From there, the provider is sent a notification letter explaining the potential billing error and requesting supporting documentation.[112]

In September 2012, CMS implemented a three-year prepayment review demonstration program for the RACs.[113] The prepayment demonstration was limited to eleven states with either high levels of improper payments or high claim volumes for hospital inpatient short-stay claims.[114] In the demonstration states, certain Medicare Severity Diagnosis-Related Groups (MS-DRGs)[115] were flagged for review before the claims were paid. Then, in April 2013, therapy claims were also added to the RAC prepayment demonstration.[116] In these cases, prepayment review was required when therapy services for a beneficiary reached a threshold in a calendar year. RAC prepayment review of inpatient short-stay claims ceased effective for discharges occurring on or after October 1, 2013, following the Two Midnight rule billing policy for short-stay hospital admissions set forth in the FY 2014 Inpatient Prospective Payment System final rule.[117] Similarly, the prepayment review of therapy claims stopped in February 2014 in preparation for procurement of new recovery audit contracts.[118] CMS subsequently tasked the Supplemental Medical Review Contractor—

111. *Id.*

112. *Id.*

113. Dec. 13, 2013, Prepayment Review Demonstration Status Update, *available at* http://www.cms.gov/Research-Statistics-Data-and-Systems/Monitoring-Programs/Medicare-FFS-Compliance-Programs/Recovery-Audit-Program/Downloads/2013-Prepayment-Review-Demonstration-Status-Update.pdf.

114. The 11 states included in the prepayment demonstration are California, Florida, Illinois, Louisiana, Michigan, Missouri, New York, North Carolina, Ohio, Pennsylvania, and Texas. Dec. 13, 2013, Prepayment Review Demonstration Status Update.

115. The (MS-DRG) classification system is a refinement over the DRG system of classification. There are three levels of severity included in the MS-DRG classification system, which are: major complication/comorbidity; complication/comorbidity; and noncomplication/comorbidity. These levels are calculated based on clinical factors—principally the patient's secondary diagnosis codes (such as pneumonia or sepsis) in addition to the primary diagnosis (hip fracture). Earlier iterations of DRG systems focused more on the institutional side, with the computational logic guided more by resources used rather than the diseases and patients treated.

116. Dec. 13, 2013, Prepayment Review Demonstration Status Update.

117. CMS-1599-F, 78 Fed. Reg. 50195-51040 (Aug. 19, 2013). *See* https://www.cms.gov/Research-Statistics-Data-and-Systems/Monitoring-Programs/Medicare-FFS-Compliance-Programs/Recovery-Audit-Program/Downloads/2013-Prepayment-Review-Demonstration-Status-Update.pdf.

118. https://www.cms.gov/Research-Statistics-Data-and-Systems/Monitoring-Programs/Medicare-FFS-Compliance-Programs/Recovery-Audit-Program/Historical_Programs.html.

discussed in greater detail below—with performing targeted postpayment medical review of claims that exceed the annual therapy cap limits.[119]

One of the key distinctions between RACs and other contractors is that they are paid on a contingency fee basis. The contingency fees, which initially ranged from 9 to 12.5% for Medicare FFS claims, are a percentage of the improper payments recovered from, or reimbursed to, audited providers.[120] RACs are required to return the contingency fee payment for claim determinations overturned at any level of the appeal.[121] One of the RAC program enhancements expected to be incorporated as part of the new RAC contracts includes a directive that RACs will not receive a contingency fee until after the second level of appeal is exhausted.[122] This delay in payment of the contingency fee is intended to motivate RACs to ensure that their claim determinations are correct based on the applicable statutes, regulations, coverage determinations, and manual provisions.[123]

Although RACs may review all claim types, CMS expects that they will focus on identifying improper payments that have the greatest impact on the Medicare Trust Fund.[124] Their contingency fee arrangement further incentivizes RACs to target claims with the potential for high-dollar value overpayments. Before a RAC undertakes a new issue for review, it must first "validate" the issue with CMS. CMS or its RAC Validation Contractor must review and approve the issue before the RAC is permitted to issue ADR letters to providers and suppliers requesting documentation.[125] Once an issue is approved, the RAC is required to post a description of the issue on its website.[126] In conducting their claim review activities, RACs are limited to a three-year look-back period from the date the claim was paid.[127] The RAC look-back period is limited to six months from the date

---

119. Section 202 of MACRA extended the therapy cap exception process through Dec. 31, 2017, and eliminated the requirement for manual medical review of all claims exceeding the therapy thresholds. The law also prohibited the use of RACs to conduct the therapy reviews.

120. OIG Report, August 2013 (p. 2); Medicare Fee-for-Service Recovery Audit Program Myths http://www.cms.gov/Research-Statistics-Data-and-Systems/Monitoring-Programs/Recovery-Audit-Program/Downloads/RAC-Program-Myths-12-18-12.pdf.

121. RAC Final Statement of Work, Sept. 1, 2011.

122. https://www.cms.gov/Research-Statistics-Data-and-Systems/Monitoring-Programs/Medicare-FFS-Compliance-Programs/Recovery-Audit-Program/Downloads/Recovery-Audit-Program-Improvements-November-24-2017.pdf

123. *Id.*

124. RAC Final Statement of Work, Sept. 1, 2011.

125. *Id.*

126. *Id.*

127. *Id.* Apart from the limitations placed on the RACs, the regulations provide generally that claims may not be reopened more than four years from the date of the initial determination, although claims determinations that were procured by fraud or similar fault, and claims determinations based a clerical error, may be reopened at any time. 42 C.F.R. § 405.980.

of service for patient status reviews in cases where the hospital provider submits the claim within three months of the date of service.[128] This change intends to give hospitals time to resubmit Part A inpatient claims for Part B payment within the one-year time limit for the timely filing of claims.

The RAC Statement of Work encourages the use of statistical extrapolation for some claim types, particularly those claims with a low dollar claim value, requiring complex review and a history of having a high error rate.[129] The Statement of Work directs that the use of extrapolation must be approved for each issue prior to beginning.[130]

CMS also requires RACs to maintain an accuracy rate of at least 95% for claim determinations—failure to do so results in a reduction in the ADR limits permitted.[131] CMS -established ADR limits based on provider compliance, providing that those providers with low claim denial rates will be subject to lower ADR limits than those with higher claim denial rates.[132] On May 3, 2016, CMS issued an update to the ADR limits for Medicare institutional providers allowing RACs to increase document requests based upon a provider's denial rate.[133] A provider with a denial rate between 0 and 3% will have a reprieve from document requests for three forty-five-day cycles while a provider on the other end of the spectrum with a denial rate between 91 and 100% could be subject to document requests up to 5% of all paid claims.[134]

Congress now requires the Secretary to retain a portion that does not exceed 15% of the RACs' recoveries, which is to be used to reduce the Medicare claims error rate. The retention of a portion of the recoveries cannot have the effect of reducing the RACs' fees that are otherwise due. [135]

---

128. https://www.cms.gov/Research-Statistics-Data-and-Systems/Monitoring-Programs/Medicare-FFS-Compliance-Programs/Recovery-Audit-Program/Downloads/Recovery-Audit-Program-Enhancements11-6-15-Update-.pdf.

129. RAC Final Statement of Work, Sept. 1, 2011. RACs are directed to follow the procedures for statistical sampling and extrapolation set forth in the MPIM, as well as Section 935 of the MMA.

130. RAC Final Statement of Work, Sept. 1, 2011.

131. https://www.cms.gov/Research-Statistics-Data-and-Systems/Monitoring-Programs/Medicare-FFS-Compliance-Programs/Recovery-Audit-Program/Downloads/Recovery-Audit-Program-Improvements-November-24-2017.pdf.

132. https://www.cms.gov/Research-Statistics-Data-and-Systems/Monitoring-Programs/Medicare-FFS-Compliance-Programs/Recovery-Audit-Program/Downloads/ADR-Limits-Institutional-Provider-Facilities-May-2016-revised-12-21-18508ao.pdf.

133. *Id.*

134. *Id.*

135. Section 505 of MACRA.

F. Medicare Parts C & D RACs

Section 6411(b) of PPACA amended Section 1893(h) of the SSA to provide the general authority for CMS to contract with RACs to identify improper payments in Medicare Part C (Medicare Advantage) and Part D (Prescription Drug Benefit). Applying the RAC program concept to Medicare Part C presents challenges due to the prospective nature of Medicare Advantage payments. On December 22, 2015, CMS issued a request for information and proposed statement of work to collect feedback on the expansion of the RAC program to Part C utilizing risk adjustment data validation audits in two ways--comprehensive and condition specific audits–to validate accuracy of diagnosis data submitted to CMS by Medicare Advantage.

The Part D RAC employs a similar model to that used in the Medicare Parts A and B RAC program.[136] The Part D RAC reviews previously paid individual Medicare claims to sponsoring organizations or pharmacies to determine if an overpayment or underpayment was made, and reports information to CMS to prevent future improper payments.[137] If any potential fraud findings are identified during the RAC audit process, they are referred to the National Benefit Integrity Medicare Drug Integrity Contractor–(NBI MEDIC), as explained below. Similar to the new issue validation process used in the Medicare FFS RAC program, the Part D RAC program utilizes a data validation contractor. In addition to reviewing suggested new audit issues, the Part D Data Validation Contractor confirms the RAC's improper payment findings and measures the RAC's accuracy rate. Specifically, the Data Validation Contractor analyzes random samples of prescription drug events identified by the RAC to contain improper payments, and either concurs or disagrees with the RAC's findings.

V. Medicare Program Integrity Contractors

Previously, FIs and carriers performed Medicare benefit integrity functions. The Health Insurance Portability and Accountability Act of 1996 established the Medicare Integrity Program in an effort to strengthen CMS's ability to detect and deter potential fraud, waste, and abuse in the Medicare program.[138] Therefore, CMS

---

136. https://www.cms.gov/Research-Statistics-Data-and-Systems/Monitoring-Programs/recovery-audit-program-parts-c-and-d/Audit-Process.

137. https://www.cms.gov/Research-Statistics-Data-and-Systems/Monitoring-Programs/recovery-audit-program-parts-c-and-d/.

138. Section 202(a) of the Health Insurance Portability and Accountability Act of 1996, P.L. 104-191, enacted section 1893 of the SSA, 42 U.S.C. § 1395ddd, establishing the Medicare Integrity Program and providing the statutory basis for CMS to enter into contracts with entities to perform work to address potential fraud and abuse. MLN Matters, Number SE1204, http://www.cms.gov/Outreach-and-Education/Medicare-Learning-Network-MLN/MLNMattersArticles/downloads/SE1204.pdf.

created new entities, known as Program Safeguard Contractors (PSCs), to perform program integrity functions.[139] Subsequently, PSCs transitioned to new entities known as ZPICs to carry out program integrity activities in seven regional program integrity zones[140]

The ZPICs handled program integrity functions for Medicare Part A, Part B, DMEPOS, Home Health and Hospice, and Medicare-Medicaid (Medi-Medi) data matching.[141] A separate contractor, the Medicare Drug Integrity Contractor (MEDIC) handles program integrity efforts for Medicare Part C and D.[142] MEDIC works under the direction of the Center for Program Integrity (CPI) in CMS.[143] CMS transitioned ZPICs and Medicaid Integrity Contractors (MICs) to Unified Program Integrity Contractors (UPICs). UPICs audit both Medicare and Medicaid claims.[144]

A. Zone Program Integrity Contractors (ZPICs)

ZPICs (f/k/a Program Safeguard Contractors) identified and developed cases of suspected fraud and took immediate action to ensure that the Medicare Trust Fund monies were not inappropriately paid and mistaken payments were recouped.[145] The focus of ZPICs was responding quickly to suspected fraud or abuse and employing administrative actions. ZPICs were organized with a Medical Review (MR) Unit and a Benefit Integrity (BI) Unit. ZPIC BI Unit had a number of responsibilities for preventing, detecting, and deferring fraud, waste, and abuse in both the Medicare and Medicaid programs in collaboration with the (Medi-Medi Program), including:

(1) preventing fraud or abuse by identifying program vulnerabilities;

(2) proactively identifying incidents of potential fraud or abuse that exist within its service area and taking appropriate action on each case;

(3) investigating (determining the factual basis of) allegations of fraud or abuse made by beneficiaries, providers, suppliers, CMS, OIG, and other sources;

---

139. MLN Matters, Number SE1204, http://www.cms.gov/Outreach-and-Education/Medicare-Learning-Network-MLN/MLNMattersArticles/downloads/SE1204.pdf.

140. *Id.*

141. *Id.*

142. *Id.*

143. In 2010 the Medicare and Medicaid program integrity functions were brought together in the newly created Center for Program Integrity. http://www.cms.gov/About-CMS/Components/CPI/Center-for-program-integrity.html.

144. https://www.mgma.com/MGMA/media/files/advocacy%20letters/MGMA-Medicare-Audits-Fact-Sheet.pdf?ext=.pdf.

(4)   exploring all available sources of leads of suspected fraud or abuse in its jurisdiction, including those emanating from the Medicaid Fraud Control Unit (MFCU);[146]

(5)   initiating appropriate administrative actions to deny or suspend payments that should not be made to providers where there is reliable evidence of fraud;

(6)   referring cases to the OIG's Office of Inspections (OI) for consideration of civil and criminal prosecution and/or application of administrative sanctions;

(7)   referring any necessary provider or supplier and beneficiary outreach to the Provider Outreach and Education staff at the Affiliated Contractor or MAC;

(8)   initiating and maintaining networking and outreach activities to ensure effective interaction and exchange of information with internal companies as well as outside groups;

(9)   partnering with State Medicaid Program integrity units to perform all actions listed for the Medi-Medi Program;

(10)   working closely with CMS on joint projects, investigations, and other proactive anti-fraud activities.[147]

The ZPICs were also responsible for processing complaints alleging DMEPOS fraud within their region or zone.[148] ZPICs were required to use both—proactive and reactive techniques—to address potentially fraudulent, wasteful, or abusive billing practices depending upon the leads they received.[149] ZPICs were directed to refer cases of potential fraud to the OIG/OI.[150]

Once the ZPIC, or the referring contractor, identified patterns of claim submissions or payments that indicate potential problems, the ZPIC could utilize prepayment or postpayment review to verify the potential errors.[151] Whereas medical review activities for MR purposes focus on evaluating the correct coverage or coding determination, medical review for BI

---

145. MPIM, 100-08, ch. 1 § 4.2.

146. A MFCU is a single identifiable entity of state government, annually certified by the Secretary of HHS, that conducts a statewide program for the investigation and prosecution of healthcare providers that defraud the Medicaid program. In addition, a MFCU reviews complaints of abuse or neglect of nursing home residents. http://www.namfcu.net/about-us/about-mfcu.

147. MPIM, 100-08, ch. 4 § 4.2.2.

148. MPIM, 100-08, ch. 4 § 4.2.3.

149. MPIM, 100-08, ch. 4 § 4.2.2.

150. *Id.*

151. MPIM, 100-08, ch. 3 §§ 3.2 and 3.6.2.

purposes may focus on identifying possible falsification, evidence of a trend to use higher codes, obvious or nearly identical documentation, or evidence of alteration to the records, among others.[152] In cases where an overpayment is identified, the ZPIC referred the overpayment to the appropriate MAC, which was required to issue a demand letter and recoup the overpayment.[153] Like the MACs and Medicare RACs, ZPICs were authorized to use statistical sampling to calculate and project the amount of the overpayment across a larger universe of claims.[154]

ZPICs also had the ability to suspend Medicare payments to a provider.[155] When the ZPIC received approval from CMS to suspend payments to a provider,[156] the ZPIChad to coordinate with the appropriate MAC to institute a payment suspension.[157]

B. Medicare Drug Integrity Contractor (MEDIC)

The MEDIC detects and prevents fraud, waste, and abuse in the Medicare Part C and Part D programs. The MEDIC program has evolved considerably over the last decade. In 2007, CMS contracted with three regional MEDICs to handle potential fraud and abuse in Part D.[158] Then, in 2009, the MEDIC program transitioned from three regional contractors to two. In addition to reducing the contractors in the program, both contractors were also given oversight responsibility for Medicare Part C.[159] Further, in 2010, the program restructured into two national—rather than regional— MEDICs, one tasked with National Benefit Integrity (NBI) and the other with Compliance & Enforcement (C&E).[160] The NBI MEDIC prevents and detects fraud, waste, and abuse in Parts C and D nationwide; and the C&E MEDIC has nationwide responsibility for compliance and enforcement activities.[161] CMS subsequently continued the NBI MEDIC activities, and the C&E MEDIC was tasked with performing special and ad hoc studies and ongoing technical support for CMS and the NBI MEDIC.[162]

---

152. MPIM, 100-08, ch. 4 § 4.3.

153. MPIM, 100-08, ch. 8 § 8.2. *See also* 42 C.F.R. § 405.376.

154. MPIM, 100-08, ch. 8 § 8.4. *See also* 42 U.S.C. § 1395ddd(f)(3); RAC Final Statement of Work, Sept. 1, 2011.

155. 42 C.F.R. §§ 405.371, 405.372. *See also* MPIM, 100-08, ch. 8 §§ 8.3.1 and 8.3.1.1.

156. ZPICs must submit to CMS a draft suspension notice and a summary of the evidence justifying suspension and receive explicit approval from CMS before initiating a suspension. MPIM, 100-08, ch. 8 § 8.3.2.1.

157. MPIM, 100-08, ch. 8 § 8.3.

158. 2013 OIG Report, http://oig.hhs.gov/oei/reports/oei-03-11-00310.pdf, (p. 1).

159. *Id.* at 1-2.

160. *Id.* at 2.

161. *Id.*

162. *Id.*

Focusing on the NBI MEDIC, the MEDIC Statement of Work outlines the following responsibilities:

(1)   review the fraud and abuse components of Part C and Part D sponsoring organizations;

(2)   process Part D and Medicare Advantage workloads to identify and deter fraud, waste, and abuse;

(3)   assist CMS in developing a "watch" list of entities requiring future monitoring;

(4)   evaluate inappropriate activities through claim and drug utilization patterns and detection of outliers, such as services not rendered, services not medically necessary, off-label drug use, inappropriate coverage of drugs, and inappropriate changes in formularies;

(5)   conduct reviews and audits;

(6)   conduct complaint investigations;

(7)   conduct preliminary investigations into potentially fraudulent enrollments, eligibility determinations, and benefit distribution;

(8)   investigate aberrant behavior and develop and refer cases to appropriate law enforcement agencies or recommend administrative action;

(9)   identify vulnerabilities in the Part C and Part D programs;

(10)   provide support to law enforcement agencies in connection with investigations.[163]

The MEDIC is directed to use proactive data analysis, as well as to investigate external referrals of potential fraud. If the MEDIC substantiates a fraud allegation, it then refers the allegation to law enforcement. Where a case has been referred to the OIG/OI, the OIG/OI has ninety (90) calendar days to either accept the referral, refer it to the Department of Justice (DOJ), or reject the case.[164] If a determination is not made by the OIG/OI, the case is then referred to the Federal Bureau of Investigation (FBI) or another investigative agency with interest in the case.[165] In cases where the OIG, FBI, or another investigative agency does not accept the case or render a decision, the NBI MEDIC remains responsible for taking any actions to protect the Medicare Trust Funds.[166]

---

163. National Benefit Integrity (NBI) Medicare Drug Integrity Contractor (MEDIC) Statement of Work—DRAFT, July 2013 § 5.5.1.

164. *Id.*

165. *Id.*

166. *Id.*

A 2013 OIG Report found that Medicare Part C investigations and case referrals accounted for a small percentage of the MEDIC's BI activities due to the lack of a centralized Part C data repository, an inability to share information with other program integrity contractors, and limited ability to recover payments from plan sponsors.[167] CMS responded that it expected to provide the MEDIC access to a central repository of data and offer guidance on appropriate situations in which to share information with ZPICs and state agencies in the future.[168]

C. Benefit Coordination and Recovery Center (BCRC)

The Medicare Secondary Payer (MSP) program ensures that Medicare is aware of situations in which it should not be the primary payer of claims.[169] In situations where a beneficiary has Medicare and some other health insurance, Medicare's coordination of benefits (COB) rules decide which entity pays first.[170] Sometimes, after payment on a claim has already been made, CMS may receive new information indicating that Medicare made a primary payment by mistake because it was not the primary payer. Previously, CMS utilized the Medicare Secondary Payer Recovery Contractor (MSPRC) to make efforts to recover these payments. On February 1, 2014, CMS consolidated the MSPRC and the Coordination of Benefits Contractor into the new Benefits Coordination and Recovery Center (BCRC).[171]

All MSP claims investigations are initiated from and researched by the BCRC.[172] The BCRC handles COB actions for group health plans (GHPs),non-group health plans (NGHPs), and recovery activities for NGHPs.[173] If a GHP is the proper primary payer on a claim, the Commercial Repayment Center (CRC) seeks recovery from the employer and GHP.[174] If

---

167. 2013 OIG Report, *available at* http://oig.hhs.gov/oei/reports/oei-03-11-00310.pdf.

168. *Id.*

169. http://www.cms.gov/Medicare/Coordination-of-Benefits-and-Recovery/Coordination-of-Benefits-and-Recovery-Overview/Overview.html.

170. *Id.*

171. What's New Archive, http://www.cms.gov/ Medicare/Coordination-of-Benefits-and-Recovery/Coordination-of-Benefits-and-Recovery-Overview/Downloads/2014-COBandR-Overview-Whats-New-Archive.pdf.

172. http://www.cms.gov/Medicare/Coordination-of-Benefits-and-Recovery/ProviderServices/.

173. https://www.cms.gov/Medicare/Coordination-of-Benefits-and-Recovery/Coordination-of-Benefits-and-Recovery-Overview/Coordination-of-Benefits/Coordination-of-Benefits.html.

174. http://www.cms.gov/Medicare/Coordination-of-Benefits-and-Recovery/Coordination-of-Benefits-and-Recovery-Overview/Overview.html. The CRC is not a separate contractor; it is the division of the BCRC responsible for GHP recoveries. The CRC utilizes a web-based portal that allows employers, insurers, and third-party administrators electronic access to manage their GHP recovery activities. http://www.cms.gov/Medicare/Coordination-of-Benefits-and-Recovery/Coordination-of-Benefits-and-Recovery-Overview/Group-Health-Plan-Recovery/Group-Health-Plan-Recovery.html.

an NGHP is the proper primary payer, as may be the case with liability, no-fault, and workers' compensation claims, the BCRC is responsible for the recovery of mistaken payment if recovery is pursued from the beneficiary, whereas the CRC is responsible for recovery of payments pursued directly from a liability insurer—including a self-insured entity, no-fault insurer, or workers' compensation entity.[175]

VI. Medicaid Contractors

A. Medicaid RACs

Section 6411(a) of PPACA expanded the RAC program to Medicaid.[176] Each state Medicaid program was required to establish a RAC program by contracting with one or more entities to serve as the Medicaid RAC, or otherwise seek an exception. Like the Medicare RACs, the Medicaid RACs identify underpayments and overpayments, and recoup overpayments for the states. The Medicaid RACs are paid on a contingency fee basis, with the specific contingency fee rate set by the state up to a maximum specified by CMS.[177] If the state exceeds the maximum contingency fee without obtaining a waiver from CMS, the amount exceeding the maximum rate is not eligible to be paid with federal funds.[178]

Whereas the regulations allow the states flexibility to craft Medicaid RAC programs that fit their specific needs, the regulations also impose several requirements. The states must set limits on the number and frequency of medical records reviewed by the Medicaid RACs[179] and are responsible for setting the timeframes for provider responses to documentation requests.[180]

Likewise, the Medicaid RAC must hire a medical director and certified coders, unless it is determined that coders are not necessary for the review of Medicaid claims.[181] The Medicaid RAC is also required to provide a

---

175. http://www.cms.gov/Medicare/Coordination-of-Benefits-and-Recovery/Coordination-of-Benefits-and-Recovery-Overview/Overview.html. CMS recently transitioned a portion of the NGHP recovery workload from the BCRC to the CRC. Previously the BCRC was responsible for recovering payments where an NGHP was determined to be the proper primary payer, regardless of whether recovered from the beneficiary or a liability insurer, no-fault insurer or workers' compensation entity. *See* What's New Archive, 10/5/2015, https://www.cms.gov/Medicare/Coordination-of-Benefits-and-Recovery/Coordination-of-Benefits-and-Recovery-Overview/Downloads/COBandR-Overview-Whats-New-Archive.pdf.

176. Section 6411of PPACA did not extend the RAC program to CHIP.

177. 42 C.F.R. § 455.510.

178. *Id.*

179. 42 C.F.R. § 455.506.

180. https://www.cms.gov/Medicare-Medicaid-Coordination/Fraud-Prevention/MedicaidIntegrityProgram/Downloads/Medicaid_RAC_FAQ.pdf.

181. 42 C.F.R. § 455.508.

toll-free customer service number and accept provider submissions of electronic records on CD/DVD, or through facsimile if requested.[182] The Medicaid RACs are limited to a look-back period of three years from the date of the claim—unless they receive approval from the state.[183]

States were required to have a signed contract in place with a Medicaid RAC entity by January 1, 2012, or submit a state plan amendment to CMS by that date.[184] The nature of current Medicaid RAC audit activities varies by state and is best assessed by reviewing the individual state's Medicaid RAC contractor information.

B. Medicaid Integrity Program (MIP)

The Deficit Reduction Act of 2005 created the Medicaid Integrity Program (MIP) under Section 1936 of the SSA. The program is a comprehensive federal strategy to prevent and reduce provider fraud, waste, and abuse in the Medicaid program–the costs of which are shared by the state and federal governments.[185] Previously, the states were primarily responsible for identifying and stopping Medicaid fraud.

At the inception of the MIP, CMS hired three types of contractors—known as Medicaid Integrity Contractors (MICs)—to perform review, audit, and education functions.[186] Review MICs analyzed Medicaid claims data to identify whether fraud, waste, or abuse occurred or was likely to occur.[187] The Review MICs then referred the leads they identified to the Audit MICs to perform postpayment claim review to ensure proper payments were made and identify any overpayments.[188] CMS also contracted with Education MICs who were responsible for educating providers, beneficiaries, and managed care entities on program integrity and quality of care issues.[189]

An OIG Report from March 2012 identified several challenges that limited the effectiveness of the MICs. First, Review MICs struggled with identifying audit targets due to missing or incomplete data in the

---

182. *Id.*
183. *Id.*
184. https://cms.gov/Medicare-Medicaid-Coordination/Fraud-Prevention/Medicaid IntegrityProgram/Downloads/Medicaid_RAC_FAQ.pdf.
185. http://www.cms.gov/Medicare-Medicaid-Coordination/Fraud-Prevention/ MedicaidIntegrityProgram/index.html?redirect=/MedicaidIntegrityProgram/.
186. 42 U.S.C. § 1396u-6.
187. 42 C.F.R. § 455.232.
188. *Id.*
189. *Id.*

Medicaid Statistical Information System (MSIS).[190] Due to missing provider identification information, adjustments that corrected claims and service and beneficiary descriptions, the Review MICs were incorrectly identifying potential overpayment targets.[191] Once potential targets were identified, CMS assigned the audit targets to the Audit MICs to conduct postpayment claim review. If the Audit MIC identified an overpayment, it submitted a draft audit report to CMS, which reviewed the report for quality assurance and submitted it to the state and provider for comment.[192] Upon receiving the comments from the state and provider, the Audit MIC made any necessary revisions to the report and submitted the final report to CMS.[193] The 2012 OIG report analyzed the audit activities of the Audit MICs for a six-month period between January 1 and June 30, 2010, and concluded that 81% of the MIC audits did not–or were not likely to–identify Medicaid overpayments.[194] The ineffectiveness of the Audit MICs attributed to the inability of the Review MICs and CMS to identify audit targets.[195]

In response to the MICs' limited effectiveness, CMS made several changes to the program. In February 2011, CMS stopped assigning audit targets to the Audit MICs based solely on data from the MSIS. In addition, CMS allowed all Review MIC contracts to expire.[196]

CMS's current Comprehensive Medicaid Integrity Plan for FY 2019-2023 focuses on greater flexibility, stronger accountability, and enhanced program integrity by employing both new and evolving initiatives.[197]

---

190. MSIS is a nationwide Medicaid eligibility and claims data source containing a subset of data elements from state data systems that states report quarterly to CMS. MSIS data are a specified subset of fields extracted from each state's Medicaid Management Information System. MMIS enables states to process claims and monitor use of services. MSIS includes four Medicaid claims files: (1) inpatient care; (2) long-term care; (3) prescription drugs; and (4) all other claims, along with files of eligible Medicaid enrollees. http://oig.hhs.gov/oei/reports/oei-05-10-00210.pdf, p.3.

191. http://oig.hhs.gov/oei/reports/oei-05-10-00210.pdf, p.3.

192. *Id.*

193. *Id.*

194. http://oig.hhs.gov/oei/reports/oei-05-10-00210.pdf, p. 10.

195. *Id.*

196. FY 2014-2018 Comprehensive Medicaid Integrity Plan. http://www.cms.gov/Regulations-and-Guidance/Legislation/DeficitReductionAct/Downloads/cmip2014.pdf.

197. The plan is available at https://www.cms.gov/files/document/comprehensive-medicaid-integrity-plan-fys-2019-2023.pdf.

C. Payment Error Rate Measurement Program (PERM)

The Improper Payments Information Act (IPIA) of 2002[198] requires federal agencies to annually review programs they administer and identify those that may be susceptible to significant improper payments, to estimate the amount of improper payments, to submit those estimates to Congress, and to submit a report on actions the agency is taking to reduce the improper payments. The Office of Management and Budget (OMB) identified Medicaid and the Children's Health Insurance Program (CHIP)[199] as programs at risk for significant improper payments. CMS developed the Payment Error Rate Measurement (PERM) program to comply with the IPIA and related guidance issued by OMB.[200] Similar to the Medicare CERT program, the PERM program measures improper payments in Medicaid and CHIP and calculates error rates for each program. Error rates are based on reviews of the FFS, managed care, and eligibility components in the programs for a fiscal year period.[201] The error rate calculation is a measurement of the payments that did not meet statutory, regulatory, or administrative requirements, but not necessarily fraudulent payments.[202]

The 2015 Improper Payments Report describes the process used by the PERM program to measure improper payments. PERM uses a seventeen-state three-year rotation cycle to measure improper payments.[203] To calculate the error rates, CMS measures a third of the states each fiscal year. The reported Medicaid and CHIP program error rates for a given fiscal year include findings from the most recent three measurements to reflect findings from all fifty states and the District of Columbia.[204] The

---

198. Pub. L. No, 107-300, amended by Improper Payments Elimination and Recovery Act of 2010, Pub. L. No. 111-204.

199. The Children's Health Insurance Program provides health coverage to eligible children, through both Medicaid and separate CHIP programs under Title XXI of the SSA. CHIP is administered by states, according to federal requirements. The program is funded jointly by states and the federal government. The CHIP funding ended on Sept. 30, 2017, but through the Healthy Kids Act of 2018, Pub. L. No. 115-123, was extended retroactively from October 1, 2017, through September 30, 2023.

200. https://www.cms.gov/Research-Statistics-Data-and-Systems/Monitoring-Programs/Medicaid-and-CHIP-Compliance/PERM/

201. http://www.cms.gov/Research-Statistics-Data-and-Systems/Monitoring-Programs/Medicaid-and-CHIP-Compliance/PERM/index.html?redirect=/perm.

202. 42 C.F.R § 431.960.

203. Medicare and CHIP 2015 Improper Payments Report, https://www.cms.gov/Research-Statistics-Data-and-Systems/Monitoring-Programs/Medicaid-and-CHIP-Compliance/Downloads/2015MedicaidandCHIPImproperPaymentsReport.pdf. The 2015 Report is the latest version available at the time this article went to press.

204. *Id.*

PERM program uses three contractors, the Statistical Contractor, the Review Contractor, and the Eligibility Review Contractor.[205]

VII. The Future of CMS Contracting

A. Supplemental Medical Review Contractor (SMRC)

The Supplemental Medical Review Contractor (SMRC) is contracted by CMS to perform a variety of tasks focused on lowering improper payment rates and increasing medical review efficiencies across the Medicare and Medicaid programs.[206] The SMRC achieves these goals by identifying provider noncompliance with coverage, coding, billing, payment policies;, performing medical review and statistical sampling activities at the direction of CMS.[207]

One of the SMRC's primary tasks is conducting nationwide medical review activities assigned by CMS. Specifically, CMS selects services and provider specialties to be reviewed by the SMRC using, but not limited to, data analysis, issues identified by CERT reviews, professional organizations, other federal agencies, and comparative billing reports.[208] The SMRC's medical review activities are subject to the guidelines set forth in the *Medicare Program Integrity Manual.*

Upon completion of an SMRC medical review, the provider receives a Review Results letter outlining the specific review findings associated with the claims.[209] The SMRC offers providers the opportunity for a Discussion/Education Period intended for review of the specific claim denials, delivery of rationale and education for the claim determinations, and to provide information regarding avoiding similar denials in the future.[210] If the provider has additional relevant information or documentation regarding the claim at issue, it may be submitted at this time to support payment of the denied claim.[211] Requests to engage in the Discussion/Education Period must be made in writing within fourteen days of the date of the Review Results letter.[212] After completing the medical review, the SMRC notifies CMS of the identified improper payments and CMS directs the appropriate MAC to initiate claim adjustments or overpayment

---

205. https://www.cms.gov/Research-Statistics-Data-and-Systems/Monitoring-Programs/Medicaid-and-CHIP-Compliance/PERM/Downloads/RY2019CycleKickOff.pdf.

206. MPIM, Pub. 100-08, ch. 1 § 1.3.1.

207. MPIM, Pub. 100-08, ch. 1 § 1.3.8.

208. MPIM, Pub. 100-08, ch. 1 § 1.3.1.

209. https://www.noridiansmrc.com/discussion-education-period/

210. *Id.*

211. *Id.*

212. *Id.*

recoupment.[213] Providers are advised to contact their MAC regarding appeal rights and overpayment recovery issues.[214]

The SMRC is required to maintain a website that lists the types of issues under review, together with a link to relevant reports on the issue. Providers are notified of SMRC audits through ADRs requesting documentation.[215]

B. Unified Program Integrity Contractors (UPIC)

In 2015, CMS created the Unified Program Integrity Contractor (UPIC) to coordinate federal program integrity work and to consolidate Medicare and Medicaid data analysis, audit, and investigation work.[216] The UPICs perform fraud, waste, abuse detection, deterrence, and prevention activities for Medicare and Medicaid claims processed throughout the country. The functions performed by UPICs include, but are not limited to:

(1) proactively identifying potential fraud, waste, and abuse that exist within their jurisdictions;

(2) investigating allegations of fraud made by beneficiaries, providers/suppliers, CMS, the OIG, and others;

(3) coordinating with state Medicaid agencies and the MFCUs to detect fraud;

(4) referring and/or recommending appropriate Medicaid administrative actions to state Medicaid agencies where there is reliable evidence of fraud, including, but not limited to, overpayments, payment suspensions, and terminations;

(5) referring cases to the OIG/OI for consideration of civil and criminal prosecution and/or application of administrative sanctions;

(6) partnering with state Medicaid Program Integrity Units to perform the above activities for the Medi-Medi Program and Medicaid-only investigations.

UPICs perform program integrity activities associated with the following types of claims: Medicare Parts A, B, DME, Home Health and Hospice, Medicaid, and the Medi-Medi data match program. The UPIC contracts

213. https://www.cms.gov/Research-Statistics-Data-and-Systems/Monitoring-Programs/Medicare-FFS-Compliance-Programs/Medical-Review/SMRC.html.

214. *Id.*

215. MPIM, Pub. 100-08, ch. 3 § 3.2.2.

216. FY 2014-2018 Comprehensive Medicaid Integrity Plan, *available at* http://www.cms.gov/Regulations-and-Guidance/Legislation/DeficitReductionAct/Downloads/cmip2014.pdf.

operate in five (5) separate geographical jurisdictions in the United States and combine and integrate functions previously performed by the ZPIC, PSC, and MIC contracts.

The goal in unifying Medicare and Medicaid efforts is to achieve enhanced detection and prevention of fraud, waste, and abuse, which will require the UPICs to coordinate activities, not only with CMS and its partners and contractors, but also with agencies at the federal, state, and local levels of government.[217] Pursuant to the UPIC Umbrella Statement of Work, the UPICs perform a variety of functions to detect, prevent, and deter specific risks and broader vulnerabilities to the integrity of the Medicare and Medicaid programs including those resulting from payment reforms and healthcare innovations, such as electronic health records.[218] The UPICs operate in specific geographic jurisdictions defined by individual task orders.[219] The five UPIC regions are as follows: UPIC Northeastern Jurisdiction; UPIC Mid-Western Jurisdiction; UPIC South-Eastern Jurisdiction; UPIC Southwestern Jurisdiction; and UPIC Western Jurisdiction.[220]

VIII. Conclusion

The number and focus of CMS contractors continue to evolve as new programs are established and existing programs are reevaluated. Although the landscape of contractors is vast, it is important for healthcare providers and their counsel to understand the underlying goals of the various CMS programs in order to better understand the focus and actions of the contractor with which they are dealing.

---

217. *Id.* at 7.
218. *Id.*
219. *Id.*
220. https://www.cms.gov/Research-Statistics-Data-and-Systems/Monitoring-Programs/ Medicare-FFS-Compliance-Programs/Review-Contractor-Directory-Interactive-Map/#ks; *see also* https://integritym.com/wp-content/uploads/2015/04/J-8-Unified-Program-Integrity-Contract-UPIC-Map-of-Jurisdictions.jpg.

Chapter 10

PHYSICIAN EMPLOYMENT CONTRACTS FROM THE PHYSICIAN PERSPECTIVE

BY: JENNIFER A. JOHNSTON TERANDO, R.N., ESQ.

I.   Introduction

With physician shortages in the United States on an upward trajectory, there is fierce competition by physician employers to both attract and retain physicians. According to data published by the Association of American Medical Colleges, the United States could see an estimated shortage of between 54,100 and 139,000 physicians, including shortfalls in both primary and specialty care, by 2033.[1]

Physicians have already begun seeing and will continue to see generous signing bonuses, salaries, relocation expenses, and retention bonuses. The attractive compensation packages, coupled with the fact that the shortage offers the corollary benefit of providing physicians with their first-choice location, have provided physicians with strong bargaining power in the physician job market.

At the same time, over the past thirty years, there has been a growing trend in physicians being employed by hospitals, instead of in "private practice" as either the owner or employee of a physician-owned practice. As of 2018, according to the American Medical Association's (AMA) Physician Practice Benchmark Survey, hospital-employed physicians outnumbered private practice physicians for the first time.[2] Given the evolving and streamlined delivery of healthcare in the United States, including the ever-evolving body of laws and regulations that govern healthcare, the number of hospital-employed physicians is expected to experience continued growth.

However, at this time, close to half of the nation's physicians are in private practice.[3] While the contracts of physicians employed by hospitals and in private

---

1. "The Complexities of Physician Supply and Demand: Projections from 2018-2033." Prepared for the AAMC by IHS Markit, Ltd., (June 2020) https://www.aamc.org/media/45976/download.

2. Apoorva Rama, PhD, *2012-2018 Data on Physician Compensation Methods: Upswing in Compensation through the Combination of Salary and Bonus*, AMERICAN MEDICAL ASSOCIATION (2020), https://www.ama-assn.org/system/files/2020-12/data-physician-compensation-methods.pdf.

3. *Id.*

practice share many of the same provisions, there tends to be greater variance in the sophistication of the contracts in private practice. Oftentimes, there is more room for negotiation in private practice contracts, likely attributable to the intimacy of the business relationship in small private practices. Accordingly, this chapter shall endeavor to provide a detailed analysis of physician contract terms, applicable to all physicians, with a level of specificity in areas in which physicians may want to negotiate terms or request assurances. The latter may particularly beneficial to physicians in private practice.

Physician employment contracts can range in length from a few pages to upward of one-hundred pages. Contracts can be drafted by an experienced lawyer, specifically for an individual physician, or they can be a form contract where the physician's name has been inserted. Either way, it is imperative that a physician conduct a detailed analysis of the contract terms, ideally with the assistance of an attorney well-versed in physician employment contracts.

From a practical standpoint, the physician employment contract encompasses terms surrounding two distinct phases of the employment: the duties owed and benefits provided while the physician is employed by the group/practice/hospital (employer); and the termination of the contract. The former terms are routinely given more consideration by physicians when they are embarking upon the employment relationship. However, the termination of an employment agreement can result in significant financial and practice implications. Thus, the review of a physician contract must be two-fold and accordingly, this chapter is intentionally divided to address these two distinct phases: the first containing a synopsis of the terms of employment, and the second addressing the terms triggered upon termination of the contract.

Most importantly, the primary goal of this chapter is not fear of hidden contract terms, but how to conduct a thorough analysis of a contract so that the physicians can make informed decisions whether the position will meet their expectations and allow them to lead a satisfying career. The chapter will conclude with a discussion on negotiation strategies for a collaborative negotiation of contract terms with the physician's future employer.

II. Letter of Intent

After a physician has participated in serious employment discussions with an employer, but before all of the details are negotiated and set forth in a contract to be signed by the parties, an employer may provide the physician with a letter of intent (LOI.) An LOI is not a contract per se, and in fact, usually includes language to this effect, but if the parties sign the letter, a physician runs the risk that the employer may deem it a written agreement. For example, if the LOI defines the salary and the physician signs it, if the physician later attempts to negotiate the salary, the employer may feel that the salary is no longer negotiable.

Additionally, the LOI likely will only address the "main" terms of the contract, such as agreement to employ and salary, but will not address other issues that can have a significant impact on the physician, such as malpractice coverage or restrictive covenants. Thus, the LOI should make it clear that the acceptance of the contract will be dependent upon reaching an agreement on all terms.

This chapter is focused on the details of the physician employment contract, but the issue of an LOI is being raised since physicians should be aware that an LOI is not a simple letter. A physician must carefully review an LOI to assure that they are in agreement with all of the terms set forth in the LOI and that it is clear that the LOI is non-binding. A physician who plans to utilize an attorney to review and negotiate their employment contract would be wise to retain have the attorney review the LOI prior to signing.

III.   General Principles of Contract

From a legal standpoint, a contract is defined as an agreement between private parties creating mutual obligations, which are enforceable by law. The basic elements required for the agreement to be a legally enforceable contract are: mutual assent, expressed by a valid offer and acceptance, adequate consideration, capacity and legality.[4] Consideration is defined as something bargained for and received by a promisor from a promisee.[5] In the case of a physician employment contract, the promisor/employer bargains for and receives the services of the physician in the treatment of their patients, while the promisee/physician bargains for and receives compensation, including salary and benefits, and the staff, facilities and supplies necessary to practice medicine. Generally, the contract will define the parties and the period of time it covers. Some contracts may be for a defined period of time, such as a one or three years, while others may auto-renew annually until one of the parties exercises their option to terminate the contract.

The contract typically will also include "basic" or "boilerplate" terms found in most types of legal contracts. Even a contract provision deemed a standard term can have major ramifications down the road and its risks and benefits must be included in the contract analysis. The following is a summary of standard contract terms:

- Assignability: The terms of the contract cannot be assigned to any other parties without written consent. This means that in the event of a sale of the practice, the contract would need to be renewed by the new employer and the physician, unless otherwise provided.

---

4. Cornell Legal Information Institute, https://www.law.cornell.edu/wex/contract. (Last visited Feb. 14, 2021.)

5. Cornell Legal Information Institute, https://www.law.cornell.edu/wex/category/business_law?page=21. (Last visited Feb. 14, 2021.)

- Amendments: There will be a statement that the written contract encompasses all of the terms of the contract and that the contract can only be amended in writing.

- Severability: If any of the terms of the contract are held to be unenforceable, the remainder of the terms will still be enforceable.

- Notice requirements: When notice is required under the contract, such as notice of a breach with time to cure, notice of termination, or the option to exercise the alternative dispute resolution (ADR) clause is invoked, the notice requirements section sets forth the details of how notice will be provided.

- Choice of law. The contract will indicate which state laws govern the term of the contract, which are usually the state in which the employer is located.

Finally, the AMA Principles of 2019 address the potential conflict of interest a physician may experience between their patient and their employer. The principles provide that an employer should never interfere with medical decision making and that a patient's well-being must always take precedent.[6] Further a physician should not be deemed in breach of their contract, nor retaliated against, for exercising their medical decision making.

IV. Physician Employment Contract Terms Concerning the Employment Term

A. Representations

The contract will commence with a series of representations the physician agrees to, including:

- that the physician is a duly licensed physician in good standing with the medical board of their state;

- the physician is board certified/eligible;

- the physician possesses a current DEA license;

- the physician is a member in good standing (or will become one as a condition of employment) of the medical staff of named hospital(s);

- the physician has never had the medical staff privileges of any hospital denied suspended, revoked or terminated;

---

6. AMA Principles for Physician Employment H-225.950 (2019), https://policysearch.ama-assn.org/policyfinder/detail/AMA%20Principles%20for%20Physician%20Employment%20H-225.950?uri=%2FAMADoc%2FHOD.xml-0-1535.xml (last accessed March 5, 2021).

- the physician is Medicare eligible/a participating provider with no sanctions or exclusions;

- the physician has have/will participate in any third-party payor credentialing required by the practice;

- the physician has have no disciplinary actions and has never been the subject of an investigation by any medical board; and

- the physician has no criminal convictions.

As part of the employment on-boarding, physicians should expect that the employer will verify all of the representations, run background checks, have them undergo physical examinations, including drug testing, and check all of their references.

B. Scope of Duty

The scope of duty clause sets forth the physician's duties. This section of the contract should provide sufficient detail in an effort to prevent any ambiguity. The scope of duty clause is highly correlated with job satisfaction. Many physicians report leaving a position, based upon working more hours than anticipated or being unhappy with the high amount of non-clinical responsibilities a job entails. Accordingly, a carefully reviewed and negotiated scope of duty clause will lend itself to higher job satisfaction. This section will review the components of a well drafted and/or negotiated scope of duty clause. It is important to note that each medical specialty and further, each physician, have varying requirements and expectations. There is none-size-fits-all arrangement. Rather, it is important for each individual physician to analyze the scope of duty in terms of their area of practice and personal preferences.

1. Clinical Responsibilities, Hours, Call Schedule, Facilities, and Equipment

The scope of duty section should specifically delineate the days and hours the physician will be scheduled to be physically present in the office and/or hospital setting. If a physician is contracting for part-time employment, it is especially important that the days and hours are well-defined.

With large scale groups, which have multiple office locations and contracts with multiple hospitals, this section should also set forth which location the physician will work at and any requirements that they cover the other locations. Of these set days and hours, the scope of duty clause should further specify which hours will be assigned to patient care and how this time will be allocated. For example, in an office-based setting, it may address how many appointments will be scheduled, how much time will be allotted for appointments, and how many add-on patients the physician may have. For a surgeon or other procedure-based physician, the scope of duty clause may set forth how many days per week they will have scheduled procedures. There is also usually a statement that the physician will close all patient encounters in a timely manner and include documentation to support billing codes to assure the employer can collect appropriate reimbursement for the services rendered by the physician, including assigning all of their billing rights to the employer. Many employers will also allot a certain amount of time for physician education, such as a half-day once a week or once a month.

One of the biggest sticking points of the scope of duty section is on-call coverage. The clause may provide a general statement that the physician agrees to take call per the group assignment or it may specifically state how many weekends per month, or days per week, the physician is required to take call. This clause is usually given very little attention in the negotiation stage, but can end up being one of the breaking points of the employment. Physicians should request clarification as to how often they will be required to take call. For call-heavy specialties, such as surgery and obstetrics, and for small group practices, the physician should seek to have a well-defined on-call commitment, including addressing how call will be handled when another physician is on vacation, maternity leave, or medical leave.

The contract usually includes a statement that the physician will provide medical care in an ethical manner in accordance with the applicable standard of care for physicians in their specialty, including compliance with all of the employer's policies and procedures and compliance with any peer review proceedings. Many hospitals/health systems have religious affiliations. When they do, the scope of duty may include a statement of common values that the physician must agree to. The statement of common values may include the employer's position on abortion, reproductive technology, physician-assisted suicide and other matters. The physician must carefully review this statement and make a decision as to whether they can practice medicine in accordance with it.

The facilities and equipment clause is most commonly a general acknowledgment that the employer will provide the necessary facilities, including staff, and equipment. However, in the case of a physician who requires specialized equipment for their practice, such as specific robotic surgical equipment or gamma tiles for prevention of brain tumor recurrence, it would be wise to have as much specificity as possible included.

2. *Administrative Responsibilities*

Physicians are frequently required to assume other duties in a medical practice beyond clinical activities. This can be especially true if they are joining a small practice. The administration of a medical practice itself is a full-time job, so physicians should have a clear understanding of what they are contracting to perform. Some physicians are required to interview physician candidates and/or candidates for staff positions. This may involve making employment offers and participating in the negotiation of contracts. Administrative duties may also extend to conducting staff reviews and handling disciplinary incidents.

Particularly in a small physician practice, other duties may include working with an accountant to oversee the practice finances and payroll and negotiating and managing multiple vendor contracts. There may be a need to hire and work with an attorney for any legal issues the practice encounters, including counsel for regulatory issues, given how highly regulated the practice of medicine is. It is easy to imagine how this may entail a significant time commitment on the part of the physician.

If a physician must dedicate many hours per week to administrative duties on top of their clinical care duties, they may find that they are working more hours than expected. Additionally, if the physician has a productivity model of compensation and they are spending more time conducting administrative duties, their salary may be less than they initially projected. Thus, when evaluating the physician employment contract, the physician must consider exactly what administrative duties they are responsible for and how much of their professional time will be allocated to these duties. When the administrative duties contained in a scope of duty clause are thoroughly vetted and negotiated by both sides, a harmonious working relationship is more likely.

3. *Marketing Responsibilities*

The scope of duty clause should address any marketing responsibilities the physician will have. These may include attending activities, such as health fairs to attract new patients and/or the preparation and conducting of CME (continuing medical education) programs for other practices and/or specialty groups who may be a patient referral source for the practice. Marketing activities may also include an active presence on social media. Similar to the administrative duties discussed above, the best practice is for the physician to clearly understand what they are agreeing to.

4. *Outside Work*

Physicians may wish to work part-time in urgent care, hold a teaching position at a university or work as a legal consultant or expert witness. The contract should address whether or not the physician is permitted to work outside of employment. When the contract demands that the physician devote all of their medical/professional time to the employment, the clause is often referred to as an "exclusivity clause." If outside work is permitted, the type of work allowed and whether there is a limit on the amount of outside work should be outlined.

In addition to authorizing work, the contract should indicate who receives the income from the outside work. Some contracts permit the physician to work outside of the practice, but state the practice is entitled to all of the income from the physician's outside endeavors. This may be acceptable to the physician who holds an associate professor position. However, if a physician wants to perform legal work, which the physician may want to do because of its lucrative enature, the physician would want to review the contract and negotiate terms allowing the physician to keep the compensation received from that work.

The contract will also require most physicians to obtain their own separate professional liability insurance for any medical work outside of the employment, such as urgent care work.

5. *Intellectual Property*

Many physician contracts will set forth that any inventions or intellectual property created by the physician during the term of employment are the sole property of the employer and the employee conveys all rights, title and interest to any invention or intellectual property, including patents, trademarks, and copyrights to the employer. For the majority of physicians, this clause will be of little significance. However, any physician working in the development of a medical device or with plans to start a medical device company would be wise to negotiate terms providing that any inventions or intellectual property developed completely outside of the employer's time and not utilizing any employer resources or trade secrets remain the property of the physician. When the physician has a medical device or other invention already in progress when they commence employment, they would be wise seek the advice of intellectual property counsel and obtain an express acknowledgment stating which devices, inventions, or other projects are excluded from the terms of the contract.

C. Compensation

The attractiveness and competitiveness of physician compensation packages appear to be increasing in sync with the physician shortage. This section discusses the various ways physician compensation may be structured. It should be noted that the focus of this chapter is the bona fide employment arrangement and does not address independent contractor or professional services agreements, which hospitals and other entities may enter into and that have their own unique attributes.

1. *Base Salary*

A straight base salary is the exception, not the norm, when it comes to physician compensation packages. A physician, new to the employer, may be offered a base salary for the first couple of years of employment and then their compensation will change to a productivity model. This allows the physician adequate time to build their patient panel, which should allow them to see enough patients to earn their base salary or higher when they switch to some form of a productivity model of compensation, discussed in more detail below.

2. *Productivity/Quality Payment*

In a productivity model of compensation, the physician receives a portion of the employer's revenue. Although some employers pay physicians on a straight productivity model, the most common model of physician compensation seen in the United States today is a base salary coupled with a productivity bonus. Some employers will also provide physicians with a set monthly or bi-monthly "draw" which is adjusted, once productivity is calculated. In this instance, the physician should set the draw low enough that they are owed funds, rather than being in a position of owing money.

Regardless of the structure, it is extremely important for both physician and employer that the contract sets forth in sufficient detail how the productivity payment will be calculated, minimizing any grey areas. The contract must define with specificity how revenue is determined, what percentage of revenue the physician will receive and how often productivity payments will be distributed. This includes whether the productivity is based upon gross or net revenue and whether the productivity is based upon the entire practice's performance or the physician's individual performance. In the case of a productivity payment, which deducts overhead costs, the contract must define with detail how the costs are calculated. And if productivity is based upon the physician's individual performance, the contract should further delineate what portion of the overhead costs are attributed to the physician. From a physician standpoint, a productivity bonus that deducts overhead costs should include either monthly/regular reporting regarding the practice costs or at a minimum, provide a physician with a right to audit cost records. As more and more physicians are employed by large groups, the overhead deduction is less common.

Many practices today calculate physician compensation according to the Medicare Physician Fee Schedule (MPFS.) Via the MPFS, physician tasks and procedures are assigned a Work Relative Value Unit (wRVU), which is applied to a physician fee schedule conversion factor to determine Medicare reimbursement. Many employers utilize the wRVU in calculating productivity compensation. For example, a physician may be paid a set dollar amount for any wRVU billed over a certain amount. As of January 1, 2021, the conversion factor is $34.89 per wRVU.[7] While the dollar amount of the 2021 conversion factor is less than the 2020 conversion factor, many wRVUs have significantly increased, meaning some physicians could see increased compensation if their employer calculates productivity compensation based upon the total amount of wRVUs generated.

With Medicare's transition to a quality payment program, pursuant to the Medicare Access and CHIP Reauthorization Act (MACRA),[8] wherein physicians may have positive or negative adjustments to their Medicare reimbursement or receive incentives to provide high-quality cost-effective care, physicians should expect to begin to see the payment program reflected in their compensation clauses with incentives for rendering quality care, leading to higher reimbursement rates for their employers.

Additionally, pursuant to MACRA, physicians have a score attached to their National Provider Identifier and the employer has a group score, reflecting the physicians working for them. This should be anticipated to have a two-fold implication on employment contracts. Employers will be interested in evaluating the physician's score during the hiring process, as the physician's score will become part of the employer's score if the physician is hired. Additionally, physicians will want to evaluate the employer's score as it will be an indicator of future earnings, dependent upon the employer's quality-based performance.

---

7. 85 Fed. Reg. 84472
8. *See* The Medicare Authorization and CHIP Reauthorization Act of 2015, Pub. L. 114-10 (2015).

Therefore, one of the most prudent moves a physician can make is to request reports from the employer regarding the spectrum of productivity/quality bonuses the practice has paid out over the past five years and the data used to determine the amount of the bonuses. The contract should address whether the physician must be employed for the entire productivity/bonus period, or what percentage of the bonus period that they must be employed, in order to qualify for the bonus.

Physicians should also inquire about the payor mix the employer has with third party payors. It is best if the physician contracts with several different payors, as reliance on one major payor may decrease the employer's bargaining power in contract negotiations, leading to lower reimbursement rates. There is also the risk that if the employer loses the contract with the third-party payor, the physician's earning ability could be severely impacted.

3. *Discretionary Bonuses*

It is common for physicians to also be eligible for a discretionary bonus. Typically, a physician will be offered a base salary, a productivity bonus, and a discretionary bonus. However, the physician may only be offered a salary and a discretionary bonus, allowing the employer to exercise more control in the amount of money the employer pays out. Like the productivity bonuses, physicians should determine the qualifications for the bonus, including whether they must be employed the entire bonus period, or a certain percentage of it, to qualify for the bonus.

Additionally, while the bonus is deemed "discretionary," there tends to be set criteria for determining them. Thus, when a physician is negotiating their compensation package, it is important to make several key inquiries regarding discretionary bonuses, including:

- the amount of the discretionary bonus? (Examples include: patient satisfaction surveys, employment reviews and overall productivity.)
- Of the other employed physicians, what percent received discretionary bonuses over the past five years?
- Of the other employed physicians who received discretionary bonuses over the past five years, what was the range of bonuses received and what was the average bonus?

By making these key inquiries, the physician will have a better understanding of what they can expect to receive in terms of a discretionary bonus and accordingly, will be able to make a better assessment of the overall compensation package.

4. *Signing Bonus*

Over the last few years, signing bonuses have become a fairly standard component of physician compensation. While the amount of the bonus varies amongst specialties and the significance of physician shortages in the geographic location of the employment, it is safe to say many bonuses are in the range of the high five figures to low six figures. Thus, they account for a significant portion of the compensation package.

As will be discussed in more detail in the termination section of this chapter, signing bonuses are usually structured as a forgivable loan. The loan is provided as an untaxed lump sum at the beginning of the employment and is gradually forgiven over a term of years. Physicians must be aware that the money becomes taxable as it is forgiven and if they leave before the loan is fully forgiven, the outstanding balance will be due immediately.

5. *The Pandemic's Effect*

Moving quickly, the Centers for Medicare & Medicaid Services (CMS) extended reimbursement for telehealth to broadly include providers beyond rural providers and by allowing patients to attend telehealth appointments from their homes, rather than be required to report to an originating site, such as a rural hospital.[9] This allowed providers and patients to quickly move many appointments on-line and reduced some compensation loss. Unfortunately, while both providers and patients adapted to the virtual office visit, CMS' extension of reimbursement will expire, returning availability to solely rural providers.

Many organizations also stepped up during the pandemic and provided compensation guarantees. In turn, physicians have been required to be flexible in their work roles during the pandemic. In New York, physicians with lower office volumes or who were unable to perform elective procedures stepped up to assist in intensive care units, treating coronavirus patients. In California, physicians such as plastic and orthopedic surgeons, unable to perform elective surgeries, instead spent time in their facilities, administering the coronavirus vaccine.

---

9. Center for Medicare & Medicaid Services COVID-19 Emergency Declaration Blanket Waivers For Healthcare Providers, (March 30, 2020), https://www.cms.gov/files/document/covid19-emergency-declaration-health-care-providers-fact-sheet.pdf (last accessed March 5, 2021).

Despite these quick adaptations, there were many physicians who lost a good deal of compensation as a direct effect of the pandemic. This raises the question of compensation clauses being expanded to address a similar situation in the future to prevent such losses. Will income guarantees be requested by physicians to address potential decreased productivity through no fault of their own? On the other hand, will employers insert force majeure clauses? Only time will tell what has been learned by the unprecedented impact of coronavirus on the healthcare system.

D. Benefits

1. General Employment Benefits

General employment benefits that will be outlined in a physician employment contract include vacation and sick time, which in many instances is defined as Paid Time Off, paid maternity/paternity leave, health insurance, dental insurance, life insurance, disability insurance/leave, and retirement benefits.

2. Benefits Specific to Physicians

There are significant costs associated with being a physician and medical practices vary regarding which of these costs they cover and which of these costs the physician covers. The primary benefit specific to physicians is malpractice, or professional liability, insurance (covered in more detail in its own section) and in almost every instance it is covered by the employer. It should be noted that in the case of a claims-made policy, whether or not the practice provides tail insurance is a separate issue and either way, the issue should be specifically spelled out in the employment contract. (This topic will be covered in more detail in the termination section below.)

Expenses specific to the practice of medicine may include fees for state licensure, Drug Enforcement Agency license, hospital staff dues, memberships in professional organizations, subscriptions to professional journals, CME (including travel expenses,) and subscriptions to smartphone applications, such as UpToDate and Epocrates. The cost of these benefits adds up quickly. Whether or not these benefits are covered by the employer is up to the employer and may be a term of the contract, which may be subject to negotiation. The value of the benefits provided by the employer should be analyzed as part of the physician's overall compensation package. Physicians should also forecast what their out-of-pocket expenses will amount to. It should be noted that many of these benefits, when paid out-of-pocket by the physician, will qualify as an itemized tax deduction for the physician and the physician should consult with their accountant to gain an understanding of what tax benefits may inure from their out-of-pocket expenses.

3. *Malpractice Coverage*

Physician malpractice, or professional liability, coverage is arguably one of the most important/highest value benefits provided by the employer to the physician. What is important to understand about malpractice coverage is that it comes in different forms, which can greatly impact the physician. It should be noted that in some instances, the physician may be responsible for obtaining their own coverage, but that is the exception, not the norm. Additionally, it should be noted that the amount of coverage required may be dictated by state laws and the physician must verify that the coverage provided is legally compliant.

Traditionally, the majority of medical practices in the United States have been insured by claims-made policies for the simple reason that the premiums are significantly less than other policies.

Claims-made coverage provides malpractice coverage for the physician for any claims made, arising from the physician's employment, between the physician's first day of employment and his or her last. Where claims-made coverage can get tricky is when a physician treats a patient while they are employed at the practice, but the patient files a malpractice claim after the physician is no longer employed by the practice. Because the physician had claims made coverage, the physician does not have coverage for this malpractice claim.

In order to have coverage for the claim, it is necessary for the physician to have tail insurance, frequently referred to as a "tail." This is a policy of insurance purchased to cover the physician for any malpractice claims. The tail endorsement can be for a set period of years or perpetual. Indefinite coverage assures coverage expands beyond the standard statute of limitations to encompass both statutory notice provisions and statutory tolling provisions for minors, which can ostensibly extend the statute of limitations for many years.

The tail is purchased from the insurance company that provided the claims-made coverage, as it is an extension of that policy. As will be discussed in the termination section of this chapter, tail insurance comes with a one-time premium payment, which can be quite expensive for the physician. Therefore, it is extremely important for the physician employment contract to set forth in detail whether the physician or employer is responsible for the premium or whether they will share the cost.

An occurrence policy provides coverage for any care rendered while the physician was employed by the medical group or hospital. For example, assume a physician was employed by medical group A from January 1, 2020, until December 31, 2020, at which time the physician resigned from medical group A and accepted a job with medical group B. Also assume a claim of negligence arose from treatment the physician rendered at medical group A on March 15, 2020. If a lawsuit was filed on January 15, 2021, the occurrence policy from medical group A would cover the physician for the claim of negligence. In contrast, had medical group A had a claims-made policy, the physician would only have coverage for the claim, if the physician had purchased a tail, when the physician left medical practice A to work at medical practice B.

GOOD EXAMPLE!

As the practice of medicine in the United States is evolving from small private medical practices, which employ a handful of physicians, to large corporate managed medical groups that sometimes employ thousands of physicians, the trend is moving from claims-made insurance to self-insured entities, or captives, which make the need for a tail obsolete. Rather than contract with a private insurance company, exchanging premiums for coverage, these large entities have "reserves" to cover the cost of attorneys and any settlements or judgments should one of their physicians be sued.

Self-insured entities operate much like occurrence coverage in that when the physician leaves the self-insured medical practice, there is no need to obtain tail insurance. The self-insured entities offer this benefit to their physicians, both as an enticement of employment, but also because, in the event of malpractice litigation, the self-insured entity typically prefers to manage the entire defense on its own, likely resulting in litigation cost containment and the benefit of managing the entire defense when multiple physicians and perhaps the hospital are named defendants.

A physician entering into an employment contract with a self-insured entity must confirm that in the event of a malpractice action being brought after they have left the employment, they will still be provided coverage for both legal costs and any settlement or judgment. This confirmation should be in writing.

E. Ownership/Partnership

A physician who is joining a practice may do so with the intention of spending their entire career with the employer. If this is the case, they will be interested in when they can "buy-in" to the practice as an owner or be named a partner. While an initial employment contract is highly unlikely to include any guarantee of ownership or partnership, before committing to the position is an excellent time to gather intelligence on the buy-in/partnership process. Physicians can inquire about the general time frames and qualifications that make a physician eligible for buy-in or partnership, such as: how long they need to employed to be considered; what percent of physicians hired go on to become owners/partners; and have physicians been passed over for ownership/partnership and what were the reasons. Physicians can also request to review a buy-in/partnership agreement, which will yield valuable information about what their future will look like if they are considering remaining with the employer for the duration of their career.

While practices ill not offer guarantees of buy-in/partnership in the initial contract, some practices are willing to contract to an agreed review for buy-in/partnership after a set term of employment, such as three or five years. This is a good mechanism to get the review process going and get an offer extended. Finally, a physician should feel comfortable asking about the buy-in/partnership, as it demonstrates a long-term commitment to the employer and having the employer and physician on the same page prevents disputes down the road.

V.   Regulatory Issue Spotting

It is no secret that the practice of medicine is one of the most highly regulated professions. Physicians must adhere to a multitude of federal and state statutes and regulations, many of which are covered in detail in other chapters of this book. The penalty for violations can range from civil monetary penalties to suspension or revocation of Medicare privileges or a medical license, and in the worst-case scenario, imprisonment.

Given the severe penalties surrounding regulatory issue violations, it is a judicious move for physicians to have their employment contracts undergo a review by an attorney familiar with regulatory issues for the purpose of regulatory issue spotting. This includes assuring that the employment arrangement qualifies as a bona fide employment arrangement and that compensation is at fair market value. In the instance where regulatory issues do arise, this will allow the physician to have those issues properly reviewed and negotiated by a health law attorney who specializes in that area of practice.

Physician recruitment agreements, which are discussed in detail in this book's chapter on Evolving Trends in Physician Hospital Contracting, are separate agreements, entered into when a hospital or entity recruit a physician to relocate to their geographic service area. Due to the unique financial relationship involved in a recruitment agreement between a hospital and a physician, recruitment agreements can be particularly prone to regulatory scrutiny. Should a physician be offered a recruitment agreement, having a detailed legal analysis conducted to assure the agreement adheres to regulatory requirements, particularly the Stark Law exception for physician recruitment, is a necessity.[10]

VI. Physician Employment Contract Terms Concerning Termination of Employment

A LinkedIn study revealed millennials will change jobs an average of four times in their first decade out of college, compared to about two job changes by Gen-Xers, during their first ten years out of college.[11] Additionally, the Bureau of Labor Statistics reports that on average, people held 11.7 jobs between age 18 and 48. (Noting about 27 percent of them were particularly prone to hop, holding 15 jobs or more, while 10 percent held zero to four jobs.)[12] While these studies do not directly address physicians, the message remains poignant. It is statistically improbable that physicians will remain at the same position for their entire career. No matter the stage of their career, in addition to the possibility of a physician resigning, physicians must also consider and plan for such possibilities as the group or practice closing, being sold, or merged with another group or practice, and for the possibility they may be terminated.

There are several contract provisions that can be triggered upon the termination of the employment contract. It is imperative that these terms be carefully considered by both the employer and physician at the time of the contract negotiation, as the ramifications can be far reaching for all parties to the contract.

A. Reasons for Termination of Physician Employment Contract

There are several reasons physician contracts are terminated. This section addresses both no-cause termination and termination for cause.

1. No-Cause Termination

No-cause termination is the most common reason for termination of employment contracts. It occurs most commonly with the physician electing to resign, usually because the physician has found a new

---

10. 42 C.F.R. § 411.357 (e)

11. Jeffrey R. Young, *How Many Times Will People Change Jobs? The Myth of the Endlessly Job-Hopping Millennial,* www.edsurge.com (July 20, 2017), https://www.edsurge.com/news/2017-07-20-how-many-times-will-people-change-jobs-the-myth-of-the-endlessly-job-hopping-millennial.

12. *NUMBER OF JOBS, LABOR MARKET EXPERIENCE AND EARNINGS GROWTH: RESULTS FROM A NATIONAL LONGITUDINAL SURVEY,* www.bls.gov. (Aug. 22, 2019), https://www.bls.gov/news.release/pdf/nlsoy.pdf.

position or is relocating outside of the geographic area of the employment. However, an employer can also terminate the employment contract for no-cause. The most common situations in which an employer terminates a physician employment contract for no cause occurs when a practice is closing, perhaps due to a senior physician's retirement, or when the patient volume is not sufficient to require the services of the physician.

The employment contract should set forth the specific requirements for no-cause termination. The primary requirement is a notice requirement, which is typically an average of ninety days. In the case of a physician terminating the contract, this ninety-day notice will allow the employer adequate time to interview and hire another physician to prevent an interruption in patient care. In addition to the interviewing and hiring process, there must be adequate time for the new physician to obtain medical staff privileges at any hospitals and to be approved for the employer's third-party payer panels. Similarly, in the case of a practice electing to terminate the physician for no-cause, the notice period allows the physician adequate time to locate a new position. In some contracts, the employer will reserve the right to pay the physician for the notice period, but elect to no longer have them working. When a physician is on a productivity compensation model, this payment should be negotiated to reflect the lost opportunity to earn productivity pay.

2. For-Cause Termination

For-cause termination of the employment contract occurs when there is either a reason for immediate termination or breach of the contract. What qualifies for immediate termination should be spelled out in the contract with a good level of specificity. Reasons tend to include: negligent care; creating a risk to patients; suspension or revocation of license or hospital privileges; inability to maintain professional liability insurance; criminal charges; an act of dishonesty/moral turpitude; substance abuse; disability or death of a physician or closing of practice; and/or filing of bankruptcy by the practice.

If the reason for the breach of the contract is not listed in the reasons for immediate termination, then the contract should require that the physician will be provided with a formal notice of the alleged breach, allowing a specified amount of time to cure the breach. If the breach is not cured, the employer can terminate the physician. In the case of a breach with time to cure, the physician is typically not meeting one of the terms of their contract, such as qualifying for a third-party payer panel, not completing their medical records so they can be billed to third party payors, or another act that is interfering with their ability to meet the terms of the employment contract. Given the benefit of having a time to cure the breach verses facing immediate termination, it is a smart move for the physician to carefully negotiate the actions that authorize immediate termination.

3. *Disability of Physician*

Physician employment contracts must also address the termination of a physician employment contract if the physician is no longer able to provide services due to disability. It is in the best interest of both physician and employer to define how a physician will be deemed totally or partially disabled. This will include how accommodations will be determined for a temporary or partially disabled physician and when the physician may be terminated for disability. This may occur following a defined amount of consecutive days of missed work, such as one to two months. In some instances, the employer may provide pay to a disabled physician for a set period of time, also generally one to two months, or the contract may state any pay/benefits are solely to be determined by the disability insurance carrier.

B. Contract Provisions Triggered by Termination of Contract

1. *General Obligations*

Regardless of the type of termination, the contract should outline the physician's general obligations, such as returning any identification badges, keys, phones, computers, or other property of the employer and the obligation of the physician to maintain confidentiality of patients and trade secrets of the employer. The triggering of more specific contract terms via termination are discussed in detail below.

2. *Repayment of Bonuses*

Dependent upon how long a physician has been employed at the time of the termination of the employment contract, the physician may be responsible for repayment of signing bonuses. Often, the signing bonus is structured as a forgivable loan, sometimes referred to as a retention loan. It is most typically provided in a lump sum payment, which is forgiven on a sliding scale based upon years of service.

For example, suppose a physician is provided a $50,000 signing bonus. The money will be distributed as a lump sum loan at the time of signing the employment contract or with the first paycheck. After two years of employment, 25 percent of the loan will be forgiven. At four years of employment, 50 percent of the loan will be forgiven. At six years of employment, 75 percent of the loan will be forgiven.

Finally, at eight years of employment, the entire loan will be forgiven. If the physician leaves the practice before working there for eight years, any amount of the loan which is not forgiven is due in full immediately. It should also be noted, that as the loan is forgiven, the forgiven amount is deemed imputed income and becomes taxable.

When negotiating an employment contract, the physician should address with the employer what will happen in the instance of the physician being terminated prior to a signing bonus being completely forgiven. In some instances, if the physician is terminated through no fault of their own, such as the practice closing or not having a sufficient patient base, the physician and employer can negotiate that the balance of the loan will be deemed forgiven.

3. *Tail Insurance*

As mentioned earlier in this chapter, the issue of tail insurance arises when a physician practicing under a claims-made malpractice policy leaves their employment. Physicians need to be certain they maintain malpractice coverage for any claims that arise after the physician exits the practice concerning the care and treatment of any patient the physician furnished while employed at the practice. If the physician's new employer has malpractice coverage through the same liability carrier, it may be possible to have the physician's policy carry over. However, in most instances, it is necessary for them to obtain tail insurance.

The biggest sticking point with tail insurance is the cost. A tail can range anywhere from $20,000 to $100,000 or more, which is most usually due in a lump sum payment immediately. Some insurance companies may offer financing and the physician's new employer may offer an interest free or low interest rate loan. Also, many insurance companies will provide tail insurance to a retiring physician who has been insured by them for at least ten years, provided they have not had a significant number of claims.

Physicians have also been able to negotiate contract provisions that make the employer 100 percent responsible for the tail insurance premium should the employer terminate the employment contract without cause, such as the practice closing. If such deals are reached between the physician and employer, the employer will usually include a clause providing that the physician is 100 percent responsible for obtaining their own tail insurance if they are terminated for cause. Due to the high cost associated with tail insurance, these contract provisions are best drafted in a way that the reasons for termination are sufficiently outlined and leave nothing open to interpretation.

Some states provide statutory indemnification for expenses or losses incurred by an employee related to the discharge of his or her duties, even when the employee is discharged for cause.[13] Pursuant to such an indemnification statute, in the instance where a malpractice action is brought against a physician, and they do not have tail insurance, they may file an action against their former employer for both the expenses incurred in defending against the malpractice action and the cost of any settlement or judgment. Accordingly, although an employer may legally decline to purchase tail insurance for a departing physician, if such an indemnification statute exists, they may be subjecting themselves to significant exposure. This may provide leverage in negotiation for any physician leaving an employer and physicians and their attorneys should be aware of the indemnification laws in their state.

As the physician shortage in the United States continues to grow, physicians are gaining clout with negotiating tail insurance provisions. Similar to the forgiveness of the signing bonus as already discussed, physicians have seen some success in negotiating similar contract terms regarding coverage of tail insurance. For example, a contract provision setting forth the shared responsibility for the cost of tail insurance might look like this: If a physician is employed at the practice five years or less and terminates the contract without cause, the physician is 100 percent responsible for the cost of tail insurance; if the physician is employed at the practice between five and ten years and terminates the contract for no cause, the physician and the practice split the cost of the tail insurance premium equally; and if the physician is employed at the practice ten or more years and terminates the contract without cause, the practice will cover the full premium.

Additionally, when a physician leaves one position to accept another, the new employer may contribute to the tail insurance premium in a couple of ways. Occasionally, the new employer may be able to extend nose coverage, which occurs when the new employer's malpractice insurance covers any claims made from the time the physician left the first employer regarding any care and treatment the physician provided at the first employer. It may be possible for a physician to negotiate a higher signing bonus at their new position to cover the cost of the tail insurance. The new employer may be inclined to do this when the signing bonus is structured as a forgiv-

---

13. For example, see, e.g., California Labor Code, section 2802(a).

able loan, because it reduces the new employer's risk that the physician will accept money toward their tail insurance and shortly thereafter, terminate the second employment contract. While it is extremely rare to see a new employer directly cover the cost of tail insurance, this may be a recruitment strategy on the horizon, in the face of the physician shortage.

4. *Productivity Compensation Due*

Due to the lag time from the time patient care is rendered until third-party payors are billed and provide reimbursement, physicians who receive productivity pay must assure the contract addresses how accrued productivity pay will be handled following termination of the contract. The physician may receive a final payment from the employer once payment is received and productivity is calculated, even though the physician is no longer employed. A reasonable time-frame for payment should be included in the terms to increase the enforceability of the contract term.

5. *Restrictive Covenants*

Restrictive covenants address what physicians agree contractually not to do following the termination of the contract with the rationale being non-harm of the employer by preventing the physician from competing with the employer for a period of time after leaving their employ.

a. *Validity*

When reviewing restrictive covenants, the first line of inquiry is their validity in the state where the contract is being entered into. States vary in their enforcement of restrictive covenants with some of them declaring them invalid, favoring the public policy rationale of access to medical care, including patients being able to see the physician of their choosing. If the restrictive covenants are not enforceable, but nonetheless are present in the contract, they must be negotiated out. Although their presence in a contract in a state that does not recognize them may seem incomprehensible, the primary cause is often an uninformed employer downloading contracts or borrowing contract language from the internet.

b. *Non-Compete Clause*

A non-compete clause forbids a physician from practicing medicine in a defined geographic area for a prescribed amount of time, after leaving the employment. While a non-compete clause may appear benign at first glance, it has the potential to cause serious interference with the physician's ability to earn a living. If the physician violates the terms of the non-compete agreement, the employer can obtain an injunction whereby the court can enforce the terms of the non-compete or the physician may be subject to steep civil penalties. Therefore, it is of great importance to understand the full reach of non-complete clauses within a physician employment contract and to negotiate the terms before signing the contract to minimize the impact these provisions may have upon the physician.

Consider the following example. A pediatrician contracts with a private pediatric practice and has an employment contract, which contains a non-compete clause stating that once they leave the practice they cannot practice medicine within 50 miles of the practice for two years. If the pediatrician leaves this position but lacks the ability to move for new employment (perhaps the physician has a spouse with a job they cannot leave or children they do not wish to uproot,) by the terms of the above described non-compete clause, the pediatrician would be unable to work within 50 miles of the practice for two years, which may equate to them not working at all.

The best strategy, in this example, would have been for the pediatrician to negotiate the term "practice medicine" to "practice medicine in a private pediatric office." It would have served the legal intent of the non-compete in preventing the pediatrician from opening a new office or joining another practice, and thereby enticing the practice's patients to leave. But at the same time, it would have also opened up the opportunity for the physician to work as a hospitalist or in an urgent care, while the clock ran on the non-compete.

Further, in this example, both the scope of geography and time were likely overreaching. It likely would have been possible to negotiate the terms of the non-compete to one year and twenty-five miles. Accordingly, the physician would have been able to handle commuting twenty-five miles for one year, allowing the pediatrician to earn a living, while not being unduly punished by the terms of the non-compete agreement. Finally, the physician should attempt to negotiate a non-compete that does not apply if the physician's employment is terminated for "no-cause." Some non-compete clauses will include a buy-out clause, whereby the physician can pay a certain sum as a settlement of the non-compete. These clauses may be negotiated at the time of contract termination, but often come with a high price.

Courts will generally "blue-pencil" or reduce the scope of a non-compete, if they find its terms are too far reaching. However, in order to achieve such a ruling by a court, the physician would need to hire an attorney and undertake significant and expensive litigation, which also may take longer to resolve than the terms of the non-compete. It is often difficult to appreciate the effect a non-compete will have, until it is too late. Thus, it is always a wise move to negotiate the specifics of a non-compete clause upfront.

c. Non-Solicitation Clauses

Physician employment contracts may also include non-solicitation clauses. These forbid a physician from recruiting their patients to follow them to their new practice. It also forbids the physician from recruiting staff from the employer to accompany them to their new position.

While non-solicitation clauses are often enforceable, the employer will usually notify the physician's patients that the physician will no longer be with the employer assigning them to a new physician within the employer In the age of the internet and search engines, patients are easily able to determine where their physician has relocated, based upon a simple search. Patients are then free to go to the physician of their choosing. Thus, in most instances, non-solicitation clauses are less impactful upon a physician than they were twenty or thirty years ago. However, the non-solicitation of staff clause may include a liquidated damages clause for employing any staff from the departed employer for a set period of time.

6. Medical Records

The contract typically provides that the medical records are the property of the employer, but that the employer will make the records available to the physician to defend themselves in a malpractice action, disciplinary action, or other investigation. Additionally, as the employer cannot be reimbursed for services rendered until the physician has completed the medical records in order for the medical billing department to generate their bills, the contract will often include a clause providing that the physician will close all of their encounters before final productivity pay is released

VII. Alternative Dispute Resolution

ADR clauses are routine in physician employment contracts. It is no secret that litigation entails high costs and a good deal of time for a case to work through the court system. The cost and delay of resolution is of no benefit to either physician or employer. It should also be noted that as of the time of the printing of this chapter, the coronavirus pandemic has created significant delays across the U.S. court system, which is anticipated to take years to undo. Accordingly, an ADR clause is more relevant and necessary than ever before.

The ADR clause typically applies to any and all disputes arising from the terms of the employment contract. These may include disputes over compensation, such as money due from productivity pay or bonuses. Other examples of disputes may relate to disagreements over the scope of duty, disputes within the workplace, including claims of harassment, and/or wrongful termination. The ADR clause will describe the process for initiating ADR. Most commonly, mediation is required initially and if it is not successful, arbitration is to be utilized, although some contracts may provide for only one or the other. Mediation involves the hiring of a third-party neutral, who is trained in mediation, and is usually a retired judge or a practicing attorney. The parties will agree upon the mediator and reserve a block of time with the mediator, who is generally available within a matter of weeks. The parties will be responsible for the mediation fee and the cost of an attorney, if they choose to be represented during the mediation.

During the mediation, the mediator will facilitate a discussion between the parties regarding the dispute and possible resolutions. If the mediator is able to assist the parties in reaching a resolution, a written settlement agreement will be created and so long as the terms of the settlement agreement are met, the dispute will be deemed resolved.

The primary benefits of mediation are both the cost savings and the swifter speed of resolution in contrast to a litigated case, which could consume years. Still, perhaps the greatest benefit of mediation is the fact that the parties remain in control of the outcome of the matter and through a facilitated discussion create and agree to a settlement that they design and accept the terms of. This is in contrast to participating in an adversarial court case where ultimately a judge or jury will decide the outcome of their matter.

If the parties are unable to reach a resolution in mediation, the contract will usually require the parties to attempt another form of ADR: arbitration, where a retired judge or an attorney will hear the evidence and arguments from both sides related to the dispute and render their finding or verdict. The arbitration clause will set forth whether the arbitrator's decision is binding or not. If it is binding, it is deemed a valid contract between the parties and litigation will be forbidden. However, some contracts provide for non-binding arbitration agreements, meaning once the arbitrator issues their opinion, the opinion is binding only if both parties agree to it and adopt the decision as a settlement. If either party disagrees with the arbitrator's decision, the parties then may proceed to litigation.

One criticism of arbitration is that it can also be a costly process, which is the reason that the trend today is to attempt mediation as a first resort, arbitration as a second, and litigation as the final resort to dispute resolution.

The ADR clause may include an attorney's fees provision stating that if the dispute is not settled by mediation and proceeds to arbitration and/or litigation, the prevailing party will be entitled to recoup their attorney's fees from the other side. Given the benefits of ADR, these clauses are usually accepted by both parties.

VIII. Negotiation of Physician Employment Contracts

The best time to negotiate a contract is before it is signed. Often, physicians discover terms they would like to negotiate after they have been working in the position for a few months. Already bound by the terms of the signed contract the physician is in a disadvantaged bargaining position. Thus, regardless of whether a physician will negotiate independently or hire an attorney to do so on their behalf, physicians must be well prepared to negotiate the terms of their contract prior to signing. Studies show that underprepared negotiators make unnecessary concessions and overlook sources of value.[14] Although it is impossible to predict how a negotiation will unfold, those who study negotiation agree that negotiation encompasses more than simply two sides trading proposals back and forth. Nor is negotiation about one side winning and one side losing. This rings especially true in the case of the employment contract where the parties are just embarking on a professional relationship, where the process of negotiation should ultimately lead to both parties deriving the intended benefit from the contract. The following section will discuss ways physicians can prepare to enhance their negotiation strategy.

A. Gather Feedback

The less unknowns there are about the process, the more mentally prepared the physician will feel to negotiate their contract.[15] Increased confidence in the negotiation process will likely lead to better outcomes. Physician peers serve as an excellent resource for physicians as they prepare to negotiate a contract. Physicians who have recently gone through the same process, especially if it was with the same employer, are in a great position to provide feedback on the process. The feedback may range from the logistics of the negotiations to which areas the employer was or was not open to negotiation.

---

14. PON Staff, *Are You Ready to Negotiate? Know When the Time is Right to Negotiate. Program on Negotiation Harvard* (Feb. 1, 2021), https://www.pon.harvard.edu/daily/negotiation-skills-daily/negotiation-skills-are-you-really-ready-to-negotiate/.

15. *Id.*

B. Create Value

It is human nature for self-doubt to creep into the negotiation process. Physicians may feel guilty or uncertain about asking for more money or other changes to the terms of their contract. Negotiation experts recommend both taking time to reflect on other times one has been successful in negotiating and to conduct an inventory of their skills.[16] Taking the time to reflect on skills and what strengths they will bring to a position will prepare physicians to articulate the value they offer when they are asking for more.

C. Address Weaknesses

On the flip side of articulating value, physicians also need to be prepared to address any perceived weaknesses. For example, if a physician has a gap in their resume that they are hoping the interviewer will not notice, or they have not published any articles and they are interviewing to work in a group of physicians, who are highly published, they must be prepared to address these perceived weaknesses. To illustrate the effectiveness of an explanation: perhaps they took a year off while serving in the Peace Corps or to care for an ill family member. And if they may not yet be published, they can share a concrete plan for articles or research they intend to work on. These issues may never arise in the negotiation process. However, having worked their responses out, rather than worry about questions arising, the physician can focus his or her energy on negotiating the terms that are important to them.[17]

D. Creative Solutions

When addressing non-monetary terms of contracts, creative solutions are often successful. For example, a physician may feel very strongly about only taking call one weekend per month, but the contract they are negotiating calls for two weekends of call per month. If the practice provides services to a rural hospital and the practice is in need of coverage at the rural hospital, the physician could propose that in exchange for only being assigned one weekend of call per month, they agree to work at the rural hospital a certain number of days per month. This extra commute time could be provided in consideration for having less weekend on-call time and can be a win-win for both physician and employer.

E. Salary Negotiation

Physicians can grow accustomed to being viewed as pleasant hard-working committed individuals, and may simultaneously be of the belief that requesting more compensation is an affront to these characteristics.

---

16. *Id.*
17. *Id.*

However, physicians must realize that even a small salary increase can impact lifetime earnings dramatically.[18]

In terms of salary negotiation, it is advisable for a physician to interview for more than one position if possible. By virtue of having other employment opportunities, the physician will experience increased confidence in the negotiation process. Having other job opportunities gives the physician their "best alternative to a negotiated agreement" (BATNA). In a nutshell, having a BATNA provides the physician with the knowledge of what their other best option is, if they are unable to reach an agreement in the negotiation. Understanding their alternatives assists them in knowing how much they want to ask for and when it is a better option to walk away without a negotiated agreement, electing to go with their BATNA.

To take a further look at the concept of a BATNA, one can assume a physician has two job offers. Their first-choice position is offering an annual salary of $275,000 and their second-choice position is offering a salary of $300,000. The physician may elect to negotiate for an increased salary in the first-choice position, knowing that if the negotiations fall through, their BATNA would be a $300,000 job offer. This has been proven to increase confidence in the negotiation process. Even if the physician does not have another job offer, it is still possible to develop a BATNA by conducting job market research and speaking to other peers who are familiar with the state of the job market.

Anchoring is another negotiation tactic that may benefit physicians when negotiation their compensation. Anchoring is often discussed in the context of settlement negotiations, but can also be utilized in salary negotiations. Here is an example. If a physician has interviewed for another position or has done their market research, they may know that the position they are interviewing for has a salary range of $250,000-$300,000 per year. As part of the interview or negotiation, they may be asked for their salary requirements. Rather than commit to a specific number, the physician may make a general statement that he or she believes the salary range for the job is $300,000-$350,000 annually. Although the employer is unlikely to go above $300,000 if that is the range of the job, including the higher number will create an anchor which will steer negotiations toward the upper end of the $250,000 to $300,000 range.[19]

---

18. Tanza Loudenback and Skye Gould, *The first big career choice you make can haunt you for years and cost you 1 million.* Business Insider (Sept 22, 2017), https://www.businessinsider.com/how-to-negotiate-salary-earn-more-2017-9/.

19. Katie Shonk, *When Considering How to Negotiate Salary, Job Candidates Sometimes Make Decisions that Go Against Their Best Interests. Research Suggests Guidelines for Effective Salary Negotiation.* Program on Negotiation Harvard (Nov. 3, 2020), https://www.pon.harvard.edu/daily/salary-negotiations/negotiate-salary-3-winning-strategies/.

F. Summary

The physician should generally assess their comfort surrounding the negotiation process. Considering the importance of the contract that they are negotiating, it is likely in their best interest to retain an attorney who can conduct the negotiations on their behalf. The attorney is also in the best position to assure all agreements achieved through negotiation are accurately reflected in writing.

Either way, in achieving a successful negotiation, it is vital that the physician still go through all of the steps recommended for knowing their value, addressing their perceived weaknesses, having a clear BATNA, and considering what aspects of the contract are non-negotiable and what aspects of the contract they are willing to compromise on. The more planning conducted for the negotiation, the more successful it is likely to be.

IX. Considerations Beyond the Face of the Contract

It is important to note that there are non-contractual factors that influence the success of the physician employment relationship. In addition to a thorough review and negotiation of the physician employment contract, every physician must also give careful consideration to the non-contractual factors. This includes the practice culture, which will ultimately determine job satisfaction. It is recommended the physician spend time shadowing another physician at the practice/employment setting, obtaining a sense of how physicians and staff interact with one another and how the practice/employment setting runs in general. The physician should also look to outside sources to obtain as much information as possible about their potential employer. This can include reading online reviews and speaking to other physicians in their professional networks who have worked at the place of employment or are familiar with the practice. The physician may also wish to consider taking one of the employer's physicians out to lunch to get to know them and learn more about the employer. All of this information combined will empower the physician to make the most informed decision about their future employer.

There are also many factors outside of the employer that will impact the physician's satisfaction with the job. It is recommended the physician consider the housing market and cost of living and look at education options if they have children. The physician should consider the distance the employment is from extended family and the extent to which that may influence their desire to remain long-term at the employment. Additionally, assessing whether the employer is located in a thriving or depressed area will provide information about how the employer is anticipated to perform in the future.

No matter if it is a physician's first job out of residency or fellowship, or if it is a mid-career change, careful consideration of the contract terms, coupled with a general assessment of the non-contractual factors, greatly increases the odds of the physician and employer embarking on a collaborative and successful working relationship.

X.   Conclusion

One thing is for certain, physician contracting is not stagnant. There are a multitude of forces at play, from the upward migration of physicians in private practice to being employed by hospitals and health systems, to CMS's evolving reimbursement models from straight compensation to a value-based model, to potential changes to telehealth regulation and reimbursement, to physician shortages, to knowledge acquired through the pandemic. Physician compensation and contracting will continue to evolve, requiring close monitoring by physicians and their attorneys.

ABOUT THE AUTHORS

Violet Anderson

Violet Anderson is in-house counsel for CHRISTUS Health, a Catholic health system ranked among the top 10 Catholic health systems in the United States by size with more than 40 hospital and facilities in seven U.S. states, Chile, and six states in Mexico, and assets of more than $6 billion. For the past 10 years, Ms. Anderson has extensively provided CHRISTUS Health counsel on matters involving healthcare compliance, regulations, and transactions, including, joint ventures, acquisitions, telemedicine, affiliations, and information management.

Prior to joining CHRISTUS Health, Ms. Anderson served as general counsel for Acadiana Computer System, Inc., a Louisiana physician management organization. She is a graduate of Louisiana State University and Tulane Law School and is admitted to practice in Texas and Louisiana.

Daniel Angres, M.D.

Dr. Angres is a national expert in psychiatry, addiction, and physicians' health programs. Currently, he serves as the medical director of the Positive Sobriety Institute, as well as chief medical officer of RiverMend Health Addiction Services. Dr. Angres has been a nationally recognized expert in addiction and dual disorders evaluation and treatment medicine with a specialty in working with addicted professionals for 30 years. He has lectured at major academic medical centers across the United States. His work has helped change the field, addiction treatment methods, and outcomes.

Dr. Angres has been published in peer reviewed journals, referenced by other leaders, and has authored two ground-breaking books on the subject of chemical dependency, *Healing the Healer* and *Positive Sobriety*. He has been active in teaching and research in Chicago and is an adjunct associate professor of psychiatry at Northwestern Feinberg School of Medicine's Department of Psychiatry and Behavioral Sciences.

Hilary H. Bowman

Hilary Bowman is an attorney in the Research Triangle Park office of K&L Gates LLP where she practices health law. Ms. Bowman advises healthcare providers on structuring physician and vendor arrangements to comply with the Stark Law and Anti-Kickback Statute. She conducts due diligence and drafts transaction documents for acquisitions of various types of healthcare providers. She also advises healthcare providers and pharmaceutical companies on compliance with registration and reporting requirements under the Controlled

Substances Act. Prior to entering private practice, Ms. Bowman served as a law clerk to administrative law judges at the U.S. Department of Justice—Drug Enforcement Administration (DEA).

Clay J. Countryman, J.D.

Clay Countryman is a partner with Breazeale, Sachse & Wilson, L.L.P. in Baton Rouge, Louisiana. Mr. Countryman concentrates his practice on representing physicians and other healthcare providers on compliance with federal and state regulations and business transactions. Mr. Countryman has extensive experience in assisting physicians, physician practices, and other providers with structuring joint ventures and other transactions to promote business objectives while addressing compliance concerns of specific healthcare laws and regulations, such as the Stark Law, the Federal Anti-Kickback Statute, False Claims Act, Medicare and Medicaid coverage, and reimbursement requirements, licensure and accreditation requirements, HIPAA, and state health information privacy and security laws.

Mr. Countryman has served as legal counsel to several types of healthcare providers, including physicians and group practices, health systems, hospitals, diagnostic imaging facilities, ambulatory surgical centers, physical therapy providers, healthcare management companies, and healthcare trade associations.

His experience in representing physicians has included negotiating and working with physicians and hospitals to establish joint ventures, form clinically integrated networks, employment and independent contractor arrangements, co-management service line agreements, medical director agreements, call coverage agreements, and recruitment agreements. Mr. Countryman has also represented physicians in commercial litigation and administrative matters, including conducting internal investigations, responding to government audits and investigations, returning overpayments and making self-disclosures, and implementation of compliance programs.

Mr. Countryman is a member of the American Bar Association, the Louisiana State Bar Association, American Health Lawyers Association, Medical Group Management Association, Louisiana Medical Group Management Association, Louisiana Hospital Association–Society of Hospital Attorneys, Health Care Compliance Association, Healthcare Financial Management Association, and the Louisiana Ambulatory Surgery Center Association. He received his J.D. from the Loyola University New Orleans School of Law, and a B.B.A. from the University of Oklahoma.

Mehrnaz Hadian

Dr. Hadian is an internist who is board certified in critical care medicine, hospice and palliative care medicine, and neurocritical care. Her academic interest is in the development of educational courses and seminars on different aspects of intensive care medicine and ICU procedures for medical students, residents, and critical care fellows and physicians. Dr. Hadian's main clinical research interests have been in the area of circulatory shock and resuscitation, different methods of hemodynamic monitoring in critically ill patients, bioethics in clinical research, and end-of-life issues in the intensive care unit.

Amy M. Joseph

Amy Joseph is a healthcare attorney in the Boston office of Hooper, Lundy & Bookman, P.C. Ms. Joseph advises health systems, academic medical centers, teaching hospitals, and a wide variety of other healthcare providers on business and regulatory matters. A significant portion of her practice is focused on fraud and abuse compliance, including counseling on compliance with federal and state anti-kickback and self-referral laws, and serving as lead deal counsel or regulatory counsel on mergers, acquisitions, and other strategic affiliations. In addition, Ms. Joseph frequently counsels both providers and health information technology companies in the digital health space. Ms. Joseph regularly presents and writes on these topics.

Kelsey U. Jernigan

Kelsey Jernigan is an attorney in the Research Triangle Park office of K&L Gates LLP where she practices health law. Ms. Jernigan's practice focuses on healthcare regulatory and transactional law for hospitals, health systems, and other healthcare providers. She advises healthcare providers on operational, regulatory, and compliance matters, including Stark Law and Anti-Kickback matters, internal investigations, EMTALA issues, hospital and physician contracting, medical staff matters, and hospital acquisitions and joint ventures.

Jacey LaManna

Jacey LaManna is senior counsel for UHS and its subsidiaries. She has primary responsibility for all transactional and regulatory matters for UHS's behavioral and acute facilities, including state licensing and Medicare compliance, mergers and acquisitions, joint ventures, affiliations and reorganizations, healthcare contracting, licensure, antitrust planning and compliance-related issues. Jacey is also responsible Medicare and Medicaid reimbursement issues.

Jacey joined UHS in 2010 as associate general counsel and was promoted to senior counsel in 2014. Prior to joining UHS, Jacey spent 11 years in the Healthcare Division of Stevens and Lee. She is vice chair of the Reimbursement Interest Group of the Health Section of the American Bar Association and speaks nationally on healthcare issues. She is also a member of the American Health Lawyers Association and the American Bar Association.

Jacey graduated from Dickinson College with a B.A. in 1996 and received her law from the Dickinson School of Law of the Pennsylvania State University in 1999.

Gabriel Scott

Gabriel Scott is an attorney in the Research Triangle Park office of K&L Gates LLP where he practices health law. Mr. Scott's practice focuses on resolving Medicare and Medicare reimbursement issues for hospitals, physicians, and post-acute providers, with an emphasis on counseling compliance with the Stark Law and Anti-Kickback Statute; providing guidance on payment and delivery system reform efforts, including rules and regulations created by the Medicare Access and CHIP Reauthorization Act and the CMS Quality Payment Program; analyzing payment and quality issues for providers associated with participation in federal and commercial bundled payment programs and accountable care organizations; and advising on telemedicine payment matters. Prior to entering private practice, Mr. Scott worked for the Centers for Medicare and Medicaid Services, where he focused on the development of bundled payment programs, analysis of Stark Law self-referral disclosures, and the design of fraud and abuse waivers for alternative payment models.

Jeremy D. Sherer

Jeremy Sherer is a healthcare attorney in the Boston office of Hooper, Lundy & Bookman, P.C., and co-chair of the firm's Digital Health Task Force. Jeremy counsels healthcare providers and technology vendors on matters involving regulatory compliance, transactions, and business arrangements, with particular emphasis on telehealth, healthcare technology, and fraud and abuse compliance. His clients include hospital systems, provider organizations, telehealth platforms, and digital health startups across the United States. Jeremy received the American Bar Association Health Law Section's "Emerging Young Lawyer in Healthcare" award in 2019, and was named one of "12 Health IT Attorneys You Should Know" by Health Data Management in 2017.

Patrick D. Souter

Patrick D. Souter is Of Counsel with the law firm of Gray Reed & McGraw, LLP in Dallas, Texas, where he is a member of the Healthcare, Corporate and Securities Practice Groups. Mr. Souter's practice focuses on representation of business clients who are involved in both healthcare and nonhealthcare ventures. The vast majority of Mr. Souter's practice focuses on transactional, administrative, regulatory, and antitrust matters for healthcare providers and suppliers. In particular, his representation includes organizational and operational issues with specific emphasis on the areas of fraud and abuse, licensure, reimbursement and compliance. Mr. Souter is licensed to practice law in the State of Texas.

Mr. Souter is a frequent speaker and author on healthcare matters. He is an adjunct professor at Baylor University School of Law in Waco, Texas, where he teaches Healthcare Law, Healthcare Fraud and Abuse, and Regulation of Healthcare Professionals. Also, he is an adjunct professor in the MBA Program at the Baylor University Hankamer School of Business Robbins Institute for Health Policy and

Leadership where he teaches Healthcare Law and Ethics, Healthcare Law: Applications and Strategies and Business Law: Applications and Strategies.

Mr. Souter obtained his B.B.A. in finance and J.D. degrees from Baylor University in Waco, Texas, and his M.B.A. in health services management from the University of Dallas in Irving, Texas. He is currently a candidate for his Master of Laws in the Health Law and Policy Program at Hofstra University in Hempstead, New York. He is a member of the American Health Lawyers Association, the Texas Health Lawyers Association and the Dallas Bar Association.

Michael C. Stinson

Michael Stinson, is the vice president of government relations and public policy for the Physician Insurers Association of America (PIAA), where he oversees all aspects of the association's interactions with various levels of government and advises on interactions with other policy-related organizations. He also serves as the chair of the Health Coalition on Liability and Access, the largest coalition in Washington, D.C., dedicated to achieving federal medical liability reforms.

Prior to joining the PIAA, Mr. Stinson had extensive federal public policy experience having worked on the legislative staffs of four U.S. senators, including six years as the health and judiciary policy advisor to Sen. Dirk Kempthorne (R-ID). He later served as the associate director for health and welfare in Gov. Mark Schweiker's (R-PA) federal affairs office.

Mr. Stinson received a bachelor of science degree from the University of New Hampshire and a J.D. from the George Mason University School of Law.

Jennifer Johnston Terando

Jennifer Johnston Terando, R.N., Esq. is a nurse, attorney, and mediator in private practice in Los Angeles, California. Her boutique law and mediation practice concentrates on medical-legal litigation and health law matters for physicians. Early in her career, Jennifer represented physicians in malpractice litigation and, over the years, many of her former clients requested her services with contract review and negotiation. Jennifer prided herself on conducting physician contract review and negotiation with a goal of securing the best terms for her clients, while negotiating in a style which recognized the physician and employer were embarking on a long-term collaborative relationship. Ultimately, seeing a need for resident physician education in the area of physician contracting, Jennifer developed the talk, *Physician Employment Contracts, Ten Points to Consider Before You Sign,* which she presents to resident physicians and other physician groups.

Believing in the importance of resolving disputes outside of the courtroom, Jennifer developed an interest in alternative dispute resolution. As a mediator, she conducts private mediations of litigated cases and is also an advocate for physicians to attempt a form of alternative dispute resolution for contract disputes prior to filing a lawsuit. She is a panel mediator for The Mediation Center of Los

Angeles, The Center for Conflict Resolution in Los Angeles and The American Health Law Association, and a mediation fellow with the American Bar Association, Dispute Resolution section.

Jennifer received her BSN with honors from the Frances Payne Bolton School of Nursing at Case Western Reserve University and her J.D. with a certificate in health law from Case Western Reserve University School of Law, where she served as an associate editor for the Health Matrix-The Journal of Law-Medicine. She has also completed extensive training in mediation and negotiation.

Emily Weber

Emily Weber is the office managing partner of the Denver office and health care lawyer with Foley & Lardner LLP. Emily takes great pride in, and is nationally sought out to represent hospitals, health systems, academic medical centers, schools of medicine, physician groups, and health care technology companies, Emily focuses her practice on complex health care regulations and transactions, governance, fraud and abuse, health innovation, HIPAA, and data privacy matters. Emily is a member of the firm's Health Care Practice Group and Health Care Industry Team.

Having advised in both in-house and outside counsel roles, Emily applies a hands-on experience of operations and regulatory compliance to her law practice. Her unique experience allows her to translate business requirements into exceptional legal solutions for her clients, including effecting collaborations between universities and health systems for academic affiliations, intellectual property sharing between academic medical centers and for-profit entities, innovative collaborative relationships to change health care delivery both in the health care innovation arena and in the traditional outpatient clinic and pharmacy clinic setting, electronic health record licensing, securing and conducting clinical trials, and negotiating agreements with medical manufacturers and pharmaceutical companies. She has a proven track record of handling data security compliance and governance for personalized medical programs.

Prior to joining Foley, Emily was a shareholder and a partner at a prominent Denver-based law firm. She also served as an associate general counsel at the University of Colorado Health.

Ashley Wheelock

Ashley is an attorney with Locke Lord LLP in Austin, Texas, and is licensed to practice in both Texas and Louisiana. Ashley concentrates her legal practice on transactional and regulatory health care matters, counseling healthcare providers and healthcare industry companies on a national basis. Ashley is adept in mergers, acquisitions, joint ventures, and reorganizations within the health care sector. Ashley also regularly advises clients on matters involving HIPAA, Anti-Kickback Statute, Stark Law, healthcare contracting, change of ownership and other licensure and regulatory filings, corporate practice of medicine, telemedicine and telehealth, and reimbursement.

Tammy Woffenden

Tammy Ward Woffenden is a partner with Locke Lord LLP, in Austin, Texas. Her practice is dedicated to transactional, regulatory, and administrative health law matters. She advises clients on federal healthcare compliance, including HIPAA, Medicare and Medicaid regulation and policy, payment audits, and fraud and abuse such as the Anti-Kickback Act and Stark. She also advises clients on a variety of state regulatory and administrative matters, including compliance with laws relating to state corporate practice of medicine restrictions, scope of practice, fee splitting, telemedicine, provider and facility licensure and compliance, licensing and change of ownership, privacy and data security, Medicaid and state provider contracting, and fraud and abuse laws. She represents a variety of healthcare providers and payors, including individual hospitals and hospital systems, pharmacies, home health agencies, hospice, assisted living facilities, laboratories, mobile health providers, therapy clinics and rehabilitation agencies, individual providers and group practices, managed care organizations, and other businesses and providers that operate within the healthcare industry. She also represents private equity firms and other investors on healthcare transactions.

Ms. Woffenden routinely advises covered entities and their business associates on HIPAA data privacy and security issues, including compliance with the Privacy Rule in areas such as data sharing and disclosures, marketing, and vendor / business associate arrangements. She also helps clients navigate obligations regarding the HIPAA Security Rule, risk assessments, breach analysis and notification, and OCR inquiries. Ms. Woffenden writes extensively on matters involving health information privacy and security, including requirements of HIPAA and the HITECH Act.

Ms. Woffenden is a member of Locke Lord's Health Law practice group as well as the firm's Life Sciences and Privacy and Cybersecurity industry groups.

Kenya Woodruff

Kenya Woodruff is a partner in Katten Muchin Rosenman's Health Care practice in the Dallas office. Her practice is dedicated to healthcare regulatory counsel and the design and execution of related merger, acquisition, and joint venture strategic partnerships. Kenya focuses on the creation and maintenance of compliant healthcare operations and structures for physicians, hospitals, home health and hospice providers, accountable care organizations and clinically integrated networks. Her practice also includes advice on compliance with Health Insurance Portability and Accountability Act (HIPAA), the Health Information Technology for Economic and Clinical Health Act (HITECH Act), Stark Law, Anti-Kickback Statutes, and other applicable fraud and abuse laws. She has more than 20 years of experience in health law, having served as a compliance officer and privacy officer of a national publicly traded radiology services company and as deputy general counsel of a large urban academic medical center.

She was recognized in *Chambers USA* for "Healthcare" in 2015–2019; featured in *D Magazine's* "Best Lawyers" list for "Health Care Law," 2014–2019; selected for inclusion in "Texas Rising Stars in Healthcare Law" in 2009 and 2013, and "Texas Super Lawyers in Healthcare Law" in 2014–2018. In 2011, she was reappointed by the governor of Texas to her second six-year term as a public member on the Texas Board of Chiropractic Examiners. She has held each of the executive team roles in the Dallas Bar Association, Health Law Section, culminating in her tenure as Chair in 2010. In 2012, Kenya was selected as a member of the board of directors for Prism Health North Texas, a local nonprofit institution committed to the wellness and care of those impacted by HIV and AIDS. She received her J.D. from Duke University School of Law in 1999 and her B.A. in philosophy and political science from Emory University in 1996.